PENGUIN BOOKS

OFF THE ROAD

Carolyn Cassady received a B.A. in drama from Bennington College. After World War II she earned an M.A. in fine arts and theater arts from the University of Denver. There she met Neal Cassady, Jack Kerouac, and Allen Ginsberg. In 1948 she married Neal; they had three children together, Cathleen, Jami, and John Allen (named after Jack Kerouac and Allen Ginsberg). She now lives in London, where she writes and paints.

Carolyn Cassady

OFF
THE
ROAD

My Years with Cassady, Kerouac, and Ginsberg

PENGUIN BOOKS

PENGUIN BOOKS
Published by the Penguin Group
Viking Penguin, a division of Penguin Books USA Inc.,
375 Hudson Street, New York, New York 10014, U.S.A.
Penguin Books Ltd, 27 Wrights Lane,
London W8 5TZ, England
Penguin Books Australia Ltd, Ringwood,
Victoria, Australia
Penguin Books Canada Ltd, 2801 John Street,
Markham, Ontario, Canada L3R 1B4
Penguin Books (N.Z.) Ltd, 182–190 Wairau Road,
Auckland 10, New Zealand

Penguin Books Ltd, Registered Offices:
Harmondsworth, Middlesex, England

First published in the United States of America by
William Morrow and Company, Inc., 1990
Reprinted by arrangement with William Morrow and Company, Inc.
Published in Penguin Books 1991

10 9 8 7 6 5 4 3 2 1

Grateful thanks to the following for permission to quote material in this book: Allen
Ginsberg, Gregory Corso, Sterling Lord, the University of Texas, and Creative Arts Book
Company (for excerpts from *As Ever: The Collected Correspondence of Allen Ginsberg and Neal
Cassady*, 1977).

THE LIBRARY OF CONGRESS HAS CATALOGUED THE HARDCOVER AS FOLLOWS:
Cassady, Carolyn.
Off the road : my years with Cassady, Kerouac, and Ginsberg /
Carolyn Cassady.
p.   cm.
ISBN 0–688–08891–0 (hc.)
ISBN 0 14 01.5390 X (pbk.)
1. Kerouac, Jack, 1922–1969—Relations with women—Carolyn
Cassady.   2. Cassady, Carolyn—Relations with men.   3. Ginsberg,
Allen, 1926–   —Biography.   4. Cassady, Neal—Marriage.   5. Beat
generation—Biography.   6. Authors, American—20th century—
Biography.   I. Title.
PS3521.E735Z594   1990
810.9′0054—dc20   90–5588

Printed in the United States of America

To
Helen and Al Hinkle

For He shall give His angels
charge over thee to guard thee
in all thy ways.

Psalm 91:11

In the middle of the journey of our life I
came to myself in a dark wood where the
straight way was lost.

Ah! how hard a thing it is to tell what a
wild, and rough, and stubborn wood this
was, which in my thought renews the fear!

So bitter is it, that scarcely more is death;
but to treat of the good that I there found,
I will relate the other things that I discerned.

Dante, *Inferno*, Canto I

Part I

One

A little past two o'clock on that Saturday afternoon in March of 1947, the phone rang in my hotel sitting room. Bill Tomson's affected tough-guy drawl was unmistakable.

'H'lo, doll, c'n I come up for a minute?'

I hesitated. Bill was becoming a nuisance. Though not enroled in the University of Denver, he'd been turning up on campus nearly every day, and I found his impromptu appearances increasingly tedious. Out of curiosity I continued to see him, but I had so far failed to find any subject he'd discuss seriously. He confined his conversation to smart retorts, abstract bravado or stories of exploits designed to impress me, either his own or those of a friend, one Neal Cassady. To Bill, Neal was a hero whose praises needed singing. Bill told me of daring escapades in cars, near-brushes with the law, deep intellectual and musical safaris.

Having been raised in fear and reverence of existing social codes, I was amazed to learn that there were men who actually dared live like those in books or movies . . . if, of course, Bill was not exaggerating. In any case such a life was remote and unthreatening to me; I wasn't about to fall in love with Bill, and he told me Neal was in New York studying at Columbia University with two friends, Jack Kerouac and Allen Ginsberg, the one a famous football player, the other a poet.

Bill looked vaguely like some movie star whose name I'd long forgotten, and this afternoon I could easily visualize him leaning on the lobby counter, his free hand twisting knots in the phone cord, the cigarette dangling from his lips, one eye squinting from the smoke, the other from the thick straight hair that refused to stay back no matter how often Bill tossed his head to tame it.

After a lengthy pause, I responded. 'All right, Bill, but only for a minute. I have a lot of work to do.'

When I opened the door at his knock, I saw he was not alone. Behind him stood another man, who now strode past me into the room, his eyes quickly cataloguing the contents before he turned to acknowledge Bill's introduction.

'Cari, this is Neal Cassady.'

I could only stare, flustered by seeing the myth made flesh. Neal nodded, and in that instant the sweep of his blue eyes made me feel I had been thoroughly appraised. Inwardly I cursed Bill's failure to warn me.

The advance publicity on this man had already made him unique, but I was not prepared for his appearance—not so much the physical aspects—which were all pretty average—it was his suit. Though not authentic 'zoot', it had the same aura, and I'd never been closer to one than the movie screen. It gave him a Runyonesque flavor, a dangerous glamor heightened by the white T-shirt and bare muscular neck.

Neal walked across the room to the phonograph and turned to me, a statue by the door.

'Bill tells me you have an unusually large collection of Lester Young records.' His eyebrows sloped upward and inward quizzically.

Bewildered, I stammered, 'Who? Lester who? I, uh . . . no . . . unusual, yes. I'm afraid I've never heard of him. All I have are leftovers from college . . . swing mostly . . . big bands.' And I glared at Bill for this additional embarrassment.

Neal too looked at Bill, but only for a second. Then, cool and smiling, he sat in the rocker and began flipping through the albums.

'That's quite all right. What have we here? Ah, yes, I see . . . Artie Shaw, good, the Dorseys, Harry James . . . Nat King Cole . . . ah, Stan Kenton, the Duke . . . hmm, lots of Ellington, Goodman, yes indeed. Very nice. May I play something?' Again his eyebrows sloped upward as he looked at me.

'Of course . . . please . . .'

As he placed the record carefully on the turntable, I dove to the floor to gather together the model of stage scenery I was working on. Bill stopped pacing and sat by the window opposite Neal. The record

2

spun and no one spoke. I glanced up at Neal and quickly down again. As he rocked, his eyes were fastened on me so intently I felt a physical stab. I was sure he sensed my discomfort, but I felt those eyes, like lasers, unwavering until the record ceased. Moving to change it, his manner eased. He made comments to Bill, and I stood up and puttered about the room, straightening nothing really.

'Ah, what's this?' Neal held up a boxed album by Josh White.

'Oh, that's *Southern Exposure*. It's about as radical as we ever got in college. We were impressed by Josh and his protest songs on poor housing and "Jim Crow" trains. It's banned in the South, I hear. When I lived in New York I knew Josh a little, but to my surprise he didn't want to talk about the issues in his songs.' Words tumbled out in my nervousness, but Neal listened with such empathy and respect I felt special, my every word a gem. Beneath his subtle charm I sensed a taut energy that was subdued and restrained, like a drawn bow.

Soon it became apparent that Neal was restless, and Bill had begun to fidget. Neal looked from Bill to me.

'Well, now. Do you two have any plans for this afternoon?' I wistfully surveyed my project materials. 'Couldn't it wait?' he continued. 'Just for an hour or so? I'll bet you need some fresh air. Look—why don't you come with me? I just got off the Greyhound, you see, and I have to get my things from the house where I used to live. Then we could go downtown—or anything you like.' Neal spoke at a rapid rate, not pausing for a reply, and moved toward the door. He turned to me with the question in his eyes.

Bill got up. 'Come on, Cari, get your coat.'

Over and above my discomfort was a compelling desire to see more of this man. I got my coat.

Two

On arrival at his former lodging, Neal busied himself about the house, collecting and packing his belongings while Bill and I waited in the old-fashioned cluttered parlor. Neal had a disarming way of looking at me sideways whenever he passed, yet he said nothing.

His looks and the silence were generating a humid magnetism which was close to stifling me, when on one of his passes he handed me a typewritten love poem 'by Neal Cassady'. Although no judge of poetry, I could tell the poem had been written by someone who was, and my admiration jumped another notch.

When Neal had finished, we walked to the corner to catch a bus downtown. The first stop was a small, shabby hotel. We went directly to the second floor and entered an unlocked room where Neal deposited his suitcase beside an unmade bed. Feminine clothing and cosmetics were strewn about, and these intimate accessories of the absent owner made me feel as if I'd intruded on a ghost. No explanation was offered.

We then walked a few blocks to a tiny short-order café, and Bill and I waited on the sidewalk while Neal went in. Beyond the open door, from which wafted a strong smell of onions and cooking oil, I could see Neal having a heated discussion with a pretty young girl behind the counter. My curiosity overcame my scruples and I badgered Bill until he ran out of dodges and blurted out, 'It's his wife, LuAnne.'

His *wife*? My heart dropped suddenly, making me aware of the extent of the attraction Neal already held for me. Married! I could not reconcile the impression I had been forming of Neal with the restrictions of married life, especially at his tender age of 21. Why hadn't Bill told me an important fact like that? And, if he were married, why had he been looking at me in such a distinctly unmarried manner?

There was no question in my mind that that was definitely that. Married men were off-limits, and besides I now faced the other taboo I'd been trying to ignore—Neal was nearly three years younger than I. The afternoon seemed much less sunny than it had.

When Neal rejoined us, he made no mention of his encounter with LuAnne, and smiling broadly he suggested we go to a music store and listen to records, since 'I've no place for a phonograph of my own.' I walked as fast as I was able, with Bill keeping pace with me, but Neal skimmed on ahead, every now and then wheeling to face us, walking backward but never breaking stride. He shouted remarks and flashed his remarkable teeth, his light brown hair ruffling in the wind, then he pivoted again to swing onward down the street, his suitcoat flapping. He appeared caught up in observing everything and everybody on every side, but he had not ceased his intimate glances at me with those talking eyes. More than ever now I avoided his gaze.

Finally we came to the music store and Neal bustled about, guiding us into a glassed-in booth and rushing out again to return with several records—not Lester Young, Dizzy Gillespie or Charlie Parker, but selections prompted by my own collection, the most cherished in our memory of that day being Benny Goodman's 'Sing, Sing, Sing'.

Neal was fascinating to watch as he listened to the music. He was passionately involved with every instrument, every note, every phrase. He shared his delight by insisting that I, too, become as engrossed as he, repeating nuances I might have missed, calling my attention to an impending riff, while—his face glowing in a wide grin—he exuded 'aaaahhh . . . hear *that*?', or, with eyes closed, 'Listen . . . now, *listen*, hear it? WhooooweeeEEE!' followed by gleeful giggling and shaking of his head while he clapped his hands on his bouncing knees in time to the beat.

We must have been thus absorbed for two or more hours. I supposed he was waiting for LuAnne to get off work, but again neither Bill nor Neal enlightened me, and I was still too spellbound by this bewitching man to think for myself.

Once more in the street, Neal halted, furrowed his brow, then brightened.

'I know . . . why don't we all have dinner together? I'll see if I can get Al Hinkle and his girl, Lois, to join us. I haven't seen Al yet . . . we'll meet at the usual place, huh, Bill? How about it, Carolyn?' And before I could answer, Neal had swept off down the street, pirouetting to flash that smile.

Bill and I waited at the appointed restaurant until we were too hungry to hold out any longer. As we sipped a final cup of coffee and I began to feel irritable, a tall blond man leaned over our booth and said softly, 'Hi.' Bill and I moved over to let Al and Lois sit down, and Bill introduced us. Al apologized for not getting the message in time to join us for dinner, and he also passed on an excuse for Neal.

'You see . . .' Al stopped, embarrassed. 'Since Neal only arrived today, this is the first time he's seen LuAnne for several weeks, so, uh . . . they were . . . delayed when she went to the hotel to change.' His eyes scanned my face for a reaction and found it blank. 'But,' he hastened on, 'we're all going to get together at your hotel room, Neal said, to celebrate his homecoming.'

My surprise at this bit of news as well as my shyness prevented me objecting, but I thought, why *my* room? And I mentally surveyed the disorder I'd left it in. They were all natives of Denver; didn't any of them have a home?

I hurried Bill through buying Scotch and ice, anxious to straighten the room ahead of the others. When they did arrive, all except Neal had on their party faces. A different man from the one I'd been with that afternoon, he was grumpy, silent and brooding and dropped heavily into an armchair. Al was obviously glad to have Neal home and talked glibly to him of his own activities while Neal had been away, but he was unsuccessful in his attempts to get Neal to respond and do likewise.

LuAnne, on the contrary, was gay and bubbling. I didn't think her particularly pretty that night. Her bronze hair, was unbecomingly parted in the middle and pulled back to a clip at her neck—in an effort, I supposed, to make her look older than her just-16 years. Her dress was shapeless, so her figure was unrevealed. Try as I did, I could not see her as the type of girl Neal would marry, considering all I'd heard about his intellectual and educational pursuits along with the rather formal manners he'd displayed.

LuAnne, Lois and I sat on the floor, LuAnne gushing about how happy she and Neal were and what an ideal marriage they shared. She thrust out her left hand, wiggling her fingers.

'And see? Look at this beautiful diamond solitaire Neal gave me.

He is the most wonderful husband! We have so much fun together! Did you know he took me to New York for our honeymoon? It was so exciting, and we met such interesting people, like Allen Ginsberg and Jack Kerouac who are *writers*.'

'Yes, Bill told me,' I managed to get in. 'How long has Neal been enrolled at Columbia?'

LuAnne looked lost for a second, then, undaunted, continued: 'Gee, I forget. But he came home just to marry me, and then we went back to New York together. He's so sweet . . .' I could tell she enjoyed saying 'New York.' 'But he has his funny quirks, too. One of them is he *hates* to get his trousers mussed and lose the crease . . . can you imagine? Watch, I'll show you.' And she bounded up and flounced onto Neal's lap, twining her arms about his neck. Neal growled and shoved her off angrily, but she bounced back to us, delighted with her demonstration.

Although I didn't doubt her story, Neal was not confirming it. He now paced about, deep in thought, or else stared out the window with gloomy pre-occupation. I was not enjoying myself particularly either, and the strange feeling of apprehension that had clung to me through much of the day persisted. It was a relief when Al suggested it was time to go.

Everyone except Bill filtered out the door and down the hall toward the elevator. I was about to shut the door when Neal turned back abruptly and, taking a step or two toward me, raised two fingers in an urgent gesture. Then he spun around and joined the others. What could he mean by that? But for the moment I was more concerned with how to get rid of Bill.

Alone at last, I changed into my pajamas and washed my face slowly, reviewing the perplexing day. Then as I lowered the hideaway bed from the closet, more than ready to climb in, I was startled by a soft knock on the door. My clock read 2:00 a.m. Who on earth? Cautiously I opened the door a few inches and was face to face with Neal, suitcase in hand.

He eased past my catatonic figure, dropped his suitcase and calmly seated himself on the couch, his knees brushing the foot of the bed. I grabbed my robe, squirmed into it and sat on the opposite end of the couch, ardently wishing I had not lowered that bed.

7

Three

'What is it, Neal? Why have you come back? Where's LuAnne?'

I was babbling questions like a child clutching at bubbles. Neal leaned forward resting his elbows on his knees and turned a serious face to me, his wide blue eyes filled with woe.

'I'm really sorry, Carolyn, to drag you into this. The truth is, you see, LuAnne and I are finished. We've been separated for months. I had hoped that today when I returned we could work it out, but it's no use. She threw me out when we got back to the hotel. I've nowhere else to go . . . and at this late hour . . .' and he leaned back with a gesture of futility. 'It was foolish of me to marry her. She's way too young, but I felt sorry for her . . . her mother . . .' he trailed off.

My mind reviewed LuAnne's testimonial of the evening, but I tried to sound sympathetic and still hang onto some detachment.

'I'm sorry, too, Neal . . . LuAnne led me to believe she was the happiest of married women.'

'Ah, yes, well, you know . . . she was overwhelmed by you, and she wanted so badly to make a good impression . . . she is inclined to bend the truth now and again . . . it's a pity.'

'Well, what will you do now? Go back to school?'

'Uh, well . . . no-o. I don't think I can afford to go back now. I'll have to stay in Denver and get a job. But . . .' He looked at me forlornly, 'if you'll let me, I'll just stay here tonight and find a place to live tomorrow.'

8

I got up and paced the small area not occupied by the bed.

'Look, Neal, I'd be glad to help you out, but you don't realize the bind I'm in with this hotel. The elevator man hates me because I don't tip him every time he pilots me three floors. He'd love to catch me at something and then tell the manager . . . But, oh my God, how did you get back up here?'

'It's okay, don't worry. The elevator was closed, and the night clerk asleep. I walked up the stairs . . . didn't see anybody.'

I checked the clock. A quarter past two—I had no choice.

'Now it really is too risky for you to be seen at this hour . . . I'm afraid you will have to stay.' Defeated without benefit of battle, I waved my hand over the couch. 'This is pretty narrow, I'm sorry, and probably too short, but it's . . .'

Neal stood up and walked to the side of the bed.

'Yes, well, I am awfully tired. I don't sleep well on buses, and what with all the strain with LuAnne . . . this bed is too wide for one person, isn't it? It seems ridiculous to waste all that perfectly good space, don't you think? We can both sleep in it, and no one will have to be uncomfortable . . . you *do* agree?'

Cool, reasonable, open-eyed, he looked at me not expecting any answers, and proceeded to sit on the bed and untie his shoelaces. I opened my mouth in an 'Ah, but . . .' but Neal smiled up at me in such innocence that any argument I could have come up with would have sounded obscene. Seeing my stricken look, he stood up and held my shoulders like a big brother.

'Now, now, don't you worry about a thing. I'll be a good boy, I promise.' And he laughed, showing me he'd anticipated my preposterous concern.

When he'd removed all but his T-shirt and shorts, he flopped down, pulled the covers to his chin, and was asleep before I had reached the other side of the bed. I crawled in gingerly and lay stiff and half-awake the rest of the night. Occasionally he turned in his sleep and his arm flopped over me. Not knowing whether it was intentional, I nevertheless removed the arm and inched ever closer to the edge of my side of the bed.

I must have slept some, because I was startled awake by the bright sunlight whitening the lacy curtains and inching across the flowered carpet. My clock showed five minutes to ten. Rarely had I been so glad a night was over. As I tiptoed past his side of the bed, I noticed uncomfortably how handsome Neal looked asleep. I climbed into the shower and turned my concern to the uncharted day ahead.

The shower off, I heard the radio and knew Neal was up. He was rummaging in his suitcase when I emerged but turned to acknowledge my 'Good morning', rivaling the sun with his radiant smile.

After Neal had showered and shaved, I informed him apologetically that we'd have to do without breakfast as I was afraid of him being seen before noon.

'That's perfectly all right,' he said cheerfully,'I quite understand. And anyway, I'd like to stay. That is, if I'm not interfering with your plans?'

I told him of my intention to work on the model set I was constructing for a class, and he listened with care.

'Perhaps I can help you, if you show me how.'

'Well, of course, if you're sure you want to.'

Somewhat nervously I showed him the design and explained that the play was about insects, a bedewed spider-web a prominent feature of the set. I had finished part of the wire structure and had begun threading it with tiny transparent glass beads.

'Surely, I should be able to do that?' he said and reached for the wire and beads. 'I've taken up so much of your time, I owe it to you to help.'

He smiled again and sat down in the rocker, having understood exactly what had to be done and set about it with apparent ease. I collected more materials and sat down on the floor.

'Now then.' Neal settled down to work. 'Here we are, sentenced to remain together for a period of time—all too short, I fear—and so you must tell me all about yourself.'

'Well, um . . . what do you want to know? My life has been pretty ordinary—not nearly as exciting as yours from what Bill tells me.'

'Bill, ha! All lies, I'm sure. No, no, I insist. Tell me a story.'

The soft breeze sighed in the curtains at the open window, the sunlight splashed about the room; but I was only half aware of these things as Neal achieved an effect of a genuine warm interest in me, and I slipped into a feeling of contentment and wholeness I had not known before. He was casting his own web around me as surely as he was constructing the spider's.

Four

The telephone's peal startled me back to reality. I answered, then covered the mouthpiece and turned to Neal.

'It's Bill—downstairs. I'd just as soon he didn't find you here. Would you mind if I go down? I'll get rid of him.'

'Why, of course. Take your time. I'm happy.'

I paused at the door looking back. 'You don't have to go on stringing those beads forever, you know. I appreciate all you've done already, but there are books and magazines—please do what you'd like. I'll hurry.'

I found Bill at the bar, dismally sucking on a Scotch and looking altogether the rejected lover. Did he know about Neal? I approached warily and took a stool beside him, waving the bartender away. Bill didn't look at me.

'Well, Bill, what is it?'

'Oh, nothing, really. I just wanted to see you. Here, come on, have a drink.'

'No thanks, really, Bill. I've too much to do to sit here for no reason. What did you want to see me about?' How he could irritate me!

'Look, Cari, I feel punk. It seems to me the least you could do is have one measly, lousy little stinkin' drink with me.' And his voice began to rise on its way to a bellow, which he knew I detested.

'Okay, Bill, okay, calm down. Let's go sit in a booth, then.' I skimmed off the stool and made for a far corner booth. Bill followed me with two drinks. He bullied me into staying with him for at least half an hour, then suddenly acquiesced to my insistence that I return upstairs.

As I swung open the door to my room, I froze. Bill's ploy was now clear. LuAnne sat on the edge of the couch, her hands in her lap pulverizing a damp tissue, her face blotchy and glistening. Neal crouched before her, one hand on her knee, the other brushing back the hair from her face. 'Now, baby . . .' he was saying, but when I came in, he straightened and walked to the window. LuAnne looked up at me with a weak attempt to smile. My insides went hollow, and now I was glad I'd had that drink. I'd almost forgotten Neal was married still, happily or not, and I had dropped my guard. During the morning he had slipped into our conversation subtle hints that he could tell already I was the girl he had been looking for, and LuAnne merely a youthful mistake. I had tried to ignore these insinuations, but how easy it is for a romantic to fall for a man's insistence that you are 'different.'

To my surprise, LuAnne, although still sniffling, turned to me eagerly, and instead of the angry attack I expected for having 'stolen' her husband, she proceeded to tell me how glad she was that Neal had found me, that I was exactly what he needed, that she and Neal would never be able to get along, he was far too smart for her, and on and on. In spite of her emotional state I was doubtful of her sincerity, still remembering her performance of the preceding evening. Besides, I'd made no commitments to Neal, I told her and myself, so I couldn't see that it mattered, and where had she gotten the idea that it did? Even my vanity found it difficult to credit her act, but in the end I felt maternal and sorry for her, patted her, wished her well and afterwards admonished Neal to see that she was properly taken care of.

From then on, I saw Neal nearly every day. His company being far more satisfying than any other, I voluntarily gave up other involvements and waited for his call, which never failed to come when expected. When he couldn't be with me, even though I didn't ask, he insisted on telling me precisely where he was going, why and for how long. He must have already guessed I'd never doubt or check. By treating me as though I had the right to know his every move, he created the impression that ours was a more binding relationship than it actually was. I reminded him that he was married and not responsible to me, and that I had no authority to monitor his actions even if I cared to, but he paid no attention to my message, pretending I was putting on a noble act.

This attitude of his affected me deeply. I'd never before experienced such solicitude, or such thoughtfulness and diligence in being agreeable. At this time, I accepted nearly everything told me as the truth, mainly because I'd never to my knowledge been lied to in matters of significance. And anyway, why would Neal tell me he loved me if he didn't? What was to be gained? I knew of nothing I had that he lacked or would like to acquire. Barring a slight uneasiness with regard to LuAnne, I believed him and never thought of being suspicious or of interfering with his activities when he was not with me. I respected his freedom of choice as I did my own. I didn't want a love that could be commanded or demanded, but only one that couldn't be denied.

Neal's manner was always formally polite. There was no hint of sensuality, only a restrained affection, as though he considered our relationship to be on a higher plane. Soon I learned to stop arming myself against the kind of siege I'd been subjected to from men in the past. I found that I was enjoying most of the features of my nineteenth-century novels, and I loved it. When any anxiety crossed my mind about Neal's apparent lack of passion, I assumed the physical attraction would naturally develop as love ripened, building in intensity as our relationship bloomed.

In college, I had hoped that by developing my intellect I might offer another means of attraction besides my body. Since my parents were both educators, and most of their friends also members of university faculties, I'd been raised in an environment of lively debates. These were always objective, never personal, mind-fencing only, and no one ever got hurt. I had always found it exciting to follow the arguments through mazes of logic, seeking meaning and clarity of ideas. The men I'd met, however, either resented any intellectual competition or were bored. But with Neal I had at last found a man who could lose himself with me in intellectual give and take. So stimulating, so exhilarating were these mental tapestries we wove, I far preferred this mutuality to that of sex.

Neal encouraged me to talk of my past experiences, but for several months he was somewhat sketchy about his own. The scraps I collected were that he had been born in Salt Lake City while his parents were traveling, and that his mother had died when he was 10. She had been married and had had eight children before she married his barber father. Even though the chronology of his patchy narrative confused me, a grim picture emerged of living off and on with a wino father, sadistic treatment at the hands of older half-brothers, and running away from Boys' Town—to me, a tale rivaled only by those of Dickens.

'Poor Neal! What a miracle you've managed to overcome all that horror. I suppose yours is one of those hardship cases that produces strength of character, like Andrew Carnegie and the like.'

Neal hemmed and hawed. 'Ah, well . . . maybe. My godfather was a Monsignor, and I served as an altar boy, too.'

When I asked Neal what he intended doing as a career, he said that when his education was completed he expected to write like Jack Kerouac and that Jack had promised to help him. There were few things he could have said that would have pleased me more.

Limited financially and not requiring alcohol, we seldom spent evenings drinking and dancing as I'd been accustomed to in the past. Neal said he didn't dance, but he loved movies and sports. Once we sneaked under the tent of the Great Western Rodeo and spent the whole day and evening there—I didn't want to leave my first real taste of the Old West.

There was one sport which Neal enjoyed and I did not, and that was auto racing, but by accompanying him once or twice a week to see the Midgets, I was given the chance to demonstrate my devotion to him. For Neal it was a major source of ecstasy. For me the choking fumes, the smell of gas, grease and oil, the skull-shattering roar of the engines, the squealing tires and bawling crowds were painful, but since he was so eager to share his pleasure with me, to watch his enthusiasm was compensation enough.

As the cars swirled and growled around the track, Neal yelled a running commentary and analysis of every sight and sound, including the names and histories of the drivers and the cars and the characteristics of both. As these became more familiar through repetition, my pleasure increased, but I was happy anyway just standing in the grandstand on those clear, cool nights, the lights blazing and the speakers blaring, sending us romantic ballads or country tunes between announcements. Neal hugged me and swayed us to the rhythm while singing along with 'Peg o' My Heart,' not altogether on key.

Occasionally we partied with Al and Lois and Bill Tomson, who still sullenly shadowed me. His company was even less agreeable now that I'd fallen for Neal, and he was drinking more. Jim Holmes was

14

the only other of Neal's friends I met, and he, I was told but couldn't believe, made his living gambling on pool and card games. Jim had big sad eyes and was so sweet and quiet I couldn't credit his occupation, which to me was equivalent to 'gangster.'

Most of the time, however, we were content to be alone and talk.

Five

In spite of Neal's open and innocent façade, he was not telling me about all of his movements when he was away from me. I was not to learn of these until long after we were married, partly from Jack Kerouac's books and partly from letters Neal wrote to Jack and to Allen Ginsberg. This knowledge came to me in a series of electric shocks.

In a letter to Allen, written in the early days of our relationship, Neal confided a fatherly concern for LuAnne, who 'due to our separation . . . has fallen into a complete apathy toward life. Her inability to meet even the most simple obligations is almost terrifying. Her life is a constant march of obsessions . . . Her attitude . . . constitutes continual lying.' Years later I might have said, 'It takes one to know one,' but in 1947 my naïvety was securely rooted.

Similarly, Neal was simultaneously courting and straight-arming Allen: 'I need you more than ever, since I've no one else to turn to . . . Let us find . . . the great heights of complete oneness . . . I really don't know how much I can be satisfied to love you . . . I want to become nearer to you than anyone. I still don't want to be unconsciously insincere by passing over my non-queerness to please you.'

Neal had agreed to join Allen in the summer on a trip to Texas to visit Bill Burroughs, but after meeting me, he inserted in his letters to Allen vague excuses and warnings, gradually preparing the way for the revelation of their cause.

Neal was also securing his friendship with Jack, though anxious about how to approach him to ensure his continued approval and brotherly affection. After expressing doubts as to his own qualifications, Neal spelled out elaborate instructions on the way in which they should write to each other to guarantee sincerity. Once, he accused Jack of 'just a hint of falseness' in his previous letter, while he himself displayed an affected style in his own 'missives' to Jack. He signed his letters to Allen 'Your other half,' and to Jack 'Your brother.'

To Jack, Neal described how the problem of keeping LuAnne and me from knowing about each other was but one factor plaguing his peace of mind. He was threatened with eviction from his 'ideal' basement room because his landlady had discovered he brought girls home for the night. He had managed to sweet-talk her into forgiving him for damaged sheets, but then a new and bizarre threat nearly landed him in jail and necessitated a change of lodging anyway.

Years before, while Neal had been living in New York, a friend in Chicago was stealing cars and money as well as impregnating a minor, and all while using the name 'Neal Cassady'. After Neal's landlady told him that the police had called, and after he had skipped about a bit to avoid them, he found out the charge. He was genuinely frightened by this ironic twist of fate, since he'd 'faced the Police Chief on similar charges before'. So frightened was he, he even told me about it, wishing to establish his innocence with me before he was arrested. Luckily, he was able to clear himself by tracking down enough evidence to show that he had been in New York at the time of the crimes. I would never have believed Neal capable of such behavior.

Throughout all this, Neal was frantically hunting work for himself and a job and lodging for Allen, who planned to come to Denver in June. Neal began and quit several jobs, then settled into happy employment driving a jitney for the May Company, transporting shoppers to and from their parking lot. He made a point of showing me he was capable of working at anything and could manage to procure an income at any time until his writing proved profitable. Work never interfered with his capacity for living.

His life then began to take some sort of shape, but he found nothing definite for Allen, and he wrote him less often as his involvement with me increased. As the time of Allen's arrival drew near, Neal could procrastinate no longer. At the end of a long letter, he casually added almost as an afterthought,

I have met a wonderful girl. Her chief quality, I suspect, lies in the same sort of awareness or intuitive sense of understanding which is our (yours

17

and mine) chief forte. She is getting her masters at DU. For some strange reason she came to Denver last year, abandoning better places, because she could make money at DU. But she's not really as vulgar as she sounds. Her lack of cynicism, artificial sophistication and sterility in her creative make-up will recommend her to you. She is just a bit too straight for my temperment [sic]; however, that is the challenge, just as that is the challenge in our affair. Her basic inhibitions are subtle psychological ones tied up indirectly with conventions, mannerisms and taste; whereas, mine with you are more internal, fearful and stronger. She knows all about the Theater, draws a fine line, and is quite popular. Don't feel that I am overawed by her, though I would have a justifiable right in being subjective to that. Somehow, my respect for her seems unimportant; I feel the only reason, really, that she affects me so is the sense of peace which she produces in me when we are together. Secretly, she is the reason I am postponing the trip to Texas until later in the season—wait till you meet her.

In mid-June Allen arrived. I was under the impression that he and Neal had known each other for years, not months, nor was I aware of the nature of their relationship or of Allen's love. Neal brought him to my room in the evening and, with much bouncing and bubbling, introduced us. Allen was a slim young man, close to Neal's height, with a shock of thick black hair and intense round black eyes encircled by dark-rimmed glasses. The narrowness of his jaw was emphasized by wide, full lips. His manner shy, he nodded to me with no change of expression in response to my sincere greeting: 'I'm so happy to meet you.'

'Hello,' he said softly, his voice deeper than his slight frame would suggest, and although his owl-like gaze made me self-conscious, I sensed a note of sad kindness in his tone that soon put me at ease, and I was eager to know him better. This was to be rapidly accomplished, quite unexpectedly.

Neal turned to me intently and said, 'Well, now, my dear, Allen just arrived this afternoon after a very long bus trip, so, of course, he is naturally tired. You know I've no room for him at my place, and what with hotels so expensive, I assured Allen you would be pleased to let him sleep on your couch . . . so . . . we'll just leave his things right here for the moment . . . because Allen and I have to go out for just a wee while to check on one more possibility, but I'm sure we'll be right back.' He didn't wait for an answer but kissed me flamboyantly, placed Allen's suitcase by the couch and ushered him out.

It was nearly eleven when I heard them at the door, giggling and softly talking. I hurried to let them in, my love for Neal once again overcoming my fear of the hotel management. They looked like a pair

18

of leprechauns, grinning gleefully, their eyes sparkling and very pink. I supposed they'd been drinking, though I smelled no alcohol when Neal nuzzled my neck. Then *both* men began undressing.

I gasped, did a bit of two-step, my mind racing, but I couldn't think how to object in front of Allen. Neal saw my shocked expression, I was sure, but he said only, 'I'll just use the bathroom a moment. Allen will help you get down the bed.' When Neal came out of the bathroom, Allen went in. I pounced.

'Neal—you don't mean to stay here, too? What have you told Allen—that we are lovers? That we sleep together all the time? How could you?'

Neal wrapped me in his arms and pecked kisses up and down my throat as he talked. 'Now, now, darling—isn't it about time? How much do you think I can stand? I've been a good boy, now haven't I? But you *know* how much I love you—please, darling, don't be upset, it'll be all right. What can we *do* with Allen here?'

When Allen was tucked in on the couch and the light out, Neal climbed into bed beside me. We lay still until it seemed Allen was asleep, me quivering. I wanted some buildup, some preliminaries— why, Neal had never even touched me except for a few hugs or to kiss or hold my hand. All too soon Neal moved close to me and kissed me while slowly removing my pajamas. My thoughts flurried like snowflakes, and my emotions refused to fall into the proper groove for surrendering to passion, so acutely conscious was I of Allen not two feet from my feet. How often I'd visualized our initial blending—but not like this! I prayed Allen was a sound sleeper as Neal threw back the covers and removed his shorts.

The instant my knees were raised, my nerves electrified every muscle to attention in a futile attempt to resist the pain, and a cry escaped me like an uncaged bird. Where was the tenderness he'd shown before? Who was this animal raging in lust? Crushed and bewildered I could only brace myself against the onslaught, fighting back tears and the threatening scream. How could he not help but notice my stiff frigidity? Even after he'd collapsed beside me, I felt chiseled from stone, except for the still-searing pain. My astonished ears heard whispers of glowing profound delight, and then he drifted off to sleep. Numb, I slipped weakly off the bed and sought refuge in the bathroom and bathed my lap with tears.

As morning approached, I had not solved this puzzle, so, not willing to admit defeat, I told myself I would not despair. So fervently did I wish to return to my former state of bliss, I convinced myself there had to be an explanation and a cure. Next time would be better, I'd be in the mood and ready . . . I'd see to that. Allen would not be there. For now, FORGET IT!

I wooed sleep, but I'd been staring at the ceiling for some time when Allen woke and turned toward me with a doleful 'Good morning.' I returned his greeting. He rose from the couch and began folding the blanket, not looking at me.

'It's nice you and Neal are so compatible,' he said. I must have blushed for the first time in years. What did he mean? 'Uh, oh . . . I'm sorry, Allen . . . did we keep you awake? How awful . . . I'm embarrassed . . . uh . . . I don't know what to say . . .'

'That's all right. It's okay . . . I didn't mean . . . it's just that I'm glad he makes you so happy.' What a lamentable tone. I searched his face to see if he were joking. He looked serious enough, even tragic. So he must think my cries were . . . of ecstasy? Was it possible? Yet, how could I deny it—Neal would surely find out. I said nothing at all, and Allen trudged into the bathroom while I put on my robe and went to stand looking out the window. Neal woke and bounded to me. He hugged me with such genuine joy, I was able at least to renew my faith in 'next time.'

Allen stayed in my room reading and writing while Neal was at work and I at school. I grew increasingly fond of him. He was open and frank, yet quiet and thoughtful. And always kind. He took a sincere interest in my studies, often helping me with papers or assignments.

One Saturday afternoon I asked Neal if I could make a sketch of him while Allen read to us. They both thought this a good idea—provided I'd draw a full figure, nude. I was not nearly so nonchalant about nudity as later became fashionable, and the suggestion not only shocked me, but embarrassed me too. As usual, however, my arguments were deftly overcome. After all, they said, think of the Greeks, my drawing-class models, etc.—same thing. I knew it wasn't, but I couldn't squirm out without appearing unreasonably prudish, so I tried to remain detached and concentrate on the drawing itself.

Neal stood much like a Greek statue, one knee flexed, the hip dropped, but with a twinkle in his eye. It took me several hours, and at least they both feigned an academic attitude, Neal even dressing hurriedly when I finished.

Although I valued that sketch for many reasons, I gave it to Neal at his request. Some years after we were married, I inquired about it, and he said he'd lost it, but one day I found it crushed in the back of

20

his closet. Of course I was hurt that he hadn't revered it as I had. He tried to persuade me otherwise, saying it was Allen and LuAnne who had fought over it, thus damaging it, but that didn't make me feel any better. To that he said, '*You* have *me*.'

On one of Neal's days off, he and Allen came to the campus. It was a warm day, and we lounged on the lawn in the sun, watching the students and comparing colleges we had known. Perhaps it was the unusual setting in which I now saw Neal, but something made me study him in a more objective way.

Why was this man the only one I'd ever met to whom I was willing to resign my total being? I didn't think I believed in predestination, but somehow I knew positively that our relationship *was* predestined. Maybe it was simply that he was the first man I'd fallen in love with without physical attraction or romance being the dominant factor. A good sign, I decided; I was being rational and intelligent for once, my mind unclouded by desire. Neal appeared even more unique and special. All at once I felt an inner chill, and I shuddered. On a level much deeper than the mental, I was made suddenly aware that I had already surrendered my will unconditionally. Physically I felt the cogs mesh in the wheel of fate.

Six

Allen displayed an appealing sensitivity and awareness of the feelings of others, so it surprised me to find him sometimes negligent in this respect when in public. The three of us often went to a little side-street café for coffee. There were few other customers as a rule, there being only one short counter and two white booths by the window.

The compactness made us conspicuous and easily overheard. Allen would talk and laugh loudly or suddenly burst into uninhibited song, accompanying himself by drumming on the metal tabletop with his fingers, unconscious of the startled or irritated reactions of other customers. I would shrink into the corner of the booth, hoping to disappear into the plastic upholstery. This made me doubly miserable: as well as my embarrassment, I felt sure Neal would disapprove of my lack of total acceptance of his friend.

It was here in this café that I was first introduced to the world of mind-altering drugs. My former circle of friends had all found their escapist pleasures in the seclusion of murky bars, but since Neal's early childhood memories contained a good deal of sorrow connected with alcohol, this pastime did not appeal to him, and he rarely indulged in anything stronger than beer.

One afternoon, we were the only customers in the café. I was sipping my coffee when one of the men produced a Benzedrine inhaler. I knew its purpose was to clear the nasal passages and was quite familiar with its use. Now I was to learn of the secret powers hidden within this innocent remedy for the common cold. With much ceremony and evident glee, the two men demonstrated the process of disemboweling the inhaler's plastic casing to get at the two-inch-long roll of paper that was saturated with the magic liquid. From this they tore off a mere quarter-inch strip which was again wadded into a ball and swallowed with coffee 'to kill the taste.' This small amount, they told me, was sufficient for eight hours of transporting delights. They were kind enough to warn me that the price of this treat was another eight hours of deadening depression—but I was not to worry, the pleasure of the 'high' was worth it, and Neal would be with me to steer me through the rough spots.

So as 'not to disturb Allen again,' Neal had devised a plan: he would rent a room for the two of us in a hotel. 'Not for what you're thinking,' he assured me, his voice dropping. '. . . All sexual desire and prowess is eliminated when you're on "benny." We'll just talk all night . . . think of it, darling . . . you'll see!'

In spite of feeling uneasy, I agreed. We were so rarely alone together now, and I was happy he wanted to be. Anyway, he could do no wrong; I trusted him implicitly. I swallowed the pellet, drank my coffee and stepped forth into the gathering dusk, ready for anything.

In the room alone together, Neal declared we must undress and lie on the bed to be free to talk comfortably. He removed his clothes as matter of factly as usual, and I hurriedly followed suit and slunk under the bedclothes. It was a warm evening. Neal opened the window and then climbed into the bed beside me. 'Really, it's too hot, isn't it?' and he sat up and threw the covers over the foot of the bed. Instinctively, I covered my chest with my arms.

'Hey, now, what's all this?' he said gently. 'A body like yours and you're ashamed of it?'

'Well, yes. I've never been very fond of it. It always seems to betray me.'

Neal laughed. 'How do you mean, "betray" you?'

'Well, for instance, lots of times it gets fat. Then it keeps sending out messages to men without my permission or approval, and I have to deal with these false promises. And I suppose a lot of it is just having been brought up in a Victorian home where I never saw *anybody*, not even my sisters, undressed. Do you realize . . . since I was a baby, I've never sat on my father's lap, and I have no recollection of ever having kissed him?'

I suddenly became aware I was prattling, and Neal was smiling and giggling, because he knew that's what the drug did. I stopped talking, embarrassed again, but then had to laugh, feeling freer than I could ever remember, less afraid each moment, but unable to control the push of a million thoughts, all of which it seemed so terribly necessary to communicate at once. Neal urged me on, saying, 'You're so expressive!' because I made a lot of faces.

I was deep into schoolday memories when I caught myself again. 'No, now, please stop me, Neal. Besides, it's your turn. Which reminds me, you never told me where you went to high school—here or in New York?'

'Well . . . actually, you see, I didn't finish high school. I quit in the tenth grade. Later I got a certificate of equivalency from the Army.'

'You were in the Army? Where were you during the war?'

'Um, no, you see, not really . . . I was, actually, in jail.'

'Jail? *Jail!*' I sat up and looked down at him. It was a joke. Jail was as remote to me as the stars. 'What on earth for?'

'All a mistake, really. I was living with this friend and working nights, so I hardly ever saw him. One day I was home sleeping when big knocks are on the door and 'Open up! It's the police!' woke me. Of course I was naturally scared, but not having done anything, I jumped up and let them in. They asked me a lot of questions about where I worked, where I'd been at a lot of different times, and I'm trying to remember accurately, when the other cop, who's been poking around, opens this closet and starts dragging out all sorts of stuff . . . radios, tires, toasters, record players . . . and I'm standing there staring in disbelief. I'd never seen all those things before. Naturally, they didn't believe me, so they took me in. They got the other guy, and even though in court he testified to my innocence, they sent me up anyway for "knowledge of stolen goods." '

'Why, that's not fair, that's terrible! Is that actually the law? You poor *deeaarr!*'

'Yeah, well, so when the Army sent my draft notice, I had to tell them I was sorry, but I had a previous engagement.'

This struck us as hilariously funny, as did the picture of all those stolen objects suddenly materializing. When we could stop laughing, I said, 'Well it's a blessing you missed the war . . . except for also missing out on G.I. benefits. Me, too, dammit. I thought I was so clever to choose to be an occupational therapist for the Army rather than the Navy, because you had to join the WAVES. I did exactly the same work as the Navy O.T.s did, but got no benefits afterward. Not so clever, me. But, go on, how did you get the high school certificate?'

'Just walked in and took the test. They assumed I was one of them.

It was a snap.' He paused to kiss me and giggle some more, then, 'But, actually, darling . . . just to be perfectly honest with you, I should tell you I've been in jail a time or two since . . . mostly for dumb stuff like that time . . . misunderstandings, you know. Once I was working on a parking lot in L. A , and I used to borrow the boss's car all the time with his blessing, so one night he wasn't there to ask, but I thought nothing of it and borrowed it again. It broke down a few miles outside town, and I got out and hailed the next car. It was a cop car.'

'You hailed a *cop* car? Oh, no!' Once more overwhelming laughter interrupted his tale. He had chosen the proper time to tell me these stories; I doubt they'd have been so funny as a cold confession.

'. . . Of course, he didn't believe my story and accused me of stealing the car. When I got to court, believe it or not, there was a bailiff who'd been there three years earlier when I was sent to a Hollywood work camp and from which I had escaped and never been caught. Boy, I knew I was in for it now, because I could see he recognized me, too. However, somehow I got inspired and talked my head off to that judge with such a rational explanation, he actually dismissed both charges.'

'Wow, that is hard to believe . . . so, you didn't go to jail that time . . . but what were you doing in the Hollywood camp?'

'Oh, yeah, well, that was another case of a borrowed car . . . and then there was the time I broke my nose, see?' He pushed down the end of his nose which appeared to have no cartilage. 'It's the bane of my existence. I can't breathe properly . . . it drives me nuts. Anyway, this time I was in a car my buddy used to rent so we could take out our girls. All four of us were in the front seat, his girl on his lap. We're coming down this steep hill—I'm driving, of course—and I motion him to take the wheel while I grab my girl. He thinks I'm saying 'Watch this now,' so he watches me instead of taking the wheel, and I'm kissing up a storm. We ran smack-blam into a telephone pole . . . split the bumper in two, flattened all the tires, his girl broke a rib, and since we couldn't pay the damages, we all went to jail.' Both of us howled and hooted over this one until we cried and our stomachs hurt.

Oh, I was having a fine time. I felt so vibrant, brilliant, witty. What fun it was to lie side by side on the cool sheet, giggling, talking, singing and watching the play of neon lights outside the open window, the flimsy net curtains billowing into the shadowy room, the two of us entirely wrapped up in the world of each other. The sudden mood-dives that occasionally hit me were tolerated because Neal bounded in with lovely words to distract and reassure me and bring me up again.

Gradually, Neal began tentative, apparently purposeless caresses, more like a gentle massage of the back of my neck and shoulders. The result was to relax me so completely that, by the time I realized his intent, resistance was out of the question. A wisp of remembered pain floated across my mind, but I couldn't grasp it, and soon all thought ceased in willing surrender. Then, again, the sudden thrust and violent pounding and virtually no body-to-body contact. Again my mind swirled in shocked dismay as I endured the pain. 'Why, oh why?' I thought. 'It should be perfect this time. What kinds of women had he known? If this is what he liked, would he ever like it my way? And why was I so inhibited I couldn't talk to him about it?' When at last he lay still on top of me, I stroked his head weakly, my hopes for an ideal sex life shattered in bits around me.

The lightening sky made the window a raw gray rectangle against the darkened room. Chill, damp air brought colder reality to my aching head and heart. Slowly we dressed in silence, both deep in our own but very different thoughts. The 'drag' had set in, too. Each movement demanded extra and concentrated effort.

Neal was buttoning his shirt sleeves and didn't look up when, low and breathlessly, he said, 'How'd you like to marry me?'

Again, my emotions vied with reason. How odd that here, after a rending disappointment, his proposal produced in me the traditional heart-skip of the girl who finally wins her one-and-only. At least, I consoled myself, Neal felt the experience significantly good to link it in his mind with marriage.

'How can I answer that when you're already married?' I had not seen nor heard of LuAnne since the homecoming episode. Neal had told me she had gone back to New York, and I had all but forgotten her. No more was said now.

He put on his jacket and meticulously arranged a straying hair in the mirror. Then, taking my elbow, he guided me down the creaking staircase and out into the cold and empty streets of the Denver dawn.

Spring was slow to arrive in that high, thin-aired city. The wind from the snowy mountains was harsh, and just as well—I found it difficult enough to keep my head. The enormous difference between Neal's and my approach to sex was seldom out of my thoughts. I analyzed, probed, rationalized. Obviously, there was no one who could help me, not even Neal—and this was the unkindest cut of all. Although I managed to avoid letting him know the extent of my anxiety, it remained a bewildering enigma to me, a cruel irony of fate.

'But,' I said to myself, 'when we're married it will work out. I'll find a way . . . *we'll* find a way, for then I'll be able to discuss it with him.'

Neal acted as though I had said 'Yes' to his proposal. It was all settled, and he demonstrated a new possessiveness. Unaware of my dilemma, he was more affectionate than ever, and we indulged in cozy talks, projecting images of our future life. He heartily endorsed all my requirements for happiness . . . the rural home, the books we'd read together, the trips we'd share, the sports we'd play, the family we'd raise in heaven.

Now he concluded it would solve a lot of problems if we lived together. So we rented a room with kitchen privileges in an old Victorian house in an obscure neighborhood far from the campus, which pacified my Puritan ethics. He assured me he would contact LuAnne and ask her again to arrange for an annulment—a simple process since she was under age and her mother hated Neal. A few days later he said she was back from New York, and in a borrowed car we picked her up downtown and drove her to her mother's home. She promised to see to the annulment right away. What a forlorn child she looked that day, I thought, so young and bedraggled as she sat in the back seat of the car, her hair in pigtails, no makeup, and wearing a rumpled dress, bobby socks and saddle shoes. I was uncomfortable sitting in front beside Neal—her husband—yet it was evident we were doing the best thing for all concerned, erasing an error to write anew.

Seven

Jack Kerouac had written from New York that he would be going to San Francisco and would stop in Denver to see old friends from Columbia as well as Allen and Neal. It must have been quite a surprise for him, I mused, to arrive and be introduced to the girl Neal intended to marry when, only a few months before, he'd met Neal's new bride.

Jack's brooding good looks and shy, gentle nature were comforting and attractive to me, but I considered him only as a friend of Neal's. He had clear blue eyes, emphasized by his black hair and eyelashes. His complexion was darker than Neal's, whose skin was fair and extremely sensitive. We got along well in our roles of mutual friends of Neal, both equally programmed for monogamy and fidelity when it was a matter of matrimony. Jack came several times to the campus theater to watch rehearsals of the two plays some madness had possessed me to act in. I had discouraged Neal's attendance: his opinion mattered too much, and I had no confidence in my ability as an actress, feeling only that the experience would be valuable in rounding out my career. Jack was complimentary and interested in the plays, and I was envied for the attention of this handsome stranger from New York. We were both shy and kept our conversation to general subjects, comparing tastes in playwrights, authors and movies and our impressions of New York and New England. When we rode home together on the streetcar, he would intrigue me by his astute observations of the people and places in the passing streets. He'd often jot down these impressions in a little five-cent notebook which, he told me, he carried with him at all times to capture details for his books.

Jack had nothing but praise for Neal, yet he revealed few facts. Nothing was said about Neal's attendance at Columbia, but I did learn that Jack and Allen were no longer enrolled. How different were these three—Neal, Jack and Allen—from the men I'd known during and after college. Jack was older than I; Neal and Allen younger. Small wonder I was confused as to which was or wasn't in college; the classes I taught as a Teaching Assistant at Denver University were filled with war veterans older than myself. School and age no longer matched. Every man I'd met since World War II had required at least one whole evening to rehash his wartime trauma before any other topics of mutual interest could be introduced. Here, now, were men who had no war experiences to relive. Jack had been with the Merchant Marine, but that had not worked out, and he was reluctant to discuss it. Also, this homelessness of so many was new to me. All my past acquaintances had had families with a sustaining attachment, either positive or negative. In the lives of these three, 'home' didn't seem to be a major factor of the past or present, only of their future dreams.

At Jack's suggestion, one evening Neal, Jack and I went to a tavern. There was a juke-box and a little space for dancing, and since Neal wouldn't, Jack felt free to dance with me off and on between conversations in our booth. As we did, Neal bounded around the room talking to other patrons at the bar, and he monopolized the juke-box selections. One or another tune would bring him leaping back to Jack, and they'd lose themselves in an excited contrapuntal dialogue on music. They were as much fun to watch as to listen to. Both mimics, they matched their words with facial contortions, vocal gymnastics, wild gestures, and every now and then broke up in laughter at the other's antics. Both had infectious laughs, sort of a combination chuckling-giggle, but the rumbling sound was of the deep, true merriment that travels from heart to heart.

Dancing with Jack was the only time I felt the slightest doubt about my dedication to Neal, for here was the warm physical attraction Neal lacked. This realization disturbed me and was difficult to brush away. Jack's manner was tender without being suggestive, although he did betray some tension. As though he had read my thoughts, he said softly in my ear, 'It's too bad, but that's how it is—Neal saw you first.'

Shortly thereafter, Jack became totally involved with other friends in Denver whose plans did not include Neal, and he left for San Francisco without my seeing him again.

My confidence in Neal's sincerity was welded by the attentiveness and pride in me he had displayed when we were with Jack, and I wrote in my weekly letter home that I was engaged to be married. I omitted mentioning that the man in question was already married, but I thought the fact that it would be a long engagement should reassure my parents. I knew they'd be disappointed, nonetheless, for they had already chosen my ideal mate, an Englishman named Cyril, and hoped I'd come to my senses and accept his repeated proposals. I stressed Neal's credits from their point of view: his literary aspirations as a student at Columbia University, his sterling qualities of character and his aversion to alcohol.

Their response was immediate. One of my brothers was a PhD candidate in nearby Boulder, and shortly after the news reached home he called to ask if he could meet my intended. I knew he'd been assigned to check out Neal and report home. He came over to Denver one evening, and since I could hardly invite him to our room we met in a cocktail lounge, where Neal nursed a beer while my brother and I gulped Scotch.

Neal was magnificent. He was poised, reserved, intelligent and articulate, and he talked brilliantly on any subject my brother introduced—except one: the war.

My brother was no exception to the veterans who liked to talk about their military experiences. He'd been a lieutenant commander in the Navy and believed a man's service record was of primary importance in evaluating his character. Neal was prepared. Looking properly remorseful and disgusted, he admitted he had been classified 4-F for a paltry thing resulting from his broken nose, and the painful subject was dropped. Sports was safer, and Neal's phenomenal memory for names, dates and details stood him in good stead in this discussion. I watched in growing admiration and love. The report went home that Neal was 'satisfactory.'

For awhile Neal and I enjoyed playing house. I was glad to cook again and pleased there was nothing he wouldn't eat with gusto and praise. The room itself was small, the bed occupying most of the space, but Neal said, 'What else do we need, hey, baby?'

Then Neal's behavior changed mysteriously. He became moody and frequently distracted, yet would admit to no cause. Three incidents occurred in the last month of that fateful summer that should have been entirely sufficient to cure me of my blind faith in Neal's love and open my eyes to our future, but he had cast his spell too well. The first was one night when he didn't come home for dinner, nor did he call. I knew of no place to look for him and was not comforted by the realization that if anything had happened to him, I would be the last to know. 'That's what you get for living in sin,' I told myself. Late that night, after I was asleep, I was awakened by Neal and a friend he'd brought home along with several six-packs of beer and a guitar. Neal knew of my heavy schedule and early rising hour, so I was dumbfounded by this lack of his usual consideration.

The second incident was a highly anticipated excursion to Central City to see the old mining town and the summer opera. On the bus he was moody and silent, then immediately after we arrived he left me to wait and weep until I could find a ride home, which was not until long after the opera (which I couldn't bring myself to watch) and all the revels had ended. When I got back to Denver, I found him asleep in our bed.

Both times when I confronted him he simply offered such logical and innocent excuses that my concern appeared selfish and uncharitable. Repeatedly, he insisted that his devotion to me was as strong as ever. Since I still couldn't see why he would say so if it weren't true, I believed him. For myself, I wondered if perhaps the meeting with my brother had brought home to him the extent of my naïve trust or the degree of permanence with which I regarded marriage, and he was getting the traditional cold feet. Perfectly natural, I thought.

When my Denver job ended in August, I planned to join Cyril and two British friends of his to drive to Los Angeles. I was grateful for the free ride. I knew that when I left Denver with no teaching position in sight and none sought, I'd no longer be able to rely on my parents for financial support. Anyway, I had my heart set on becoming a movie costume designer and had already made appointments in Hollywood.

This plan of mine allowed Neal to reveal to me one of his own. He said he had reconsidered and agreed, after all, to go with Allen to Texas. I had been expecting him to follow me to Los Angeles and thence to the altar, but he pointed out how impractical that would be. 'I couldn't very well accompany you and your lover to L.A., now could I, darling? So, it works out perfectly, you see. While you're fol-de-rolling with your veddy, veddy British blokes and setting yourself up as a new Edith Head, I'll redeem my commitment to Allen, whom I let down so badly and disgracefully by not keeping my promise at the beginning of the summer. Why? Because I fell in love so completely with the most beautiful and hip chick that ever came out of Nashville . . . It's all your fault, really, darling, so you see you must agree, because you have a teeny-weeny bit of guilt in this matter as well . . .'

Neal was expert at producing laughter to smooth over sticky situations, and now I appreciated his wish to soften the blow of our enforced separation.

'Besides . . .' He hesitated, 'Uh, you see . . . Allen is . . . well . . . Allen is in love with me, too.' And he looked demurely down at his hands.

'Allen? You mean . . . ? My God, Neal . . . you knew this when you had him sleep in the same room with us? Why, that's positively sadistic! How could *you* be so mean? Aha, and now I see . . . the drawing he asked me to make of you in the nude . . . so that's why he asked for it.' I had not been at all prepared for this sort of thing.

Neal looked at me suddenly with new concern. 'Wait now, you don't imagine . . . of course, you know, we don't . . . I mean, we'd never . . . now, really, Carolyn, nothing like that.' In fact, I hadn't even considered that actual sex might be involved, not having run into homosexuality before; and Neal certainly wasn't homosexual, so his reassurance wasn't necessary.

It was Neal's turn to be shocked now, by my lack of resistance to his going off in the opposite direction from me. Quite honestly, and with resignation, I responded that I would not dispute his choice. Since he wasn't free to marry anyhow, perhaps a separation would prove if our love were strong enough to withstand one. I still felt Neal was the only man for me, but unless he felt the same way, coercion I knew would defeat my goal.

Then occurred the third and what should have been the last incident to set me straight about Neal.

My final week in Denver was hectic, and to top it all, I had to perform in an extra showing of Maeterlinck's *The Blue Bird* for a group of children in a downtown movie theater. It was the morning of the day I was to leave for Los Angeles. I had moved out of our room the day before, and stayed with a fellow teacher near the campus where Cyril would pick me up. I rose early and returned to our room in order to have one last farewell with Neal over breakfast.

I tiptoed up the stairs and, hoping to surprise him, gingerly turned the doorknob. He did the surprising. The scene before me stunned my senses as if I'd run into a wall. There in *our* bed, sleeping nude, were

LuAnne, Neal and Allen, in that order. Neal raised his head and muttered something, but my feet were already stumbling back down the stairs and out.

Somehow I performed my role in that sweet, allegorical, interminable children's play, in which I depicted, of all things, 'Light.' If there was anything I needed, that was it. My mind was a blank except for that scene in the bedroom replaying over and over against my will, while I prayed for some illumination to come to me. I had no frame of reference, no related experience — real or fictional — on which to draw, and I could hardly discuss the incident with anyone else.

On the afternoon of 22 August 1947, as our jolly party sped westward, Neal and Allen prepared to depart for the east, and 'never the twain . . .' So it was over, another 'summer romance.' Surely, I told myself, nothing more was needed to convince me I had been gravely misled. I should be grateful that I had escaped in time. I would forget the past six months and the man I'd met and loved, Neal Cassady.

Eight

Cyril and his friends took me back to the world I'd known before Neal, a world that was stable, dependable, ordered. The scene I'd witnessed faded slowly into a part of my mind for half-remembered nightmares.

The carefree excursion provided a salve for my wound, but although we laughed a good deal, it did not lift the stone sunk in my midriff. Neal's ghost accompanied me, and I inwardly communicated to him all my observations. In Los Angeles, while Cyril and I danced in the Biltmore hotel ballroom, Cyril pleaded with me once more to wake up and realize that he and I belonged together. I told him I could sympathize with his feelings because I felt exactly the same about someone else. Here was a man offering me everything on the surface I'd dreamed of, yet every bit of me yearned for Neal.

After we'd explored the movie studios, my three British friends continued their tour on into Mexico. Alone again, I couldn't help sharing my experiences with Neal as I'd done all summer, and I filled all my spare and lonely hours writing to him in Texas—just as a friend now, telling myself I'd learned not to think of him as a husband. When I was promised the next vacant job at the Western Costume Company, a required preliminary step to the studios, I went to San Francisco to wait, preferring to live in that city. I had an older sister there with whom I could stay until I found work and my own accommodation.

Two letters from Neal awaited me, filled with words even more warm and loving than his verbal avowals of undying devotion, and as equally convincing in his apologetic explanations and remorse. Instantly I forgave him and was whole once more. The wheel of fate cranked on.

Neal wrote that, in partnership with another man, Bill Burroughs had bought a 'ranch' in New Waverly, Texas, and it was here that Neal and Allen were staying. In Neal's words, it was a 'crazy spot', a ramshackle affair of wooden shacks on ninety-seven acres of land, and its chief virtues lay in its cheapness to run, its isolation, and its space for growing marijuana. With Bill lived Joan Adams and her two small children, and staying with them was Herbert Huncke, a sometime heroin addict from New York.

After Allen and Neal had settled in, Neal wrote that he helped with the chores, had built a fence, repaired the garage, laid a cement floor and dammed the creek. He did not mention the marijuana again, nor that Bill was also a heroin addict. He did, however, refer to Joan's need for at least eight whole Benzedrine tubes per day, a drug Huncke enjoyed as well, with or without large amounts of Nembutal. Neal drove the sixty or so miles to Houston regularly to collect these and other supplies.

Bill spent many hours testing his shooting ability with one or another of his firearms by setting, or having Neal set, tin cans on the houseyard fence for Bill to pick off from the porch or from his rocking chair behind the front room window. Benzedrine tubes were potted on the mantelpiece with his air gun. Bill was proud of his marksmanship and his gun collection, the care and cleaning of which occupied much of his time.

The composite picture was as revolting to me as anything could be.

Neal confessed that, although one purpose of his trip with Allen was to try to meet his demands as a lover since it meant so much to Allen, he had found that a satisfactory physical relationship with his friend had, after all, proved impossible. Allen, crushed, was planning to sign on a ship and at least earn some money. Now that this issue had been settled, all Neal could think of, he wrote, was rejoining me and making up for his foolishness in ever having allowed us to separate. He had promised Bill, however, that he would drive them all to New York, so this must be done first. Then, when he could raise the fare, he would race to San Francisco and me.

Allen missed the first ship to which he'd signed on, so Neal and Huncke waited with him for another. After four hours and '. . . after

35

tender goodbyes, Huncke and I left Allen . . . reading Henry James and musing on his fate.' Allen finally got a ship bound for Dakar, Senegal, on which he wrote 'Dakar Doldrums,' the sequel to his 'Denver Doldrums,' and not the last poem to be salted by the tears that the crucible of that summer created.

I had learned to love the Bay area when training with the Army at Mills College in Oakland, but San Francisco held a special charm. I reveled in the openness of the city, the air that smelled washed with soap, the casual, friendly people—far more sophisticated a place than Denver, and a striking contrast to New York. Beset with fears myself, I longed to be more like these defiant, courageous folk, who dared to construct buildings on hills so steep that cars parked sideways and steps, not sidewalks, flanked the pavement. The clear blue of the sky and sea brought exhilarating nostalgia for my beloved Michigan waters, and even the moan of the protective fog horns recalled those on Lake Michigan, reviving memories of my secure roots.

I got a job selling jewelry in a big store, and for a couple of weeks I lived in a quaint house on Telegraph Hill with a wild woman who rented me a cot and a chest in a corner of her glassed-in front porch overhanging the bayside cliff. My landlady was in her 70s, the widow of a famous artist. She wore her platinum-dyed hair in thick bangs and a long page-boy bob, fluttered long claw-curved fingernails enamelled in brilliant red, dressed always in Oriental pajamas, and drank gin all day. By the time I got home after dinner each night, she'd be staggering wildly and frequently just barely avoided catapulting out the front porch windows into the Bay. She would sit in her rocker opposite my cot, flailing away at a ukelele to the accompaniment of a radio, set at a jumble of sound between stations. After learning to sleep through this cacophony, I was often wakened later by her one-sided telephone conversations, carried on at the top of her lungs—in Chinese. Sometimes she'd mistake me for her long-lost daughter and weep over me in bed, clutching me to her bosom; on other nights she'd insist I stay up late into the early hours and drink mug after mug of tannic acid—'Tea like they make it in India,' she'd say.

I didn't really mind any of this; to me, she was a San Francisco 'character,' whose antics I used to relate for the entertainment of the girls at work. And besides I loved my prized address with its magnificent night-time view of the glittering lights on the hills of

36

Oakland and Berkeley, linked by the jeweled bracelets of the bridges across the Bay.

With Neal due to arrive in San Francisco shortly, however, I jumped at an opportunity which arose to share the rent of an elegant two-bedroom apartment in the Richmond district with a seafaring friend who was about to leave on a six-month voyage.

Nine

Although it seemed like years, when Neal stepped off the bus in San Francisco on 4 October only five weeks had elapsed since we had parted in Denver. The day of his arrival simply crawled; I took countless cigarette breaks, chewed my cuticles, and was inattentive at my job. A woman to whom I was showing the last of many necklaces suddenly threw it in my face, huffing, 'Well, you certainly don't want to sell it very badly!' True enough, but the blow jolted me back to reality. When six o'clock dragged around, I fumbled into my coat, and even passed the door inspection although I'd forgotten to remove the store's earrings.

Emerging into the lowering dusk and fog, I braced myself against the raw, wet wind and walked around to the front door to find Neal leaning against the marble storefront and looking almost as I'd first seen him. He wore the same suit and T-shirt and looked handsome, his hair ruffled over his forehead and his face ruddy from the wind. When he saw me his pinched expression vanished in the warmth of his broad smile. We were both awkward and suddenly too shy to embrace. Beside him was the familiar suitcase, roped together, and two cardboard cartons. My belief in his devotion was again confirmed when I heard he'd ridden all the way from New York on a *bus*—more so when he shyly revealed how careful he'd been to keep his coat tucked under him so as not to get it wrinkled. The cartons, he told me, were full of records given him by a 'gone singer.'

Impatient to have him alone and to tell him about our new apartment, I persuaded him to let me hire a cab. As I gushed on, he held my hand and gazed at me, or nuzzled my cheek with his cold nose, smiling.

After appropriate exclamations of wonder at our new apartment, Neal showered and changed while I prepared the setting and the meal I'd rehearsed mentally a hundred times. He cooperated with my mood, surpassing every movie hero I'd ever adored.

When we finished eating, a question surfaced in my mind which I'd been too happy to notice, but which now needed banishing with an answer. Neal lit a cigarette and leaned back in his chair with a satisfied sigh. I swirled the wine in my glass and squinted through the red glow of the candle's flame.

'Did you see LuAnne in Denver on your way? Has she gotten the annulment?'

Neal was apparently absorbed by the end of his cigarette. 'Uh, yes, well, of course, darling, we *must* talk about that, but let's do it in the morning, can we? Right *now* . . . so's to continue this marvelous homecoming eve and not to bring us down . . .' he leaned toward me over the table and took my hand '. . . I've got a super-special, extry-ordinary, sen-sa-tional treat for *you*! Yessirree . . . the best is yet to come. Now, you just put those couple of dishes in the sink and come right back here and sit down.'

He stood up and took his Oliver Hardy pose: chin tucked in, elbows flapping, thumbs under his armpits, his fingers rippling on either side of his extended chest, while rocking on his toes and heels. His eyes twinkled and crinkled, his lips compressed in that smug smile.

Tonight I couldn't object, and he helped me remove the dishes to hurry me up. 'Can your surprise wait until I change?' I asked. 'I can't possibly relax in this straitjacket of girdle and hose.'

'Why, certainly, my dear, you go right ahead and "slip into something more comfortable," as they say, while I make a few *preparations* here, heh, heh, heh.' And now he was Uriah Heep, churning his hands and grinning wickedly.

When I returned in my new nightgown and robe, Neal was perched on the edge of the couch, a piece of newspaper spread before him on the coffee table filled with a dull green mound of twisted miniature vines, somewhat dry, interspersed with little smooth, round seeds and tiny twigs. The latter he delicately removed and deposited in the ashtray. The seeds were scooted to one side with his forefinger, but carefully saved. In his right hand, he now cradled a cigarette paper;

with his left he picked up a pinch of leaves and spread them along the paper. I knew this must be marijuana, although I have never seen it before, and my heart gave a little jolt of fear, remembering the stories I'd heard as a teenager of this 'devil weed,' but remembering also that this was Neal, who was about to become my husband and care for me all my life.

With a flourish he moistened the paper's edge with his tongue and pressed it down the full length of the skinny cigarette, stroking it and gently rolling it back and forth to even out the lumps. His eyes glittered like some devilish witchdoctor's as he carefully twisted one end of the paper and just as carefully pinched the other end flat. Holding it before him, thumb and forefinger grasping its center, he turned to me. With a somber expression, he held my eyes with his.

'Now, darling, listen to me. You must have no fear, hear me? It is completely harmless, I promise you. All the tales you've doubtless heard are entirely false, perpetrated by Anslinger and his boys to keep up employment in the narcotic squads. All this does is heighten your sensory perception, awaken your own true awareness and speed up your thought processes while giving the impression that time has immeasurably slowed. You'll see more and see better . . . colors . . . patterns . . . you'll hear every note of every instrument, simultaneously. You'll be amazed at how much you usually miss. Oh, ho, ho . . . just you wait. You think you've heard music? You've never heard it until you hear it on tea.' His own description so excited him that his attempt to be serious disintegrated into smiles and chortles of delight. 'Then, after a while, we'll dig into that delicious pie you've made and which we were too full to eat, and you'll *taste* as you never have before . . . pure ambrosia, you'll see.'

Unable to sit still, he had hopped up and was striding around the room, accompanying his speech with extravagant gestures and rolling eyes. 'Ah, yes, but to return to your fears, darling . . .' And he crouched beside me on the floor, growing serious again. 'I must emphasize this point: the most important thing for you to remember is that you are always in control. Anything you have to do, you can do. Hear me? Remember that. Another thing: you can't tell in advance how you're going to feel—that is, what you'll feel like doing . . . Sometimes you'll want to talk or maybe not at all. Other times everything seems funny, and you'll laugh all night. But, as I said . . . if you have to do something, you always can.

'*And* . . . you can't take it just one time and know how you are on it. You must use it every night at first—say, for a week. That way you'll find out your own different moods and reactions. Then you won't have to worry about getting paranoid someplace, because you'll know how it affects *you*, see?'

I drank in every reassuring word.

'Now then, watch closely, m'dear. You can't smoke these like cigarettes.'

He held the joint away from him while he applied a match to the twisted end and waited for the paper to burn off. Then he put it between parted lips and drew in short, noisy breaths without closing his lips, inhaling more deeply on each gasp until his lungs were fully expanded. He held his breath, becoming red in the face. When he could hold it no longer, he exhaled, very little smoke being expelled.

'You see? Keep it all in. Now. You noticed I took in as much air as smoke? Too strong otherwise, burns your throat too much and you lose some—cooooo, myyyy . . . this *is* good shit . . . oh, I beg your pardon, darling . . . excellent product this, yas indeeed.' His eyes had turned quite pink as his gaze wandered upward. 'Ah, but the point is, mustn't waste any, see, get all you get, dig? Now, you try. Prepare yourself for the awakening of your latent mind and senses . . . you never even *knew*, ho, hooo.'

I did my best to imitate him, but had only inhaled the first weak puff when the unexpected searing of my throat made me cough. He patted my back. 'Here, here, never you mind, everybody does that the first time.' Neal was growling through his clenched teeth and held breath, having frantically retrieved the joint from me and puffed rapidly to keep it lit. Nodding urgently, he thrust it at me again. This time I was more careful and managed to get some smoke and hold it in. My first sensation was a sort of cool feeling inside my chest. There was a pungent, earthy tang to the taste and a generally expanding feeling of wholeness throughout my body.

I moved an ashtray closer to him, but he shook his head. 'No need, see? The ashes are just fluff.' He brushed the end of the joint with his little finger, and only a small piece of unburned paper floated down. It had gone out, a frequent occurrence. (In later years, I could tell when he'd been smoking pot, or 'tea' as he called it, by the quantity of tell-tale matches in the ashtray.) When I'd had another couple of respectable puffs, he decided that was enough for a beginner. Everything he had described proved true, my favourite part being the sense of extended time.

After savoring the pie, we lay flat on our backs by the phonograph, the music vibrating every cell.

Neal sighed. 'Ah, my love, we are going to have a beautiful life together. I can just see us at 80, sittin' on the veranda, rockin' in our chairs, and we'll never say a word . . . just look at each other, smile or nod . . . we'll know exactly what the other is thinking, just like mental telepathy. We'll be so *one*, so in tune we can communicate without words at all, eh?'

I smiled all over but got up. 'You must be exhausted, honey, but you've given me such a lovely time. I've missed you and am so happy to have you back.'

'For good now, baby . . . it's you and me from now on out, right?' He hugged me close, and we stood entwined for many minutes in silence. 'And now, my love . . . beddy-bye. Ah, haa.' Smirking, he twirled an imaginary mustache and brought our laughter back.

Neal kept his word and put me through a week's indoctrination.I enjoyed the time extension and second-by-second awareness, as well as the physical feeling of well-being, but I never got over the fear of being caught in an illegal act, and eventually came to resent the control of my mind by an outside agent and so gave it up.

Ten

The next day Neal wrote to Jack, now back in New York.

My conviction that Carolyn was enough is, I find, correct—so don't worry about your boy Neal, he's found what he wants and in her is attaining greater satisfaction than he'd ever known . . . I am finding it easier to lead a more productive life, having escaped the fixation on my need to write. I now find I'm relaxed enough to start plugging away at it; this seems to fit my temperment to a greater extent than the old frantic unreasoning drive . . . Just got a great letter from Allen; he calls me down plenty, and I'm sure he's right; now don't you agree with him; well, I agree with both of you but not enough to come back to New York until next year. So *that's settled.*

When Neal had left New York for San Francisco, he had left a note for Allen who was still at sea, a note that Allen found 'harsh.' 'I suppose I must say goodbye, then,' Allen wrote, but 'I don't know how.' But he didn't say goodbye, and letters were again exchanged, although not as frequently as before. Allen suffered a long time over Neal's rejection: 'I have protected myself, armored . . . from grief or too much self-pity, and as a result saw my mind turn more than ever before . . . into isolation and phoney goodness—to the point of retiring from the world, which I have not, yet, to a furnished room to write cold hot poems.' He made one more all-out agonized appeal to Neal to come back to him in a letter that must be classed as a symphony of unrequited love.

Allen did not address me directly for several years. I was sorry to lose his friendship, and who could understand his feelings better than I? An accident of gender was all that put me where Allen wanted to be. I was genuinely sorry for him, especially since there seemed no ray of hope, and his poignant letters affected me deeply.

The night following our reunion, I came home from work to find Neal restless and preoccupied, and when I'd done the dishes he didn't get out the tea right away. He was lying on the couch devouring a news magazine. I sat on the floor, leaned back against the couch and lit a cigarette. Throwing down the magazine, Neal raised himself on one elbow and put his arm around my shoulders, his head against mine.

'I've got to tell you something, sweetheart . . . um . . . you see, I did stop in Denver, as you know . . .' He sat up, swung his feet to the floor and began pacing. 'Well. I finally found LuAnne, and . . . well, the bitch . . . she's got some dumb reason why she can't—*won't*—get the annulment . . . says she won't have the money for a couple . . . three weeks. And since *I* don't have any . . . but she promised she'd definitely do it.'

He saw I was about to speak.

'Now, now, don't you fret. What's a couple of weeks when we have our whole life? It won't be long, you'll see, and I'll keep needling her,' and he turned up my face and pecked little kisses all over it so that I couldn't reply. 'Now then, let's forget all about her and all her nonsense.'

He bounded up again to bring out the tea, and the evening's education began.

Although I wondered why LuAnne hadn't gotten the annulment long since, feeling as she did, I trusted Neal and felt it was his responsibility, never doubting he was as anxious as I was to tie the knot. LuAnne again faded from my mind.

San Francisco offered us a cornucopia of exciting activities to share, and Neal always added another dimension to any entertainment. No matter what amusement we indulged in—table games at home, movies, plays, lectures, concerts, the zoo, the galleries, Chinatown or simply watching sailboats in the Bay—his mind elaborated on the scene before us and expanded my enjoyment, sometimes swooping and soaring on wings of fancy, like the ever-present gulls, at others relating his observations of obscure minutiae to corresponding ideas in other areas of life, literature, philosophy or history.

After a lecture we attended, he wrote to Jack;

I saw the great, one and only Thomas Mann day before yesterday. He gave a terrific lecture on 'Nietzsche in the Light of Modern Experience.' It was not a simple rehash of stock thought and inept handling of our Frederick, but rather, pushed into the real 'rarified air' of *true* understanding; not abstract nonsense and trashy, trite inquiries into his motives, etc. . . . but honest dealment with the problem . . .

I was interested in the local little theaters, and Neal accompanied me gladly to several plays, a new experience for him. He could hardly sit still, seeming to enter into every actor and role on stage, as well as being aware of all the accoutrements. Again to Jack he wrote:

Of late I've become more aware of the theater as a release; I love to do take-offs on everybody . . . Chaplin, Barrymore, etc. I feel the urge and jump up and act out, stage, direct, costume and photograph an entire Class-B movie; all this in a hurried, confused dialogue and pantomime which is mixed with frantic rushing from one side of the room to the opposite as I progress with the epic. Scene after scene rolls out; one coming from another, and soon I'm portraying everybody from the script writer to the temperamental star; from the leader who arranges and conducts the music for the soundtrack to the stage hands who dash in and out with the sets.

As he was writing, he was, as usual, high on tea and had Dizzy Gillespie's 'Salt Peanuts' bebopping at full blast. Intermittently, between record changes or scene shifts, he would bolt to the refrigerator, grab an open quart of beer and pour great glugs down his throat with trickles down his chin and bare chest, so eager was he to continue unfolding his thrilling saga. That day I was at home, and during one of these breaks, I continued the letter:

. . . (Jack, Neal is now gorging himself with the aforementioned Class-B movie. This time, he is sprawling on the couch, as usual nude, gazing into cross-eyed space, wheezing 'I retreat! I retreat!'—to Tibet, that is, accompanying each 'retreat' by flailing the arms and legs alternately about. He becomes annoyed with me now . . .)

Dear Jack . . . this fiend, Carolyn, has just swiped my typewriter for 30 seconds while I explained *The Razor's Edge* in its entirety.

Such were the glorious and fulfilling days of our first two months. Sex had not improved to the extent I had hoped, but I resigned myself to that one flaw in an otherwise perfect life. Besides which, around the first part of November Neal got a job. It was with a service-station chain that had a 'revolutionary' approach and high-powered promotion. Their idea was for five men to hit a car at once and see how fast they could service it, including washing the insides of the windows and vacuuming the floors. This was the kind of challenge Neal responded to, even if he disapproved of their methods. Soon he had memorized the massive journals of sales procedures and was out-smiling and out-cheering the other employees, impressing the bosses (though not the other employees) and getting raises more frequently than anyone else. As a customer I found their method startling, if not frightening, when one wasn't expecting the onslaught,

Monday was my day off, and on 1 December I was at home. That afternoon Neal and I were cozily relaxing over a game of chess, when the doorbell rang. Answering it, I was confronted by two girls standing on the stoop. It took a moment for me to recognize one of them as LuAnne and the other as Lois, Al Hinkle's Denver girlfriend. This LuAnne was not the little girl in pigtails I had last seen. Here was a beautiful, sophisticated young woman, well groomed and chic. Her hazel eyes were shadowed by thick black lashes, her complexion waxen smooth, her wet red lips curved in a stunning smile over those glistening perfect teeth, all framed in a huge white fox-fur collar. She was breathtaking.

'Lu*Anne* . . . and Lois! Do come in, why, what a surprise . . . Neal, look who's here.' The girls teetered on their high heels over the thick carpet. Neal just stared as LuAnne went toward him, her hand outstretched. 'Well, Neal, aren't you going to say hello? How've you been, anyway?'

'Yes, of course.' Neal ignored her hand. 'You're looking well. What are you doing in San Francisco?'

'Let me take your coats. Do sit down,' I put in.

As I went to the closet, LuAnne answered Neal. 'Well, I really don't know yet. We just got here a few days ago. We drove out with George . . . you remember him, don't you? Ever since you left he's been nagging and nagging me to marry him. Of course, I don't want to do *that*, but I did accept when he asked if I'd come to San Francisco . . . provided, I said, I could bring Lois along as a chaperone.' And she giggled at her own joke, her eyes twinkling as she teased Neal. The more she laughed and chattered, the surlier Neal became, it being quite obvious where the new look had originated.

I asked them both to stay for dinner, and they accepted, offering to help.

'No, no, that's all right.' I was glad to have something to do. 'You stay in here and tell Neal all the news from Denver.'

Throughout dinner, LuAnne's manner was gay and charming despite Neal's continued glowering and short replies. She was evidently doing some getting even, and I had to admit that Neal deserved it. She played her cards well and got just what she wanted: Neal was angry on all counts, including a few unknown to me at the time. I was more amused than anything by her performance, and in spite of her new glamor, I felt no threat to our solid and secure marriage—for in my mind we already were married. The only burning question still unanswered was whether or not she'd obtained the annulment. When Neal returned from seeing them to the car, he said she had not, and it was to this I attributed his now open fury.

A few days later he wrote to Jack:

On December 1st LuAnne arrived here. She was quite changed, affected a more sophisticated air, came on hep and moved with improved poise. After some preliminary skirmishing we reverted back to an old naturalness of relationship and it was with great difficulty I finally managed to extract the commitment of desire to gain an annulment from her. The process of becoming legally free rests now on money. After the 5th I'll have some and forward it to her mother in Denver to start the divorce.

I think, dear Jack, we've underestimated money. I predict a lucrative year for me, since I'm goin' to make money one object of this year's struggle. Hear me?
        So long.
        N.

Eleven

Soon Christmas was in the offing, and I had gifts to buy, wrap and mail to my extensive family. Having grown up with wonderful Dickensian Christmases, this holiday represents all that is the most sentimental for me.

Gifts began arriving for us, postmarked from all over the country and beyond. Along with colorful packages came boxes of traditional food—home-smoked country ham from Tennessee, cheese from Canada, my mother's annual English plum pudding and a huge box of international cookies, some even retaining their original shapes in spite of the efforts of the U.S Mail to reduce them all to crumbs.

Neal was dumbfounded by such a display of family affection, especially since each member included a gift for him. Even though no one imagined we lived under the same roof, he had been accepted as a family member when I'd announced our engagement.

In the course of becoming top candidate for promotion at work, Neal had burned himself out: his ardor wained, he became lax and his attendance lagged. He also had another problem of which I was blissfully ignorant. I would have been stunned to learn that contributing in large measure to his state of mental and physical fatigue was LuAnne. I had not presumed that sex was what Neal meant by the 'naturalness' of their former relationship. She toyed with him, taunted him and flaunted her lovers and their gifts. It was an extremely effective campaign. She managed to plunge him into agonies of desire and jealousy, since Neal felt 'once his, always his,' and, after all, she *was* still his wife.

The Christmas display at home and the torture meted out by LuAnne stirred his ambivalence again, the tension erupting in huge hives all over his body. He had not written to Allen for six weeks, but on 30 December he summed up his condition in a letter he kept private from me:

> On December 1st LuAnne came to town and since then has been a constant thorn; she is with an old beau and a girlfriend and together they all live in a downtown hotel. Since she doesn't work (although the other two do) and does nothing, even read, she has much time to come by my station in his car, call on me at home in the morning while Carolyn is away and before I go to work; in short, my efforts toward an annulment have been little rewarded. However, now that I've at last (during several emotional scenes) made it plain to her that all is finished, she has again promised to have her mother gain our legal separation.
>
> . . . I am moving by myself again because Carolyn has practically gotten married to me in the eyes of her family, and unless I break quickly things may become drastic.

The puzzle I never solved was why Neal never gave me any hint of this attitude toward our impending marriage. I had no reason at the time to suspect he didn't really want something which, before, he had so strenuously promoted.

His physical pain and resultant despondency caused him to have new doubts about writing as a career for him. He discussed it with Jack on paper:

> There is something in me that wants to come out; something of my own that must be said. Yet, perhaps, words are not the way for me . . . I have found myself looking to others for the answer to my soul, whereas I know this is slowly gained (if at all) by delving into my own self only. I am not too sure that the roots of the impulse to write go deep enough, are necessary enough for me to create on paper. If, however, I find writing a must (as you've seemed to) then I know I must build my life around this necessity; even my most indifferent and trivial hours must become an expression of this impulse and a testimony to it.
>
> I have always held that when one writes, one should forget all rules, literary styles and other such pretentions as large words, lordly clauses and other phrases as such—rolling the words around in the mouth as one would wine, and, proper or not, putting them down because they sound so good. Rather, I think one should write, as nearly as possible, as if he were the first person on earth and was humbly and sincerely putting on paper that which he saw and experienced and loved and lost; what his passing

thoughts were and his sorrows and desires; and these things should be said with careful avoidance of common phrases, trite usage of hackneyed words and the like. One must combine Wolfe and Flaubert—and Dickens. Art is good when it springs from necessity. This kind of origin is the guarantee of its value; there is no other.

Jack was then working on his first novel, *The Town and the City*, writing in an academic and traditional style. Neal's observations were to affect Jack profoundly, as his later works, and he himself, testified.

Since I was kept in the dark regarding LuAnne, I attributed Neal's allergy solely to overwork. He had told me about LuAnne and Lois coming to the service station, and about his anger at her delaying the annulment, yet his physical reaction was too severe a consequence to ascribe to that and I urged him to leave the job and seek one less demanding. Upon resigning, he did improve, but the acquisition of his first very own car may have had some part in it. He summed up his condition to Jack:

> I crushed my hand, but it's OK. I took my pills so my hives are OK. I settled LuAnne and Carolyn (inadequately) so that's OK. I guess I'm OK. Twenty years ago General Motors, Chevrolet Division, made a car with a 4-cylinder motor. I now own a copy of same. The paint job is original, the motor's original, the upholstery's original, the wheel's original; in fact, the only thing that didn't come with the car when it left the factory in Flint, Michigan is the license plates. Price? Gulp—225 dollars. How much have I paid? 100 dollars. Come to think of it, I'm not OK; I'm broke and in debt up to my ears.

Despite debts, Neal's health problems and the unfortunate experience of his taking a short-lived job as an encyclopedia salesman, these were months of great happiness for me. But they were about to come to an end. I missed a menstrual period.

My feelings gyrated from one extreme to the other. I had expected to have a family with Neal, but not yet. More important at that time was the shame I knew I would bring upon my family. I went to a doctor without telling Neal, and the doctor said, 'Congratulations!' I knew Neal would be no more overjoyed than I, but I also knew he'd stand by me and we'd work it out together.

I told him that night at dinner, and he did very well in almost convincing me I had not misjudged him. When he told me the next day that he thought he'd found a way to 'take care of it,' I was crushed.

'Shh, shhhh, now, now, darling, don't cry,' he said as he swooped me in his arms. 'It's just that it worried me, you understand . . . no job, no money. We're not ready to have a baby yet, are we? You don't want one now, do you? There's so much more we have to do together before we start a family. I was only trying to think of us and what's best for our baby. Forgive me, now, love . . . sshh, you know I love you . . . you 'n' me, baby, right?"

He lifted my chin and kissed my wet cheeks. Even though he'd said all the stock phrases I believed him again and felt relieved, pushing back the question of why he hadn't discussed the idea with me first.

Twelve

For Neal's birthday on 8 February, I looked forward to cooking him a special dinner and making as much of it as our finances would allow. I had learned already that he took special dates seriously, almost religiously, and some sort of ritual to mark them always appealed to him.

But when I emerged from the store into the twilight, he wasn't parked in the loading zone as usual. He'd never been late before. I searched the streets looking for his car without success, then settled to wait by the side door of the store, wrapping my coat about me against the wind and gusting fog. Funny he hadn't called, but I supposed he'd had a flat or something. After another fifteen or twenty minutes I was so chilled I walked up to Geary Street to board the streetcar, fear beginning to creep up on me.

I liked the ride out to the avenues on the big open streetcars, and this evening as we clicked along the tracks and clanged at the crossings, I tried to relax with a cigarette in the fresh damp air. I reassured myself by supposing that maybe Neal was planning a surprise himself for his birthday celebration. It was not yet dark when I walked across the broad street and down the block to our apartment house.

The I saw the car by the curb. At least he was home—must be something wrong with the car. I quickened my pace. Just as I turned into our walk, from the corner of my eye I saw a movement in the back seat. I swung around and looked in. Neal . . . What on earth? . . . Was he hurt? I yanked open the door. 'Darling, what is it? Why . . .?'

'Go away,' he barked. A tone I'd never heard before: gruff, hateful, chilling. Stunned, I backed away as though hit, only then seeing the silver revolver in his left hand. I flung the door shut and ran down the walk and up the steps to the apartment. I was shaking now, violently. I paced rapidly around the rooms in an effort to control my pounding heart and chattering teeth. A gun! Neal with a gun! He'd always felt as I did—violence of any kind sickened me, but firearms terrified me. I'd only seen one pistol up close in my life; my father wouldn't allow any sort of gun in our family home. How and where could Neal have found one? And, more important, why? I didn't know how to begin to unravel the nightmare, nor what to do next. I sat down, desperate to calm myself and think constructively.

The front door opened slowly, and Neal came in, the pistol dangling in his hand, his face pale and drawn. He slumped down on the chest beside my chair and held out the gun, with the butt toward me.

'Here, you do it . . . *please*, Carolyn . . . you do it . . . help me. I've tried all day. I can't do it.'

I sprang from my chair as though it were on fire to get away from that awful object.

'Oh, Neal—what *is* it?' I managed to croak weakly from the other side of the room. 'What on earth's the matter? Are you ill? What ever made you consider such a thing? *Why*, Neal?' Now I feared for his sanity.

He sat rocking his head in his hands, not answering. He had dropped the gun in the chair so I summoned all my nerve and picked it up gingerly and placed it high on a shelf of the bookcase.

'Where did you get it?'

'It's Al's.' Neal leaned back heavily against the wall.

'Al's? Al Hinkle's?' This was equally mysterious. 'What would Al want with a gun?'

'I don't know. I think he bought it in Texas. I found it in his glove compartment and took it.' So we were back at the start, and he wasn't answering the right questions.

I was still trembling but managed to hang up my coat while trying to think of what to do now. Get Al. I dialed the number in Oakland and he answered, thank God. My tone of voice as I said 'It's Neal' was all he needed to hear. 'I'll be right over.'

I sat down and rested my head on the chair back. Neal got up and went to look out the window, apparently much calmer now.

After a lengthy pause, he spoke without turning around. 'Please, Carolyn, forgive me. I didn't mean to frighten you. I really am sorry. I'm okay, don't worry. I haven't lost my mind, though I thought I had for a while.'

Then he came over and knelt beside me, laying his head in my lap. I stroked his hair but could say nothing, incapable of making sense of this Neal I'd never seen before.

When he heard Al's rapid footsteps on the walk, Neal jumped to his feet to open the door and greet him, putting on a jovial voice in an effort to clear the air.

'Come right in, old buddy. Ahem, just having a little family crisis here, you know—heh, heh, nothing to be concerned about really . . .'

It was a feeble effort, and Al looked past him to me, searching my face and then Neal's.

I pointed to the gun. 'Is that thing yours?'

Al reached up and took it from the shelf. 'So that's what happened to it. I forgot to lock my car. I was afraid someone had stolen it . . . wow.' He began emptying the chambers.

'I can't imagine you owning a gun, Al. Why would you want one?'

'Oh, I dunno. I just saw it in a pawnshop window, and it was so cheap I bought it. Guess it's a leftover from my cowboy hero days.'

Al put the gun on the table and turned his attention to Neal, but I had to go over and pick it up, somehow fascinated, as by a dead rattlesnake. Cautiously I turned it over in my hands, trying to fathom the horror it held for me. When I barely grazed the trigger and it released, I dropped it, more frightened than ever. Neal's finger had been crooked around that trigger the whole time.

Al could tell Neal was uncomfortable, so he talked in his quiet way about other things and suggested a game of chess. His presence and his homilies did much to soothe me, and he seemed to be having a healthy effect on Neal as well. I guessed Al might know something of the causes that I did not. I left them and went to prepare dinner, hoping to add to the appearance of normality.

Neal did not refer to the incident again, and I didn't believe in demanding an explanation. I would simply have to be as patient and loving as possible until he felt like unburdening himself. At least I was confident his conflict was in no way related to us.

But it was to Jack, five months later, that he did unburden himself—or tried to, and without my knowledge. He had not answered any of Jack's letters during that time, because, he wrote,

54

'describing my tortures by mail would result in my becoming too overbalanced or too distastefully, incoherently mad.' Having failed several times to write to Jack about his 'ache and distorted vision of flesh and latest most terrified stupidities,' he listed chronologically events 'which are strangely, entirely removed from my being . . . almost as if I were telling of another person . . . I've nearly gone crazy the last half year or so, so please try and understand that fact (though you know not the cause) and do be good and forgive me.' He told Jack that after he'd quit the service-station job he was so out of his head, so saturated with grief, he would tear across busy intersections in the car, right through red lights, hoping to get hit. He made an effort to write about his suicide attempt, but said words were no use.

> I don't feel I need new words to merely translate my private knowledge—I need to preach a new Psychology, a new Philosophy, a new morality . . . what a task—how can I expect to speak in a letter? This madness has been unlike any I've ever known, *entirely* different—I feel as if I've never had any life before—I do childish things—I think in new distorted, over-balanced levels, I burn with agony—I sense a loss of most all wisdom I ever had. When I see a girl, I tremble, I spit, I'm lost.

In the days that followed his birthday, Neal was quiet and sweet, but distracted and never happy. Even the tea didn't seem to elicit the usual euphoria. He read and wrote, and I let him be, trying to adjust my moods to his, ready for whenever he would care to confide in me. Perhaps he was simply subject to fits of depression? He had told me of several attempts at suicide in his younger days, each having ended as did this latest one, in self-disgust.

The truth of that day was mercifully withheld from me for twelve years, until Al and LuAnne filled in the missing details. Tormented, Neal had driven to Oakland, hopeful that 'sensible Al' could lift his depression, but to no avail. Finding the gun, he had decided on more desperate and final action. LuAnne's taunts were driving him wild, and he drove to her hotel and woke her, demanding at gun point she go with him to Denver. She lured him into bed in an unsuccessful attempt to change his resolve. He forced her to get in the car, drove to a wild section of the beach and raped her, she said. When he let her crawl back into the car, he drove her back to her room and ordered her to change and pack—he'd pick her up at noon and drive her to Denver. She changed and packed all right, but then fled to her new fiancé's apartment.

Thirteen

On the last day of February, Neal had an idea that brightened his mood considerably. He would drive to Denver himself, make LuAnne's mother start the annulment and, at the same time, pick up the books and other belongings I'd had to leave behind. He'd only be gone a week. The idea seemed rather rash and expensive to me, but I toned down my objections in view of the welcome return of his high spirits. He assured me it would cost 'nothing,' and we spent a happy tea-enhanced evening for the first time in a month.

Next morning Neal dropped me off at work and sped away. It was our first separation in San Francisco, and that evening, alone with my thoughts, I tried to foresee the future. I even allowed myself to doubt whether this time Neal would come back. My spirits sagged. Never had I felt so isolated and alone. No man, I felt sure, could ever understand the helplessness felt by an unmarried pregnant girl. Yet I was luckier than many: I had a man—I hoped. But it was tempting to resent him, too, if only because, like everyone else, he was so safe and free. His guilt need never be known. Mine would be visible for all to see. Only death was as inevitable and immune from human aid.

Why had it happened to me? I did not approve of premarital cohabitation in general, but in our case it had seemed the only practical thing to do. I felt that sin, like everything else, had to be judged in the light of common sense, and my only regret was the pregnancy—and that on account of others. Not much common sense had gone into that. But I did wonder why it had not happened to LuAnne (who conceived the minute she married)—or to me before Neal arrived in San Francisco. These thoughts added a modicum of weight to my idealized notion that Neal and I were already married in the eyes of heaven.

I debated with myself whether or not to tell my parents. At first I had not done so, praying some miracle might cause me to abort naturally so they'd never have to know. But now I remembered how shattered they had been when my sister had eloped, thinking they wouldn't understand, and the pain that had caused them. I had watched their suffering as well as the forgiving reunion a year later. I decided now to give them that chance to understand. Any emotional support from my mother would moderate my remorse considerably.

So I wrote to her and anxiously awaited consolation. It did not come. Instead, at the week's end, a letter arrived pouring out her disillusion and disgust, with rending accusations of my wantonness and selfish irresponsibility. For Neal I had dishonored my family. And where was Neal?

I spent a damp and dismal night. Neal did come back, just as he'd said he would, but he found a pitiful *hausfrau* awaiting him. Recovered himself, he set about altering my state of mind with a frantic and hilarious description of his trip.

'Thirty-three hours, baby—just think of that! It's two thousand eight hundred and ninety-four miles, y'know! I really had that old clunker mesmerized . . . hee, hee, heeee, yeaaah. You shoulda seen me going over Donner pass—ha! Of course, I didn't have my chains on, so I just barrelled right up that mountain, full throttle, and it was snowing hard. Right on top—now get this—on top, see, there were these two snowplows. They'd stopped to yell at each other—out there in the dark and snow, another human bein' . . . They stopped opposite each other . . .' He drew diagrams on the table in his intensity. '. . . I couldn't slow down, of course, or I'd never get up my momentum again, so I just whooshed right in between 'em before they even knew what passed them . . . hee, heee . . . and imagine their faces! Then, just over the summit, the damn car quits. There I was . . . no antifreeze, you realize. I just sat there seven hours . . . *seven hours*, mind you . . . freezing my ass off . . . It was eight degrees below zero, my love. Imagine that ! Finally, when I thought my wish to die had come true, a bus came along . . . they'd opened up the road behind me, and I *made* him give me a push so I could coast down the mountain. He had to, you see . . . couldn't leave another human in

57

that cold . . . he'da had it on his conscience for . . . Anyway, on the way down, my windshield wiper broke, see, and I had to stick my head out the window the rest of the way . . . the windshield being thick with snow and it being dark and all. Well, when I got to Denver, the whole side of my head was frozen, and I still can't hear too well out of that ear . . . but, by golly, I made it, hey? I never let up for an instant . . . never hit the brakes the whole way down the mountain . . . yesssirrr . . . *thirty-three hours!*'

'Oh, Neal,' I wailed, 'you could have frozen to death.'

'Not me, baby . . . indestructible Cass, they used to call me, yassir—and we know it's true now, don't we? What with all that nonsense awhile back? But listen to *this* . . . I even made it back in thirty-*six* hours . . . how about that?' And, grinning, he lunged across the table and planted a big kiss on my mouth, his eyes sparkling as of old.

'Uh . . . were . . . you successful in your mission?' I hated to sound a sour note, but this was the important part to me.

'Why, of course, darling, it's all arranged. LuAnne will go back, get the annulment and let us know the minute we're free. So . . . *now,* my pet . . .' He pulled me up in a hug, but I drew away.

'You'd better get some sleep, don't you think?'

'Right you are . . . as always.'

Now Neal decided to consider seriously Al's testimony to the joys of working for the Southern Pacific Railroad. One Sunday afternoon, Al drove us down the peninsula to Campbell to meet his uncle, a conductor. He encouraged Neal, spelling out the advantages of railroad life, many of which Al had already touched upon.

As a beginner, a man worked off the 'extra board,' so called because his runs were either non-scheduled or he was filling in on regular runs if someone was off. He signed on at the bottom of the list and worked up as men and trains were matched and eliminated. The drawback of the extra board was the necessity to be near a phone at all times: if you missed a call, you went to the bottom of the list again. The advantage were more hours' work and more pay than a regular run. Summer work was busiest, because of the perishable truck-farm produce from the Salinas and Santa Clara valleys. If you caught a 'local'—a freight train serving these areas—you might have to do the same job for a week or two, and even though Watsonville was the limit of the Coast Division, temporary extra trains might be needed as far

58

down the coast as San Luis Obispo in the Southern Division, and you could be sent for a two-week 'hold down' there. When your name reached the top of the extra board, you were obliged to accept whatever job was next in line. This added a certain sense of suspense and adventure.

As a beginner, you were required to start work on freight trains. In the first few years, you were likely to be laid off during the slack winter season, but most men either got other jobs or saved their money to tide them over. However when enough years and seniority had been accumulated, you could become a passenger brakeman as well, and in time a conductor, and so have enough seniority to hold down a regular job of your choice, either freight or passenger.

Other advantages of the work were that there were no bosses watching you and you had the freedom to work or not. If you gave sufficient notice, you could take off at any time, being paid only for the hours you worked. You could keep your seniority rating by working only sixty days a year. This allowed for travel, study or any other chosen activity, provided you had the money, while still keeping your seniority status and being able to return whenever you wished. It sounded too good to be true in some ways: varied and exciting, if somewhat hazardous and uncertain at the start. And though the trainmen's union was ineffectual—as we were soon to learn—the base pay was fairly good, so that if a man were willing to work hard and often, a lot of money could be made during the busy season.

It was the sort of challenge that Neal liked. He agreed to try, and Al's uncle put in a good word for him. The following week he completed the necessary examinations and, although color blind, passed the color test. Luckily, the old physician who gave the test still used the old-fashioned bits of yarn that Neal could distinguish. Even though Neal had memorized every page of the Japanese color-blind book, and I'd been testing him for days, this came as a relief. When I asked him if he wasn't worried about signal lights, he answered, 'Well, dummy, everybody knows the top one is red and the bottom one green . . . even if they look the opposite to me, what does it matter? I know what they mean.' Now he just had to wait two more weeks for his training trips, for which he would not be paid.

At my own job, I began the game of announcing my wedding plans—no one knew I was pregnant—and gave in my notice. I worked at being the glowing, happily expectant bride-to-be, and even convinced myself sometimes. It was going to be a far cry from my sister-in-law's early vision of me sweeping down the spiral staircase in an ice-blue satin gown. On Saturday, 27 March, I bid farewell to my co-workers with no reluctance whatsoever, except perhaps for missing the weekly check. But I was confident, as usual, that security would be a simple matter; Neal would soon be working regularly, and as a babe in the financial woods, it seemed to me that our small savings were more than adequate.

Neal and I spent a carefree weekend as of old, enjoying the city and Golden Gate Park, then going to hear Flip Phillips in concert one night and Perez Prado the next. Neal yearned more than ever for a musical outlet of his own.

I slept late on Monday morning, and when I awoke I saw that Neal had already gotten up. Mystified, I padded to the kitchen and found a sweet note saying he had 'errands' to do but would return soon. 'Soon' turned out to be late in the afternoon, and I had to rebuff threatening memories of his birthday. But then he came bursting in the door in a frenzy. LuAnne's mother had arranged for the annulment, he declared, and LuAnne had agreed to go with him to Denver to sign the papers . . . tomorrow. Neal was his old self once more. I piped the usual anxieties and warnings, but this was the kind of thing that made life worthwhile to him: a challenging drive with a couple of deadlines and no end of obstacles.

With all the old loving, reassuring words, he roared off the following morning in an old Packard he'd traded for the Chevy. He'd promised to pay $1,195 for it, had paid only $200 so far, and had driven it 14,000 miles in eighty-five days. It couldn't hold out much longer. I couldn't help worrying, remembering his last trip, and now he'd have LuAnne with him. She said she was engaged to marry a seaman, but I doubted if she felt any obligation to Neal, and maybe she saw this just as one more chance to torment him. My confidence in Neal's love for me was intact, however. I was sure he and I were equally concerned about the future of our child.

Forty-eight hours later Neal was back, held up this time by a minor accident on the way into San Francisco. He let himself in and came to sit on the bed. I awoke and grabbed him, relieved, surprised and thankful. He was jubilant—free at last, and we already had our marriage license. Better yet, LuAnne had stayed in Denver, a piece of news that made my happiness complete. 'So—get up, get up—we gotta have a big celebration breakfast.'

Once I was dressed and had prepared something to eat, he reached across the table and took my hand. 'So now, my one-and-only, you and I will blast down to the courthouse tomorrow morning and get hitched at last, eh wot? Hey, baby? You 'n' me forever, like I said, right?' He lifted my hand and planted a big egg-yolkey kiss on it. I could only manage to smile, nod and reach for the coffee pot.

Fourteen

At work at the jewelry counter, I had struck up a friendship with a weekly shopper who collected and sold antique jewelry. She had often shown me pieces that were elaborate and unusual, and was herself a living image along the same lines. When I'd told her that I was leaving the store and getting married, much to my surprise and delight she had begged me to let her provide our wedding rings. I was to call her when I would need them. I was excited, trying to imagine what marvels she'd find for us. So, while Neal was away I telephoned, and although it was short notice, she responded warmly and told me to meet her at the side door of The White House at ten on the morning of the wedding, when she would bring the rings.

That much was settled. Now, what to wear? Besides the two 'basic blacks' I had for work, there was only one other dress in my possession: a plain light-green woolen my mother had made me for Christmas. Little did she suspect she'd made my wedding gown. It came with a navy coat which was lined in the dress material and was loose enough to conceal my swelling front.

Next morning I was awake early. I dressed as carefully and as prettily as possible and left the apartment before Neal, agreeing to meet him at the City Hall at eleven. When he'd first gone job-hunting, I had bought him a suit, only the second he'd ever owned, and for his birthday I'd added a white shirt and a couple of ties, so he had no problem deciding what to wear. The Denver trip had finished off the Packard, so we were both dependent on public transport.

It was a cold, grey morning, with clouds of fog chasing each other between the hills and buildings. I stood outside The White House in the biting wind, regretting my habit of always being early. To kill time and get warm I crossed the street to Woolworth's. There was a display of fake diamonds just inside the doors, 'newly discovered' stones that 'defied comparison' with the real thing. This reminded me of my reason for being there, and I looked the stones over, smugly pleased that I didn't have to wear the traditional 'solitaire'. I'd never liked diamonds by themselves, and I was happy my benefactress dealt in more exotic items.

When I was warmer, I crossed back over to the appointed meeting place. It was ten-fifteen and I had begun to think she had been bluffing when I saw her hurrying along on the opposite side of the street, hanging on to her flowered hat and veil, her head bent against the wind that ruffled her fox-fur collar. I nearly called out, then checked the impulse as she bustled directly into Woolworth's. Could she have forgotten she'd said The White House? Should I follow? Before I could decide to move, she emerged, darted into the traffic and made her way to me. She blossomed into a broad synthetic smile and opened her purse to paw through its generous womb, bringing out a small box in her gloved hand. She pressed it into mine and held on. 'My *very* best wishes, my dear,' she oozed warmly. 'I hope you'll be very happy. He's a lucky man—and thank you for letting me share in this happy occasion. I hope you'll both like the rings.'

I was impatient to see them, so I disengaged my hand and tore off the wrapping. I lifted the lid of the box and could utter only a weak 'Oh.' With great effort I cracked my face into a smile. My few words of gratitude came out with a hollow ring. Here was a set of rings straight from the display I had scorned in Woolworth's. I was crushed, bewildered, and wanted to cry. Even I could have done better—even Neal! I thanked God *he* hadn't presented me with this trash; I'd have had to wear them forever.

By now it was so late I had to hail a cab or be late meeting Neal. It was money I hated to spend. I sat in the cab and looked at the pathetic molded silvery rings and tried to figure why she'd bothered, why she'd offered in the first place. Mostly I thought, 'What have I done to deserve this?' I was sentimental and symbols were important to me the way dates and resolutions were to Neal. But then I had to laugh as my 'wedding day' became more and more a grotesque parody of my youthful dreams.

Seeing Neal waiting and smiling at the curb renewed my joy. This was all that really mattered, after all. And from behind his back he flipped out a little gold flower box. So completely unexpected was the gesture that I could only gape and stammer. This mark of affection more than made up for my disappointment with the rings. I pinned the three gardenias on my coat as we mounted the steps of the ominous gray building.

We had to wait in the anteroom until the judge was free, and as we sat on the big black leather couch I told Neal about the rings. When I showed them to him, he gasped, and we fell prey to those irrepressible giggles that one only gets at times of great solemnity.

Presently we were told by a bored underling that the judge would see us in his chambers. 'JUDGE CLAYTON GOLDEN' a little plaque on the door declared.

In the small chamber, nearly completely filled with a large desk and chair, our unrehearsed and varied emotions were amplified by the awkward space. We became eager to get the ceremony over, instead of gazing into each other's eyes and savouring the significance of the words as we had planned. The judge was cool, detached and mechanical: '. . . I now pronounce you man and wife. That will be ten dollars.' Neal turned on me such a blank look, I nearly broke into laughter again. Panic prevented it. I came to with a snap and fumbled in my purse until I found my wallet, from which I withdrew the only bill in it—fortunately a ten. I felt as though I'd just bought a husband—but it was cheap at that, considering my need.

Once outside we let loose all our tensions and howled with laughter as we ran down the steps into the plaza and out into the now bright April sunlight, scattering pigeons and dodging startled passers-by. 'No wonder his name is "Golden",' Neal yelled.

'We can't just go home,' Neal said when we reached the curb. 'What shall we do to redeem the situation? If that judge hadn't fleeced me, I'd ask my wife to join me in a glass of champagne and an elegant lunch.'

'Oh yeah? It was *my* ten dollars.'

'Now my dear, let's not be petty. All for one and one for all, right? Let's just see what we have left.' He poked through his pockets, and I got out my change purse to pool our resources. 'Well, now. This I keep for carfare. That leaves . . . let's see . . . why, that's a heap! Ahem, my dear wife, would you do me the honor of sharing a lunch at that quaint little diner across yon street? Hmmm, Mrs. Cassady?' He stuck out his elbow and bowed with Charlie Chaplin flourishes as we pranced across the street oblivious to the other pedestrians.

The diner was tiny, a bit grimy and crowded, but we squeezed into a table and did our best to create some romance, lighting the candle in spite of the daylight all about. Neal turned on all his charm, held my hand and gave me his full attention. I sniffed my gardenias and glowed. The champagne turned out to be a bottle of beer apiece, but it was spiked with spirits of joy.

As we walked out, Neal spied a small grocery store. 'Hey, I think we have enough left for a six-pack, by gum. We'll have a celebration yet.'

Fifteen

That was 1 April 1948—April Fool's Day, it occurred to me. But at last I was Mrs. Neal L. Cassady, and even though I'd already been using the name for quite a while, it was an enormous relief to be honest about it.

The day after, Neal began his unpaid railroad student trips. He found the work something of a strain at first, but on the whole it agreed with his temperament, and, as usual, he distinguished himself and became a favorite with the older 'heads.' His diploma came in the form of an official pocket-watch, iron-toed shoes, retractable key chain for switch keys, and a big freight lantern. He displayed them to me with as much pride as any Cub Scout showing his mother his badges.

Neal was ready for work, but work wasn't ready for him; the season had not yet begun. For two weeks he tried locals in Watsonville, but with no luck, he returned home disgusted, announcing he'd go to sea.

'But Neal,' I wailed, 'you'd be gone for months—the baby born without you?'

'I know, I know, darling, it sounds awful to me, too. But it'll only be until the railroad picks up . . . I'll send you all my pay. What else can I do?'

His question had a ring of rising desperation, and I backed down.

Two days later he was a full-fledged Ordinary Seaman. 'Not so "ordinary" to me, my love,' I said. He had papers, an ID card with his name and new title, and a funny picture of him taken on the boardwalk under souvenir banners of San Francisco. Two more days and he had signed on a ship going to Arabia; it might as well have been Mars. I felt the rug being pulled from under me, but I said nothing.

But fate intervened when Al telephoned to say he was going to the Southern Division where there were definite jobs. Neal decided to join him, keeping his seaman status in reserve, and once more he was generated into hyperactivity and good spirits at the chance to be on the move. The fact that Bakersfield maintained the highest temperatures in the state was of no consequence to him . . . yet.

The bad news arrived the week after he left. Mike, our housing benefactor, returned to announce he was getting married again. His bride-to-be already had an apartment, so he would move his furniture there immediately. So that I wouldn't have to move while Neal was gone, he generously paid the rent until 15 July and left us the fold-out couch, our bed and one chest. My foolish pride wouldn't let me tell him how broke we were, or that Neal would not be paid for at least another two weeks. I was down to my last five dollars.

It was an unusually hot May for San Francisco, and after Mike left I sat and surveyed the bright white, echoing apartment. After dark, stark overhead lights replaced the sun. In the kitchen only the stove remained, but I had nothing to cook except water and nothing to cook that in. I recalled my sister telling me that she'd once existed on peanut butter and lettuce, so I followed her lead, adding milk for the child. In a mockery of my plight, a newlywed couple moved in next door and invited me to view the slides of their honeymoon in Bermuda; I sat glumly amid the warm, rich surroundings and the aromas of their just-finished dinner.

My pregnancy was into the sixth month, and I had no maternity clothes. I found some cotton curtain material and sewed by hand a gathered skirt. This and one of Neal's white shirts comprised my entire wardrobe. The heat was getting to me, so I stayed up later at night when it was cool and napped in the afternoon.

As the money dwindled, I searched our belongings for something to sell. A used-record store apologetically bought our entire collection for $2.50. Tearfully, I saved a few Billie Holiday's and mambos, sentimentally too attached to part with them. After that, I hunted through the closet, but the only garment of any value appeared to be my fur coat from college days, a mink-dyed muskrat. I tramped the hot streets of San Francisco in the blazing sun, being brushed off with snobbish sneers at the fur department of elegant stores, finally thrusting the coat upon a man who remade long coats into jackets. He didn't want it either, but he took it and gave me 25¢. I accepted it for carfare and because I couldn't face lugging that hot fur all the way home.

Looking back, I am appalled at how I had to walk on such thin ice, but that was not how I felt then. I was proud to be 'enduring' for 'us.' I was sustained, too, by the almost daily loving letters from Neal, which described an ordeal far more severe than mine, a grueling routine in intense heat. After a month, he was not released as expected but sent to Pixley to work a potato local, and I couldn't even find that town on the map. 'Daily routine:' he wrote, 'up at 8:30 a.m., work from 9–7 p.m. Sleep in the outfit car here—eat in a café across the street, read, write, think and smoke.' His paycheck had been delayed for no known reason.

My situation was becoming critical when Al Hinkle suddenly appeared at the door, bearing Neal's first check. Because of Al's higher seniority, he'd been called back to the Coast Division again, but he said Neal had been lucky to get so much work already and would be paid well when he was through.

As Neal's peace of mind improved, he wrote at last to Allen from Pixley, and Allen answered:

> . . . the great event was your letter—we had assumed you were in jail or something—of course, I had fantasized you dead, more or less, and even suspected suicide some months back. Myself, this spring has been one of madness, much like yours . . . What finally pulled me out—to name an external cause—was Jack's novel. It is very great, beyond my wildest expectation. I never knew.

Neal also wrote to Jack, summarizing the major events of the previous six months and relating his tortures, if not their cause, and adding, 'I make no attempt to answer your letters; I'm insisting on a copy—with autograph—of the great, perfect and loving tome of yours . . .'

On Neal's exultant deliverance from Pixley at the end of June, we set out at once to find another apartment. Our days of luxury were over. We took the first one we found for $50 a month, in a converted old house high atop a hill overlooking Castro Street, on one aptly named Alpine Terrace. Steep concrete steps rose from the street to the front door, from which you looked down on the tops of the telephone poles. Had we been less hurried, we'd have noticed it was at least six blocks uphill from the nearest market or laundromat. But once again love made all things possible, and I was eager to build a nest for Neal and our child. I was happy and secure once more, and set to work decorating with painted muslin, enamelled orange crates, tatami mats and peasant designs on the kitchen cabinets.

Now that Neal was working steadily I learned to adjust to the railroad's unusual demands. We didn't mind the irregular hours — I liked having him home during the day sometimes — but the chief drawback was being tied to the telephone. If he went out at all, he had to keep calling the crew clerk for an estimate of his next run, and it wasn't easy to predict accurately — sometimes it was only hours away, other times, days. The job was now familiar and it suited his restless nature, with its stimulating variety of action and suspense as well as periods of quiet riding when he could write or think. Occasionally it offered a bonus in vegetables scattered off boxcars — manna from heaven, though it was sometimes hard to dispose of eleven heads of lettuce all at once.

Neal loved all the characters and the whole new language. His imitations would have me holding my sides — for example, his description of a tagman on a local job: 'We picked up the switchlist, see, and this guy'd say, "Wall, Neal, let's get two behind three off one, then double to four to set out the east cars, spot the express reefer, pull five and kick seven down the lead. Then it'll be a tray, deuce, four, another deuce, five aces and a tray, hand the head car and come to fifteen to shove that rail, then set the crummy off the limey and we'll cross over tie eight . . .' Neal would get giggling so hard himself he'd have to stop. Then he'd translate slowly, but still too fast for me to remember past the telling.

His *joie de vivre* was restored to full force, and he wrote to Jack, '. . . For the first time in more than three years my soul has faltered in its black, purposeful dash to sick ruin. It's not a cycle . . . for God has once again touched my seed — it blooms, I blossom.' Giddy descriptions were resumed, detailing all the simultaneous creative projects he'd accomplish, and Neal even confided, 'I am working seriously on a short thing about a man digging — oh, well, if I finish it I'll talk about it . . . I have a little thing I've done. If you've time I'd be pleased to send it on to you for any opinion you could give.'

And I, too, now free of a daily job and with the apartment in a livable state, relaxed and felt the urge to paint. I bought supplies and began a 'formal' portrait of Neal in spite of cramped quarters and poor light. I suggested to him, since he could do all those impossible artistic stunts he'd outlined to Jack, that he should try oil painting.

Much to my surprise he went about it with painstaking precision, painting stiff, abstract designs, rigid and tight, flat color bordered by flat color. In no way could I get him to loosen up and enjoy splashing paint about.

The same restraint showed in another letter to Jack. After writing, 'Carolyn is doing a tremendous portrait of me, 4 ft. by 5 ft. [how he loved exaggerating sizes!]. It'll take her 6 months, I'm sure.' He admitted:

> I feel somewhat forced in writing to you and thereby stunted in growth with you . . . I ask directly can you think of a way to make *me* speak more freely to you, and, in doing so, improve my *direct, simple* style of writing? Any suggestions of this literary question will be gratefully received. Thank you, Mr. Rilke, I want to be a cowboy, a ranch hombre. I'll grow a beard like 'Gabby' Hayes.

Whether or not this remark started it, I can't remember, but Jack wrote to Neal of his ambition to buy a ranch for all of us to share, and Neal answered with enthusiasm:

> Your ranching is beautiful! If you're serious and want a man who will make $350–400 a month on the railroad every year from May to January—and his wife and his child and his knowledge of ranch work and his love for you and your mother—then take me. Seriously, now, Jack, stop and think of it—it's easy really to do. I *know* your mother (you must bring her) and Carolyn would get on together famously—and for us to build a ranch, a great spread, together, would be better than renting rooms for $50 the rest of our lives—we had better start right now—we always put off too much—start *now*—bring your buddies, we'll have 7–8 bedrooms—your mother (Bless her) and Carolyn (Bless her) are exactly alike—Carolyn's a great worker, and interior decorator—I'm convinced it's easy—and I'll get the money. A home—to go and come to—to grow old in—to make into a great place—you'll never do it if you don't do it now—please think!

To me he said, 'Listen, Carolyn, I figure it should take us about two years to achieve the actuality of living in our Shakespearian house. After this month and next, we should have all our bills and the baby things paid off. Then, starting September, we should be able to save $100 every month . . . the baby shouldn't cost too much the first six months, should it? So, by the first of the year we oughta have $500, if we really scrimp, eh? Then when I get cut off in January, I'll go to sea till May and get something over $200 per—or, if not, I can get $25 a week unemployment here . . . maybe I could get another job under an alias . . .' He saw my scowl. '. . . No? Well, okay, anyway, we'll see how it looks in January.'

In several subsequent letters to Jack, Neal rhapsodized still further on this idea; he even sent for every pamphlet offered by every bureau he could find to learn more about ranches, water rights, land permits and so on. This dedication to the cause and his ardent visions of our bucolic life deepened my sense of peace and joy. I had a few reservations in regard to the kind of communal living he began to outline to Jack as he added more and more 'guests' or 'ranch hands':

To fantasize a bit. I envision Holmes, one Bill Tomson and, depending again, one Allen G., grubbing, scrubbing to aid, for they come in as they wish. No hard and fast, naturally, rules or obligations or expectancies or any such bourgoise [*sic*] strains in our veins toward them. The nucleus of our family then (financially, wholeheartedly): you, your mother, Paul, his wife and child, me, Carolyn and our offspring (*and* your wife?). That totals 8 or 9, figure 9, all living, striving. First cousins to our family, then, will be (as they wish from one week to one year) your great GB . . . George?, remember? Allen, Holmes, Tomson, and dear beautiful brother Herbert Huncke. This may seem to be becoming overdone, but, to continue, I don't really mean to include Burroughs (a probable impossibility anyhow) but I do love him and Joan so much you know . . . pure speculation, but maybe visits at any rate. So, that's another 9 counting Julie and Bill junior. That makes a house that, at one time or another, ought to hold 18 people. How many rooms is that? Anywhere from 10 to 13. Kitchen, living room (which must be huge or we'll need two), dining room, figure about 7–8 bedrooms, nursery room or rooms or some such, you understand, Jack. Huge garden . . . Well, I'll stop. I'm sure you have the idea, in fact, better ideas, and you decide the limitations if any, on our household from guests to residents, location, etc., etc.

But I encouraged him for all I was worth and joined him in games of pennypinching. For once he didn't buy another car; instead, he bought a bicycle and rode the long length of Market Street to the depot no matter the weather, the hour or his state of fatigue.

Sixteen

The baby had been scheduled for August, but August came and went. I was hot, heavy and ready. Neal was all I could wish for in attentiveness and help and seemed to look forward to the child with genuine pleasure. He had written to Jack: 'My dear, sweet, great little wife—my perfect Carolyn . . . is now 7 months along and will present me with a child I shall keep, raise, and glory in—needless to say, dear Jack—if my baby is a boy, I shall name him after you—and Allen. If it is a girl, I can't, for a name like Jacqueline . . . is unbearable to think of.' On 20 August he wrote to Allen: '. . . if it is a boy I shall name it: Allen Jack Cassady. I anticipate him always signing his name thus: 'Allen J. Cassady.' If my child is a female, I have decided to name her: Cathleen Joanne Cassady.'

Late in the evening of 6 September, my hour arrived. Neal contacted a railroad friend who drove us to the hospital. For my first baby, I would have appreciated Neal's presence and support, but he was not allowed to come in with me, nor was he allowed to visit during my week's required stay since the previous week there'd been a case of childbed fever.

During the labour I asked about anesthetic. 'Not this week,' the young doctor replied smugly. 'We're trying it without. Besides, we think women should have this experience'—'we' meaning men, I assumed.

Cathleen Joanne Cassady was born at 12:29 a.m. I'm sure of the time, because those twenty-nine minutes were the cause of my having to stay an extra day. They were the longest eight days I can remember, in spite of the entertaining company of eleven other wardmates. Neal sent flowers and a lovely card, but that's the only contact I had, and fearful thoughts assailed me as to his activities.

Once I was home with Cathy, Neal erased all such suspicions. He was completely immersed in his daughter and wanted to be a part of everything concerning her. He made her food formula, changed diapers, took the wash to the laundromat, fed her, bathed her and studied Dr. Spock as thoroughly as he had his former interests. While he fed her a bottle, I beamed at the sight of that tiny pink mound no longer than his forearm nestled against his bare, muscular chest. He was beside himself with delight in her, repeating often 'I never knew . . . I never knew.' He wrote to Jack: 'I can't tell you the blubbering glee I've been gurgling since Cathleen's arrival (and before) . . . She's a month old today, has gone out into the world 3 times . . . and is thriving in general. She's now 21 inches long and weighs 8lbs, 8ozs. I love her like mad.' And later: 'I cannot learn sadness from you, Jack, my capacity for it is lost. (I think sadness is gone forever from me— Ah, how sad.) . . . I used to be truly indefatigable . . . sex drove me . . . now, I like music and am sterile. Maybe my girl, Cathy Jo, will continue to make me content and strong.'

Allen responded to the announcement with a note that cheered me, too:

Congratulations on your little child. How does it feel to be a father? (I mean it even if it sounds simple.) It certainly feels fine to be a grandfather. If you send me some details surrounding the psychic atmosphere of her birth, I'll write you a triumphal ode . . . I've put little Cathy in my will . . . I'm seeing my lawyers tomorrow. She will inherit zillions of dollars when I die. P.S. Blessings on my daughter-in-law for a change, and on you, too, son.

Then one afternoon two months later, Al and Neal came in and acted strangely self-conscious and nervous. I could hear them go into the bedroom mumbling and whispering. After awhile, Al came out and sat on the edge of the couch, fidgeting with his cigarette package. 'Uh, I've got a . . . surprise for you,' he stammered.

'Have you, Al? What is it?'

'I'm going to get married.' He looked up at me and smiled.

'Married! Why, Al—to whom? Why haven't I met her? You haven't told me you have a steady girl.'

73

'I don't, that is . . . I just met her day before yesterday.' This was more surprising still; Al was the stable type. 'When do you plan to be married?'

'Well . . . Saturday morning . . . in a church!' His eyes widened.

Neal emerged from the bathroom during this exchange. 'Yeah, what the hell,' he said. 'Why does she insist on a church wedding, anyway? Come on, Al, let's see if we can't think of something to speed her up.' His tone was nasty; I couldn't imagine why, nor what business it was of his. But he hurried Al out, Al calling back: 'I'll try and get her to come back with us.'

It was late in the afternoon when they returned with Helen, for that was her name. I was more mystified than ever when I saw her. I would have bet money Al would choose only a sweet, young, pretty thing, but here was a woman of indeterminate age (although Al said she was 22) and rather stolid of figure, a Mother Earth type. Her face looked tired now, her dark brown eyes round and as puzzled as mine. Perhaps I was not what she expected in Neal's wife, either. She had rich brown, thick, wavy hair pulled back to a bun, and she wore a tailored brown suit. She was nervous, seemed to feel awkward, and she answered my polite inquiries rather grumpily. Why wasn't she glowing? I had to assume she had so much on her mind, she'd prefer not to sit making small talk with Neal's wife, especially since, I gathered later, she'd taken an instant dislike to him. Her eyes appealed silently to Al, and he got up to lead her out.

The next day Neal dashed in and out, preoccupied, evasive and jumpy, protesting that he was helping Al get ready for the following morning's ordeal. Late in the afternoon he bounded into the apartment, grinning broadly, eyes shining and rubbing his hands.

'Come with me, baby . . . I've got a surprise for you. Come on, now . . . I'll show you . . . just wait till you see . . .

He appeared ready to burst. Now what? I stopped folding diapers and followed him down the inside then the outside steps. At the sidewalk, I said, 'Where are you taking me? I'm not dressed . . . and Cathy . . .'

'Nowhere, my baby, we're *here* . . .' Neal interrupted. 'Right here, my dear! Now, look at *that*, wouldja?'

He waved his free arm in a broad gesture toward a shiny, brand new, two-toned metallic maroon and gray car. Seeing my blank expression, he leaped into action, tearing open the door on the driver's side (he had parked it on the wrong side of the street).

'Just look at this, honey, see? The floor is sunk below the door frame

74

. . . it's a step-down living . . . I mean . . . *driving* room, how about that? And look at that dash—like an airplane, eh? See? Radio . . . oh, and baby, it drives like a dreeeeeam, smooth as silk. Just wait till you ride in it. Come on, I'll take you for a spin.'

Each word was like a giant demolition ball, crushing all my hopes. He had started to take my elbow to lead me around the car, but I wrenched free and bolted up the steps and into the apartment. He ran after me and found me on the couch, my head in my hands. He sat beside me and put his arm about my trembling shoulders. He spoke quietly (because of the sleeping baby) but urgently.

'Now, now, Carolyn, look here, you don't understand. Al and Helen are getting married tomorrow, right? They have to have a honeymoon, but they have no car. Now, then, Jack wants to come out, but he hasn't the money to get here. So, see, ol' Cass to everybody's rescue. We'll kill both birds with one basket, so to speak. I'll whip over to New York to get Jack, break in the new car, and at the same time Al and Helen get their honeymoon, see? But the best part is, Helen is loaded. She's paying all our expenses! It's a free ride, don't you see?'

'Did she pay for the car, too? Where did you get it?'

'Why, I bought it, naturally, my dear . . . or the downpayment, of course. It's for you, you and Cathy, so you can take her to the doctor and the store and . . .'

'You mean . . . you used our savings? The ranch money?'

I leaped away from him and stared at him. He got up to pace, the strain beginning to show in his face.

'Well, our savings, yes, but look, I can make that much back in two months when I'm on the railroad again next spring . . . easy. The monthly payments are practically nothing. It'll be a cinch, honest, baby. You know we need a car with the baby and all, and this one won't be breaking down all the time. Soon as I get back, I promise you I'll get another job until they call me back. It's *all right*, Carolyn . . . you'll see.'

He made it sound so logical, but it couldn't be. Here we were living in a cardboard dump with orange-crate bookcases, yet we had a brand new car, no savings, no income, a new baby, and he was talking about driving clear across the country.

'I see. So all the rush about the wedding is just to get Helen and her money to finance *your* trip?'

'Well, ye . . . no . . . not entirely. It just works out neatly that way. And I promised Jack . . .'

75

I started to cry. 'I seem to remember you promising me a thing or two, like loving and cherishing. What about *our* honeymoon? Oh, no, we had to save our money so we could have a home . . .' I bit my lip.

Neal tried to come to me, but I dodged him, trying to collect myself and wipe my face. More calmly I said, 'When do you leave?'

He paused until he'd lit a cigarette. 'Well . . . uh . . . right after the wedding.'

'You mean . . . *tomorrow*?' Panic struck. He was serious. This was really happening. He was going to leave us stranded. 'But Neal, what about *us*? How will we live with no money?'

'Now, honey, don't you worry. I've thought of that, of course. I have it all arranged, so don't fret. Ardo is going to look after you while I'm gone. He'll bring groceries . . . just give him a list. He'll take the wash, too, see? There's nothing to worry about. I'll pay him back when I'm working. It's all okay, and I'm only going to be gone a week, at most two.'

'You really mean to tell me it's more important to you to keep a promise to Jack than to your family?'

'It isn't that . . . good God, it's just a short trip. Don't I deserve any vacation after I've worked so damned hard?'

I spun around like a wounded animal and snarled: 'What about *me*? What have I been doing? Can you even imagine what it's been like for me?' Renewed tears made my voice shrill.

His face looked pained, but he said nothing. In a moment he walked to the closet and began hunting for his suitcase. This concrete evidence was too much for me. I dropped on the couch again and wailed: 'Oh Neal, don't, please don't leave us!'

'Now, Carolyn, I'm not *leaving* you. I'll be right back.' And he continued to sort clothes.

My fear turned to fury. Something snapped inside me. I've never forgotten that feeling of a physical tear . . . in my mind? my heart? where? All the discipline of my early upbringing to keep control, bite the bullet, never to hurt anyone, never to express anything rude or derogatory—all gave way like a bursting dam.

'How can you, how *can* you? Have you no heart at all? How could you lie about loving me . . . use me . . . make me bear your child? All you do is take advantage of people . . . You'd just walk out with all our money? Leave a *baby*? Oh, you bastard, you lousy *bastard* . . . You don't care for us . . . *My* car! What a riot *that* is . . . You're finally showing your true colors . . . You've a heart of stone if you have one at all—you're nothing but selfish . . . I should have known—you're

76

nothing but a *guttersnipe*, after all . . . How *stupid* I've been . . .'

All control had abandoned me, I was sobbing, bawling, screaming, wallowing, shaking and feeling sick with self-disgust and fear. When he turned to face me, my degradation was complete—for he was crying, too, his face contorted in pain.

Quietly he said, 'I have feelings, too, you know.' He actually said that. He had *feelings* . . . Oh, God, how insane it all was. I threw myself on the couch and sobbed on.

Of course, Cathy woke up. How could I move? Why must I? But I had to, and I dragged myself to her and performed all the automatic movements to attend to her needs, the sight of her tiny helpless form squeezing out fresh tears.

As I came back from the kitchen with her bottle, she on my shoulder, Neal approached us, his hand held out, concern on his face. His suitcase was in his other hand. I backed away and spat out: 'Just go, if you're going. Get out, now! I never want to see you again—not ever!' And Cathy started to scream.

All I wanted was for him to stay; all I could do was to tell him to go. For the first time, I was afraid of life, yet every word and action was aimed at driving him farther away. Neal dropped his hand but still looked lovingly at us. 'Oh, don't look like you *care*,' I said. 'You can't fool me again.'

I listened to his departing steps, the closing apartment door, his feet on the stairs, the closing outer door, the front steps, the engine starting and the roar of the departing car—the breaking cord. Gone. Really gone. I was all alone. My ears were ringing, my body and mind drained. I held Cathy like a doll, feeding her, her tiny eyes scanning my face coolly, her feeble fingers probing my wet face. Without her, what would have happened? Her needs caused me to keep going through the motions, but I didn't know how or what to think. Of course, without Cathy, I'd have been free; I'd never have gone back to Neal. I'd have gone to work and moved away. How simple. Yet this tiny creature could make me so helpless and enslaved. At least it never occurred to me to resent her for it.

Seventeen

The next morning the telephone startled me awake, and it was a minute or two before the horror again established itself in my awareness. I leaped at the phone to keep it from waking Cathy, and softly said, 'Hello.'

'Now, darling, keep calm . . . listen to me. I feel terrible. I understand how you feel. I see now, and I'm sorry. I do love you, you know I do . . . and Cathy Jo. Please don't fret. Honest, baby, I'll be right back. I can hardly wait. I'll hurry.'

How I loved his voice; how I ached to have him back; how I hated him. I must be strong. Don't be deceived again. Don't listen to him or your heart.

'Where are you?' was all I could say with safety.

'Just outside of town. I just had to stop and call you. Everybody's waiting in the car, but I had to talk to you. I love you. Please don't fret, promise me?'

'Outside of town? Then . . . what do you mean, "right back"?' For one wild instant I thought that he meant he couldn't do it.

'Just as quick as I can make it, baby. You know me, I'll drive my greatest. I'll really hurry, and with this car, it'll be like no time, you'll see. I'll be back 'fore you know it . . .'

'Oh, *shut up!*' I interrupted, now realizing he was still on his way, that he was simply salving his conscience with good intentions, hoping to get my blessing so he could really enjoy himself. 'I never

78

want you to come back. Don't you dare come back here—*ever!*' I slammed down the receiver.

My venom turned to self-pity and sobs took me over again. Cathy woke and began to scream. 'Stop it!' I yelled, then guilt and shock at my outburst sobered me. I picked her up and we wailed together.

With less than two weeks until Christmas, every day's mail brought packages—my family's abundant offerings again, and this time, Cathy as well as Neal was included. It was the final irony. I took off the mailing wrappers but left on the pretty coloured papers and ribbons, and put the presents on top of the low bookshelves in an ever-growing array. My marriage over, I had no desire to open them or read the cheery sentiments.

In a few days, Ardo arrived. He was a young colleague of Neal's from the railroads. My emotions toward him were mixed: I resented him since he represented the loss of Neal, but at the same time I was relieved to open the door and see him balancing boxes of supplies. Neal must have given him a well-considered list, and Ardo had not stinted on quality or abundance. I was far from gracious. I thought him a fool and told him so. He adored Neal, and I did my best to disillusion him as I had been disillusioned. He must have thought Neal all the wiser for having left such a shrew.

'Can't you see he's using you, too, Ardo?' I asked scornfully. 'He'll never pay you back . . . how can he? Who knows if he'll ever even *come* back."

'Oh, yes, he will,' Ardo averred with fervor. 'He's been wonderful to me. He wouldn't lie to me. He's helped me so much at work. I know he'll keep his promise.'

'Ha!' I battered at this staunch faith. 'You and everyone else. Sure, he's just great when he wants something from you. Boy, can he be everything you want and say all you want to hear. Don't *I* know! But you'll see, just as I have. How can you believe a man who deserts his wife and baby?'

'He didn't desert you—he's just gonna be gone a couple weeks.'

Trust shone in his pale blue, pink-rimmed eyes. He looked such a babe in the woods, I had to soften a little, torn between the need to keep Ardo's help and the desire to vent my pain and humiliation. I thanked him weakly.

As Christmas day drew near, I knew I'd have to tell my sister. I couldn't think how. Such shame, such misjudgement to confess. I had been so proud of Neal, so sure. But she'd have to know; we were expected there for Christmas dinner.

By the time we left her apartment on Christmas night, my sister's English stoicism and enduring optimism had helped pacify my anxieties somewhat, and as I walked outside to her husband's car, I could see a little of the sprawling city lights and realize there was something outside myself that was not entirely hostile. But when I entered my own dark, close rooms, so permeated with memories of Neal, weakness and fear threatened me again; the task looked too great. I had no motivation even to attempt it.

I sat in the big chair and gave Cathy her bottle, the room lit through the single window only by the reflection from the night sky of the surrounding city lights. Through my tears, the shiny papers and Christmas trimmings on the still-unopened gifts made gay, glittering prisms of color before my eyes. If only we could pass out of life right now, Cathy and I. If only time would stop, tomorrow never come.

But mornings continued to come round and, with my returning consciousness, the need to cope. Ardo, too, came around like the days of the week, his being Saturday. I continued to be cool as he reopened my wound and tried to convince me that Neal was faithful and true.

One day he triumphantly produced a postcard, waving it before me. 'Look, see? I told you so! I got this card from Neal. He does think about us and he will come back.'

I took the card, a desert scene. It read: 'Great car. Doing 800 miles a day. Made it here in two. All's well, see you soon.' Then I saw the postmark: Denver. A new flash of pain, another surge of shock and realization. Denver = LuAnne. So that was what this was all about. I threw the card at Ardo and smashed all his cheery hopes of changing my mind.

As Ardo looked at me in dismay, little by little the events that had puzzled me during the previous year knitted themselves together: Neal's moods, his restlessness, the suicide attempt, his frequent absences and trips. I buried my face in my hands. He had not really loved me at all—only her. Angered with shame at my blind, trusting stupidity, I laughed in derision at myself, then succumbed anew to self-pity. Tears I had thought expended gushed afresh. I had forgotten Ardo, and when I caught sight of his face, dumb and uncomprehending, some pity went out to him as well. He must have thought me quite insane as well as hateful. Although he had provided me with new ammunition against Neal, it was too painful to use. 'Never mind me, Ardo, I'll explain later. I'm sorry. Now, please go.' No doubt this was the softest tone he'd heard from me, and he was only too glad to comply.

When my landlady defied rent controls and showed frightening signs of insanity, I moved with a neighbour girl into an apartment a few blocks from Mission Dolores and one block from a small park. The girl had stayed with Cathy while I hunted for a home, but soon after we moved in, she moved on.

My few items of furniture looked bleak in the one huge room, which had high Gothic undraped windows with a panoramic view of the city and the distant bay, at night a carpet of jewels. I was once again facing life alone. Ardo still did his duty and was my only contact with the outside world, except for an occasional phone conversation with my sister. She had loaned me the money for rent, and had informed me about welfare. To get to the welfare office meant riding miles and miles, transferring from streetcars and buses not once but three times, carrying Cathy, of course, and having to wait hours to be seen. After days of these voyages, this ray of hope was extinguished, without explanation, and the only suggestion made to me by the welfare people was that I should put Cathy in an 'infant shelter' while I went to work. That I could not do. (Years later, when appealing again to this agency, I was to ask them to check back and tell me why my previous request had been refused. The astonishing notation read: 'No apparent need.')

Neal had telephoned me several times on his trip. The first time was from Washington, DC, and I had immediately let him know that I knew about LuAnne. 'LuAnne who?' he asked. My insistence that we were through didn't phase him, and he continued to call and talk as though we were both desperate to be together again—he might have been away on a business trip. When I'd hang up, I'd start weeping all over again. When once he called to say he wanted to send me $18.00, I had to give him my new address. His delay in returning had been necessitated, he said, because he'd had to help Jack move his mother from North Carolina to New York. Helen apparently had been left in Tucson, Arizona, but Al was still with him. Why this was, I couldn't make out, but one thing I didn't want to hear were details of that trip.

Sometime during the last week of January, there Neal was at the door, all smiles and effervescence, ready for the grand reunion. Arming myself with superhuman determination, I presented only frost and indifference, while my whole being reached out to him. He looked so good to me. But pride must be preserved, so I did my best to pretend I was capable of managing by myself and not at all frightened—an empty bluff.

'Now then, darling . . .' He spoke as though I had welcomed him with open arms, but as he looked around the gray apartment he was not deceived, and his cheer was dampened. 'Yes, well . . . so this is the new place? Ah, yes . . .' He poked his head into the unheated bathroom with its ancient fixtures and bare linoleum floor, then strode over to lean down to coo at Cathy in her crib. Then he said, seriously, 'How is she?'

'She's as well as can be expected with no father, no money and no future,' I retorted acidly.

'Now, now, darling. That's no way to talk. The past is past, and I'm back to take over.' He came to sit beside me. I knew I must avoid his touch, so I jumped up and walked to the daybed opposite. 'Just go back to LuAnne, Neal. I don't want to start it all over again.'

'LuAnne? Not a bit of it, my dear. I don't know anything about her nor where she is. It's you and me, baby, you know that. I'll get a job right away and get you and Cathy out of here. Everything will be all right. Trust me, darling. Come on now, you and me, remember?'

'Oh, I remember all right. No, Neal, it's no use. I can never trust you again. The spell is broken. My faith is gone. Better to stop now when a break has already been made. Cathy will never know you nor what she lost.' My voice began to shake. 'Please go . . . now, and quickly.'

'Go? Go where? I have no place to go.'

'Oh, Neal, come off it.' Anger stopped the tears. 'I'm sure LuAnne is with you . . . and where's Jack, the whole excuse for this great sacrifice? Where's the great man that means so much to you?'

'I left him downtown, so's I could see you alone.'

'Sure, with LuAnne. Just go, will you? Leave me alone.'

'Okay, okay . . . I'll call you.' He could see I wouldn't bend and strode to the door. I watched him run down the walk and heard the car zoom away. With it went another hunk of myself.

I lit a cigarette and flopped face-down on the bed. Somehow, though, in spite of my resolve, I didn't feel quite so desolate. At least he was back . . . reachable. I wanted him to find a way to make me believe him, but how? How could he, without erasing completely what he'd just done? I couldn't allow myself to be made a fool of, and why wasn't what he'd done enough to kill my love for him? Why wasn't I like other women who'd get hurt or betrayed once and that was that? Turn it off, go on to someone else, pride and honor intact, the lesson learned. Why couldn't I change that image and conviction in my mind that he was my husband, my only husband?

Cathy began her hunger whimper, so I got up and put her bottle on the stove to warm. The sun had set, and as the sky turned to deeper blue the city lights began to blink on like Midwestern fireflies. I changed Cathy in the dusk, then sat watching the show of deepening darkness and polychrome lights while she drank her milk, her little body warm against my stomach. With my free hand, I dropped the needle onto the turntable besides the couch and let Lady Day say it for me: 'No good man/Ever since the world began/There've been other fools like me/Born to be . . . in love with a no—good—maayann.'

Eighteen

When I awoke in the morning, I turned the record over, as usual: 'Good morning, heartache/Here we go again . . .' This morning was, however, a little brighter than the last dozen had been; there was *something* to expect . . . good or bad. With this anticipation, I took an interest in straightening and cleaning what I could. Around noon the telephone rang. It was Neal.

'Good morning, my sweet. Now, listen to me, look here, I mean to say . . . dammit, we have to figure this thing out, now don't we, Carolyn? After all, Cathy has to be cared for properly. I understand, of course, your feelings and all that, but nevertheless, something has to be done. I have to get a job, and you see, darling, I haven't any money, you understand, and neither has Jack . . . though he's wired his mother and will have soon. But we can't stay here. Now just purely for economics, my dear . . . you do and feel just as you like . . . I won't bother you at all . . . anything you say, but we'll just have to have a place to stay until I can get enough money, you understand.'

I couldn't help thinking that it was rather stupid of me to be so harsh when we needed his support and he was willing to give it. What other solution was there? But my pride made me stall. 'Where's LuAnne?' was all I could think of saying.

'Now, darling, I *told* you. I don't know where she is. How should I know?'

His voice was edging towards anger; he didn't *like* lying over and

84

over. After all, I was only guessing and trying not to be dumb again
. . . but what if he were telling the truth?

'Well, I suppose I have no choice. As long as you clearly
understand it is strictly a business arrangement and only until we can
make another. Surely Jack had some plan when he sent for you?'

'Yes, yes, of course, darling. We'll talk about that.' He had gotten
his way again, so he couldn't be more agreeable. 'He won't be in the
way again, you'll see, and I've got all the Sunday papers right here—
we'll start job hunting this very day. I'll go see Ardo first, then we'll
be over. Bye, sweet, I love you.' I replaced the phone, torn in two
again, happy and afraid.

Around five o'clock Neal and Jack bounded in, loaded down with
bags of groceries, courtesy of good ol' Ardo. Neal danced around the
small kitchen, tossing cans to Jack and hoping to ease all our
embarrassment with constant chatter. 'You know, Jack, it's strange,
but you and I have never played catch and so on . . . so I could show
you my magnificent arm. Seventy yards I used to throw the old
pigskin, yessir . . . an unmeasured distance with a baseball. I
developed this special hop, you see, and I'd astound my buddies with
the distance I could peg a rock . . . too small an area here to
demonstrate properly—' A can crashed against the wall. '—Oops, too
bad. Like most southpaws, I'm slightly erratic in accuracy.' Jack
chuckled and tossed back, imitating exaggerated football action.
Without wanting to bring them down too much, I tried to shush them
for Cathy's sake and realized I'd not considered all of us living in one
room.

Jack and I were more awkward and shy than ever on this, our
second encounter. Not knowing all he knew about the trip and
LuAnne, nor what Neal had told him about me, I felt humiliated and
at a loss. Jack was embarrassed to be considered the possible cause of
my pain and poverty and couldn't defend himself without further
incriminating Neal. Realizing each other's position only made
communication more difficult.

The first evening the two men sat in the built-in booth in the
kitchen and tried to be jolly as I did the dishes, but it was an up-hill
effort. What could we talk about? I was being the wronged woman,
and they only knew painful secrets. Luckily, they were both tired and
content to retire early. I had the day bed and offered them the double
couch, but Jack preferred the floor.

The following day Neal accepted another selling job, this time a
new line of aluminum cookware. He came home with a huge carton of

all sorts of brand-new pots, pans and pressure-cookers with piles of pamphlets, recipes and instructions.

'Hey, honey . . . whooooeeeeey! Looka hyar what I got.' And he staggered in and dropped the carton on the bed. 'Now you an' Jack just sit over theah, and I'll show you the greatest breakthrough in the annals of cooking in this century . . . yas, yaass indeedy.'

Off he went into a W.C. Fields patent-medicine routine with each pan, exaggerating all the 'unique' features and adding a few of his own invention until Jack and I were both laughing aloud. When Neal saw he had managed some defrosting, he dropped the pan in his hand and climbed and stumbled over all the stuff on the floor and pounced beside me, gurgling, giggling, hugging and kissing me, with me trying to pretend to resist. Then, thoroughly giddy, he sprang back to his demonstration with renewed glee and elaboration.

We all knew this job was completely out of character for Neal— selling cookware, being invited to dinner parties in order to demonstrate, etc.—yet I could never be too positive about what he could or couldn't do.

Jack opened the quiz when Neal showed signs of running down. 'What are you *doing*, man?' He was still giggling. 'Where did you get all that stuff? You didn't steal it, did you?'

'My dear Jack, ahem, how can you say such a thing? Even *think* such a thing!'

'But, Neal . . .' I cut in. 'Not selling again. Have you forgotten the encyclopedias? Do you get a salary or only a commission? Is it door-to-door? What will you wear? How can you . . . ?'

'Tch, tch. Just you relax and leave it to Daddy here. I've been briefed and checked out, and see here . . . here's the booklet tells you all about these wonderful little beauties . . . nuthin' to it. And besides, my dear, *you're* supposed to use them and tell me more about how great they are, see? Your old Daddy has already brought home . . . if not the bacon itself, at least something to cook it in, eh? Not bad, eh?' He walked around in a circle, beaming at us.

This time, however, my instincts proved accurate. For the first two or three days Neal got up early and, taking Jack along, set out with gusto. A few rejections and slammed doors were all that was needed to discourage him. He began to sleep later or sit around reading the papers, never quite getting out. One day the supervisor called, and Neal simply told him he was through. The man came to pick up the pans which I had collected into some sort of order.

It was difficult for all of us confined in that room, especially with a

86

baby sleeping most of the time. Neal and Jack soon mustered the nerve to go out 'to dig jazz,' and I reverted to feeling like a neglected wife, even though this time I could hardly justify or express it. At the end of the first week, the jig was up. The telephone rang, and when I answered, LuAnne's sweet voice asked for Neal. I handed him the phone and went into the kitchen, tears streaming into the sink as I washed Cathy's diapers. Neal was so angry, his face turned pale, his jaw set, and he snapped only a word or two into the receiver, growling under his breath 'The stupid bitch' as he slammed down the phone. Marching into the kitchen to me, he started with 'Now, honey, don't go thinking . . .'

'Just go. Just go! Don't say another word to me . . . ever!' I wrung the diapers with a vengeance.

Neal paced around the living room, swearing to himself. Jack had been out but now returned to walk right into the hornet's nest. When I was unable to answer his 'Hello,' he went in to Neal for enlightenment. I could hear Neal's explosive answer and curses at LuAnne. Jack, too, was angry with her. She had made a date with him, and then, right before his eyes, climbed into a Cadillac with an older man. 'She pretended not to see me, but I know she did. You're right, she's nuthin' but a whore.' It gave me some slight satisfaction to hear them malign her, yet I know it was because they *cared*. And she was free, free to take 'em or leave 'em, and I envied her the more.

Whatever had been Jack's reason for coming to San Francisco, if he'd ever had one outside Neal's plans for him, it didn't materialize. When his mother sent some money, he decided to use it to return to New York. He bought a loaf of bread and some cold cuts and made a huge stack of sandwiches to take on the bus, and Neal drove him to the station. My instructions were for them both to keep going.

Back I went to figuring out how I got where I was and how I could possibly have become involved in such a sordid mess. Where had I gone so wrong? My feelings still seemed programmed by the stoical family behind me, even though I was now cut off from them. I could never tell them all this, and for some time I'd avoided any reference to trouble in my weekly letters home.

One morning the following week I heard rapid footsteps and looked out the window to see Neal walking up the path from the street, grim determination on his face. He burst in and danced around, holding his left wrist with his right hand, bending up and down in pain. He was hurt. Well, you can't kick a man when he's down, I told myself, feeling genuine sympathy.

'What's the matter, Neal? What happened to you?'

'Now look, Carolyn, I'm coming back here and I'm staying.' Neal only ever called women by their given names in times of extreme emphasis or stress—perhaps because he knew he talked in his sleep. 'I'm through with LuAnne forever, that bitch, absolutely and completely, do you hear me?'

He continued to sway, breathing hard and hanging onto his wrist. I finally got him to hold still long enough for me to look at his left hand. It was swollen from the wrist down, and the thumb was strangely bent.

'It looks broken, Neal. How on earth did you do that?'

'LuAnne . . . I hit her . . . stupid broad.'

'LuAnne? You *hit* her? Neal! How could you? Where is she? How is she?' This was more serious than I had imagined.

'That thick-skulled bitch . . . *she's* just *dandy*! Nobody could hurt that hard head.' He repressed further swearing in expressions of disgust, once again prancing about. 'But, look, don't you think I should see a doctor or something?'

I came back to reality. 'Yes, of course, you must. Come on, I'll drive you to Mission Emergency.'

I had not driven 'my' car yet, and Neal forgot his pain as he instructed me. I parked opposite the emergency entrance, and Neal went in alone. Once more, warm reassurance washed over me. This must really signify the end of their relationship, if he could stoop so low as to actually hit LuAnne.

Now he was running toward the car.

'What did they say?' I called.

'Nothing yet. I have to wait. Listen, love, have you got a nickel? I'll call LuAnne and tell her to put my things together so I can pick them up. Thanks.' He grabbed the coin I offered and ran back into the building.

My moment of rapture was brief. A cab drove up and out of it sprang LuAnne, consternation on her brow. She ran toward the entrance, and out of the shadows Neal appeared. She held his hand and clucked, and by their nodding heads and fervent looks. I knew I'd been deceived again. Neal walked back into the hospital where Cathy had been born.

LuAnne turned and, seeing me, waved and crossed the street. I forced a smile, and we greeted each other like long-lost sisters.

'How's your head, LuAnne? How terrible for you. I can't believe Neal would do a thing like that.'

She laughed and leaned on the car door.

'Oh, I'm all right. How have you been? I think it was rotten of Neal to go off and leave you like that, and I told him so.'

'Why don't you get in?' I motioned to the other seat, although I felt maybe I should move over myself. After all, it was more her car than mine, since she'd been riding all over the country in it. She went around and got in just as Neal came running over to the car again. 'They've taken X-rays, and I have to wait to get a cast on. Why don't you wait for me at the apartment. I'll call when I'm done.' Then he disappeared back into the hospital.

'What do you say, LuAnne? I don't like to leave Cathy too long . . . a neighbor is listening for her.'

'Yes, that would be nice,' she answered. 'I haven't seen the baby yet, and I want to very much.' Just as if she were my dearest friend.

'Would you like to drive?'

'No, no, you go right ahead.'

She settled back in her seat and took out a cigarette. It was dark now, and I had to ask her to show me the lights switch. I felt altogether crumby.

Back at the apartment, LuAnne cooed over my shoulder as I checked Cathy. When we sat down opposite each other, the dim light from the windows behind me fell on her face, and the lamp accented the red-gold of her hair, hanging in careless burnished ringlets on her shoulders. It might have been because I felt so dowdy, but I'd never seen a more luscious girl, and she seemed to grow prettier as we talked. As an artist, I was far more conscious of her beauty than she was, and it affected me both with aesthetic pleasure and personal pain. I knew I'd never be able to compete with her physically.

She began relating a series of tales about the many times Neal had disappointed her, each revelation piercing me acutely. In a way, I welcomed this punishment, hoping *something* she told me would be bad enough to cure me of my own attachment to him. In all her narrative, however, she deleted any reference to physical abuse.

After an hour or more the telephone rang at my elbow, and I grasped it quickly, now trained to think of Cathy. It was the hospital; Neal was ready to leave, and I said I'd be right there. LuAnne, however, said, 'Let him wait.' She didn't finish her reminiscences for at least another half hour, and when she decided he'd waited long enough we drove back.

She probably expected him to be storming up and down in another rage, but instead he was sitting bent over on the curb, his head leaning on his arms. My heart went out to him, but I sat still. LuAnne ran over and touched his shoulder. He lifted his head groggily and then staggered to his feet, holding on to her to make his way to the car. 'God, I'm sick,' he muttered. 'Been throwing up for hours.' LuAnne whispered to me, 'Ha, serves him right.' Gently I started the car and drove to the apartment.

I knew how wretched Neal could be when nauseated, and it was all I could do not to smother him and that grotesque cast with solicitude. It took both LuAnne and me to get him up the stairs and onto the daybed. I covered him with a blanket, asking him if there was anything he wanted. He shook his head and was soon asleep.

I offered LuAnne some coffee, and she sat down for another chapter of confession and condemnation of Neal. I expected Neal to nap some and then be well enough to accompany her to her hotel. He certainly wouldn't expect to stay with me now, and I was thoroughly tired of the emotional ping-pong.

Then LuAnne put down her cup and stood up. 'Well, thank you. I must be going now.'

'Oh, well . . . I'll wake Neal then.'

'Oh, no, don't do that. He's better off as he is.'

'But . . . he can't stay here, you know. He'll have to go with you. You can drive him . . .'

'*I* don't want him back . . . I can't. My fiancé is due back in San Francisco at any time now. It would never do for him to find Neal in my room!' And she laughed at the mental picture.

So she deceives him, too, I thought. 'How will you get home at this hour? I don't think I should leave . . .' For a second I feared she might take the car.

'No, no, don't worry. I'll get a cab on Dolores.'

As I walked her to the stairs I asked, 'Will you live in San Francisco when you're married?' I hoped not.

'Oh, yes, I expect so. I met him when I was here before with Lois, and we've been writing while I was in Denver. He asked me to meet him here and marry him — that's the only reason I went with Neal, to get a ride out here.' I didn't add 'by way of New York'.

Back in the shadowy room I looked down at the sleeping Neal, wondering if I should wake him. How helpless he looked and how incapable of inflicting such pain. Well, at least I should be convinced now that he could never be trusted. Sighing, I opened the couch and climbed in, turning out the lamp. The high ceiling flickered rainbow colors from the city's lights. Although it wasn't right, he was here, the apartment was full, and we were a family again, even if only on the surface.

The next morning my defenses returned, but I put off attacking him until his health improved, and this gave me some relief. He felt rotten, his head splitting, his hand throbbing. Codeine disagreed with him, aspirin would only inflame his empty stomach, and the thought of food nauseated him anew. He was punishing himself enough.

'You seem well enough to go back to LuAnne now,' I ventured, pretending I knew nothing of her affairs and attempting to get our relationship on a proper footing. He answered me as though I were an irksome child who had persisted in playing the same game too long. He, too, was depressed, not only by the physical discomfort, but by the whole sorry mess. Now that he was injured, he couldn't work. This meant Ardo couldn't be repaid, the car would be repossessed, LuAnne was rapidly getting out of his reach, not to mention that he had a wife and child who were dependent on his support. I didn't overlook the opportunity to point the lesson.

'Well, Neal, I hope it was all worth it to you.'

Nineteen

~~~~~~~~

There seemed no solution other than for him to take care of Cathy
while I worked, and he assured me he could handle it. The day after
his injury he felt well enough to take the car and leave it on a side
street. He was two payments behind, and the finance company didn't
have his address. It was all a mystery to me and seemed a terrible
waste.

So out came the old green dress again, and I began a survey of
doctors' offices. The first afternoon I was lucky to be hired by a
Hungarian radiologist in his mid-50s. When he asked if I could begin
at once, he also tactfully inquired if I'd like an advance on my salary.
Evidently, my wedding outfit had lost its glamor.

Neal was somber and subdued. Then one day I came home and
looked up at our window to be startled by an apparition of a man with
a bald head: Neal had shaved off his hair. Such an impulse made me
uneasy, and he could give me no reason for having done such a drastic
thing. He said he stayed in the apartment except when taking Cathy
to the park, and I was inclined to believe him. Many years later I
learned that LuAnne often accompanied him.

Since I was still nursing my disillusion, we didn't have the
animated discussions of previous times, and we hadn't money enough
for entertainment. We'd sit behind our magazines or discuss Cathy.

With her he was wonderful and conscientious. On 15 March 1949, he wrote to Allen:

I'm lonely and restless . . . Action in the sense of continuity of purpose is now quite impossible. I lead a shallow simpleton life, little agreements of mind and emotion escape my endeavors. Long or involved speech, coherence of logic, literate leadership or conversation; all quite beyond me. I'm listless without reason; I sit as would Rodin's statue were his left arm dangling. (*The Thinker*'s brow is false.) I sigh with looking out the window over the city—to the east—and north, horizons, clouds, the street below me. I'm as far west as one can go; at a sloppy ebb-tide.

I'm free of LuAnne, my friends are my friends; but I have a child. My life's blood she is, lovely and perfect—she wakes at this very moment. I stop to kiss her. So, I live in the child for as long as possible, that's my stand; after that: the world, you, saxophones and hardened struggle to succeed. You see, it's all very simple: I will take care of Cathy as long as Carolyn will allow me, which may be, I hope, forever; where she severs relations I will lead other lives, until that time—Cathleen Joanne is my charge.

With a regular salary the first aim was a new home. This time I found a house nestled under the brink of Russian Hill and near all the parts of San Francisco that constituted the city's essence for me: Aquatic Park, North Beach, Fisherman's Wharf, Telegraph Hill, Chinatown. In the opposite direction was Nob Hill with the Mark Hopkins and Fairmont hotels—not that I could go there anymore, but they held memories of spendthrift wartime revelries.

The house, built on three levels, was on a quiet street only a block long, and we had the only patch of grass and garden. A grocery store was a half-block away, and the cable car clanged its musical bell up and down Hyde Street and took me to and from work. It was more like an amusement park ride than a means of transport—a delightful way to begin and end each day.

The change to a decent home, partly furnished and with even more 'possibilities' than the previous ones, improved my relationship with Neal, and he too became more settled, less morose. He began writing what was to become *The First Third* in spite of the handicap of the cast on his dominant hand into which a traction pin had by now been inserted. I couldn't allow myself to be as happy as I'd been before his trip; my wariness persisted, as did a false pride which I believed honorable and necessary. Still, I yearned for the old closeness, but I didn't know how to achieve it.

Then osteomyelitis infected the bones of Neal's thumb, presumably caused by contamination when washing diapers, and required daily injections of penicillin. To avoid extra medical bills, I convinced the doctor I was capable of administering the shots. Many were the times I regretted that request: Neal was not only fussy and defensive, but his buttocks were so lean and taut that it was difficult for me and painful for him. His sensitive skin caused him to yelp and swear.

In April our wedding anniversary and my 26th birthday came and went almost without notice except that my boss, whose attentions and gifts I'd hitherto been staunchly refusing—a policy incomprehensible to Neal—presented me with perfume and an ornate, embroidered Chinese smoking jacket for Neal, who loved it. He wore it solo; it reached about an inch below his bottom, and he strutted about, pretending his cigarette was a cigar and harumphing like Major Hoople.

In May, Allen wrote: 'Are you too occupied to write, or don't you want to for some reason concerning your relationship with us in New York? . . . The golden day has arrived for Jack, and he has sold his book . . .' and he gave details of the contract. Then, 'he is not mad at you; as a matter of fact 5 of the 15 sandwiches he denied you in Frisco went bad before he could eat them.'

After signing the contract for *The Town and the City*, Jack had gone to Denver to see his friends again. He was disappointed to find most of them out of town, and he wrote to Neal for comfort, advice and amusement.

Neal was now capable of compiling the many unmailed letters he had begun since Jack had left San Francisco.

Your Book sold! I sit here thinking of my elation and how best to let you know. I come up with but one word: Glad. Glad, Glad, Glad, oh, so damn Glad, Gee, I feel so Glad. I'm Glad . . . Try Five-Points in Denver for bop, the Rossonian Hotel, and a couple of places across the street on Welton between 26th and 27th streets. There may be a spot or two downtown or on the north side . . . Other than that I just look for good juke-boxes. Strangely, last night had big dream about Slim Gaillard. Perhaps you might remember the mixed feelings of admiration and inability to be close to him I felt. I was unable to tell him how dumb I felt not to be coherent about my admiration. That's how the dream ended, with me just sitting there watching his face and wishing I could speak.

God, just heard that great George Shearing, remember God Shearing, Jack? God Shearing and Devil Gaillard. That's us, Jack, a mixture of George and Slim. The images we struck of George, a sightless God; of Slim, an all-seeing Being . . .

May as well say it: started *The First Third* again . . . family history; got as far as 1910 when my pop was 17.

My lack of cooperation with the doctor's amorous advances eventually caused him to become unreasonably picky and demanding of my work, so when Neal declared he'd been idle as long as he could stand it and wished to go back to work, I was overjoyed to be able to give my notice. Neal found a job curing recapped truck tires, hard work in blistering heat, but he grabbed the chance as usual. He described the job to Jack: 'The cast weighs heavy. Sweating makes the thumb gooey, and it sticks to the plaster-of-p. I do *impossible* task; my job is so difficult, it saps everything from strong, two-fisted men, yet with one hand I throw the heavy truck tires in a real frenzy of accomplishment. I'm amazed.' My own feelings were not so much of amazement as of anxiety about his stamina and endurance.

Neal was now beset with further physical problems as well as those of his thumb. Again, in a summarizing and somewhat exaggerated letter to Jack, he wrote:

Jazz-hound C. has a sore butt. His wife gives daily injections of penicillin for his thumb, which produces hives, for he's allergic. He must take 60,000 units of Fleming's juice within a month. He must take one tablet every four hours for this month to combat the allergy produced from this juice. He must take codeine-aspirin to relieve the pain in the thumb. He must have surgery on his leg for an inflamed cyst. He must rise next Monday at six a.m. to get his teeth cleaned. He must see foot doctor twice a week for treatment. He must take cough syrup each night. He must blow and snort constantly to clear his nose, which has collapsed just under the bridge where an operation some years ago weakened it. He must lose his thumb on his throwing arm next month.

Sun. p.m.: Sitting on a sore ass in my kitchen with the ball game, gurgling daughter, grass-watering wife, full belly from two dollar steak . . . Reading a new book, *Escape from Reality* by Norman Taylor is fairly interesting and deals with all forms of junk, stuff, coke, tea. Just started reading *Dr Faustus* by T. Mann. Despite the reviews, I find it the best thing I've ever read by him, except possibly *Magic Mountain* (which I read when young and it influenced me a lot). Strange to discover his latest work starts much as mine . . . My terrific, darling beautiful daughter can now stand alone for 30 seconds at a time. She weighs 22 lbs. and is 29 inches long. I've just figured out she is 31¼% English, 27½% Irish, 25% German, 8¾% Dutch, 7½% Scotch. 100% wonderful.

So serenity was returning day by day. Neal had assured me continually that there was no way he would or could see LuAnne anymore, and that spring, she married. As Neal wrote to Jack: 'LuAnne has married Ray Murphy who has sharpened a sword and is dashing about town trying to find me so he can cut my throat.' I hoped such a violent husband would watch LuAnne with a passionate possessiveness.

Allen wrote with news of a less than cheery nature: Bill Burroughs had been arrested and faced a jail sentence for possession of narcotics and guns: 'If he gets out, he will have to leave Texas and La. as it is hot there for him.' Allen, himself, was allowing friends to use his apartment as a base of operations for 'various schemes' of an illegal nature. He had planned to sublet the apartment to them and use the money to visit Bill, but the latter's arrest 'casts a shade on that . . . I can't seem to put my foot down,' he complained. His letter ended:

What are you doing? When will your heart weary of its own indignity and despotism and lack of creation? Why are you not in N.Y.? Can you do anything away from us? Can you feel anybody as you can feel us, even though in N.Y. you did your worst to surround yourself with a sensate fog of blind activity? Are you learning something new? Wherever you are now? If you wonder the motive for these questions, don't undercut it with suspicion of sexual motives of mine; I have none now and was not dominated by them when you were last in N.Y. I am writing a set of psalms; they begin

> Ah, still Lord, Ah, sweet Divinity,
> Incarnate in this grave and holy substance
> Circumscribing the hexed endless world
> Of time . . .

The next thing we knew, Jack wrote that Allen was in a mental institution and Herbert Huncke was in jail. Neal wrote back:

Bill on the border, Allen in an institution, Huncke in jail, Jack in Denver, Neal in land's end. The horizon here is the sea. I lay me down on the brink, the West end. Frantic Frisco, yes, frenzied Frisco, yes Fateful Frisco. Frisco of frivolous folly; Frisco of fearful fights. Frisco of Fossilization. Frisco: Fully Fashioned Fate.

Allen—I conjure up things, I wonder how and why? The details, the details I want. Wot hoppen? Bill I knew would end in Texas, Huncke too; no surprise once he was busted again. But Allen? How, why, where, etc.?

Two things throw reality into sharp relief: Your successful sale and Allen's commitment. The whole bugaboo of external forces I've evaded so purposefully for three years is brought close once again. This has much bearing to me; not directly but as a point of Philosophy, if you will. Your bookselling means success, you see, or, in competition with the world of big boys, recognition. This bears on the whole idea of constructive involvement and the like. You understand. Star on the forehead, etc. Now, Allen's internment means the force that so painfully involved you to some

96

degree. This is the force I've evaded with success for three years, almost four. As a preamble to getting to the point, however, I will say I fear you can't feel the deep involvement I have had in this negative fashion. All the struggle for the book, all your constructive involvement has been the prime thing with you. Even thru your period in the nuthouse with Big Slim, your deep anchor has been this submergence in writing, which unwillingly threw you into the other camp. The camp had your mother, father and other factors. To be blunt, you were never in jail so many goddam times you had nightmares of future arrests. You were never actually obsessed with the year-by-year, more-and-more apparent fact that you couldn't escape the law's stranglehold. You, in short, were never where Huncke is now. I was not where H is now, not for the first few years, anyway. I stole over 500 cars in the period from 1940–44. I was caught but three times for cars. Good average, you see; no cause for obsession.

We heard nothing from Allen for nearly a year, and the only details we ever got on how he had come to be committed were those contained in John Clellon Holmes' book, *Go*. According to Holmes, Allen's anxiety had increased to such a point that he had decided to remove his precious letters and journals from his apartment, which was rapidly filling up with stolen goods, and take them to his father's home in Paterson, New Jersey. In the car (stolen) with Vicki and Little Jack, Allen sat in the back seat, his papers on his lap, surrounded by loot, while Vicki chattered away, telling of their most recent escapade. Then Little Jack made a wrong turn into a oneway street in the middle of which sat a patrol car, the driver talking to another officer leaning on the door. This patrolman walked out to wave Little Jack into turning around. Little Jack panicked, stomped on the accelerator and roared full speed ahead, just grazing the patrolman. The patrol car swung into hot pursuit, siren blaring. Little Jack hung another left turn, far too fast. The car overturned and Allen was thrown to the floor, his papers and letters showering around him and his glasses lost. All he could think of was that Huncke must be warned—the police were sure to arrive, since Allen's address was plastered all over the scattered letters. He dashed away from the scene, and hid in doorways until he found a telephone. He told Huncke to destroy the narcotics and hide the stolen goods. Vicki also ran off toward the apartment, but poor Little Jack was out cold behind the steering wheel.

When Allen arrived, Huncke was languidly sweeping the apartment. Nothing had been touched. Allen raced about doing his best to flush away evidence, but seconds after Vicki arrived so did the police, and all three were arrested. Little Jack was already in custody and he made a strong plea for insanity, being a four-time loser as a felon, and Vicki promoted her pregnancy. Allen was released to his father whose lawyer stressed Allen's involvement in psychotherapy, suggesting he be sent to Bellevue rather than jail.

Twenty

Neal was not called back to the railroad at all in 1949, and his present salary was less than we'd planned on, so I agreed to return to work. I found a job with two doctors who shared an office, one a male surgeon, the other a woman general practitioner.

I had been employed a mere two weeks when I learned I was once more pregnant. It was an even greater shock this time because I had been so extremely conscientious in following the doctor's directions for birth control.

This time Neal acted happy, perhaps trying to make up for the first time, or perhaps because he found such a source of joy in Cathy. For myself, I felt trapped, half wanting another child of his, but mostly afraid of being more dependent on Neal when I was still trying to resist him.

The surgeon felt my condition would be detrimental to his practice, but the woman did not, so she left him and opened her own office on the floor above. Neal's job was exhausting and dirty, but mine was easy; as I counted out pills or typed, I could watch the people and the pigeons below in Union Square. And I could still ride the cable car. My defenses relaxed, and again I saw that our marriage might recover. By now I should have learned to fear the calm more than the storm.

As usually happened, Neal began to miss excitement and diversity, so when Jack wrote, at a loose end and undecided where to go from Denver, Neal answered him frantically, pleading with him to come to San Francisco:

I am so excited as I punch out this plea to you . . . I am *not* going to work for at least two weeks. You see, the thumb, after three more weeks in the cast, failed to respond to treatment, and last Thursday they decided to cut it off—just the first joint. So, Mon. a.m. I get operated on. Carolyn will be working all day including Saturday, and we will have the house to ourselves. We can play music, talk, etc., etc. and in the evenings, bop, mad nigger joints, etc. . . . I want to have a perfect two weeks' vacation with you . . . I rush to mail this, I only repeat; think of all the reasons for coming here, then multiply by ten and think of our joy, and then . . . get 'On the Road.' . . . Carolyn is now three months pregnant with our second child. If it's a boy I shall name it Jack Allen Cassady. If it's a girl I shall name it Carolyn Jean.

Jack didn't answer. Instead, a few nights later, there was a knock on the door. We had already gone to bed, but Neal got up—as usual in the altogether—and opened the front door to find Jack standing on the porch. Jack broke out in laughter, saying, 'My God, man—what if it had been someone else?' and they giggled and whispered as Neal conducted Jack downstairs. The old familiar fear crept over me. I imagined a drawbridge between me and Neal being drawn up, enclosing them in their castle of delights and leaving me sitting wistfully on the opposite bank, filling the moat with tears. My fears grew as I heard their exuberant reunion, Neal becoming more forgetful of those trying to sleep upstairs.

Neal was true to the promise in his letter, and they exulted in each other like two schoolboys playing hooky. But as we had let Mrs. Davies, Cathy's babysitter, go for two weeks, I became worried about how our daughter could be properly cared for in this atmosphere. I'd come home from work and make dinner, after which Neal and Jack would jump up from the table and rush out into the night. My supersensitivity made our few encounters strained, and the more I behaved like the disapproving parent, the more they treated me as such—the mother, to be lied to and evaded.

Early in the first week, I must admit, Neal tried to break the pattern, annoyed by my constant sulk.

'Why don't you come with us, then?'

'Who'd stay with Cathy?' I asked icily.

'What do other people do?' he retorted somewhat impatiently. 'Get

Louise next door or Mrs. Davies.' I was afraid to go, but I could hardly uphold my injured air if I didn't. So, on Saturday night Mrs. Davies came over, and I agreed to join them.

My doubts were more than justified. I was a fifth wheel, like a bratty little sister who big brother has to take along with his friends. Neal talked over my head to Jack about people and places they knew in common and I did not. The first half of the evening was spent racing around the Fillmore area, which was populated chiefly by blacks. Every few minutes Neal would jerk the car to a stop, leap out, whip into a cigar store, bar or doorway, and bound back to lunge us forward again into the traffic until the next time. It finally dawned on me that they were hunting for tea, and after an hour or so, it seemed they made a 'score'.

Neal drove to a dark, tree-lined street in a residential section and parked the car. We waited, and waited, and waited. So far I was not amused, and I wondered if this was an example of the gay times I had thought I'd been missing. And what a sad far cry from our threesome in Denver two years before! After at least another hour, Neal deduced he'd been duped and, with much swearing, abandoned the vigil. The rest of the evening was divided between more waiting in a Tenderloin district hotel—where Jack and I attempted to make conversation with a friend of LuAnne's while she made coffee for us on the bottom of a flat-iron suspended on a coathanger over a wastebasket—and a grimy nightclub where we watched a variety of pathetic strippers while Neal followed up other leads. When Neal returned and flirted openly with a vocalist on the stage directly above our table, I was so hurt and mortified that I demanded to be taken home. Neal was more than happy to oblige and strode out in front of me to the car. Once at our door, he gunned the motor while I ran into the house, trying to control my tears long enough to pay Mrs. Davies. The men did not return until early morning.

There was no further suggestion that I participate in their continued revelries, and henceforth a stone wall divided us. Once I overheard Jack ask Neal what was the matter between us, but Neal was unable to explain. Sometimes he did make attempts to find out and to soothe me, but the fact that he didn't know already only made things worse. Somewhere in my mind I was vaguely aware it was not all his fault, yet I couldn't think how else to behave and still maintain my pride and righteous indignation. If he had made promises, I wouldn't believe them anymore; he must *undo* what he had done. I did so want to stop this moaning, but how? The concept of forgiveness was then unknown to me.

A small thing turned out to be the last straw. One evening Neal and Jack came home while I was giving Cathy a bath. She was surrounded in the tub by her water toys and bubbles, her baby skin rosy, the bathroom enshrouded in steam. With them was Jack's French friend, Henri Cru, and they brought him in to meet me. Henri knew nothing of our tensions and thought only that he was entering Neal's happy home. He beamed at us: 'Ahhhh—*tres jolie*! My, my, what a charming domestic scene—ah, *oui*, how verry delightfule . . .' He bowed and smiled, then followed Jack downstairs into the kitchen. It was too much for me. I dissolved into tears, bitterly resenting that our life was not as Henri pictured it. I was tucking Cathy in her crib when they all came gayly back upstairs. Jack and Henri went singing out the front door, and Neal came in to kiss Cathy goodnight. His frivolous mood made him shower me with pretty, empty endearments—not even *noticing* how miserable I was, how powerless.

I pushed him away and unleashed the only remaining weapon I had. 'Get—out! Just go—just get *out*!' I hissed though clenched teeth.

'All right, dear—I'm going.' He looked puzzled but he fled.

I lay in bed agonizing, yet with hope revived by the prospect of some kind of action—a showdown. Sleepless, I waited and waited for his return. When I heard them tiptoe in near dawn, I said nothing until Jack was through in the bathroom and had gone up the stairs to his bed in the attic. Then, with all the cold fury I could muster, I pounced on Neal and stopped him from getting into bed.

'I told you to go, and I meant it. Get that precious friend of yours out of this house and you, too. He's all you want, and that life is all you care about. What do you think I'm made of? You expect me to sit here night after night, work day after day, with nobody—just be your housekeeper? Well, I've had all I can take. If that's what you want, do it someplace else and leave me alone. Go. Now.'

Hopelessness stilled Neal's features and his voice. Silently he put his clothes back on. Wasn't he going to fight? Oh, no—now what was I to do? Why didn't he talk about it? He went upstairs to tell Jack, then I watched in dismay as he packed his old strapped suitcase, everything in me crying out for some way to stop him. Would he say nothing? He would in a day or two, at least, surely? He wouldn't go far . . . Meanwhile, this would make him stop and consider the price. I had to feel I'd made some sort of impression.

Then they were gone, the house deadly still. It had taken so little time. I thought of his unhealed hand, of Cathy, of the new one growing inside me.

The alarm went off, and I remembered work. I'd have to leave Cathy next door. Responsibility mapped the course.

Unconscious of my surroundings, I automatically rode to work and opened the office, my mind locked in a frantic quest for an answer. I'd made a terrible mistake this time. Surely Neal knew it, too—that I didn't know *how* to behave any differently. If only Jack hadn't been there, and I could have talked to Neal. But if Jack hadn't been there, there'd have been no problem. Yet, it wasn't Jack's fault, it was Neal's. Where were they now? Maybe he'd call me; he'd called the last time—but then he had been the one who chose to go—this time I'd forced the separation. He must know I didn't mean it.

The doctor was on hospital rounds all morning, and I had the afternoon off. Apart from two patients coming in for injections, all I really had to do was answer the phone and make appointments. I couldn't sit still. Mechanically, I straightened instruments and pillows.

Then, after some time, I heard footsteps outside the office—familiar footsteps. As I wrenched open the door I saw the elevator doors closing and, at my feet, an envelope. Damn fool, why didn't I run to the elevator instead of picking it up? Conditioned restraint, again. Shaking, I shut the office door and sat down at the doctor's desk. Inside the envelope were three dollars and a page torn from a 1947 calendar. In a neat, pencilled hand—not Neal's—was written:

Carolyn: Am leaving today. Won't ever bother you again. I won't come back in a month to make you start it all over again—shudder, shudder! Here is a few dollars that I can give you. You won't receive any more until Sept.
The things of mine still at the house—do what you want with. I am going to Denver, Detroit and New York City and won't ever come back to Frisco. Incidentally, I'm *not* going to see LuAnne—don't know where she is.
Writ by Helen Hinkle.

Neal

I read it several times, sifting the contents for grains of hope. Well, first, he didn't have to write me at all—or send any money. And why tell me where he was going? And, certainly, what difference could it make now if he saw LuAnne or not, if this *was* forever? Maybe, after all, he was in no hurry, maybe . . . I ran to the window and scrutinized all the shifting forms below me in Union Square, my desperation mounting. So close! I had almost seen him again—almost prevented this. Would he call? I doubted it now. But he must! Hysteria threatened; that wouldn't help. Think. Where would he go now? Helen Hinkle would know but where did she live? Al had left her, too, and I didn't have their number. I had seen neither of them since I'd first met her.

I stared dumbly at the leaden sky above the square. The soaring gulls seemed as aimless as my futile thoughts, swooping and swirling, resting, dipping, getting nowhere. I demently pulled out and pushed in the desk drawer as though I had a nervous tic. Catching myself, I looked down into the open drawer and noticed the piles of pill samples. This was where I kept the amphetamines. I had yet to get through the rest of the morning, I reasoned, and nothing mattered anyway, so if I had to live, I might as well make the best of it. Maybe some of these could wind up the clockwork inside me. Feeling somewhat dramatic, I got a cup of water and swallowed two, putting the rest in my purse.

At noon I locked the office and vacantly caught the cable car home. Our neighbour Louise greeted me. 'Come in and stay a minute—have some coffee.' I shook my head and looked around for Cathy, but Louise went on. 'Imagine Neal's leaving in the middle of the night like that . . .' Had I told her? I supposed that in my grief that morning I'd said something to her to try and make it real to myself. 'Good riddance, if you ask me,' she continued. 'It's the best thing that could happen—you should never have put up with him for so long. You'll be a lot better off in the end . . .'

I know, I know—I'd heard it all before. But my heart yelled back, 'It's not the best thing. I will *not* be better off. I love him.' But I only nodded and, lifting Cathy, backed out the door. 'Thanks, Louise. I'll come over later and we can talk.'

I liked Louise and knew she was not being a gossip but genuinely sympathetic. I also knew the whole world would, rightly, agree with her. Why couldn't I?

Twenty-one

The silence in my own house was almost suffocating. Best I get out the pills quick. After gulping them, I rushed about opening windows and the back door, turned on the radio and, yammering nonsense at Cathy, prepared her for her nap. I changed into my worn jeans and old shirt, and now there was nothing for it but to face the lonely weekend ahead. As I started back down the stairs, I heard a knock at the front door.

At first I didn't recognize Helen, and for a moment we stared at one another in nervous silence. She broke through it by getting to the point: 'I'm so sorry about Neal, Carolyn. I had to come over and see if there is anything I can do.' I came to with a snap and backed away from the door.

'Why, thanks—how nice of you. Come on in. Let's go downstairs— I was just about to make some coffee.' And I led the way, touched by her concern but somehow more distressed. Her mission seemed to indicate that Neal's departure was final. She believed it was, apparently, and she had seen Neal and written that awful note. I put the coffee on the stove while she made approving remarks about the house. Then, as she settled herself on the couch, I sat down next to the table, facing her, almost afraid to ask, 'When did they leave?'

'They just did. Did you get the note?'

'Yes.' I had to get up and turn down the fire under the pot, glad of the chance to hide my feelings. *Just* left! So he wouldn't be calling this time—this time when I would have begged him to come back. But I mustn't let her know; she was probably another woman who thought me a fool for putting up with him. Probably in her eyes, too, it was all his fault.

'I got so mad at him, Carolyn. How can he just take off and leave a wife and child? How can anyone be so irresponsible? God!'

'How did they happen to come to your place?'

'Well, you see, the *reason* was—it certainly wasn't *my* company— they had no car.'

Helen settled back and lit a cigarette. I enjoyed listening to her. She spoke with slow intensity, emphasizing certain words, and her low, mellow voice had a straightforward quality. Now I hungered for details.

'You had a car?' I handed her a cup of coffee.

'No, Lorraine did—she's the girl that introduced me to Al. She used to live next door, and Neal knew she had a car. He and Jack had been riding around all day with Bill Tomson, who had followed us to San Francisco with his new bride, but he had to go home for dinner.'

Inwardly I groaned—'*all day*'! Then aloud: 'This was last night?'

'Yes, that's right. There was this tapping on the door, and much to my surprise, it's Neal. Of course he did this little song and dance at the door about his friend and how they're leaving and going to New York. I didn't know anything about you until the next morning. Of course, I think he knew I liked Jack, so he asked if they could take a shower and wash up. Then Neal asked about Lorraine's car, so I called her.

'They wanted to go hear this fabulous combo on Howard Street and asked if I wanted to go too, so I thought, what the hell, it might be fun. Then we couldn't start the car, so we all pushed it out into the main street, whereupon the gallant gentlemen—ha, ha—hid in the back seat—mind you—while I was out pushing and Lorraine steered. It was hilariously funny, actually—*hiding* yet.'

'Why did they do that?'

'They felt—reasoned—that they would get no one to push them with two men . . .'

'Oh, I get it. They needed a *car* to push . . .'

'Yeah, that's right, but here I am pushing this car *up* hill—and in the wrong direction, bye the bye—anyway, sure enough it worked.

'Well, we finally got to this club—grimy, filled with Negroes and weird winos, and there was this wild Negro sax player that Neal liked so much. Neal would stand right in front of the bell of the horn, and

106

the guy would blow right at Neal—Neal jumping and swaying, half the time with his eyes closed, nodding, smiling to every note.

'We were perched on little stools pretty close, and there was this other guy with wild spears of black hair sticking out all over his head, and he sang "Close Your Eyes"—he was something—wow—just great.' Helen paused, remembering the moment and smiling. 'So, pretty soon you can smell tea, you know—all over the place. Now this Negro with the hair—he had *terrible* scars all over his arms and face—whew—but, he was singing to *me*. I realized it suddenly with some embarrassment. But Neal came over and grinned and jumped around and said, "Don't you dig it? Don't you *dig* it?" and I said, "Don't be ridiculous" and acted like I didn't, but, of course I *did*—but I didn't want to get lured into anything like *that*. It was sort of unnerving, you know—the *potential*, wow! But, actually, it was really a sort of sharing—and I didn't feel quite so scrumpy, dumpy and dumb—you know.' She thought about it again. 'Funny how that guy hangs in my mind . . .'

'Well, we were there several hours. It was dark when we started, so it was probably about ten o'clock then—and after awhile Neal says they're gonna take a quick run over to Oakland . . .'

I couldn't help interrupting her, laughing, 'Yeah, that's Neal—*quick* run—clear across the Bay. I suppose it was to get more tea?'

'Probably. I don't know. There was a lot of arguing, and for some reason, he really wanted us to go, too. But it smelled to me like one of Neal's plots and fraught with danger. So Neal and Jack got into this car wild with Negroes and left. So here we are again, Lorraine and I having to push her car. But we got another guy to help, and we were going to meet Neal at Jackson's Nook. I'd been there lots of times—it's an after-hours club, you know, and the musicians come over there to go on playing. I had no real expectation of seeing Neal again that night, but sure enough, in about three more hours they showed up with the same musicians. We stayed until dawn drinking coffee.

'When we got home I just asked Lorraine if I could stay with her and gave Neal and Jack the keys to my apartment. Just before noon today I went back, and they were up, so I fixed them something to eat. It was only then I noticed their bags—so they really did mean to go to New York. When Neal asked me to write the note to you, I was yelling at him for leaving you and Jack kept defending him, saying you kicked him out . . . Tell me, was his hand really so bad he couldn't have written that note?'

'I guess he could have, but it would have been a mess. He's been typing everything for quite awhile.'

'It struck me as an odd thing, and it made me feel kind of in league with him. I felt awful—wanted to say "Write it yourself!" '

'Or Jack could have.'

'Yeah, right. Why me?'

'That's Neal, part of his way of getting around people by getting them involved and on his side.'

'Well, I felt terrible writing it . . . being the *instrument*.'

'Why, of course I don't blame you. It is my own fault, really. I did insist they go . . . but it was . . . I was trying to get Neal's attention . . . you know. I think that's what I was after . . . I don't know. Life was intolerable the way it was.'

Listening to Helen, I was struck by how casually and comfortably she had joined Neal and Jack for a night out with no feeling of disapproval or of being threatened. Why had I been unable to join them as simply as she? Grateful for her company, I urged Helen to continue talking.

'Tell me about you and Al. I've always wondered about that wedding and how you happened to marry him after knowing him for such a short time.'

'Yes, it is funny, but I just knew he was the one, something clicked—I guess it sounds crazy.'

'Not to me. That's what happened with me and Neal. There was nothing to consider. I just knew.'

'Yeah, that's it.' She sighed, sadly. 'But that afternoon when Al brought Neal over . . . God . . . There he was, bopping and beeping, hitting the car, jumping all around . . . I was *terrified* of him! I remember—ha—I told Al afterward, very seriously, you know—that I thought that guy must smoke *marijuana*!' We went into gales of laughter. 'Ah, me, well it was a mad two days. I can't really remember what happened . . . I know I had to see a doctor—he gave me a diaphragm which kept popping out all over the bathroom floor—bad omen, I figured.'

There was still so much I wanted to ask Helen and she accepted my invitation to stay for dinner. After we had done the dishes and put Cathy to bed, I offered her some of my amphetamine samples. She accepted, and from then on we never let up. I can vaguely remember getting Cathy up, feeding her, changing her and putting her down again, and repeating all this over and over as the hours ticked by. Monday morning found us still sitting there, still wallowing in our grievances.

One of the most interesting revelations for me was Helen's version of her first trip with Al and Neal, and her introduction to Bill Burroughs.

'Well, of course the trip *to* Tucson was sheer *hell*. I'm still in my wedding clothes, you understand . . . my girdle is killing me, and Neal . . . well, you know Neal's *driving* . . . I was *petrified*. And of course the radio is on *full* blast, him beating on the dashboard and yelling . . . God, it was *horrible* . . . and he wouldn't, absolutely *refused* to stop at a service station for me to go to the john even . . . God, how I hated that man . . . I had hated him on sight, of course, and he returned it, too. He said awful things to me, insulted me, nasty remarks . . . went out of his way to be crude, I thought.'

'Neal? That's odd. I never heard him be personally mean to anyone . . . certainly not to a stranger or to a friend's wife. Maybe it was because you're the only woman who didn't respond to him. You saw right through him. He couldn't con *you* . . . I suppose he couldn't tolerate that, eh?'

'Maybe so, I don't know . . . but it was sure not my idea of a *honeymoon* trip. But, you know . . . he picked up a woman and her child along the way. The child was epileptic or something, and Neal was simply *fantastic*. I've never seen *anyone* be that nice, he was so *considerate* and *concerned*. I just could not believe it was the same *man*. Though of course, other times, he picked up all *sorts* of hitchhikers to get them to buy gas . . . I had to sit on Al's lap, mind you . . . yeah, and my girdle cutting me in two . . . uuggh.

'Well, I lasted till Tucson, and then I had just had it. I insisted I had to have a bath, and Al must get us a hotel room. So that's what we did—Neal making nastier-than-usual remarks, but I didn't care. When we got in the room Al and I talked, and I told him I was less than enchanted with our honeymoon and wanted out. He said he'd have to go with Neal because he'd promised, before the wedding, and had contributed money.'

I was puzzled. 'I thought the reason for the rush-rush wedding had been that Neal thought you had money, and that's why he wanted to take you and Al, to get your money to finance his trip. No?'

'Well, he may have thought so, but you see, I *didn't* have very much money, because I was at the end of my six months' leave and was just about to go back to work again. And I certainly wasn't about to put any into *his* pocket.'

'Poor Neal. Ha! That's probably also why he was so hateful to you . . . he must really have been counting on that money.'

'Yeah, well, so Al said okay, I could either wait for him back in San Francisco or go on to New Orleans and wait there, which is what he really wanted me to do. He had given me Burroughs' address, which I presume he got from Neal.

'So when Neal arrived at the hotel, I was still in bed. Neal rushes in and says "Let's go, let's go!" but Al said, "She's not going." And Neal's mouth dropped in disbelief. But he recovered and said, "Well, whaddya gonna do?" and Al said he'd be right down. Then Al begged me to proceed to New Orleans and contact Burroughs.'

'Did anybody tell you about him?'

'No, oh no . . . just a good, *good* reliable friend of Neal's who had a house and so forth. I knew nothing about his past . . . or that he was an addict . . . and Joan too.' We both laughed and for a moment mused on the contrast between her strict conventional upbringing and the new kind of life she had unknowingly let herself in for by marrying Al. 'Of course, Al and Neal were going to be back in—'

'—Oh, I know . . . just *no* time at all. Ha!'

'Yeah, right . . . five days at the *outside*, you know. So here I was. I decided I would go on to New Orleans, mostly because I just *couldn't* go back to San Francisco and try and explain this to my friends . . . you know. So Christmas Eve I'm on a *train* . . . this was a real *tragedy* to me . . . or I thought it should have been, because for us it had always been such a big *family* thing, 'cause we always opened our gifts on Christmas Eve, and it seemed like such a . . . twist of fate to be on a train alone going . . . you know . . . where?'

'*And* a new bride.'

'Yeah, yeah, ha, ha . . . but you know I kept thinking it's not all that *bad*. Funny. Well, I arrived in New Orleans and took a hotel room—I'd been in New Orleans before, so it wasn't a strange place to me. I wired Al at Jack's mother's to tell him where I was, and I told the hotel people I expected a call any minute. But the days went by and no call and Al didn't show . . . Finally the hotel staff told me that it was the weekend of the Sugar Bowl, and all rooms would have to be given up. So one of the bellhops tells me, "Now I know a little place down the street where I can get you a room," so off we go down this little alley. We came to a door and he rang a bell and we went inside, and here was this great old mysterious entryway, huge and empty except for tapestry and so forth hanging about and there was another bell to ring . . . and finally a woman showed up . . . real weird with beads, long skirts . . .'

'Like a "house".'

110

'Well, that's *it* . . . it *was*. It was a whore house. And I'm shown a room . . . a bare, pristine room off another courtyard that was full of weeds, old broken-down cars and so forth . . . and one of my first discoveries was a huge jar of *Vaseline* sitting on the mantel—ha—and two cigarette butts, you know, one with lipstick on it . . . but still I didn't want to believe it . . . and it wasn't until the middle of the night when the bells kept ringing and people were coming and going that it finally dawned on me . . .'

'Oh, you're *smart*! I lived in one in New York for two weeks and never caught on at all . . . had to be told!'

'Well, I couldn't avoid it . . . it was so corny . . . a jar of *Vaseline*, really . . . that's why I couldn't believe it . . . so *corny*. Anyway, funds are really getting low at this point and I wasn't even eating much, so after a week I had to wire San Francisco for more money—I'm still expecting Al at any minute. I decided I'd better call Burroughs, and maybe find out something. He invited me to lunch. On the phone he sounded like an ancient, ancient old man. He took me to this evil-looking dark place, Chinese, I think.'

'Where he got his opium . . . morphine?' I laughed.

'Probably . . . and we had lunch, and he talked on and on and on about—prefabricated *housing* . . . he talked a good hour, through the whole meal. I was dying to ask some questions about if he'd heard anything from Jack or Al, but, I mean, he was really eloquent when he was talking about something, impersonal, you know. But at the end he said, "Well, why don't you come out to my place" . . . just very casually. So I took one of my bags—I owed the brothel ten dollars, so had to leave the other bag there—and Bill and I took the ferry over to Algiers.

'It was a long walk to the house, which was L-shaped with a veranda all along it. I met Joan. The thing that struck me most about them was how casual they were. They gave me a room between the children's room and Bill's study, which was where he slept. It was really kind of a charming room . . . louvered shutters, a faded oriental rug on the floor, a rough-hewn, garden-like settee made from whole branches, a fireplace and a high iron bed . . . really sort of charming.'

'You said Bill slept in his study. Where did Joan sleep?'

'Well, she didn't much, of course . . . but in the front sort of entry-parlor there was a couch, and over in the corner a table that Bill had built "to last a thousand years" . . . weird. It was quite some time before I was aware of their sleeping arrangements, or lack of same. Now that I had a little money, I made myself as scarce as possible and went into New Orleans every day, going to shows, museums, walking around . . . I never ate with them. Every day I was to pick up a tube of Benzedrine for Joan, though I never knew why. Often I could see the empty tubes placed in rows on the mantel, and Bill used to sit there and shoot them off with his air gun. Anyway, one time this druggist said I could have a dozen if I wished, he was sure I wouldn't misuse them. I said, "*Misuse* them? How's that possible?" So he told me, and I said, "No, *one* is just fine." When I got back and told Joan this, she just about crapped. That was the only time I ever saw her really get excited about anything.

'Really it was all just crazy . . . Bill had this cat thing. He had six or seven cats, and each night he tied them with string . . . tying up their feet . . . and *bathed* them. You'd hear these terrible shrieks and it was all so *insane*, but they acted as though it were perfectly natural.

'Then there was the lizard tree, this grotesque, ugly tree outside which was—ugh—literally *covered* with lizards. It was one of Joan's duties to rake the lizards off the tree every night. I don't know why she didn't try poison. I'd step out on the veranda after dark, and she'd be raking lizards off the tree in the moonlight.

'I thought everybody was absolutely insane, as if there was some kind of logic they knew about that I was unaware of, and I didn't want to ask any more questions. Like, Bill would stay in the bathroom for hours, and there was always a funny odor afterward and bits of rubber tubing, teaspoons and so forth lying around.

'Joan and Bill had great rollicking fun discussions . . . they had brilliant minds and talked about all sorts of subjects, though never anything personal. Bill always wore a shoulder holster, which he was very proud of, and once in a while he'd have a hip holster thing, and he loved to get out in the yard and show you his gun and his marksmanship.'

'Yeah. Neal told me about that when he was in Texas.'

'Funny, too, Bill was always alluding to the sinister, criminal elements over in New Orleans whenever he went to the race track. But it was so ludicrous to see him . . . spindly, studious type in a suit, tie, hat . . . and a shoulder holster . . . it was like a kid playing games. You couldn't really take him seriously, even when he was just talking about guns.

'Then there were the kids. Julie was about six or seven, and the little boy not quite a year, I think—at least he was still in diapers . . . when he wore them. They were allowed to go to the toilet whenever and wherever they pleased, but particularly in their room. It had been

112

child-proofed—that is, linoleum and so forth—and every night Joan had to go in there with Lysol and scrub it down. The little girl Bill teased terribly. It wasn't that he was mean . . . you knew that there was something between them, something deep. All he'd have to say was 'Here comes Old Bull' and she'd just scream and have a fit . . . the whole relationship was so strange. She had great horrid scars all up her arms, because she chewed them at night.

'The little boy was perfectly bea-u-u-tiful, just beautiful. He and Julie could bring anything at all into their room. There were a lot of neighbor kids in and out, too, and there'd be buckets of mud, horse turds or whatever, anything the kids could drag in. Anything they wanted to do in that room they did.

'But one thing I'll always be grateful to Bill for was that he introduced me to Céline—you know, *Death on the Installment Plan*.'

'Yeah, that's a great one.'

'Well, when he first gave it to me I thought, 'God, a mystery' . . . you know . . . ha, ha, ha! That's what really kept me alive; it really helped. Periodically of course I would try to reach Al, and finally I asked Bill if he would try and call Jack's mother, because he knew them. I hated to ask him, though, because all the time Bill kept up this running criticism of Neal, and how he'd better not think he was going to "come down and con me," blah, blah. Of course, Bill didn't know *who* Al was. I remember telling Bill confidentially one night that I thought Neal smoked marijuana. Ha! Bill had only raised twenty-five acres of it or something like that! He assured me that marijuana wasn't all that *bad*—it was heroin you had to be careful of.'

'And him fixing himself up all the time! How often?'

'Oh about three times a day, sometimes only twice. I remember how there were periods when he'd just sit and dream and not say anything, but I never knew why.

'And then one day they all drove up. There was Al, looking about the same, and Jack too. They filed out, one by one, and Bill and Joan sort of looked at each other . . . and then in walks Neal through the back kitchen and says, "This is my wife." And I look at this girl . . . *wife*! You know I'd just met *you* before the trip. Well, there was some greeting and jumping around and so forth, and one of the first things Jack said was that they were hungry and he knew a wonderful recipe for crêpes Suzettes.'

'Oh, yes. That's the first thing he said when he first came to my place—must be his opener as a guest.'

'Well, it seemed to me by the smiles of Joan and Bill that they were

113

delighted, although it was hard for them to smile. They rarely showed any emotion. But they couldn't help themselves, they were grinning this time. Anyway, Al and I went into the bedroom to talk. I can't remember what I said—less than I would like to have, I'm sure—and before we'd gotten to say more than four or five words, LuAnne comes in and asks if she can watch us screw!'

'Aiyeee.' I recoiled.

'*Yeah*! She sat down on the settee, and like—well—"let's have at it," you know. Of course it was the *last* thing in the *world* I wanted to do—much less in *public*—euuck. She looked like a child, too . . . long tumbling hair . . .

'Then one time I went out to the car to talk to LuAnne about something, and we're sitting in the car when Neal jumps in and starts beating the *hell* out of her! I told him to quit—*stop it!*—and she said, "No, it's all right. I like it." Well! That just about did it!

'Another time we spent an evening in New Orleans on some sort of surreptitious business—I suppose to do with drugs, although I didn't get it then—and I can remember being in the back seat with Bill, and he had a cane that was a sword—you know, you pressed a button and a sword jumped out. Honestly!

'It had taken Bill quite some time to realize I wasn't one of them. I think he got a kick out of my thinking them all quite respectable, and they tried to sort of live up to the image, for which I was grateful in a way. Near the end I'd babysit for Bill and Joan, and they went to the first movie they'd ever seen together. He was grateful I hadn't taken advantage or lived off them or tried to "take" them in any way, and he even offered to rebuild the chicken coop so Al and I could stay there. I was tempted, finances being what they were, but Al said no. He knew about the drugs, of course. Still, I wanted to stay in New Orleans—I really liked it there—and I wasn't about to get in a car again with Neal! So we got a small apartment and Al got a job to tide us over until he was called back to the railroad.

'The next week I called Joan, partly to thank her and partly to keep up the contact, and I found out Bill had been arrested on a narcotics charge. I was sure glad we hadn't stayed with them!'

Helen and I aired all our grievances against our men and against men in general. Mostly we cemented our convictions that both of us were pretty much put-upon and innocent victims. It still seems an odd coincidence that Helen should have appeared and shared such understanding and agreement at that crucial time. When the second day rolled around and we concluded it was Monday, I realized I had to go to work. By then it had been decided that Helen would move in with me, an arrangement of mutual benefit. She could save her rent, and in return save me hiring a babysitter, which I couldn't afford without Neal's salary. Neither Neal nor I had shown much sense of responsibility in our emotional reactions, obviously, but it seemed that God, whomever or whatever that meant, was still watching over fools like me.

Helen probably saved my sanity as well as my livelihood. She was marvelous with Cathy and a sympathetic companion, and her great sense of humor prevented us from becoming completely depressed or desperate. We wouldn't have said we were happy, and we grumbled about our fate and the worthlessness of men, but somehow we usually ended up laughing when the melodrama threatened to become a farce.

Still, we made no effort to find a new constructive lifestyle, and we didn't care to survey the future. We marked time, got through it one day at a time, and played a lot of cards. Cathy had her first birthday a month after her father left. Neal didn't fail to mark the date by sending me money, but he sent no word of comfort, hope or regret. Then Al returned late in the fall from his travels with Jim Holmes, and asked Helen to come back to him. She agreed, but promised to stay with me until my baby was born in January.

And so the second Christmas of my marriage was one step worse than the first. Al and Helen and Bill Tomson and his wife (another Helen) came to my house, all reunited, all dressed up and all full of new plans for the future, while my outlook was bleaker, a lonelier year looming on the horizon.

Until the end of the year Neal sent money whenever he could, small though the amounts were. But after Christmas there were no more envelopes with the familiar, cherished scrawl, and I assumed, with heavy heart, he was determined to make the break final. But I couldn't possibly concede anything like that with his child stirring inside me.

Al went to Denver, and Helen and I returned to our solitaire, although now a door was placed before each of us, hers open, mine shut.

Twenty-two

———

Soon after the beginning of 1950 I answered the phone to hear a low, brash Eastern voice say cheerily, 'Hi! Carolyn? This is Diana Hansen in New York. I suppose Neal's told you he lives with me here? How are you? How is Cathy?'

I pulled the telephone to the couch and sat down; my heart had either stopped or was lodged somewhere where it didn't belong. 'No' was all I could utter but she surged ahead, just as though we were old friends.

'Well, as you know by now, I'm sure, you and Neal were never right for each other, and since you've kicked him out never to darken your door again, ha, ha—you're absolutely right, of course—and I know how glad you are to be free. So, you see, we want to ask a favor of you—that is, Neal asked me to ask if you'll divorce him. It seems I'm pregnant, and I know *you*'ll understand that we want to get married as soon as possible—give the little brat a name and all that, you know— ha, ha.'

A cold mass now replaced my solar plexus, and disbelief chanted 'No, no, no, no' through my head. I'd never even thought of this possibility, never. No one else could have his babies. How could it be? All my strength was needed to push sound into words.

'Why doesn't Neal ask me himself?'

'Oh, no reason. He just asked me to. I was going to call you, anyway. You and I have a lot to talk about. I've been dying to call you

116

for just ages. I hope I have a girl. If I do, I'll name her Jennifer. What do you think? Isn't that a darling name? You know, we have this great apartment, Carolyn. You'd love it. I've decorated it all up like the Village with travel posters, you know? Neal's writing his book, and he's been so good at staying at it. I'm afraid I spoil him terribly. I just wait on him hand and foot. . . and he never goes out, just likes staying here at home with me. His friends come over a lot, though. I have to admit I don't care much for his friends—awfully lowbrow, you know what I mean—except Jack. I like Jack, and then Allen, of course—that's how we met, through Allen, at a party. But the other people that hang around aren't good for Neal. They sponge, and we've barely enough money for ourselves. I work—I'm a model—I love to work . . .' And on and on and on. Through it all, the only words that stuck in my brain were 'I'm pregnant.' Please, God, make it not true.

'Well, whaddya say, Carolyn? You'll get the divorce? We'll pay for it, but how long do you think it will take?'

'I'll only do it if Neal asks me himself. Goodbye.'

This was the bitterest pill I have ever had to swallow, and it never completely dissolved. In a day or two I received a typewritten letter, signed by Neal but obviously dictated by Diana. It hurt and disgusted me that he would allow her to do this, but I supposed it was in his nature to try to give everyone what they wanted of him.

In martyred agony I hired a lawyer, but we had a problem finding grounds for a divorce. Not that there weren't plenty, rather there were too many whose nature we didn't care to air in public. The Hinkles had returned by now and Helen agreed to serve as my witness and the legal wheels were set in motion.

On Thursday, 26 January, I was alone in the office while the doctor was on her rounds, when I knew my time had come. I still felt fine, so I completed all the unfinished business in the office, then took the cable car home. I had a cup of coffee with Helen, packed my bag and called a cab.

The hospital was overflowing, so I was parked on a guerney in the hall and given a caudal anesthetic. But Jami hardly gave me time to enjoy it, for an hour and a half later she arrived, entering the world in a storeroom. She lay screaming on a counter until a nurse remembered to take her away. Her damp hair stood out from her head in long black spikes, and with her eyes swollen from the drops, she had a distinctly oriental look. Consequently, when later in the afternoon a strange man entered my room and sympathized at length for my having had a Mongoloid baby, I had no reason to doubt him

117

and merely sighed, 'What next?' When I asked my doctor what to do about it, he went into mild shock and exposed the error: wrong room, wrong Mrs. Cassady.

This time I was home in three days, and Helen left the next. I was to consider this time off from work as my two-week vacation. It was two weeks but no vacation, Cathy being only seventeen months old. The new sitter had to be paid exactly the sum I earned, but my employer proved herself an angel by installing an extension of her office phone in my house so that I could work part-time from home and split my pay with the sitter.

The divorce suit was filed exactly a month after Jami's birth. Diana wrote me every day from the time she had first called, letters written on yellow lined paper in a large childish hand. At least twice a week she'd telephone, spending $25.00 to tell me how broke she was. So nearly every other afternoon I'd type letters in reply, generally contradicting her opinions about Neal, arguing furiously at her arbitrary pronouncements and illogical conclusions about me.

But throughout, my real motive was to keep in touch with Neal, and much of what I wrote was aimed at winning his approval and convincing him of my remorse at having sent him away. At the time, however, I wasn't fully conscious of this motive, and as I was constantly bombarded with the fact of Diana's pregnancy, I tried to believe that all was really over, forever.

In spite of Diana's impatience, my day in court didn't arrive until late in June. The large courtroom, musty and varnished, overwhelmed me—I'd only seen them in the movies, and I was nervous and miserable. We drew a woman judge who was renowned in San Francisco, and I felt all the more intimidated.

My lawyer was quite timid herself, and barely spoke above a whisper. Even though her prepared list of complaints against Neal had been watered down so that I hardly recognized him, the judge became furious. Gasping, she burst out with 'Wait, wait—I'm going to postpone this hearing until we can find that young man! I want to have a talk with him. How can he be so irresponsible? Two small children!'

From the witness stand I flung a horror-stricken look at my lawyer, shaking my head. She got up and said, 'Please, Your Honor, we'd prefer to settle it now.'

The judge turned to Neal's lawyer and asked, 'Where is Mr. Cassady?'

He stood up and said, 'He's in Mexico getting married.'

I stared at my lawyer, she stared at me, Helen's mouth dropped open, and the courtroom was silent. The judge recovered first, groaned, banged her gavel and said, 'Interlocutory degree granted.' I was granted $100 a month child support and $1 for alimony; the legal reasoning behind the latter escapes me.

And so it was over. All but the year to wait for the divorce to become final. Here was another painful blow I'd dealt my family: their first divorce. After their reaction to my premarital pregnancy, I had been evasive about my married life, but I would be unable to keep this from them, even if I wanted to.

Diana was now nearly five months along. I hadn't forgotten what it felt like, and I tried to do unto her as I would be done to. After all, I too had been careless, knowing Neal was already married. But I did feel bitter towards Diana, which I thought was justified because she had known Neal had other children to care for. Only later could I face the probability that he had been as persuasive with her as he had with me, convincing her that she was the 'only', the 'right' woman for him.

Since California law required a year's wait, I couldn't see that my divorce was of much help, and neither obviously did Diana and Neal. He had gone to Mexico to obtain a quickie. I wondered where the money was coming from for all these divorces, especially when I had to hear daily accounts of their dire lack of funds. I suspected Neal had seen an opportunity to obtain a sizeable store of marijuana, and my guess was corroborated by a letter he wrote Jack later, describing his trip and his search for their old 'connection,' saying he 'picked up Elich's Gardens [one of their code names for tea] in New Victoria.'

When Neal's railroad call-back telegram arrived, he hastened back to New York, and I was allowed a blessed few days' respite from Diana's communiqués. Even with no papers to prove it, he convinced her he had obtained the divorce, and they were bigamously married in New Jersey on 10 July. Two hours later Neal took the train to 'St. Louis and the west; Carolyn and the babies my impending hope,' he wrote to Jack.

Immediately he left her, Diana was on to me again, writing me her version of the wedding and saying 'I am ashamed of myself for my "worries" while Neal was away. I shouldn't be such a baby.' She explained that Neal hadn't been able to find a job in New York to cover the 'Mexican business,' saying that was the only reason why he had returned to the railroad, and gave me another penny-by-penny account of her financial status— '. . . none of your concern as long as you get your $101.'

119

As logic is one of my standbys, and as I had a fixed desire to maintain some privacy about my own husband and affairs, every word in her letters seemed to me uncannily devised to drive me mad. 'I expect Neal will visit you and the kids this weekend,' she wrote. 'I don't know what arrangements you'll want to make about his seeing Cathy and Jami. But please be nice to him—he does love them and they *are* his children, too . . . I also think *you*'ll find him a good person . . . See you all in a month or so, I hope . . .' To see her was the very last thing I wanted. It appeared as though bludgeoning was the only way to get through to her, and I was positive I wouldn't be able to control my exasperation if I met her in the flesh.

Neal arrived on my doorstep on the afternoon of 14 July. There's no use denying that my heart leaped at the sight of him, but I did my best not to show it, and backed away from his proffered embrace . . . the embrace I'd been yearning for for almost a whole year.

I attempted some off-hand small talk, but Neal ignored it and walked slowly and softly around the house, gazing reverently at everything, like a man returned from the dead. Barely audibly he said, 'Oh, darling . . . you don't know how great it is to be *home*.'

'Unh, hunh, I'm sure, Neal, but you can cool all that. It's a bit late for such sentiments. You are entitled to see your children, of course, if you want to. You won't recognize Cathy, and of course, you've never seen Jami.' I ground a mental heel on a rising urge to share their growing up with him. 'Help yourself to coffee, if you'd like. I'll get them up from their naps.'

Neal took no notice of my reactions, persevering in his own game. And, as this history too often relates, he won me over again. He continued his silent reverence, holding and rocking Jami, while looking his special look beyond her to me. Speaking softly to Cathy and stroking her hair, he continued to try and hold my eyes with his soulful gaze. I moved about cleaning up, but he rose and blocked my path or followed me if I dodged him, building the tension between us. It was a game we both knew well.

He finally got around to the inevitable request to move back in with us, but I was firm. 'Certainly not—not a chance. After all, you were the one who wanted the divorce, not me. You've swapped us for another family now, so let's quit while we're ahead. You've really gone too far this time, Neal. I've had enough, and I've a good start on my own independence. I certainly don't want to "start all over again, shudder shudder" as you said in your farewell note.'

I tried to put some conviction into my words. Oh, I knew it was the best thing to do, all right, but why would my feelings never correspond?

I didn't let him move in, but he was there most of the time when not at work, insisting he had 'the right to get his hundred dollars' worth' as Diana had said. I had been so lonely after Helen left, and he made me feel pretty and desirable again; he was wooing once more, and all the old charm, devotion, helpfulness, kindness and consideration I'd loved him for in the beginning, was poured in my direction. I thoroughly enjoyed being sought after, but by this time I'd had enough practice to affect indifference and prolong the return of my confidence and security. I insisted on our divorced status being maintained, partly to punish Neal and partly to protect myself from my own desires, and I hoped thus to strengthen my determination to remain free.

Twenty-three

When my boss moved to a new office which was too far for me to continue with our half-day arrangement, she suggested I go on disability insurance for awhile. She would verify my illness as post-partum depression, which if I wasn't having, she said, I should be. Given Neal's conscientiousness regarding child support, I would be getting in almost as much money as if I were working.

Happily I returned to the role of homemaker and mother, if not of wife. Now, too, I would be able to begin work on a correspondence course in illustration which my parents had bought. I dove into the first assignment, determined to find a way to support myself at home and to show Neal how serious was my intention to remain independent from him.

Diana was still modeling—maternity clothes—but she managed to take a vacation—without pay—and to fly to California to spend the time with Neal; apparently there would not have been enough time if she'd used his railroad passes. Neal, who had been living in the trainmen's dorms in Watsonville, now rented a small apartment there for her visit. In those two weeks I saw him only occasionally, between trains.

The Saturday afternoon that Diana was to go back to New York she telephoned and asked if she could stop by and see us before going to Oakland to catch her plane. She *still* didn't get it. 'No, Diana, definitely not. You somehow have to get it through your head I do not want to meet you, now—or ever! The less I hear of or from you, the better I'll like it. And if that's beyond your understanding, simply take my word for it.'

'But, Carolyn—here I am in California—I don't know when I'll be back. I want to see Russell Street and the house I've heard so much about, and Cathy and Jami.'

'Dear God,' I groaned to myself, then went over it all again.

Finally, she said wistfully, 'Well . . . okay.'

My sigh of relief was premature. At about six in the evening Diana called from Oakland airport and said she'd missed her plane. *Sure* she had! 'What am I going to do, Carolyn? I haven't any money for a room and there isn't another plane until tomorrow noon . . . I'll just *have* to stay with you now, Carolyn.' Because of her pregnancy I couldn't refuse her, just as she'd known all along.

She hadn't the money for a room but plenty for a cab all that way from the airport. She gushed all over me and everything in the house and had even brought *gifts* for all of us—further proof that she'd intended to see us all along. I was seething and sullen, but she took no notice. She jabbered on and on about Neal as though we were all in some delicious conspiracy together. She had even managed to arrive at an hour when the girls were not yet in bed, and I wanted to throw up as I listened to all her baby-talk. Her attitude was insufferable, as if she had some natural right to make judgments and recommendations concerning them. During her monologue, I'd learned why Neal had been attracted to her. She came on as a sophisticated and aggressive New York model, telling him she was from an old New England family that owned lots of property in upstate New York—so she was to be an heiress as well.

She also revealed that she wasn't as sweet and ever-agreeable as she had led me to believe. She admitted now that she had once thrown a bowl of soup in Neal's face and he had hit her so hard he had broken his thumb again. She thought this was terribly funny.

I put the girls to bed as soon as I could, moving Cathy's crib into the living room where Jami already slept in the buggy. I took Diana to Cathy's room and said she could sleep on the daybed.

Gloomy, disgusted with myself and with her, I climbed into my own bed but slept little. What good was it being angry at someone, I fumed, if it didn't penetrate?

Luckily I was wide awake when the first light of day appeared or I might not have heard the soft knock on the front door. It was Neal. Ha! At once I realized he thought Diana was already in New York. I was about to get some satisfaction out of this fiasco after all.

I couldn't help smiling as he bustled past me and down to the kitchen. I followed and sat down, waiting to pounce. He puttered about making coffee, lively and elated, another plan cooking in his mind, no doubt.

'I've got a surprise for *you,* Neal, my dear.' He looked at me warily, undecided whether to be pleased or suspicious. But I am no good at cat-and-mouse. 'Diana's upstairs. She *said* she missed her plane.'

Suddenly my anger returned, and I took it out on him; it was all his fault, anyway. I ticked off a brief review of some of his former atrocities and bore down heavily on how mortifying she was to me, especially at this moment. Given Neal's present campaign of trying to win me back, this was not agreeable for him either. Now Diana had caught him red-handed, a rare occurrence he would not tolerate nor forgive.

Stirrings above told us she was awake. She would have heard us talking. Had she left on the plane, I assumed he'd be writing her love-letters full of 'Carolyn who?'

He looked grim as he went up to her room and closed the door behind him. I heard his voice angrily cursing her and became apprehensive. Well, darn. I couldn't help feeling sorry for her now. He meant as much to her, even if I didn't understand her personality. There she was, pregnant, alone and leaving him behind, and there he was, rejecting her. Now, too, she had asked for more punishment by seeing us together, and would be able to picture the whole setting at this end of the country from her lonely room at the other. By the sound of her sobs and his stony voice, I assumed his usual compassion had been turned off. Perhaps he thought a swift cut would be easier for her in the end.

He should have known her better. When she returned to New York and wrote to him, she acted as though the scene had no significance whatever:

I dropped a note to Carolyn last week thanking her for putting me up Sat. night, apologizing for my 'breakdown' & asking her about what kind of diapers are best & the meaning of all those 'pads' in the essentials list. She hasn't answered, so I guess she wants to discontinue the communication [Fat chance! I thought] . . . As for the Sun. a.m. we don't have to discuss it because I think I understood. It was just so painful and unpleasant, and I, for one, was completely worn out from the battle with the airlines . . . by

the way, 'Jennifer Jo' it will be . . . the name I know you know is a little
tribute to Cathy, whom I am quite in love with . . . I'd rather have a little
boy & Cathy the big sister. She's so full of silent real conversation and
understands so much and is so brave when she doesn't . . . If Carolyn
doesn't want her, I'll bid.

I simply could not believe her act!

Neal redoubled his efforts to be nice to me and to try to persuade
me he was through with Diana, but I still wouldn't let him move back
in. He returned to the apartment in Watsonville for the rest of the
summer. He lured LuAnne to move in with him for a time, while her
husband was away at sea, but she told me later they couldn't get
along without jealous scenes, so she came back to San Francisco. Still
in Watsonville in September, he wrote to Jack:

. . . I am going to my death. It seems to happen every autumn, more
particularly, each September of late. The realization of the things that go
to make up one's death is such a personal thing, with so heavy a pressure
on the intelligence, that it becomes unbearable agony to put word to
paper. Each one with their privacy contained in mind has within their
reach a seed of death which becomes the thing to be aware of and its use is
not to be escaped . . .

Giving up his Watsonville apartment, Neal rented one in San
Francisco on Divisadero Street, asking Diana to send him a radio and
anything of his left in New York. She now got another idea I detested:

The Divisadero St. move for you sounds just right, provided you don't get
too lonely . . . Would the apt. be any place for you, me and the baby to
stay till we find our own apt.?

I was not at all in favor of this move. I could well imagine Neal
repeating the Denver performance, as well as Diana's sickening
chumminess if we were all in the same town. I told her just that, and
she wrote to Neal in all innocence:

Gee whiz, despite all, I really hadn't worried about that—just assumed
. . . we'd just lead a peaceful life without emotional turmoil . . . Would you
really try to have an affair with Carolyn? Or try to instigate some 3-part
plan? I shouldn't think you would—too damned destructive for all of us
. . . My darling, let's be nice old bourgeois . . . with salt shakers on the
table & a Chevrolet station wagon in the garage . . . P.S. By the way . . .
can you send me the baby stuff C.'s been gathering up? Tell C. to quit
hoping I won't move to SF if I want to . . . that my marriage to you is some
temporary fly-by-night business . . .

Now that I was maintaining my independent attitude, however, Neal and I had really good times together. Although I tried telling myself we would never get back together, I was happy only when he was around showing an interest in me. To fortify my position I accepted dates with friends of Louise's, even though I had no conversation to offer, having been so immersed in Neal and in staying alive. These men *sounded* as if they were a threat, and served to keep Neal worried and attentive.

By mid-October Neal persuaded me that the cost of his apartment was extravagant, and I had to agree to let him move back to Russell Street for the children's sake—but only if he'd sleep on the couch and behave properly. I now felt strong enough to hold my own position. I don't know what reason he gave Diana for his move back, but her answer was surprisingly calm: 'Your letter today about no nice Divisadero St. was so tender—also your voice on the phone. To hell with Divisadero. It was between "Hate and Wallow" [a pun on Haight and Ashbury], wasn't it? . . . Let's not jump to any big plan . . .'

Neal, however, had already been hatching a 'big plan,' and after having thus softened her up, he sprung it. He told her that he would give each of us a 'test period,' three months of living with me and then from January to June, living with her in New York in order to allow her to prove she was the better wife. (How many men have ever had it so good?) Of course, this was a harsh bit of news for Diana, and the telephone screamed when she got the letter. From then on she doubled her daily correspondence.

My deep belief that Neal was the only man for me had still not changed, try as I might to deny it, and I found it all too easy to slip back into a married feeling with him. Yet I certainly understood Diana's panic. I also knew that her attacks on me in letters to Neal made her chances of winning him back even slimmer; he never liked hearing any criticism of or gossip about others and rarely indulged in either himself. But I would never acknowledge that Diana had an equal claim, and at that time her ability to compromise with other wives and other children was impossible for me to understand.

Twenty-four

Neal settled in and continued writing his autobiography and long letters to Jack. He bought a tape recorder and wanted Jack to buy a similar machine so they could swap tapes. They were both fascinated by voices:

Jack: the Greatest:
Unbelievable! You write me *exact* description of what I've been doing, and *how* I've been doing it! Gene Kelly, correct. I dug him that way too.

And let me tell you how I've discovered similarly the eye sockets of *all* brakemen. Sunken in so from the long hours of staring with the focus on a distant point (a mile or more away) like cattlemen and old-time farthandlers of Indian juice.

I dig you about Wolfe. I am so amazed (as usual) how *really* alike our kicks (everything, I mean, thoughts everything, not happy kicks or self-satisfied life) like, listen, Important. Look here I enumerate: 1st VOICES:

I have done and gone done the gonest thing: I BOUGHT A WIRE RECORDER! not a *wire* recorder, but, better, a tape recorder; a gone instrument which reproduces so flawlessly (you can hear a clock ticking from way over in next room when you play back recording) and so cheaply, and so *effortlessly*, and the tapes last *forever*, don't break, can save any part or all of anything recorded, etc. etc. etc. The hour tape for example is only about 5 inches in diameter and weighs only few ounces and can be filled on *both* sides, so is really 2 hour tape (I got 2 half-hour rolls too) and simply record go to nearby postoffice and mail to *ME* a LETTER, better, 2 hours of our VOICES talking to each other. Save all labor of letters for writing (SO HORRIBLY HORRIBLY SHITPOT

127

HARD FOR ME) until such time as have written, then maybe, I too, could reel off a 5000-page letter every day to you. Gawd, I sho (don't know dialect yet) does *ad*mire any of them fellers can write them books an' all Geezus Christ! Get it now? Buy an EKOTAPE tape recorder small portable size, look in telephone directory it has EKOTAPE dealers, buy on time (costs no more) and get at once, costs 150.00 dollars, down payment, say 60 or so, don't know. GET AT ONCE (184 with tape). YESTERDAY, believe it, yesterday, I picked up, for the first time in *years* Tom Wolfe and recorded his gone poem prose prologue introduction preface dedication page beginning of *Time and the River* which is so old to me in years of past knowledge of it and etc. Of course I was hi and I've also recorded all kinds of such, like recent 'hi hour with Proust' and of course a Major Hoople (me as W.C. Fields) of a little thing I tossed off on 'The Repeating Rifle in the Bulgarian Army' (All bullshit, 'Repeating Rifle' believe it, comes from *Proust!*) Etc. Etc.

'I wish Allen would write,' he added.

Allen eventually did, recounting his ineptitude at two jobs he had tried: 'Truly the real world is my downfall.' He ended with:

Hear little from Diana, she seems worried about future, etc., as well she might. So you're back with Carolyn, eh? Well, you old scapegrace you, hope you're both having a fine time, though I worry about you. Why don't you all get married ala mohammedan customs. Jesus, what the hell are *you* all after in each other?

When Neal was called to San Luis Obispo, a town on the Southern Division where Al Hinkle was already working, and I was relieved of some of the verbiage from Diana, I tried to gain some perspective on the situation. I was helped by a visit from Bud, a friend of my brother who looked me up while in San Francisco on a month's business trip. It was perfect timing. Louise, still hoping I'd find a replacement for Neal, found someone my size who loaned me a couple of substitutes for the old green dress, and Bud took me on expense-account carousing in all the beloved places remembered from affluent wartime binges.

Poor Louise, Bud had a wife and five children already, but his attention worked to my advantage since Neal responded with passionate jealousy. Cathy especially liked Bud, and after Neal's return he was infuriated by her chatter about 'Bood.' I pointed out it was a good thing for the girls to have a man around.

While Neal was away, I also tried to re-evaluate and re-analyze my own requirements for a husband, all in the spirit of the 'trial period.' I wrote Neal a long dissertation, beginning with 'First, know that I love

128

you and all I want in life is to be your wife and the mother of your children . . . but I want all that this implies . . .' My chief concern was the discrepancy between his words and his actions, and I expended plenty of words on the pitfalls of deception and the futility of pretense.

> I do not consider you as a husband and father or that you consider me a wife when two other women can still draw responses of influence or emotion from you as a result of past experience with them . . . You distinctly said, 'I can live with anyone.' . . . If it is still 'I can live with anyone' to you, then this is how you must *act* . . . I can find a way to live the compromise, perhaps, but not the pretense.
>
> The sex problem has suddenly struck me, too. I know I fail you as a 'wife' there, but know that it is because I do not feel considered one otherwise. I feel sure that were the other conditions corrected, I could remedy my failure there. But recently I saw . . . how out of proportion this phase of your life has become!

I recalled a paragraph that I had read in a letter he had written to Jack:

> I masturbate every day at least 3 times and have done so for years no matter how much I'm doing other things at the same time. Years ago I had all-day orgies where lying there by myself I think of a woman . . . & come 11 and more times in 6–7 hours. Now it's a daily habit before going to sleep . . . and a brakie sleeps never more than 4 or 5 hours until called, when business is good, and must catnap anywhere and so on. I didn't begin masturbating until the very late age of 17. I had banged for almost 5 years . . .

This confession revolted my Victorian sensibilities, and I was able to mention it only in writing, not in person:

> Frankly, I'm frightened of and for you again. Anyone who saturates his mind with that sort of thing constantly is bound to come up with a pretty gruesome effect someday.
>
> As I've told you, I think one of your major difficulties is this whole attitude of 'let it ride; it will work out.' You should see by now such is rarely the case . . . at any rate, I am no longer willing to bypass or let ride. If you won't cooperate, then my only choice is to do as I said, work toward freezing my love for you and gaining independence. But the big moves must come from you.

Ah, how smugly righteous I was. The 'big moves' certainly came from him in the years ahead.

It was something of a surprise (and a little disappointing) when

Neal answered, not in his usual reassuring and loving rhetoric, but in a rare sober mood, taking his cue from my accusation that he wasn't being 'honest.' He wrote back:

Dear Carolyn:
There are so many things not ever to be understood; certain specific differences between us which are really unimportant, but, which, under the stress each of our respective personalities put on our minds, cannot be reconciled emotionally. The particular flaws I present your mind with are now stretched from original vices to abstract notions of me, which, thru so many modifications are no longer true . . .

Love has nothing to do with it, for all processes are, by nature, intellectualizations about abstracts which are conveyed by words whose meanings are lost to the mind . . . For the first time in years I am returning to an intellectual snobbery, altho, of course, I have no right to, being incoherent as ever and more unable to be understood by anyone on questions of life. Perhaps this is because I'm here with Al and Helen and realize, once again, and more fully than either you or Diana can see, how essentially I am far in the lead of any one of us. This means nothing. Especially in the light of the horrible position I've gotten us all into, but still, I must be, cannot help being governed by these things I know . . .

This means circumstances are now so developed that no matter how we each suffer, there is nothing left but to go through with it (the plan). Not in any sense of 'truth' am I writing; there is none actually that can be recognized, and 'truth' is a matter of the understanding process *only*—read Spengler, Vol. I.

Now is a period of interruption. The present is such an iron-clad pressure on the soul that being so weakened by lazy coasting, I can now do nothing but barely summon the strength to keep the process going . . . however, in my case, no one is sure that I ever had the lost strength. It's worse than that. I know the strength that was there is gone forever, because it was illusion. This calls for strict measures. The effort to gain peace has passed, then, into an obnoxious struggle to show people something. This I cannot do; it's not there, no matter how I attempt to manufacture. So let things be; help everyone with kindness, help them to win out, since that's what they want, but, for yourself (me) suffer your peculiar hurts in silence and hope for nothing—except to be able to not regret too much and to forget . . .

Insofar as I could follow his thoughts, this letter did little to reassure me, and it made me vaguely anxious and confused in a new way. Did I really want him to be honest? I'd always believed one could work with the truth, but what I meant was 'fact,' and even that is not so simple to define. What did I want? Well, for his extravagant declarations of 'love' to be genuine, that's all, and for 'love' to be

130

guaranteed, a predictable condition of a definable quantity. *I* felt capable of fulfilling this, so why didn't he?

One night soon after this exchange, Neal had to 'make a run' to San Francisco. He arrived when Bud and I were sharing a home-cooked dinner for a change, and I made Neal stay away until Bud had left, partly to show Neal it was still my life, that he shouldn't take me for granted as before, and partly because I felt too gauche about handling their meeting. Later, the fire of Neal's jealousy gave him the super-eloquence and extra persuasion which had been lacking in his letter. He dispelled my fears, as he always had.

On 7 November 1950 Diana's child was born—a boy. Damn. Why did she have the son? Fate was too cruel, and I underwent another period of despair and humiliation. Dumb, of course, when Neal and I were supposedly getting divorced, but still it seemed unfair. The fact that she intended to name him 'Neal III' did nothing to ease my pain.

Daily she wrote to Neal from the hospital, even though he didn't answer until she'd gone to her mother's, and then only to tell her when he'd be there for the promised visit. Nothing fazed her, and her observations continued to drive me up the wall—for example: 'Give C. the enclosed brass safety-pin to wear as her badge of membership in the "Cassady Mothers Auxiliary." It's a leftover from the bracelet and belt kit, and I find it makes a neat scarf pin.' Good God, she had the skin of a rhinoceros! Could she be serious? It irked me still more that she wanted to send announcements of the birth to all of Neal's half-brothers and half-sisters and asked how to reach his father for the same purpose. Leave it to her; she succeeded where even Neal had failed, and we received a nice grandfatherly note from his father congratulating 'Neal's wife.' The poor man was unaware that there were two of us, or that he already had two other grandchildren.

While Neal was away in San Luis I forwarded his mail, and with his permission I read the letters which arrived from Jack and Allen before sending them on. One day a letter arrived from Allen with stunning news. It was dated 'Saturday eve. Nov. 18':

I got home today from Jack's wedding . . . which took place last night at 6 followed by a big party at Cannastra's pad which his wife has leased and Jack is now master of . . . He has been strangely out of town the last several months, in retirement and brooding on T alone, and when he rejoined N.Y. society he seemed to me to be more settled in reality, more sober. He talked in a more disillusioned way—not making a fettish of it as I do—but like a post 20's survivor, F. Scott Fitzgerald after the party of ego was over . . . All of a sudden appears on the horizon this J. in C.'s pad, making a vulturish shrine of it* (on the pretext that they had been great lovers) . . .

Next thing I know Jack ran into her, two weeks ago, slept and stayed on, decided to marry, and did yesterday. This is a very sketchy account, not even an outline, but I am just jotting. The main things I see is this increased wariness and caution in life of Jack, and this mad marriage: they hardly know each other. But maybe it will all work out for the rest of his life. I think he hopes for permanence.

. . . Anyway, I say . . . we all should have beautiful intelligent wise women for wives who will know us and vice versa as well as we know ourselves (one another). I say let the home be the center of emotional and spiritual life . . .

Be that as it may, we had a big party. Seymour and I sat on roof and blasted and talked about women; Bill F., Claude, and Lizzie, Holmes, Lindens, Harrington, Lenrow, lots of other unknown women, Solomon and Anson, Winnie, others from Village and elsewhere. I wandered around distracted, getting into conversations and breaking them off impatiently till at three a.m. Claude, Jack and I put our heads together and kissed and sang 'Eli Eli' and held loving symbolical conversations. But anyway, I did not feel passionate or exultant that night but dead, as did Claude and I think Jack, as we were all too old and weary to exult over anything but was new and outwidening into unknown joys beyond control, and this was not exactly like that, but anyway it did seem a big event, so that all that day Claude and I sang 'Them wedding bells is breaking apart that old gang of mine,' but without real sadness, since we knew that anyway we could break into each other's apartments still in the middle of the night.

When I get married I want everybody I know to be there and watch, including all regiments of family, in a synagogue where will be great groaning choirs of weepers, sacraments, everybody in flowers and dress clothes, slightly awed by the presence of eternal vows, chastened by tradition and individuality of marriage. Then I can go home to mad pad and have real crazy party with people jumping out of windows after. And womenfolk and menfolk separated for last goodbyes and vows of eternal fidelity . . .

'Amen,' I said. Allen and I weren't as much at odds in our viewpoints as I had imagined.

It was a great shock to both Neal and me to learn that Jack was married. Even without the doubtful tone of Allen's endorsement, it didn't strike us as a good thing. Knowing the depth of Jack's emotions, his convictions regarding women, and his sympathy with Catholic dogma, this action on his part was difficult to understand, and we felt an ominous wave of apprehension.

It wasn't easy to think of 'our' Jack married to a girl we'd never

*Bill Cannastra had recently been killed while leaning out of a subway window.

132

even heard of, and I'm sure it hurt Neal and bowled him over for a time—all his plans had been securely aimed at traveling alone with Jack in the coming months, and now it looked as though Jack hadn't cared enough to take these plans seriously.

It was at least two weeks before Neal could bring himself to write Jack, and then he did so in an unusually superficial way. The envelope itself was addressed in a most self-conscious and giddy manner, and the letter began: 'Dear Jack: for the first time truly a man of marriage and family.' But there followed several pages of intricate dream-recounting in which Jack figured, and then a lengthy description of a man Neal had met who looked exactly like Bill Burroughs. Finally, he got around to the subject of Jack's new estate:

... I'm sure happy to hear you got married, naturally I was as surprised as all git out but I knew you had to do it sometime. When a man approaches 30 (ugh) without being well on the way to have little kiddilies, it begins to become a teensy bit too late and soon all he can do is write books. It'd be fine, then, if your 'impregnated on the 18th?' is right and there is abuilding in the mixer a miniature K. with big ears and a bigger thingajigger.

He passed on some advice to the 'wonderful girl you picked out of the whole big city' to 'not get into the silly habit of worry.' He continued:

... But, beyond this bunk, tho, Jack, with all your fooleries, you can never escape your serious and overconcerned nature nor the destiny of your blood and your inclination to the Home ... and all the times you've spoken about, and otherwise revealed, to me the hankering for a family.

The letter was an example of Neal's humanitarian instincts overcoming his doubts and personal dismay.

Included in all of Neal's letters to Jack and Allen was the constant request for tea. And in this letter, too, he makes such a request, saying he will reveal all about Jack to his wife in exchange for a 'joint of honest weed (or the price of same).'

Twenty-five

Meanwhile, Neal's crisis with me and Diana had come to a head. I don't know whether it was caused by the added stimulus of Bud's visit, which had also given me more confidence in myself, or by our exchange of letters during Neal's absence, but Neal said he was tired of the game—he was sure he wanted to make his permanent home with me and the girls.

Typically, he didn't come right out with it to Diana, but began the let-down by telling her he didn't have enough money to send her all of the December allotment he had agreed to. When I objected, he insisted she had plenty of resources because she was living at home, and her family wouldn't let her starve. Besides, Cathy needed an urgent tonsillectomy and Neal felt that was far more important. At first Diana was understandably furious, and she brought to bear all the classic sad and regretful accusations of the rejected and wronged woman (I knew them all by heart). Then came a letter in the opposite vein, reminiscent of Allen's so long ago: 'I want so much for you to want me . . . I want you to feel that I'm the one for you . . . It just can't happen . . . I know that if you do not want me as a wife, no one ever will . . .' How well I knew that what she said was truly felt and I never got over my amazement that Neal could inspire in so many of us the same devotion.

Neal wrote her a kind letter and sent her what money he could, causing her to feel she still had a chance. She tried a new tack of complimenting me while at the same time revealing derogatory remarks Neal was supposed to have made about me, trying in this way to make me angry with him. Her ploy was transparent and we pitied her. She also abandoned her vow not to talk about the baby. Every day she sent a detailed description of his every move, internal as well as external, with appropriate comments to impress upon us her trials, her courage and her son's captivating appeal. Diana never quite grasped Neal's dedication to making everyone happy, to 'let them win out,' and this blind spot of hers required him to go through a lot of unpleasant actions in order to keep the peace. He often sought relief from these grim duties in correspondence with Jack.

Although Neal had mailed his response to Jack's marriage on 7 December, we received a letter from Jack written together with John Holmes on the 14th, the contents of which showed that he had obviously not received Neal's. We blamed the frivolously addressed envelope. Jack wrote that he was:

> waiting on pins and needles for your reply about my marriage Papa Treetop . . . it may be lost among Xmas rush mail—well, I feel so fine . . . my wife just grand and divine, wait till you see her . . . Have 'Road' all hogtied and thrown . . . Missing you—just heard of the birth of Neal Cassady III and am anxious for you to come back to your son and boy— Let me know exact date so can plan big do-dig . . . You must take the Blue Special and hit town by Michaelmas, okay?

Jack either didn't know about or didn't wish to mention all the decision-making Neal was going through, but it pleased me that Neal chose to spend Christmas with us, although I knew Diana's would be much like my first one without him. I was truly sorry, but I felt I had earned having my first Christmas with Neal since our two children had been born. The Hinkles shared it with us. We celebrated on Christmas Eve because they were leaving for Denver on Christmas Day. This year, of course, there were no presents from my family for Neal; we were supposedly divorced, but now he witnessed their solidarity toward me and the grandchildren, in spite of my 'crimes.'

The advent of Christmas seemed to help Diana accept the inevitable at last. She wrote pages and pages about her present tragic condition, her mother's tragic illness, the tragic financial situation, and 'I'm worried about the job-hunting because a lot of my old, old physical neurotic symptoms have returned and I get dizzy and faint when I go outside.' But after a couple more pages about the baby, she ended with 'Not much to say. I suppose sooner or later we'd better do something legal about dissolving marriage . . .' I had been amazed to learn that the law against bigamy is generally ignored unless one of the wives objects. Anyhow, it made annulment simpler. Her correspondence to Neal abated, and I tried to feel kindly toward her.

Feeling he had accomplished some sort of settlement between Diana and me, Neal sprang back into action. Writing an exuberant letter to Jack on 'Dec. 30, 1950's last gasp,' he said he'd leave on 3 January for New York but would have to 'boom' on the way in order to make some money. He had received a letter from his father who was in jail, and Neal planned to detour to Denver to be there when he was released. 'I plan for him to live with Carolyn and me. Car and money fallen thru completely, so have Diana and I, so has U.S.A.' He then set forth an elaborate plan for Jack and his wife Joan to come back to San Francisco with him. 'Carolyn thinks you're it, and all the old nonsense is finished . . .' Once again he listed the assets of living with us— '. . . I got everything you'll ever need or want . . .'

And once more the 'best-laid plans' went awry. Our finances were such that Neal felt he couldn't leave for New York on the 3rd after all; I noted the difference in his attitude from what it had been in 1948. Hearing that there was a shortage of switchmen in Oakland, he planned to hire on as such until spring.

At the end of February, he figured he could take a 'business leave' and wrote again to Jack, outlining in the same minute detail a new set of plans, insisting that Jack and Joan should immediately begin their preparations for returning with him. Chief among those was for Jack to find or save the money to buy a truck. Neal had found another '43 Packard coupe for us but was afraid it wouldn't make it across the country, and I needed a car now to take Cathy to nursery school. And he told Jack:

. . . not tomorrow, you hear, you lazy lout, but right now YOU GET A JOB! . . . Pick out the toughest tasks and do penance, grovel in the daily horror necessary for the lousy few bucks. I am sick. I shudder at the thought . . . however best you can, make it so by my birthday. Amethyst for sincerity, Violet for modesty, that's February; Boy Scouts founded in 1910, Cassady born 1926, that's the 8th . . .

After fixing the exact time he would leave and precisely when he would reach each city en route, exactly how each day would be spent in New York—including helping Jack to choose a truck and helping them pack—Neal told them there was a chance they could rent the house next door to us; if not, they could stay in our attic until more suitable accommodations could be found. 'Carolyn insists that J. become pregnant, to have kids, of course, and catch up (impossible) with us, but, to also live next door and we can swap them, tossing the little wigglies over the backyard fence . . . got Joan's fine letter to me—tell her Carolyn feels same way about Pickup, Kickup and Shackup.'

No sooner were these new plans dispatched than there was a sudden lull in the switchman's job, and Neal decided to take his leave immediately so as not to miss any work or income. In the end, he took everyone completely by surprise in New York.

By now Diana's daily communications had resumed, and she was making veiled threats and frequent allusions to her 'unbalanced condition.' I was apprehensive, and as soon as Neal left, I sat down and wrote him a long letter, hoping it would be waiting for him when he arrived in New York:

> . . . don't you ever go away again! I looked back and saw your silhouette against the train light . . . you striding across the tracks carrying that big suitcase, and I could hardly push on the gas to go. You looked so little and lonely, and it made no sense all of a sudden—I have awful superstitions that now that you've changed to doing the right thing, your so-far-so-good luck will change too. Just when everything is about to be all right . . . and since D. is so cold, she might be capable now of carrying out her threat—I almost wrote Jack to ask him to go with you when you see her. She called this a.m. and tho I didn't talk to her, since I wouldn't accept the charges, I felt she wasn't in quite that state yet, altho now maybe she's madder. I wanted to talk to her, but I realized she could buy her crib and more for the phone bills. I wrote her airmail special to show her how fast it works and that 21¢ is better that $21. So, I hope they won't harm you . . .
>
> When you get back we'll show you how much we love you . . . There's so much to be done, and the second quarter century must be as rich as the first was wanton . . . I'm going around in a fog today and feel tired, but I'll get over it . . .

Neal wrote me a postcard on the way, and after he'd seen Diana, he whisked away all my anxieties regarding her:

Dear Wife; my only one:
Writing a quickie to you while bouncing along on commute from Tarrytown to NYC. I have just left Diana after 48 hours of talk and tears. I am pleased, happy, amazed, proud, overjoyed and impatient to report to you that everything, yes, every little thing is completely perfect and absolutely OK—i.e, we have come to an understanding . . . Actually, she made all the final decisions; to gratify her is simple enuf as it consists of

137

fantasy words . . . The long trek home to you and my loved children commences on Sun the 21st . . .

He said a great weight had been lifted, and pointed out that she and I were different personalities, so that she really was satisfied and knew she didn't want him because they were so unsuited. This, of course, was in contradiction to what she'd been affirming for so long, and I didn't believe a word of it, but I tried to.

> We both want different things and feel no respect for the other's ideals or desires, i.e . . . . she thinks my writing a joke, or at best a poor hobby. That's OK, you and I feel much the same but somehow are serious about it, huh?
> Approaching NYC and night of talk with Allen and Jack and reading of Holmes' novel and other readings, etc. I am whole, happy and for the first time rushing unreservedly to my one and only family, my sweet Carolyn, I love you . . . P.S. Jack and Joan not coming with me. May follow in a month . . .

It was strange to feel so differently about this trip of Neal's to New York; although I knew he would enjoy it, I considered it primarily an errand of mercy and he had my blessing. There were many things I wanted to accomplish before his return, but my energy seemed drained, and I felt only like resting and putting off all my ambitious plans. I credited the feeling to the relief from the strain I'd been under for so long on Diana's account. Then the light dawned, and I had to write to Neal the awful, unbelievable truth, half thinking he should reconsider his wants once more.

In my letter, however, I found myself writing about everything else I could think of—the girls, of course, and coy descriptions of my problems with the car. I took the opportunity to put in a section aimed at Jack, explanations and apologies I'd never be able to speak in person, hoping Neal would pass it on, and ending with '. . . I hope it can be cleared up, and I guess it will through you . . . your only acquaintance who took me seriously and made me feel really married to you and not just the current "bed with a girl in it" . . .'

But I couldn't dodge the subject forever. '. . . I wonder about your state of mind . . . how you feel about us, etc. . . .' I wavered, but finally plunged: 'Well, damn, now then, hold tight: I still haven't had a period . . . I just don't accept it; it really burns me up, and believe me, dear, I'm going to do everything I can think of . . . after all our precautions, *it just isn't possible!*'

And that was a fact. I had even gotten an infection because I wouldn't risk taking out the diaphragm. (When the doctor scolded me, I had told him that Diana had had Neal's sperm tested, and the little devils lived for at least 36 hours.) What was a girl to do? I was very bitter, and I ranted on about society and its laws, the Catholic Church and the peddlers of contraceptives that didn't work, and the doctors who guarantee they will. I proposed to demand an abortion from my former employer with the okay from her psychiatrist associate because of my previous post-partum depression, etc., etc. 'Must we look for this every year?' I asked. Before I finished the letter, I called the doctor. 'Well, I talked to her. She says it must be fate in my case and that something wonderful must be about to happen to me—but no abortion.' Although I didn't see how she figured any of that, nor how we would manage, I thanked God that Neal had decided to stay with me. But as I wrote to him, '. . . I still think you need a lighter dose of family . . . but don't let me spoil your vacation anymore.'

This gave Neal more inspiration for magnanimous and reassuring words.

> . . . The wonderful absolute joy I know and feel at thoughts of next quarter century with you (rich, not wanton) . . . I've learned how to treat possessions! . . . WORRY ABOUT NOTHING—including the third child . . . you come first, first, first in everything—kids next--perfect just to watch you, work for you, and I'm *not* hung on lazy kicks any more!! I've got the secret of perpetual energy! . . . I'm in there with you at last too . . . Trust.

I was glad to. How could I not? For the first time since our wedding I felt comfortable, safe and loved again by the only man I wanted.

Twenty-six

Spring of 1951 came, and with it the feeling of fresh beginnings and new hope. On our third wedding anniversary, Neal buttressed my optimism by writing me a silly poem, but one which showed his understanding and awareness of my feelings. He placed it beside my plate at dinner along with a piece of coloured glass.

> To my April Fool's magnificent Ass
> So beautious, though overfull, as is your heart
> With misery. I here make present a sliver of cut
> Stained glass
> Which unable to shave your behind's blubber
> Might yet pierce your reservoir of hurt
> Enough to make our third anniversary
> A day of insight crystal clear
> Combined with knowledge thru the ear
> So that when this Sabbath sun descends
> There'll be an understanding which portends
> Henceforth a bliss that never ends
> But shows up for joke the fear
> That dread neurotic minds hold dear
> To all the while make careful file
> Of everybody's dreary food
> On which they feed of selfish acts

Only to find it does no good
For conscience never has been forgot
The pacts made three years ago this day
When each to the other did say those eternal vows
That cost ten bucks
To get from you my legal—shucks. No paper.

He watched me read, grinning while I blushed here and there. 'You think Ginsey would be proud of me? Hey?'

With superhuman wizardry Neal had vanquished my jealousy toward LuAnne and Diana, and there remained only the residue of resentment kept alive by Diana's 'daily double' of letters and frequent phone calls. I took charge of the battle with her in order to protect my home, and although Neal maintained our harmony, his conscience nagged him badly. On this anniversary he also wrote a postcard to Jack, with 'April Fool' on the date line and no signature.

I've tried to write and can't. I love you and love you, but am so bothered by other things that each letter I begin ends at first paragraph. I can send you these if you wish. I even have funny little things torn from magazines for you. This card to let you know I'm alive . . . First 10 torturous sheets of double-space done on novel. Life hard with no tea to swallow or money for anything . . . C. and D. having tremendous long distance roaring match this very minute, been yelling in frustrated rage for halfhour. I'm sick to my stomach with sorrow . . .

Diana kept holding out unfounded hopes that she'd leave us alone. She'd changed the baby's name to Curtis, but insisted on hyphenating 'Cassady' onto the end of her own last name for awhile longer. She was now trying to get to Neal through Allen, a tactic I understood, as well as her need to talk to someone about Neal. Allen wrote us:

. . . I saw Diana 3 times for lunch and she is quite upset since all is in confusion, not so much amatorily (I think she's cured) but financially . . . You are a martyr to that plaything, and Diana said wife Carolyn was due again. You can have my policeman's badge, like in the Charlie Chaplin picture. Congratulations: I hope you may have the pleasure of a boy-child now. And Jack said 2 nights ago, 'he went back to the woman that wanted him most.' Ideal image of you in my mind has replaced reality. But I send love to the reality. Allen o' the woods.

So determined were Neal and I to succeed this time, we turned to the only source of help we then knew of—we investigated the facilities for psychological therapy and began regular sessions at the Langley–Porter Clinic. Our encounters were erratic and no progress was

141

apparent. Frequent changes of therapist did little to inspire our confidence; we were encouraged to talk about anything that came to mind, but the counselors almost never made comments. Neal and I free-associated all the time anyway, in each other's company and in letters, but it was difficult to repeat all that without any goal or guidance. Our monologues became increasingly vague, unfocused and unproductive.

Neal may have agreed to this step simply to humor me or to show he was willing to *do* something to help our marriage, or it may have been because Allen had pressed him for so long to try psychoanalysis. Neal thought he knew enough about psychology and marriage already; so did I, and perhaps we both did, intellectually. He had once written to Allen,

> Scientific psychology has worked out for itself a complete system of images in which it moves with entire conviction. The individual pronouncements of every individual psychologist proves on examination to be merely a variation of this system, conformable to the style of their world science of the day . . . like everything else that is no longer becoming but become, it has put a mechanism in the place of an organism.

My own feeling was that the psychologists had missed two opportunities when it came to Neal. One was the fact that Neal could remember his dreams vividly and abundantly—he wrote pages of them to Jack—yet they were never mentioned at the clinic. (Jack meanwhile loved the dream narratives and began paying more attention to dreams of his own, many of which he would write down for Neal, who would interpret them as best he could.)

The other opportunity Neal presented to the psychologists was that of first-hand research into the effects of marijuana. Neal would have provided them with the ideal guinea pig. As it was, I knew he often—if not always—went to his sessions 'under the influence,' but whether the counselor was aware of it we never knew. In any event, Neal seemed always to beat them at their own game, and they treated him with hauteur and hostility, unable to conceal their disapproval.

Neal became less communicative. It may have been because he was talked out or discouraged by the results, or because of the tea, as he maintained. He wrote to Jack:

> My mind is utterly blank; can't think of a thing to say. It's really a form of exhaustion brought on by the steady use of t, which with its enormous number of images, contents the brain with just thoughts—terrifying tho

142

they now are—so no can write. My brain waves on this stuff must form a very pretty picture· i,e., I feel I have most surely squared the circle tho so jazzed are the jagged lines as they return to the starting point, it makes me tired.

When Allen had written his dismal letter about Jack's marriage, Neal had answered with a lengthy analysis of some possible reasons for Jack's action, and high on the list was the particular batch of marijuana both Jack and Neal had been using at the time: '. . . because I've noticed that anyone who uses it has a tendency to think the same strange things as do others who use it . . .' He deduced that by its constant use Jack had seen himself as never before, '. . . brooding alone on Richmond Hill.'

In analyzing Jack's reasons for marriage, and in re-evaluating his own, Neal did a good deal of thinking on the subject and answered Allen's confusion:

> . . . reasons *for* marriage mean less than you believe, Allen . . . A marriage such as I am inclined to believe Jack's is, and know mine were, is a combination of willful blindness, a perverted sense of wanting to help the girl, and just plain what-the-hell . . . it all depends on the attitude of each partner toward the other as that attitude has been conditioned by the various actions and ideas that have influenced each person's personality. The many compromises, even tho intellectually not begrudged, push the limits of love, and soon each person affects a static comprehension of the other, and there is no changing the viewpoint. If one is convinced of the other's integrity, all is usually OK, but, if this is gone, there is no hope . . . I could go on indefinitely from experience . . . The conflicting ideas of the partners are the crux which combined with the emotional habits of each make for the strain that, once ruptured, needs an external responsibility to save the marriage—church, family, pride, children or some such absolute. My God! I sound like the *Ladies' Home Journal* or worse, and never having done this before give that excuse.

Perhaps this involved diagnosis was an attempt at justification inspired by the sterility of the psychology interviews, but whatever it was that made his brain work overtime and pour forth so much analysis, Neal's mood was more content, our 'static comprehension' of each other was altering somewhat and our 'viewpoints' seeing some change . . . at least on the surface. To Jack he wrote:

> Carolyn and I have never gotten along so well; her whole attitude has completely changed, at last. No shit, she is really nice as hell all the time now, I can hardly understand it . . . I gave Cathy a sip ('SIP'—whole GLASS) [I typed in] of beer . . . the depraved action shocked her into a

143

prompt scream of horror, but since we no longer bother to dicker or work up any emotional sweat, she gave up quickly and at the next pass of my chair, she stooped and with a kiss ruined all the thought of this paragraph, and my viperous ideas were nipped temporarily . . .

For some reason, Neal and Jack had found it difficult to talk during Neal's brief visit to New York, and now Jack's involvement with his wife made communication awkward. Neal's letters now contained fewer personal anecdotes, but occasionally he wrote long descriptive pieces based on past experiences, enjoying the 'Proust-like re-collections.' Jack applauded lavishly every word Neal wrote, and went overboard about a long letter in which Neal described an affair he'd had with two girls in his early teens. Jack hailed the letter as a literary masterpiece. Allen was usually less expansive in his praise and tried to comply more seriously with Neal's request for constructive criticism. But about this story they both agreed. Allen wrote:

> I finally got your long letter of Dec 17, the story, by stealing it from Jack's desk when he was out. He was afraid I'd lose it . . . He said to me when he read it, 'Neal is a colossus risen to destroy Denver!' I read it with great wonder, stopping and laughing out loud every few paragraphs, so much clarity and grace and vigor seemed to shine in the writing . . . even now it's hard to say (or feel at the typewriter) how much I am impressed and astonished at the magnitude of the work you have done in the Joan Story, which seems to me an almost pure masterpiece. It's easier to speak of the flaws, which I will do . . .

For pages and pages Allen did so, giving examples from poetry and literature and including suggestions of style.

At that time Allen was also acting as an informal literary agent for Bill Burroughs:

> Am having trouble publishing Bill's book (still not finished as he decided to write more of shit). But Doubleday already says 'no respectable publisher will put this out' or 'self-respecting' it was . . . But Jack Kerouac, however, on the ball, had last week finished *On the Road*, writ in 20 days on one sheet of paper yards and yards long, that he got from Cannastra's apt once . . . Jack needs, however, an ending. Write him a serious self-prophetic letter foretelling your fortune in fate, so he can have courage to finish his paean in a proper apotheosis or grinding of brakes. He is afraid to foretell tragedy, or humorable comedy or gray dawn or rosy sunrise, needs help to understand last true longings of your soul, yet, though he surely knows. Truly, what is too foolish to be said is sung.

Neal answered with his own views of *On the Road* and a scheme for Jack's future works:

Great news that Jack's finished *OTR*; I trust in his writing, but fear for it because theme of *On the Road* is too trivial for him, as his dissatisfaction shows. He must either forget it or enlarge it into a mighty thing that merely uses what he's written as a Book 1, since what he's done doesn't lend itself to stuffing, he should create another and another work (like Proust) and then we'll have the great American Novel. I think he would profit by starting a Book 2 with the recollections of his early life as they were sent to me and then blend that into his prophetic *Dr. Sax*. Of course, I'm sure I don't know what I'm talking about, but I do worry for him and want him happy.

Then Neal foretold his 'future in fate' for the ending:

Tell Jack I become ulcerated old color-blind RR conductor who never writes anything good and dies a painful lingering death from prostate gland trouble (cancer from excessive masturbation) at 45. Unless I get sent to San Quentin for rape of teenager and drown after slipping into slimy cesspool that workgang is unclogging. Of course, I might fall under freight train, but that's too good since Carolyn would get around 40 to 50 thousand settlement from RR . . . one thing sure, I'll keep withering away emotionally at about some rate as have last 3 years . . . I'm afraid I've irrevocably slipped, however, and in my mediocrity have become precisely what Jack long ago feared was my fate: I am blank and getting more so.

Neal continued sweating over his inadequacies as a writer, although he told Allen, '. . . re Joan Letter; can do same anytime, not now, tho.' Throughout the summer, his paramount concern was how to persuade Jack to come live with us. Each letter or postcard — even telegrams — extoled the advantages of our life and what it could offer Jack:

Dear Jack:
Alright now listen you, let's get serious. You going to write another book, huh? I'm trying to write one, right? You love me, don't you? I love you, don't I? If we're so all-fired good, then think of the funny times historians of future will have in digging up period in last half of 51 when K lived with C, much like Gauguin and Van Gogh, or Neitche [*sic*] and Wagner, or anybody and how, during this time of hard work and reorientation C learned while K perfected his art and how under the tutoring of the young master K, C ironed out much of his word difficulties and in the magnificent attic K did his best work and etc. etc. etc. No, but listen now, you'd have perfect freedom, great place in which to write, car to cut around in, satisfaction of knowing you're helping me when I need it most. No bother, great books to read, music to hear, life to see, up at any hour, to bed at same, free rent, best of all, a real period wherein instead of, when you're actually at a weak point as now, going thru hassle and money spending of setting up own pad . . as you just got thru doing . . . you come to me for

145

rest and relaxation and find a spot with absolutely everything you could need already set up for you.

All you have to do is take advantage of my hospitality, like a weekend that stretches into months in an English countryside estate, and say to yourself that you need a quiet place of freedom in which to write a new book and bone up on those few things you might hanker to know while you've got the chance to just lie around doing so, a time in which to gather your strength and your thoughts, a period of recuperation wherein you solidify your soul, everything is not jazz, cunt and kicks as you know so well, and before you indulge in same by taking off for some faraway place before you're really ready, you must come here to listen to me and make into cement the liquid putty of our life.

I have absolutely greatest bed in the world on the floor of my extraordinary attic; I got books and shelves, great huge desk that's bigger than any desk could possibly be, since Carolyn made it out of 6 ft. by 6 ft. piece of plywood, with immense dictionary of 30 lbs, and foot thick proportions, and fine lamps and good radio (one downstairs too) and wondrous tape recorder made for not only endless kicks on sound but for dictaphone type writing and recording of thoughts, hi and otherwise, and golf clubs, and baseballs and (soon) tennis racquets with nearby court and all the socks, handkerchiefs and dirty pictures one could want, and perfect weather, no heat, no cold, and world famous galleries and railroad you must dig, and Al Hinkle and maybe Bill Tomson and whore houses, if you've got the money, and freedom, man, freedom, no bull, Carolyn loves you, be like your mama without you having any need to cater like to her, and coffee, gobs of expensive coffee, and clothes washed free, and your portrait painted, and front parlor for smooching with anything handy (before you go upstairs for complete privacy) and good typewriter and ribbon, and the greatest of subtle think drugs, and so soft and easy to take: Dexedrine, it's perfect and mellow and is such a mental wonder that on it I write poetry (after a fashion) I got lots of it and journals and paper and if you don't come home for days or stay in your room for days or sleep forever or stay up all night or growl or cuss or dig my gone little chicks who are positively no bother even to a child-hater like Dillinger (much less than even Julie or master Bill, Jr.) or if you want to get serious again like an idealistic youth and want to really get in there on some subject, whether by yourself or with me, or if you want to go to pot so as to be further prepared for a tropical clime, or if you want analyst at free clinic (50¢ a visit) or if you want to work on RR or any damn old thing that strikes your fancy, do all of it, it's OK, more than you can possibly realize, for you don't know what easy living is till you dig old man C's brand at 29 Russell.

As soon as you get tired of us you may, if you are prepared in your own mind, leave at once for your shangri-la, or else, if you succeed in finding a bit of peace, or in doing a work that can't be quickly abandoned, you will stay until December, at which time we will all pile into my station wagon with its roominess and very slowly dig everything as we drive to Mex City where we will stay until short money completely fades and then the wife,

146

little kiddies and I will bid you fond goodby and leave you to your own devices in that city of magic. All this with less tension and anxieties than one might experience with even Mr. Burroughs' family, for Carolyn and I, at least, are a smooth running little team, that tho we sputter and snort a bit, are compatible as hell.

Naturally, in the back of your mind must be the remembrance of the rough receptions you've received at 29 Russell in the past, in fact, less than 2 years ago, but you must concede it was not as difficult for you as a murder or suicide might have made such a brief visit. Carolyn wants to try and make it up to you. We could try by way of a few group orgies or whatever, although this might sensibly be postponed until after Oct. because she's as big as our house and the bed is only four feet across. You understand that if you don't come here now it will curse my new son forever, since you won't be here to be his Godfather, and because you will have deserted him, I would be forced to not name him John Allen Cassady as is my present intent.

And be sure and bring your Bongo drums, or you'll have to go down on O'Farrell and see the gone drums there.

Early AM
Just got back from daily passenger run . . . I'm a big passenger brakie now, with a pretty monkeysuit that looks like a tux from the rear . . . and can't think of much more to say that might entice you to cover the long trail to this end of the world for no good reason, except that it's too hot in NY or Mex and too European in France and too trite in Great Neck and too early for Siberia or Africa. Incidentally, when all is lost you and I will go to Morocco and build railroad for thousand a month. All we do is ride while African coolies dump ballast over roadbed.

Am dying to read *On the Road* so you better have it published quick or have spare ms. And if you don't come because of intellectual reasons or because you just feel you can't make it, I will understand just as I think I do about poor J, and if I pine and die away as she without you: just meant to be.

N.

The exuberance of the letter was partly aimed at cheering Jack because he and Joan had separated. It also seemed to Neal to be a particularly good time for Jack to come because the railroad was actually advertising for brakemen.

But Jack did not come—he suddenly got severe phlebitis and was taken to the hospital. I felt I could write to him myself now, although I was still inhibited and could think of little to say except to sympathize with his illness and regret the fact that he couldn't join us: 'I need your help in making life worth living for Neal, I can't make it so by myself, I guess. Can you convalesce with us? . . . Neal's mind truly a blank. (He said "verify it.")'

147

By now Neal had earned enough seniority to work passenger trains, and he was able to afford his dreamed-of station wagon and saxophone. The wagon was fine, but the saxophone turned out to be a bitter disappointment, since it was a C-Melody and '. . . the C-Melody is so unpopular that I can't find an instruction book, and there is almost no music written for it.'

His passenger work was less tiring and more sociable, and now I had white shirts to iron and new black shoes to polish. He still could not hold down a regular run, but he enjoyed the suspense of never knowing whether he'd be called for passenger or freight. He had just begun to get used to the new conditions when the trainmen went on strike. The switchmen struck in sympathy, but Neal leaped into the breach and hired on again as a switchman in Oakland. Now he was gone even longer hours.

Our divorce would have been final in June, but I received no notice or papers from my lawyer and did not contact her—I said nothing about it to Neal, merely smiled to myself as the deadline came and went.

Twenty-seven

September of 1951 brought the kind of weather we usually expected in the fall and spring: dazzling blue skies and bright sunlight with a light wind, affecting a perfect balance of warmth and refreshment. On the Sunday afternoon of the 8th, I collected Helen and her nine-month-old boy and, with my two girls drove down to Aquatic Park at the bottom of our hill. We sat in the sand and, while the youngsters splashed about, blissfully dangled our legs in the icy water. Behind us the bright green grass of the sloping lawn tempted lovers, musclemen and the elderly to bask like so many lizards and look out over the Bay, flecked with sailboats and whitecaps. I felt unusually peaceful and content.

After two or three hours of this harmony I drove Helen home, having some difficulty on the long ride because my tummy interfered with the steering wheel. Helen and Al, on their return from Denver, had rented an apartment that was the converted upper story of an old Victorian home at the other end of town. In spite of Al's railroad priority, they had been there several weeks without a phone and had to depend on the couple living in the flat below. Helen didn't drive, so I had been to see her several times, but it wasn't until that afternoon that I noticed the name under the bell below hers. It was a long Polish name, unpronounceable for me, but it stuck in my memory even though it meant nothing to me.

Around two o'clock in the morning I was awakened by the by-now-familiar signs of impending birth. The baby was not due for another month, according to the doctors, but there was no doubt it was on its way. I thought it most considerate to spare me the last hot month, but despite this, the timing seemed poor. Neal was in Oakland across the Bay, Louise had moved to the Peninsula, and Helen had no phone.

Suddenly, the Polish name of Helen's neighbor appeared in my mind. Breathlessly I ran downstairs for the phone-book—I couldn't have given the name to an operator, nor was I sure of the spelling. I found the only one similar—and it was on the right street. The phone rang and rang, my heart fluttering with every buzz. When it was finally answered, relief and apologies muddled my request to wake Helen and call her to the phone. Luckier still, Al was home, and as usual they lost no time in responding cheerfully to my distress signal, even though it meant packing up their own infant as well. While I waited for them I couldn't get over the coincidence which had saved me; it gave me a queer, indefinable feeling.

When Helen and her baby were resettled in my house, Al drove me to the hospital. This time there was no heavenly anesthetic—it was too late—but my joy became complete when finally I dared to ask what sex the baby was. The nurse answered 'It's a boy' in a tone that said, 'What else?' That was exactly how I felt; it had to be. Now I was even. I had given Neal a boy. Peacefully, I drifted off to sleep.

Neal arrived home that morning to find Helen and Al in our bed. When he learned that I had had a boy at 5:10 a.m., he slept for an hour or so and then came to see me, after which he went back home and sat down to write to Jack:

> My boy is full term and healthy, tho seems a month early. He is amazing looking with *absolutely* White Platinum Blond hair, like Jean Harlow's was, only more striking with its growing over his ears already. I have, of course, already named him after you and Allen. John Allen Cassady, J.A.C.

John Allen and I had a restful week—he was such a calm baby—and Neal brought the girls to the hospital window to visit whenever he was home, having found his younger sister Shirley to care for them while he worked.

For the first six or eight weeks after I brought John home he continued to be an angelic baby. Then one day he wasn't there—that is, he was there physically, and he indicated his needs in the same manner as usual, but that was all. It took me a few of these unresponsive days to realize that his personality (could it be his *mind?*) seemed absent. When I was sure my senses were not deceiving me I

The author in 1946.

Neal Cassady, Snr.

Neal's mother with friend, date unknown.

Neal with his older brother Jimmy, 1932.

Schoolboy Neal, 1941. He'd played hookey from school the previous day, and so had missed the announcement that ties had to be worn for the photograph the next day.

Neal's first wife, LuAnne, in about 1946.

Neal, 1948 – his merchant marine application photograph.

In love. San Francisco, October 1947.

Neal with Southern Pacific
colleagues, 1949

Sketch of Neal
by CC 1951

Sketch by the
author of Neal
typing, 1951.

Neal with Diana Hansen and family, Tarrytown, N.Y., 1950.

Christmas 1949, with Helen and Al Hinkle, and Bill Tomson

Helen Thom

With Neal, 1952 – a rather typical illustration of our relationship.

Jack Kerouac, 1952.

called the pediatrician, finding it extremely difficult to explain myself. But he calmed my fears by saying he'd heard of it happening occasionally, and the babies had all snapped out of it in time. Sure enough, in about another week John did There he was again, cooing and gurgling, his bright awareness returned.

The idea of a son growing up for whom he should furnish an example, was later to accentuate Neal's feelings of inadequacy, but while John was still an infant and Neal still young and idealistic, these fears were forestalled. He reveled in the child, writing Allen '. . . children, children, the pox of freedom and demander of money that siphons off luxury, but an enormous sponge to absorb your love and a bottomless pleasure pit into which I throw myself sometimes.'

His anxieties concerning Diana and her son could not be put off so easily. She wrote less often, but regularly, pleading for more money and rueing the day she'd met Neal. She even wrote a ten-page letter to the San Francisco district attorney including pictures of herself and Curt. When, nervous and afraid, we were summoned to meet the D.A., we explained the situation. He merely sighed and said, 'That woman should see a psychiatrist,' and dismissed us.

On the night I went into the hospital Neal had been reading the Oakland paper, and one squib sent him wildly searching through all the other newspapers hoping for more details, for he could hardly believe what he had read:

An American tourist trying to imitate William Tell killed his wife while attempting to shoot a glass of champagne from her head with a pistol, police said today. Police arrested William Seward Burroughs, 37, of St. Louis, Mo. last night after his wife, Joan, 27, died in a hospital of a bullet wound in her forehead received an hour earlier.

Bill, the perfect marksman. How could it have happened?

Two days later we got a letter from Allen in Galveston, Texas. He had gone there with his friend, Claude, after a rapid business trip to Mexico where he had visited Bill and Joan. Allen had read of the tragedy in the Texas paper, and was able to add some observations of his own:

Claude and Joan played games of chance with drunken driving, egging each other on suicidally at times, while we were there . . . My imagination of the scene and psyches in Mexico is too limited to comprehend the past misery and absurdity and sense of drama that must exist in Bill's mind now . . . or whatever he feels.

151

Although later Bill claimed a faulty gun as the cause, Allen's comments made us wonder if there had been some desperation in Joan that might have played a part. She could easily have willed—consciously or unconsciously—this fate and moved her head . . . but we didn't care to think about that.

In early January 1952, the event Neal had anticipated and promoted for so long finally occurred: Jack arrived. We had all thought about and talked of it so much, the actuality was extremely awkward for awhile. Neal bounded about showing Jack in rapid succession the wonders he'd described, overdoing the clowning until Jack was reduced to giggles. Jack and I were even more self-conscious with and strange to each other this time, never looking directly at each other without remembering the former meetings. I didn't know if it was Neal who influenced Jack or the other way around, but Jack probably thought I believed him to be the tempter. Since Neal had told Jack that I had 'changed completely,' I tried hard to justify the claim. When Neal was with us we were more relaxed; Jack would talk to Neal and include me, and his looks and tone indicated his sympathy and understanding. He avoided being alone with me, however, staying in his attic or walking around the surrounding sections of the city.

Jack and Joan had broken completely and bitterly. 'You see,' he explained, 'she was an only child, raised by women—her mother and aunts. They all hated men and taught her to, too. They were dedicated to revenge and used me to vent their anger—it's true; I'm convinced they did it on purpose. I caught her with this Puerto Rican a couple of times, see, and now she's pregnant and says it's my child—ha—it ain't my child.'

He seemed sick at heart but certain, and Joan's betrayal hurt him deeply, especially since she was his second wife. I felt really sorry for him and wondered why his judgment in choosing wives was so poor. I had heard him speak only sympathetically about women in general and quite sentimentally about marriage and family life.

He was immediately at ease with children, sharing an understanding at their level and communicating naturally without being maudlin. I never got the impression that my girls were a nuisance to him; rather he sought their company, listened intently to Cathy's prattle and told her lively stories. He was unaccustomed to small babies, however, and didn't know what to do with them. Once hearing him say something to this effect, Neal scooped up John from his crib and thrust him at Jack.

'No, man, here—babies are to *hold*, see? Just feel that. You've never known—see? You gotta *hold* 'em.'

Surprised and awkward, Jack still chuckled at this sudden outburst of Neal's and tried to do as he said. John reared his head back to study the strange face a moment, then sank against Jack's chest. Jack did his best, patting him hesitantly, but he obviously felt as though he were holding a bag of eggs and was relieved when I took John from him. Neal all the while was raving about the advantages of tiny babies over older children.

The first few weeks I didn't see much of Jack. He'd go with Neal, wander off on his own or stay in his room reading or writing. The attic worked well for him. He settled in and carefully arranged the few precious books and papers he needed to make him feel at home. As Neal had told him, I had found a huge piece of plywood and, with the aid of orange crates (which also served to hold books), constructed a great desk, the surface smoothed with several coats of dark green enamel. It could hardly fail to inspire a writer, I felt.

Only half the attic was 'finished,' but Jack preferred it that way. The rough, bare other half lent a barn effect and satisfied his craving for the natural and simple. The end he occupied was far from complete or decorated, but it was cozy and snug. A box spring and mattress made a low 'pad' and was covered with a paisley spread. The one window with its dark green shade was softened somewhat by burlap curtains. One square striped rug covered the bare floor boards and added a touch of color and warmth. He was gratifyingly enthusiastic. The only uncomfortable aspect for Jack was that the sole access to and from his lair was through a door in Neal's and my bedroom . . . as was the only route to the bathroom. It surprised me to find him so shy, old-fashioned and modest about personal physical needs or habits, but he used the bathroom only when no one was around and made arrangements elsewhere whenever possible. We all tried to cater to his embarrassment, though it was somewhat difficult with small children, and I had to be careful to be fully clothed at all times.

He had arrived at the worst time for hiring out as a brakeman, but after a few weeks Neal managed to get him a job in the baggage room at the depot. This eased things a bit, as Jack was forever fearful of imposing on us; this way he felt more independent. Neal's work was slower now, and they were able to spend more time together.

Although they tried to show more awareness of my feelings and talked reassuringly, I was no less anxious. By now, though, I realized

I had to find a means of dealing with this if I wanted to keep Neal and the family together; it seemed an inevitable condition. I mentally searched and probed for attitudes and answers that would fit some reasonable precedent in the institution of marriage. It wasn't that it was uncommon for extra or unrelated persons to live in a household . . . in fact such had often been the case in my own home; we were always taking in medical students or associates. But I knew this was different, though I tried my best to view it in a tolerant light. Each time they went gaily out the door or shut themselves up in the attic, I could not overcome the feeling of being a neglected household drudge.

It took a great deal of effort for me not to show how I felt and to search for reasonable criteria on which to base a change in my feelings, and a physical reaction soon erupted.

Neal worked the night before his birthday, arriving home about four o'clock in the morning, so I knew he'd want to sleep the next day. I awoke early and planned the day ahead, looking forward to another opportunity to wrap necessities such as socks, T-shirts, underwear and cigarettes into extravagant packages, to baking the cake and to making the trip to the store for ice cream. With Cathy now four and Jami three, they would enjoy the excitement of a birthday, especially since it was their first one for 'Poppie.' Jack's presence too would make this birthday even more special for Neal.

When John awoke I swung out of bed and into my robe, scooped him up before he could cry, and collected the girls. We all tip-toed downstairs without waking Neal. When he joined us around noon, I made him a huge brunch, and he opened his gifts. Neal's response could have been no more effusive had we given him a gold Cadillac, and he was genuinely delighted with all the attention. We spent a pleasant afternoon together, drinking coffee, reading the paper and playing with the children, being peaceful and glowing, 'like marriage was meant to be,' I thought.

There was only one small flaw. During the day, the left side of my face had become increasingly sore and stiff. I assumed it was a tooth problem and took some aspirin, saying nothing to Neal.

Dinner was to be somewhat later than usual owing to the late brunch, but also because Jack had not returned. I couldn't believe he'd forgotten the occasion, so Neal and I had a beer while we waited for him. When we could postpone it no longer, I served the steak dinner followed by ice cream and the birthday cake. Jollity prevailed.

After we'd read to the girls and tucked them into bed, my face was so painful and numb I told Neal about it. He insisted I call a doctor friend, even though it was long after office hours and a Friday night.

'You have Bell's palsy,' the doctor said, 'and you must do something about it immediately if you're going to recover. It didn't used to be curable, but it is now if you catch it in time. I'll call in a prescription for codeine . . .'

As he went on, a picture flashed into my mind—the face of the woman who had taught my sister violin. Now I understood why her face had been so askew, one eye glaring and unblinking, her mouth pulled up on one side of her cheek so that she drooled when she talked. I shuddered at the frightening prospect.

'How did I get this?' I asked the doctor.

'We're not sure what causes it,' he replied. 'Soldiers sometimes get it if exposed to cold on one side, and there's new evidence it can be caused by emotional strain or tension.'

I was annoyed, afraid and confused, but there was no doubt in my mind that it had not been caused by exposure to cold.

Neal expressed anxiety and sympathy and insisted on going out for the codeine right away. When he returned he made me go to bed, and then joined me, holding me close and comforting me. His warmth and the pills put me to sleep feeling happier than I had in some time.

Twenty-eight

The shriek of the telephone didn't scare me; we were used to it because of the railroad calls at all hours. Neal had perfected an automatic leap that quelled it quickly before it woke the children, even though it was in the front hall and about eight feet from our bed. I couldn't help hearing what he said. He sounded excited and alarmed.

'Yeah, Jack, sure—you're where? oh, my God, man, whaja do? No, never mind. I'll be right there.'

In one bound Neal was back and pulling on his pants. 'Jack's in jail. Sounds drunk. Gotta go get him out.'

'In jail? In *jail*?' I hated that word and all it implied. 'Whatever for?'

'Don't know yet.'

Neal slapped the belt-end through the buckle loop and bent to the mirror to pat his hair. In one continuous sweep he leaned down to kiss me, scooped the car keys from the dresser and was out the front door. As he left, a chill draft struck my bare shoulders. I turned out the lamp, and the darkness rushed in. I was uneasy and stared out into the blackness.

The rest of the night I spent in restlessness and increasing pain. Neal did not return, and before I realized it, further sleep was impossible: I heard the girls padding about their room and John's

156

squeaks and coos emanating from the living room. The day had begun.

When their needs were all met and they were playing in their rooms, I washed my hair and rolled it up. Just as I secured the last curler, I heard voices and activity in the front hall. When I opened the bathroom door, I saw Neal darting down the stairs and Jack escorting a young black woman up his attic steps. Stunned, I followed Neal, trying to blank my mind in preparation for reassurance.

In the kitchen Neal was busy lighting the stove under the kettle and rattling cups. He didn't look up at me as I came down the stairs. I tried to keep my voice level. 'What's going on, Neal? Where have you been? I see you got Jack out—what was it?'

'Where's the sugar?'

Neal's attempt to distract me failed. I knew he knew where the sugar was, so I didn't answer. Next he bounded to the refrigerator and peered into it as though it had an infinite depth.

'Well, actually, you see—ah—you see Jack wasn't actually in jail—' He laughed at this trivia and waved his spoon in the air. 'He was terribly drunk, and he thought—just as a joke, you know—it would be a way to get me out of the house—he didn't really mean anything by it, honey, honest.'

The sickening wave of familiar feelings welling up in me made me clamp my mouth shut and go sit down by the table. I was shaking and trying not to fly apart, but my dismay came through. I stood up and spat out in icy tones, 'You certainly don't think I'm going to put up with *that* sort of thing in my own *home*? With the children?' And I flung my head and rolled my eyes upward like some biblical evangelist, to indicate Jack and the girl. 'You just get yourself right up there and get—her—out—of—my—house—*right now*!'

I knew that I would scream or break something in another second, so I dashed for the stairs ahead of Neal and ran to hide in the bathroom. I'd forgotten how I looked. I had no makeup on and my hair was in rollers, and the face I saw in the mirror was more like the violin teacher's. I covered my face with my hands. I could hear Neal knocking at the attic door and calling up to Jack, but I couldn't hear the words. I was sitting on the edge of the tub, trembling, when I remembered the girls in their room beside the attic door. Grabbing a towel, I tried to wrap it around my head as I rushed out the door. I had to get to them first.

Too late. They were already standing wide-eyed in their doorway, and I got only as far as the corner of our bed when Jack and the woman jumped down from the steps and blocked my way. Neal was standing by the bureau between me and the hall door, so I had to step back to let Jack and the girl pass.

But the woman didn't pass. She lunged up to me flashing her black eyes, narrowing them into slits, then opening them wide with hate, the yellow eyeballs around the black center like the eyes of toy animals. Slowly she coiled words around her tongue, and they slithered out between her teeth, smashing against my ears like a string of firecrackers gone wild. I didn't really hear what she was saying, I was so startled. We all stood, frozen, while out of her poured snakes and toads of words raining down around me. To stem the torrent, I tried weakly to insert that I had nothing against her personally, nor was it any concern of mine what Jack did, but this was my home, and I'd rather they went elsewhere. She didn't listen, only mustered another barrage of adjectives, this time in a higher key. All the while the two men stood by dumbly, looking at the floor. I didn't feel at my best in my tattered robe, curlers and crooked face, but I sort of expected one of them either to defend me or to stop her. Neither moved a muscle until she had had her say. Then she walked haughtily to the bureau and picked up our car keys. Holding them out to Neal, she looked back over her shoulder for one last sneer at me and said, 'Take me home.' Neal obligingly took the keys and turned to the front door, she and Jack following behind.

Pain and self-pity got the better of me, and I couldn't stop the tears. I tried to hide them from the girls, but I had to go to them—do something. I wiped my face the best I could and tried to blubber reassurances, hurrying onto the subject of lunch and other distractions.

While the children napped I went outside and sat on the back steps and looked at our little patch of green grass in the middle of the surrounding buildings, and on up past the lines of waving wash to the square of blue sky above, hoping the sun would warm the cold ache in my middle. I just let my thoughts glide around without direction. I couldn't believe I would have to go through another awful separation, but what else was there to do? All I had to go on was righteous indignation, and I was tired of that. What good had ever come of it? I could think of nothing to do, so I would do nothing, just see what happened. This numbness was a kind of relief, and the codeine helped maintain it.

Around five o'clock, when I heard them come in the front door, my heart contracted sharply. I hadn't expected them so soon, if at all. In a few minutes all was quiet again. Curious, I went inside and up the stairs. Neal was asleep in bed, and Jack apparently in the attic, so I wasn't required to do anything for some time yet. I returned to the kitchen and began preparations for the children's dinner.

Neal was called to work, and when he was dressed he came downstairs. I went on with the routine as though nothing were different, but he saw my familiar put-upon look and understood my silence all too well. He kindly inquired about my face, but I just shrugged. In the past I had felt that if I was cheerful or pretended nothing was wrong, he wouldn't realize how *important* the episode had been, and I thought I shouldn't let him get away with it. But he was much better at pretending nothing had happened, and as he made remarks about the children, I tried tentative answers, ignoring the subject that was on my mind. I guess this time the horror was so stark, I figured even he wouldn't have to be told about it. Gradually, as I made his meal and watched him eat it and nothing happened, I found I could converse a little, though with a sense of doom behind my voice. He must have been surprised and bewildered, but he tried all the harder to be tender and at least he didn't try to make jokes. He left the house with the proper air of remorse.

That night the episode flitted back and forth in my mind among fragments of dreams, but I continued to push it away and refused to deal with it. When Neal returned home the next afternoon, I talked only about Jack and my concern that he had not stirred as far as I knew. Perhaps he had gone out while I was asleep? Neal went up to see. I heard muffled voices and then Neal reappeared.

'Dumb guy. He's sulking, I suppose, but he says he's okay and not to worry—he's reading and writing.'

'But Neal, he hasn't eaten since yesterday, unless he has something stashed up there . . .'

'Well, hell, I tried to talk him into coming down, but he just growled, so—' Neal shrugged and raised his hands in a mock Yiddish gesture. 'I'll take something up after awhile—kinda casually—he'll get over it.'

Monday morning Neal stayed home, and I went to the hospital as early as possible. The staff made me feel much better, and they promised me I wouldn't end up like the violin teacher. I began a series of treatments with heat, massage, exercise and electric needle muscle stimulation. It was no fun, but anything was worth it to know I'd be all right in six more months. They gave me a rubber band attached to a paper clip to wear over my ear and hook into my mouth, and an eye patch for my left eye which wouldn't close. I felt about as unattractive as anyone could, but I swallowed my vanity and followed their directions.

When I returned home, I noticed a book on the dressing table that had not been there when I had left. I picked it up and saw it was *The Town and the City*, the copy Jack had sent when it was published. I opened the cover and beneath Jack's original inscription was a note: 'With the deepest apologies I can offer for the fiasco, the foolish tragic Saturday of Neal's birthday—all because I got drunk—Please forgive me, Carolyn, it'll never happen again.'

So that was why he'd stayed upstairs: suffering with guilt and remorse. I was deeply touched, uplifted and eager to show him all was forgiven. A thought flashed through my mind: 'Not like Neal.' Why could I look forward with pleasure to righting a situation like this with Jack but not with Neal? Was it because I believed Jack when he said it wouldn't happen again?

I blamed Neal a good deal for the recent episode, and although it wasn't likely I'd retaliate, this crime would certainly join the ranks of all the others, ready to file in parade before him whenever I needed to remind him of his obligations to me and of my reasons for doubting his good intentions. My present state of suspended hostilities was not to be confused with 'forgiveness.'

When I'd reread the message several times, I took the book downstairs to show Neal. After reading the note himself he bounded upstairs and in wild jocularity released Jack from his prison with promises of total absolution from my hands. They came giggling down to the kitchen, Jack and I smiling shyly. Neal became master of ceremonies, opened the beer and wine, and we eagerly gave up any thoughts of sorrow or condemnation in our efforts to restore a state of mutual comradeship, even racing out into the street to take photos of us all.

That evening after dinner there was no mention of going out. They got high, talked and laughed into the tape recorder and were careful to include me in their conversation and reminiscences. Wisely, I let the sleeping dog lie.

160

Twenty-nine

———

The old pattern thus broken, the climate of the household warmed, and there began, for me, a new life, or at least a new perspective on the old life. When Jack wasn't at work or busy writing, he'd now sit and talk to me, telling me of his childhood in Lowell, Massachusetts and of his mother's tenacity in working at the shoe factory; or he would voice his regrets at his sister Caroline's intolerance of him. Jack had a loyal affection for her, and felt it was an odd coincidence our names were so similar. She was married with a son and felt Jack should get a job, support their mother and stop wasting his time playing around with writing.

Here with us, Jack was trying to finish *On the Road*. I had only read random passages of the manuscript; I was too close to the pain of the events he described, and the more Neal chortled over it, the more fearful I became that I'd feel a necessity to start something again. The only details I'd heard of their trips were those Helen had revealed, and I was blissful in my ignorance. Jack was still writing additional scenes, and he became excited with the possibilities offered by the tape recorder to capture spontaneous discussions or stories. I was beginning to think the *Road* might become an interminable highway. Jack had found that he had an audience that believed he could do no wrong, and he was happy to share his daily efforts with us. He still carried a little five-cent notebook in his shirt pocket wherever he went to note impressions or new ideas which he would type up within a few

161

days. One notebook he inscribed to me.

The liquor store was just around the corner on Hyde Street, and Jack sometimes bought a small bottle, or 'poor-boy,' of Tokay or Muscatel to sip late in the afternoon or after dinner, when he would share it with me. Sometimes I'd go with him to the liquor store to buy beer for Neal. One time when I stopped for beer alone, the proprietor said something about my 'husband's' preference for sweet wine. It wasn't until I was outside that I realized he meant Jack, and I had to laugh. If only he knew how much trouble I had keeping one husband, let alone two.

One afternoon I was feeding John in his highchair when I heard the front door open and slam shut, and Neal came clumping down the stairs dragging his jacket behind him. He threw it down hard on the couch and said, 'Shit.' He hardly ever swore in front of me, so I knew he must be really angry.

'I've got to pack,' he said. 'I've drawn a two-week hold-down in San Luis.' He stood looking out the window, clenching his jaw.

This kind of assignment was the only kind he didn't like. On hold-downs he had to go to a neighboring branch, and it meant staying in either a barren dorm, the 'crummy' (caboose) or a sleazy hotel. He had to work the same local freight early every morning for at least two weeks, sometimes longer.

Neal blew off some steam and then accepted his lot, settling down to his own cheerful self again. He would never expand on his disappointments if it meant bringing someone else down.

He hadn't much time. While he went upstairs to pack, I hurried with the dinner, and he called up to Jack to explain why dinner would be earlier tonight. I was even more sorry than Neal at this sudden development, and I guessed maybe Jack would be, too. When alone together, Jack and I had still not found a firm footing in our relationship, and we needed Neal nearby as a buffer. Consequently, during this dinner we were both nervous, eyeing each other in a new and uncharted way.

Neal stood up from the table and planted his hands on either side of his chest in his Oliver Hardy stance, looking down at Jack and then at me.

'Well, kiddies I must be off. Just everyone pray I get back in fourteen days and no more.'

He retrieved his jacket, kissed me and the children and strode to the stairs. At the landing he turned back as though he'd forgotten something, then said with a grin, 'I don't know about leaving you two—you know what they say, "My best pal and my best gal . . ." Ha, ha—just don't do anything *I* wouldn't do—okay kids?' He bounded up the stairs laughing, knowing, just as we did, that there was nothing he wouldn't do in a similar situation. I wanted to crawl under the table and disappear, I was so embarrassed, and I couldn't look at Jack. Instead, I jumped up and began grabbing dishes off the table and putting them in the sink. Jack bolted for the attic.

Jack had been taught that marriage was a sacrament, whereas my thinking was that if a person agreed to a set of rules and went so far as to choose to take vows, then he should play the game and keep the promises. Otherwise, don't do it—nobody *has* to get married nowadays. Neal, on the other hand, was torn between his beliefs and overpowering desires. Jack's courtesy and gentleness toward me resulted from my being the wife of his best friend, nothing more—at least that was all either of us could admit to, even to ourselves.

The more I thought about Neal's remark, the angrier I got and the more it hurt. Well, maybe I was jumping to conclusions again—maybe he really did mean it only as a joke. But it was no joke to me. During the next two weeks, Jack was out most of the time and rarely sat and talked to me. When he did agree to share a meal, however, it was so pleasant we'd soon forget the circumstances in the joys of conversation. But the silences brought back our discomfort at being alone together, Neal's remark hanging in the air around us.

When he returned we welcomed him with great relief. He seemed a little reserved the first evening at dinner, and I wondered if he supposed we had behaved as he would have done. When Jack hurriedly left us alone, I asked. 'Remember what you said when you left, Neal? How could you say a thing like that? Do you know how that hurt? You made me feel I was no more precious to you than—a towel or something. Can you understand that? Don't you know I'm proud to show you I deserve your trust, that I like chances to prove my loyalty? Tell me, did you sincerely feel we should have made love, Jack and I—or were you just saying that to protect yourself in case we did?'

I was peering at Neal intently, waiting for his answer. He got up from the table looking uncomfortable and started toward the stairs. Then he paused and shrugged.

'A little of both, I suppose . . . yeah, actually . . . why not? I thought it would be fine.' And up the stairs he went.

Goddamn the man! Well, I had asked for this second blow, but how could he be so unfeeling? I should know by now, I thought dejectedly.

163

Hadn't he 'shared' LuAnne—even though they were no longer married—and how many others? Again, I kept supposing I was different, meant more to him. This seemed a greater rejection even than desertion.

Dolefully, I did the dishes, mulling it over, finding no solace. When Neal came down to tell me he and Jack were going out, I got a vision once more of the future as an incessant repetition of the past, and I knew I must do something to change it. None of the old ways had worked, so defiantly, I said half-aloud, 'All right, Neal dear, let's try it your way.' And the anger drained out of me while I felt another conviction torn away as though I'd shed another skin. Suddenly I felt exposed, but with that came a coolness and a spurt of excitement mingled with fear. Never had I known how to play female games of deliberately setting out to trap a man. At least in this case it shouldn't require much aggression, just a few calculated moves. After all, Jack knew better than I how Neal would react. It was worth a try; anything was better than this.

Thirty

An evening or two later, I made a few plans—nothing elaborate or unusual, but admittedly I manipulated circumstances as best I could. I'd asked Neal about the train he was called for and its schedule. He'd be gone until the following afternoon. When the children were settled for the night, I called softly up the attic stairs. 'Jack?'

He came to the top of the steps. 'Yeah?'

'I wondered if you'd like to join me for dinner. I've made an experimental sort of pizza, and there's way too much for me. It doesn't keep too well, so—how about it?'

'Okay, sure . . .' He looked hesitant. 'Just give me a minute?'

'Oh, no hurry; it'll be another thirty minutes anyway, but there's some wine, too. So whenever you're ready.' Pausing for a minute at my dressing table, I checked my appearance—mustn't be too obvious. I was already feeling like a wanton woman and had butterflies in my stomach. Too bad I could only get away with jeans and a white shirt without arousing his suspicions; but I had been careful with my hair and makeup, and thought just a dab of cologne would be fair.

Downstairs I checked my ammunition there: new candle in the bottle, table set as usual, radio set at KJAZ, the station both Neal and Jack approved of for its ballads and progressive jazz. The oven was ready, so I popped in the pizza. I thought I'd better sample the wine to calm my nerves, and I fancy I appeared quite nonchalant when Jack descended from the attic to join me.

'Pour us some wine. Dinner will be ready in a jiffy.'

I sat down opposite him at the table, raised my glass to my private scheme and smiled.

The wine helped put us both at ease and made us garrulous. Jack praised my cooking long and loud and plunged into stories, all self-consciousness gone. For my part, I forgot my preconceived plot and was lost in genuine enjoyment. He regaled me with the impressions of Bill Burroughs he'd gained in New York, what he knew of that strange individual's childhood, education and brilliant mind. Neither of us could guess why such a man had become so attracted to drugs and firearms. He told me the story of his own first wife, Edie Parker, and the hectic times in New York when he'd met them both. He was planning to visit Bill in Mexico in the summer and eagerly looked forward to another sojourn in that magic country. He loved the music and the slow, easy-going lifestyle. To him it seemed to represent a Utopian existence without hassles, a timeless peace. He and Neal favored Spengler's word '*fallaheen*' to describe the culture, but since to them the term meant a people who weren't going anywhere but had already been and were resting before the next creative cycle occurred, it sounded to me like the impossible dream for these two men who loved dashing about looking for 'kicks.'

When we had finished eating, I knew I had to keep Jack downstairs until I'd finished what I'd started; I'd never be able to repeat it. I poured more wine and walked to the couch we kept opened out to double-bed size. As I sat down on its edge, I held out Jack's glass to him. He followed me, accepted the wine and lay back upon the couch, balancing the glass on his chest. With his eyes closed, he hummed along to 'My Funny Valentine' as it wafted from the radio.

I looked down at him but said nothing until the silence became thick and warm, then I asked, 'Do you remember when we danced together in Denver?'

He turned his head, opened his eyes and looked at me tenderly. Then, smiling, he sat up and said softly, 'Yeah . . . I wanted to take you away from Neal.' He kept looking into my eyes but he had stopped smiling.

Barely audibly, I asked, 'And do you remember the song we danced to?'

He leaned toward me: ' "Too Close for Comfort." '

At that moment I knew plots and plans were foolish; my mind and will floated away and, just as in the movies, we both put down our glasses at the same time, not unlocking our eyes or looking at the table

166

but making perfect contact. When his arms went around me, glints of light sparked in my head as if from a knife sharpening on a wheel, and my veins felt filled with warm, carbonated water.

The first morning light awakened me, and for a second I didn't know where I was. Then it came back, and seeing his form beside me a wave of remorse passed through me. What had I done? I was married to Neal, and now I felt sorry for him as well as afraid of what would happen next. The leather of the old couch was cold under me, and my muscles felt cramped. As quickly and silently as I could, I slid out from under the blanket and ran upstairs to my own bed, hoping for a few more hours of oblivion. It was no use. My mind kept frying the situation on all sides. I felt more shy of Jack than ever, and I didn't see how I could look him in the face. Would he be sorry?

I heard him getting up and come up the stairs, so I pretended to be asleep. All at once I felt his lips on my forehead, lingering, and a flood of soothing warmth poured over me as he climbed the stairs to his attic, and I drifted into sleep.

He accepted our new relationship more enthusiastically than I had expected, but I was pleased my guilt was thus diminished. Jack was a tender and considerate lover, though somewhat inhibited, and I suspected he wished I was more aggressive, but that I could never be. So our temperaments and our guilty feelings about Neal made actual love-making infrequent but more passionate. Although I could be wholly romantically in love with him, my heart still ached for Neal to be enough. Also, my compassion for anyone in Neal's position made me feel even more loving toward him, and I wavered in my resolve to teach him a lesson. I'd have sworn allegiance again in an instant, but I prodded my mind to remember his flippant words of indifference. I hoped sincerely that some lasting good would come from this, but for now there was nothing to do but relax and enjoy it.

Whenever Neal was home, Jack and I were extremely discreet, but there was no concealing the change in us. Neal couldn't help but notice, though the only evidence we had that he cared was his increased attentiveness to me.

The hope that my gamble would change the pattern of our lives was well founded. Like night changing into day, everything was showered with new light. Butterflies bursting from cocoons had nothing on me. Now, I was a part of all they did; I felt like the sun of their solar system, all revolved around me. Besides, I was now a real contributor for once; my housework and childcare had a purpose that was needed and appreciated. I was functioning as a female and my men were

167

supportive. It may have taken two of them to complete the role usually filled by one, but the variety was an extra added attraction. They were such different types. How lucky could a girl get?

I provided for whichever of them was in residence according to his individual preferences. If they were both home during the day, Neal usually slept and Jack wrote, or Jack would go out and leave the husband and wife alone. On occasion, Jack and I would make love in his attic if the children were asleep. He'd produce a poor-boy of wine and play host. I think of him now whenever I smell unfinished wood, and remember how the sun sometimes lay across us like a blanket; or how, huddled under covers, we'd listen to the soft patter of the rain close above our heads.

When both men became accustomed to the idea, they dropped their defences and joined me downstairs in the kitchen. While I performed my chores, they'd read each other excerpts from their writings-in-progress or bring out Spengler, Proust, Céline or Shakespeare to read aloud, interrupted by energetic discussions and analyses. Frequently they would digress and discuss a musician, or a riff or an interesting arrangement emanating from the radio. I was happy listening to them and filling their cups. Yet, I never felt left out any more. They'd address remarks to me and include me with smiles and pats, or request my view.

They still made forays together in search of tea or to buy necessities, but they were never gone long, and if Neal was at home, Jack and I sometimes took walks in the neighborhoods nearby. In Chinatown we marveled at the weird food displayed in the markets, the gorgeous embroidered clothing and the endless bric-a-brac in the tourist shops. Jack found an old-time Chinese restaurant with a white-tiled entrance on a little street adjacent to St. Francis Park. We'd buy steaming bowls of won-ton soup for 35¢ or fried rice for 25¢. Often we warmed ourselves thus and then sat on a bench in the park beneath the magnificent Benny Bufano steel and marble statue of Sun Yat Sen. Other times we walked down the hill to Aquatic Park and drank Irish coffee in the Buena Vista or down the Union street hill to Washington Square, taking French bread, cheese and wine purchased at the Buon Gusto market to nibble beneath the glittering gold spire of the cathedral. This reminded Jack of his childhood church in Lowell where he'd been baptized, St. Louis en l'Ile, and of his desire to see the original in Paris. On bright days we might hike up Telegraph Hill to Coit Tower and gaze out over the Bay, watching the ships, and that would be his cue to tell me of his seafaring adventures.

The times when Neal and I were alone were happier, too. We had the children's progress, illnesses and antics to discuss, as well as household economics. I felt especially affectionate toward him now, and he accepted and returned these expressions in better grace. I wondered if it was because he tended to appreciate his women more when the relationship was threatened, or whether a rival made him feel less trapped. At the moment I didn't care. Meals together amused me and gratified my ego. Here the two men were like small boys, vying for the most attention, for the best story, and felt slighted if one was allowed to hold the floor too long. Jack was the more sensitive, sometimes taking offense or sulking if Neal talked exclusively to me and behaved as though he weren't there. At times like these, Jack might stalk upstairs, and Neal would have to go and coax him back and make it up to him. Neal still had to prove he was the best man around. By and large, my cup was running over.

Already, in the first couple of months since Jack's arrival, my self-esteem had expanded as I found myself accepted as a desirable companion both mentally and physically. So I decided to go along with Jack's expectation that I would now join him, with or without Neal, on evenings out, although I was apprehensive, still conditioned by past experiences and less comfortable in the Bohemian scene than I had been when younger and unencumbered. Young people now seemed more intense, clutching, and I couldn't help feeling they took themselves too seriously. I wondered if the increasing use of drugs could account for this, but whatever the cause, 'good, clean fun' appeared to be a thing of the past. Or perhaps the aura of suspicion and defensiveness was merely a reflection of my own fears.

One afternoon Neal brought home a young man called Charlie, whom he must have met on one of his expeditions in search of tea. Charlie lived in the Tenderloin area with some pretty basic characters and had a daughter whom he housed with one woman or another of dubious genre. It was a situation that frightened me, and although we tried to help the child from time to time, I was out of my depth.

Charlie was a tiny thing, only about five feet tall with a round shining face. His age was difficult to assess, but I guessed it to be in the middle 30s. He was always cheerful and bubbling and loved to join the boys for blasting.

One evening they got together with tea, wine, the tape recorder and a variety of instruments: recorders, wooden flutes, maracas and an old harmonica. Jack never stopped drumming, whether or not an actual drum was available. He did very well on the bottoms of assorted cooking pans or oatmeal cartons, and was content with these ever since an appalling episode when he'd ruined someone else's beautiful new bongos. We'd all gone to a pay-the-rent party in a dockland loft, and in order to get in without paying Neal had persuaded the hostess that he and Jack were musicians. Saying he'd left his drums in New York, Jack was lent some and told that he could tighten them by heating the skins over the gas jet. He hadn't seen the blue flame extending high above the yellow, and, to his horror, burnt a large black hole in the drum. He was almost in tears when he secretly told me. 'What'll I *do*!' he wailed. We were both too distressed to confess, so we hastily collected Neal and raced for home. Jack had suffered for hours over that mishap, until Neal's rational analysis, and the tea he'd managed to score, cheered him up again.

On the evening that Charlie came around, I declined to indulge in the tea but was interested in studying its effect on them. They had a riotously good time, sometimes hung up on their musical impro- visations, sometimes on the replay of same, but mostly howling with laughter and appreciation over what they apparently considered an inordinate display of brilliant wit. Charlie was not in their league intellectually—his mind was inclined to run to the earthy and his comments were usually connected with sex. I decided the tea was not responsible for any exceptional cleverness, only for making them think they were being clever. In fact, it seemed to me that nothing they expressed showed any really heightened perception; they were so high that dumb things just didn't sound dumb. After a short time, I was content to bid them a bored good night and retire. Jack later inserted his transcription of the tapes of one of these conversations into his novel *Visions of Cody*.

One night two or three friends came over with a new kick. Neal was all excited and the atmosphere took on an expectant and awesome feel. They had brought peyote, which Neal and Jack had never had before. Explicit directions were given and followed; all theories and reported results reviewed. Neal watched, leaning on the table with eyes aglow, as the friend carefully chopped up the lobes of cactus as finely as its toughness would allow.

'Well, how do you take it, man? Cook it?' Neal was impatient.

'No, no . . . just eat it . . . chew it up. Only trouble is, it makes you nauseated at first, but if you can keep it down . . . wow . . . like you've never seen such colors . . . technicolor visions.'

I knew then this was an experience I would forever have to forego.

When I weighed the thought of purposely causing oneself to be nauseated against such possible 'visions,' the visions lost out. I'd have to live with my own feeble imagination. All such external administrations to the psyche make me apprehensive, but I squared my shoulders and decided I'd stick around to function normally if anyone required help.

Each participant ceremoniously chewed a tablespoon or two full of the gray-green mound and either sat on the couch to await results or ascended to the attic. I watched and waited. All was quiet. Extremely. I couldn't tell when they ceased struggling with the rising nausea and became deep in their dreams. Since dim lighting appeared to be part of the ritual, I went to bed to read, still remaining alert to any signs of distress. No emergency arose, and no one cared to communicate their sensations that night, so I gave up and went to sleep.

Even the next day, my efforts at drawing out some descriptions of their wondrous experience were mostly futile. Neither Jack nor Neal could remember anything particularly startling or revelatory. It may just have been they couldn't find words to match, unlikely in Jack's case, but it seemed the deepest impression remaining with them was the nausea. Neal's stomach was so sensitive anyway, he had lost his first dose and made himself repeat the ordeal. I doubt he was as enthusiastic on the second try. Nevertheless, they kept some peyote in the refrigerator and wrote to Allen in glowing terms, so he requested a sample for himself. The rest of the stash was finally dispersed when we awoke one morning to find ourselves criminals—possession of peyote had been declared a felony. I think they were secretly pleased with the excuse to get rid of the stuff; after all, the illegality of marijuana had never worried them.

One blustery night, Jack went out alone but came back in a few minutes and tried to get Neal and me as excited as he was about having discovered that Joan Crawford was only a block away making a movie. For some reason neither Neal nor I wanted to go, and Jack went back out with his notebook. Hours later he returned and stayed up all night writing 'Joan Crawford in the Fog.' When it was eventually published, he called her Joan Rawshanks, but when he read it to us the day after he wrote it, it was only Joan Crawford, and I was always sorry afterward I hadn't gone with him.

Another night Jack asked me to accompany him to a party, this time with Neal's benediction as he couldn't leave the phone and was content to sleep until his call. The party was in a private apartment, and there were four or five other couples. The hosts were Jordan Belson, a talented artist and film maker, and his wife Jane, and the group had been invited especially to view Jordan's latest film.

Before the film was shown, I struck up a conversation with an art student and was intent on listening to her, not noticing that two joints of marijuana had been lit and were being passed down both sides of the group seated in a semi-circle before the screen—each cigarette ended with me before being passed back up. So as not to seem prudish, I had been absentmindedly taking puffs as each joint was handed me, not realizing I was getting twice as much as anyone else.

Soon the film was shown, the first of its kind I'd ever seen, and I was fascinated and delighted. Jordan had animated line drawings and paint splotches to the music of a mambo. It had everything: humor, pathos, despair, excitement, personalities, character types, and I didn't want it to end.

When it did and the lights were turned on again, I found myself unable to move a muscle. I was absolutely rigid. 'Stoned' came to mind—so that's what it meant. But what was I to do? Rising panic made me icy cold as well. It seemed an eon before Jack turned to me and said something. He put his hand on my arm and his touch broke the spell. He turned away again, apparently not having noticed anything unusual about me. Could it be? I thought everyone in the room must be conscious of my helpless condition. I wanted to tell Jack, but now I was blocked again, couldn't think what to say, and the panic returned.

The party was breaking up. Jack and the others were moving about the room, collecting coats and making farewells. I sat like a rock. Somebody was bound to notice, yet the nice girl I'd conversed with accepted my smile as sufficient answer to whatever she'd said to me. With extreme effort I found I could lean forward slightly, but I didn't dare attempt to stand. Jack came forward to me with my coat and held out his hand. When I saw I could reach for his in return and, with his touch, was able to rise, relief swept over me. I was mobile, I was okay.

Not quite. 'Jordan wants to know if we can drive him over to Columbus Avenue, and I told him it's right on our way, all right?' I heard what Jack said, and it sounded simple, but drive! I hadn't thought of that—how could I ever *drive*? But I must go on, and I said, 'Of course' while climbing into my coat, my mind awhirl. Holding onto Jack's arm I got to the door and down the stairway, the bright light in the stairwell illuminating brilliantly colored paintings on the

172

wall and making me feel as if I were floating in a surrealistic fantasy. Jack behaved as though I were perfectly normal.

When we reached the car at last, I was about to give up and confess all to Jack and Jordan, when into my mind came Neal's original instructions on my initiation into tea: 'Remember, you can always do anything you have to do.' I grasped these words, repeating them again and again as I got in and started the car. I hadn't a clue as to what the men were discussing, but, sure enough, I drove Jordan where he wished to go, and right on through the traffic, the busy streets and up the hill to home; I even parked with no greater difficulty than usual. I thanked God or whatever was responsible, but also resolved that I'd had my last tea party.

Neal was leaving for work when we reached the house, so I said nothing of my experience to either him or Jack. Being close to Jack's naturally reassuring presence was enough for now.

Thirty-one

Work on the railroad was slow, so Neal 'bumped' a newer man in order to hold down a steady job on a daily freight local, even though he'd make less money than he could on the extra board. My blooming self-confidence developed into a daring hitherto unknown in my sheltered experience, and to help with the finances I decided to seek a night job. I wanted something which was fun and wouldn't tax the brain, a job I could quit without feeling guilty but which would let me have a go at being a 'night person.'

I knew I couldn't be a waitress; I'd nearly come apart trying that in college. After quite an education in the ways and means of night-time jobs, I finally settled for being a camera girl, even though the only income was from tips. The office was in the 'International Settlement.' Hidden down a side street below Broadway this dazzling block of nightclubs and amusement stalls was neither a 'settlement' nor 'international,' but everyone knew it was the last remnants of the Barbary Coast in San Francisco. It was shoddy, though, by today's entertainment standards, far from wicked. (Now that it has been torn down, instead of the seamier places being concentrated in one, easily avoided area, the new lust factories of San Francisco are sandwiched between the finer restaurants and jazz nooks and seep down the neighboring streets to contaminate a far larger area.)

I passed under the elaborate wrought-iron archway that spelled out its name in lights and found the boss, who gave me a quick resumé of my duties and then yelled over his shoulder, 'Hey, Joe, here's a new one. Show her how to work the camera and give her one.' I suppose it was that easy because there was no money involved. After a few minutes' instruction, I shouldered my camera and clicked my best high heels down to Sodom, or maybe it was Gomorrah.

I was to cover three clubs. One was a small Mexican café which served excellent food and had a good combo but very few patrons. The second was an intimate, elegant club with a floorshow of female impersonators; no pictures were allowed during the shows. The third club was in Chinatown, and a cab was required to reach it. This one boasted 'exotic dancers,' a euphemism for strippers; it was frequented almost entirely by regular customers whom I was forcefully forbidden to approach. Later I learned these near-impossible assignments were given to all the new girls to test their ingenuity.

I worked from six until two, and during this time Neal and Jack experimented with their 'voices' and enticed stories from each other into the Ekotape. I would come home, kick off my wet shoes and head for the refrigerator, my appetite whetted by eight hours of tantalizing aromas of Mexican, Chinese and Continental cuisines which I was forbidden to sample while on the job. Jack and Neal would make me relate the continuing saga of night life in the sinful city—at this time, their night-time ramblings centered around the black neighborhoods, and in years to come it would amuse me to think it was me who had first introduced them to North Beach. They were particularly curious about the Beige Room with its female impersonators, because, like me, they'd never been to such a club. I'd become friendly with the performers there, and would listen to them size up each male patron as he entered—'Would he, or wouldn't he?' I wanted Jack and Neal to come down and be evaluated, but they were both too self-conscious.

'Who are the customers?' they wanted to know.

'Oh, all kinds of people—even the Greyline Tours take busloads of Midwestern businessmen and their wives there. It's always crowded, but when I go around between shows and ask to take their photos, they clutch each other and gasp, "Not *here*!" even though I tell 'em I'll put it in a plain wrapper. So that's another disadvantage of that assignment. But the shows are great, and I'm glad that, during them, I can't take pictures so I can watch.'

One night I had a public screaming match with the boss and expected any minute to be fired but wasn't. Soon, however, it was obvious I was putting more nickels into this job than I was getting out, so when I got a $5.00 tip at the Chinese club I decided to quit while I was ahead. I had 'done my thing' and ultimately found it boring.

Since Jack's arrival, Allen had been writing more often. It was plain to see he envied his friends being together without him. He wrote long poems, reported the activities of everyone they all knew, and repeated stories others told him. We enjoyed taking turns reading his letters aloud and discussing them.

> Burroughs has been writing. He is lonely. Write to him. Bill says 'Meanwhile things seem kind of dreary around here. I want to get the case settled and clear out.'* His kids have been claimed by respective grandparents.
>
> Jack, please write New Directions a short note telling them how much you like Bill's book, recommending it for prose and archive value, and telling, as I did in 6 page letter, it's a great book. I have revised the version Bill sent up 2 weeks ago . . . smoother now, not so weird Reichian. If Laughlin no want, we'll peddle it to cheap paper covered 25¢ Gold Medal or Signet Books, like *I, Mobster.*
>
> Carl is serious about Neal's manuscript. Neal, get to it, honey lamb. He'll give you money, and you are a great man.
>
> How I miss both of you and wish I were there with you so that we could share hearts again. I know I am hard to get along with and proud; I insulted Jack before he left and felt many twinges of sadness . . . I only hope that you are not laughing at me when I am here away from your warmth. Write me. I think about you all the time, and have no one to talk to as only we can talk.
>
> How or when will I ever hear your records? I sit here and my soul lacks you Neal and you Jack. I hope my ship goes your way to Frisco. I don't want ever to fade from your minds.
>
> Love, Allen

His letter concluded with a poem.

> Put a kiss and a tear
> In a letter,
> And I'll open and cry
> Over you.
>
> Put a sperm and a wink
> On the paper,
> And I'll come when I read,
> I'm so blue.

*A reference to the shooting of Burroughs' wife.

Put a throb of your heart
In 'yours truly,'
With your names writ in blood
'Neal and Jack,'

And I'll open my palm
With my penknife,
And send you a bucket-
Full back.

Done in 3 minutes
A.G.

Jack was becoming depressed by the hassle with his ex-wife and her efforts to get money from him which he didn't have. He had given the $1000 advance he'd received for *The Town and the City* to his mother, and he earned very little at the baggage room. The mere mention of Joan's name made him angry, and he wanted only to run. Allen offered sensible, fatherly advice:

Carl upset you still starving, and that your mother keeps your money. Why don't you use it yourself? You are in a worse hole than your mother. I spoke to lawyer about wife and he said either change your address to keep safe or send her money (from another postal town) according to agreement. If want to stay in country safe and without anxiety, that's only way. You're letting yourself get too unnecessarily tangled up in sad fate. Let's figure a way to clean things up before it gets farther, makes writing paranoid and life lousy. It's strictly situation, external, not absolute and fixed fate for you unless you *leave* it be fixed fate. Am not being analytic-moral. None of us are fast and strong enough to battle society forever really, it's too sad and gray. Just felt you were feeling too crazy lately and am putting out friend-hand. Must not let situation drift to intolerability. We got too much else to do besides suffer.

Jack's sights turned more and more longingly to the peace and simplicity of Mexico.

In the light of the past months of comparative compatibility and serenity with Neal, I felt our married life was now built on a firmer foundation, and I let my thoughts return to plans for a family life based on the conventional patterns that had formed my own. Now seemed the time to solidify the tie with the grandparents, who had never seen our children but had shown a consistent interest in them. So, we decided to go to Tennessee and visit them, giving Neal a chance to see the farm as well. Neal, always ready to travel at any excuse, also thought it appropriate for me to accompany him on at least one 'road'—after all I had had no vacation of any kind for five years or more. Neal also thought this a chance to look up his father.

There was now no doubt that the trip was an absolute necessity, not merely a pleasure. I plunged into plans. We could survive if Neal took a month off from the railroad. We'd take with us all of the baby food and most of our own, share the driving and keep the motels to a minimum. We'd drive Jack as far as Nogales across the Mexican border south of Tucson, to start him on his way.

Everything worked out beautifully. We took out the back seat of the 'woody' and covered the floor with a cot mattress, putting John's small crib mattress across the back, which left enough room for the two girls to stretch out between it and the front seat. The sides were lined with our bags and boxes of food. There was a surprising amount of room.

Jack took a nostalgic farewell of his attic nook, leaving the bulk of his possessions in it, taking only his sea bag. He and I had no opportunity for a private talk before we left, and we all bravely minimized the impending separation by making happy plans for reuniting in Mexico in the nebulous future. It was accepted by all three of us that we would share a home somewhere for at least a part of each year.

Before pulling away from Russell Street, Neal took the girls into the front seat, and as we got underway he enhanced their excitement with a constant patter about every passing scene. Jack and I had crawled into the back with John and sat crosswise, facing each other. The space was somewhat cramped for two adults, but this suited our melancholy mood. We lapsed into a silent reverie, realizing that time was growing short. We could make no overt move toward each other without feeling sorry for Neal, so communication had to consist only of longing looks and the occasional electric touch of knees. The tension was nearly unbearable by the time we reached Santa Barbara four hours later, but it was a romantic agony willingly suffered.

We spent the first night with Neal's younger sister and her husband, and the second in Los Angeles where Neal was able to locate two older half-sisters and two brothers. We visited from house to house, and they were all most cordial, in spite of this sudden arrival of three adults and three children. I seemed the only one concerned about this breach of manners, but my objections were silenced, and at length I held my peace and relaxed on the floor next to Jack to watch television—the first I'd ever seen.

For all of the next day's drive I urged Jack to sit in front with Neal while the girls and I played games in back. I had to smile as I listened to the men, thinking what a different 'road' this was from the others they'd shared. It didn't sound as though the family presence was dampening their pleasure in the least; in fact it seemed to add to it, especially when they passed a place remembered from a previous trip and would begin at once to tell me the stories attached to it.

While the children slept, we three adults sat in front and drove all night across the desert. The sky was deep and clear, and all of us were wistful, in tune with the knowledge it was our last night together. We listened to radio dramas, *First Nighter* and *The Whistler*. During the latter Neal became so emotionally involved that Jack and I had to laugh and remind him repeatedly that it was only a play. He probably was putting us on, but his absorption made me nervous.

Later, when there was only music for background, we peered into the vast panorama of glittering stars all around us, and Neal astounded both Jack and me with a detailed discourse on the constellations and stars.

'Wherever did you learn all that?' we asked in unison. 'I didn't know you knew anything about astronomy.'

With a sigh Neal replied, 'I know everything about everything— how many times do I have to tell you?'

The stars dissolved into the pearl gray dawn, and with it came a chill. The parting was near, and we grew silent. As if by accident, I let my head drop to touch Jack's shoulder, and he stroked my hair with his hand behind my head; it was the best we could do by way of farewell. Neal drove to the Mexican border and parked the car alongside a wire fence, but I didn't see any guards or customs, only dirt, weeds and trash. Everything was gray and dreary: the weather, the outskirts of the town, and now our mood. A few yards inside the gates was a white-walled café with chipping paint, and Jack said, 'Aw, come on. Can't you have one last beer with me?' He stood forlornly beside the car with his sea bag over his shoulder.

'Sure, man,' Neal condescended, and we got out.

It was no warmer inside the one big bare room that smelled of Lysol. A brown varnished bar lined one wall, and in front of it a few metal tables and chairs were scattered. Beer before breakfast was new to me, but this morning it was a good idea and helped calm me. Jack

179

made a few stabs at cheery conversation, hopping from Mexico ahead to the adventures behind, but sensing only unrest on Neal's part, he too fell silent. I wondered if Neal's mood was less one of regret for Jack's departure than for not being in Jack's shoes, but all he said in the end was that in a few months maybe we'd all be living there together.

Neal was eager to get going, and I wanted the separation over, so we said corny goodbyes and ran back to the car, turning to wave until we'd lost sight of the sagging figure by the border fence. Later Jack wrote:

> . . . you could have come through with the car that morning . . . and we could have driven fifty miles around or anything at no charge (and bought stuff) . . . and seen a fiesta in the afternoon in the gay little city of Nogales. You have no idea what it is ten feet beyond that wire fence.

After the melancholy of the morning, we set out on the rest of the journey confident our former problems were the errors of youth. We had learned our limitations, and that gave us a new freedom. Now I could concentrate all my attention on my own little family. We were together enjoying a shared experience; I didn't want to miss a minute of it.

Neal was all I could wish. He drove carefully and slowly—almost too slowly at times, I thought, but he had some notion about a 'cruising speed' to preserve the car. Whatever it was, it dispelled my initial anxiety that we'd be bickering all over the country about his driving.

There was only one near-catastrophe on the way to Nashville: at a drawbridge near New Orleans, Neal drove under the barrier as it was descending to stop the traffic. I nearly died of fright to see the concrete highway rise up directly in front of the radiator. Somewhat hysterically, I began yelling at Neal, at which point a police officer rode up beside us and began to do likewise. I switched from scolding Neal to defending him, and in my terror inflicted the full power of my indignation on the officer. Neal wisely slid down in his seat between us, casting a hapless, henpecked look at the officer who, taken aback by my outburst, soon shot Neal a sympathetic look and rode off. My stability returned with the relief that we'd not received a ticket. 'Ha, see there? It shows there's some advantage in having a shrewish wife, hunh, honey? Forgive me—you understand.'

The two weeks with the grandparents went smoothly. Neal exhibited his good manners and thoughtfulness, also impressing my parents with his affection for and patience with the children. He listened with enthusiasm to my father's stories of the local folkways, crops and animals, and throughout our stay remained remarkably serene and agreeable, as pleased as the little girls with the horses, cattle, pigs and lambs and the sight of tobacco growing. A cowboy he wasn't, and I couldn't get him on a horse, much to my surprise, but we took walks and played in the creek. I taught him to churn butter and we toured the historic battlefields and ghost-filled mansions of the Old South as well as my former Nashville haunts.

Neal was once again my ideal companion. The only problem I had with him wasn't between us; rather it was his failure to get the appropriate slant (for a white) on how to treat black people. He'd be naturally friendly and respectful to farmhand, coal man or drugstore curb-server, and they'd freeze in instant suspicion. I explained to him how I'd had to learn the techniques and attitudes of the Southern whites, although I'd hated it and it had been a major cause of my leaving the South. 'It's no use trying to reason with white Southerners—it isn't a matter of reason or intelligence. It's all emotional and ingrained. My parents and I have close friends who are wonderful people otherwise, but that is one subject we simply have to avoid. It took me a long time to comprehend.' But Neal couldn't, and I was glad of it.

Then one afternoon shortly before our departure, I caught Neal smoking marijuana in our bedroom. I panicked, my confidence in him shaken. How could he risk any possibilty that my folks would find out? I remained nervous and on edge until we were safely away.

In Kansas City we found Neal's brother Jim, against whom Neal bore no grudge for his childhood atrocities. We had a friendly visit for an hour or two, but Jim had no room for us to spend the night, so we went to a drive-in movie and slept as long as we could before continuing across the endless plains.

Whether it was being reminded of his childhood miseries by seeing Jim again, or a reaction against his recent submission to conventional behavior, or simply his psychological imbalance, I'll never know, but before we reached Denver, Neal reverted to his old self, escaping from us twice for many hours without explanation. I responded with the same old righteous martyrdom, more sadly now because everything had been going so well for so long, and I thought I had learned that lesson.

By the time we got to Denver I was attempting to collect the shattered pieces of our relationship again, and Neal behaved as though he wished to, too. It was a bitter pill to have to acknowledge that our differences had evidently been overcome only through circumstances, not through real change.

With some reluctance, but trying not to show it, I agreed to take the children to see Neal's father. Not that I didn't want to meet him or have him see the children, but he was living in a hotel in a neighborhood that made me uncomfortable, and I couldn't imagine what we would have to talk about. I knew I had to make the effort though—it meant so much to Neal. As it happened, all went well. Neal decided at the last minute to stay in the car with the children, letting them hang out the window to wave at their grandfather while I went in alone. It was just as well; the poor dear really didn't know who I was, but as long as I kept mentioning his son, he was happy to see me. While I was there, a wonderful floozy of a woman went in and out of his room, clucking and fussing over Neal, Sr., and I was glad to be able to reassure Neal that his father was being very well looked after. Afterwards Neal went up to see him on his own, while I stayed with the children. Neal's filial affection was appeased, and when his father died a few years later he was able to return to Denver with a clear conscience to arrange for his burial.

We traveled the rest of the way home as fast as we could, resolving to return to Denver someday and review it properly—'when the children would be older and would appreciate it, too.'

We were both considerably depressed by the setbacks, but when we reached home we agreed to keep trying to find new angles. We promised each other we'd give analysis another, more attentive try. We also reached out for the hope that possibly a change of scene would help. I didn't really know how to raise children in a city—Neal had just seen the wide open spaces I'd been accustomed to—and although a city boy himself, he concurred it might be better for us all if we moved to a more rural area. It gave us something else to look forward to, more plans to make, and as we settled into our own bed again, dim hope recycled once more.

Two letters awaited us, plus one addressed to Jack—the first word we'd had from Allen for three months. In the letter he'd written first, he said he'd found a missing chapter of *On the Road* which he was forwarding to Jack, apparently unaware of our trip, writing 'Jeepers, where is Jack?' The other letter said he'd just received a 'monumental letter from Jack in Mexico' and that we were to send back the twenty-three opening pages, while Jack was sending him the rest.

Jack says you're mad at him or tired of him, Neal, is that true? . . . I'm
afraid for him in Mexico, it is a kind of lostness . . . he's smoking with
mexicans in mudhuts . . . He says you are busy and obsessed with
'complete all-the-way-down-the-line materialistic money and stealing
groceries Anxieties,' etc., etc. Also said he was happy there . . . are you in
Frisco, even? What's going on around there anyway?

Back in harness, Neal became depressed again. In those days I
didn't understand his need for change and excitement, still judging
others by my own standards. He wrote Allen a nice note, saying
'You're the same great wonderful guy and I'm more of a bum than
ever . . .' and ending with 'Why don't you come out here? Nice place
if one likes it. Be brakie and make lots of money. Or write in attic and
make love to wife and me.'

Much to my delight and surprise, Allen wrote a letter to *me*,
breaking the ice of five years:

Dear Mrs. Cassady:
How is you, after all . . . as I see things now I think maybe you been
through the mill bad, always been sorry I contributed to the privation . . .
Too bitter to forgive? Hope not. Take care of the children (that means
Jack and Neal too) as everybody will ultimately be saved, including you
. . . I plan no imminent invasion of Frisco but would like to someday and
hope I will be welcome to you and we can be friends. You always seem
alright to me. Jack likes you but is afraid of you. (you know?) I wonder
how you feel about him.
    Yours,

                                        Allen the Stranger

I answered him cordially, and he wrote to Neal '. . . Maybe a change
of scene would be good. I may come out there yet.' He also replied to
my letter and sealed our friendship.

Much thanks for your letter. Didn't expect to be so well received either. So
that dispenses that cloud. Was Jack's tip too; he not so dumb, with other
people's female notions . . . Would be interested know your process of
changes of love and thought. Don't realize too much of yr. interior of last
years except by conjecture. Thank you for child name. Never got the idea
from W.C. Fields that you had anything to do with it, but now that you
mention it does sound sort of inevitable that you might have had some
hand in naming yr. own children. Yipe! Consider my letters henceforth
addressed to you, too. Would it be possible have my epistles (like St. Paul)
read in state at dinner table in front of the children of the Church?
Constantinople here needs me so can't get to Rome temporarily, am
waiting for a Word. Understood your letter. Thanks. Shy.
                                        Allen

Immediately, I jumped at the offer to share my thoughts by pouring them out to him and requesting his comments and advice on my position with Neal and Jack. He further gratified me by setting down a thoughtful and thorough analysis of all our relationships:

Jack's attitude: a) as I haven't got all his letters here, I'll send on an anthology of statements apropos his relations with Neal when I assemble them. What *I* think about it is, Jack loves Neal platonically (which I think is a pity, but maybe about sex I'm 'projecting' as the analysts say), and Neal loves Jack, too. The fact is that Jack is very inhibited, however. However, also, sex doesn't define the whole thing.

b) Jack still loves Neal none the less than ever.

c) Jack ran into a blank wall which everybody understands and respects in Neal, including Jack and Neal. It upset and dispirited Jack, made him feel lonely and rejected and like a little brother whose questions the older brother wouldn't answer.

d) Jack loves Carolyn also, though obviously not with the same intensity and power as he loves Neal, and this is acceptable and obvious considering all parties involved, their history together, how much they knew each other and how often they lived thru the same years and crises. Jack is full of Carolyn's praises and nominates her to replace Joan Burroughs as Ideal Mother Image, Madwoman, chick and ignu. The last word means a special honorary type post-hip intellectual. Its main root is ignoramus, from the mythology of W.C. Fields. Jack also says Carolyn beats Ellie [a girl in New York] for Mind.

e) Jack said nothing about sleeping with you in his letters.

f) Jack thinks Neal is indifferent to him, however only in a special way, as he realizes how good Neal has been to him and that Neal really loves him; but they couldn't communicate I guess. However, he would love to live altogether with everybody in Mexico, I believe. He would claim right to treat Neal as a human being and hit him on the breast with balloons. I will transmit all messages immediately.

g) I did not think (even dream) from Neal's note he is bitter. I was surprised to get his invitation to visit, and thought it showed great gentility in the writing and the proposal which I accept with rocky belly for sometime in the future. Had I money I would fly out immediately for weekends by plane.

h) Perhaps Neal wants to feel like a crestfallen cuckold because he wants to be beat on the breast with balloons. I well imagine him in that position. Neal's last confession is perhaps yet to be made, tho his salvation is already assured . . . however nobody seems to take seriously the confession he has made already and continues to do so, which have always had ring of innocency and childlike completeness and have been all he knows which is more (about himself) than anybody else knows anyway. I believe Neal.

I include his preoccupation and blankness (preoccupation with R.R., household moneying, etc, as final confessions of great merit and value, representing truth to him.

184

What further sweetness and juiciness issues therefrom no one knows, even him; there is no forcing anything . . . that will be fate. Neal has already unnecessary guilt. (He does not know?) He is already on top of the world. What to do with world is next problem.

Jack probably feels no remorse, just compassion for Neal.

. . . Mexico may be a good idea for all of us when become properly solidified . . . What we must make plans to do is all meet somewhere where it is practically possible for us to live, under our various pressures, when the practical time comes. Shall we not then keep it in mind to try to arrange for a total grand reunion somewhere for as long as it can last? . . . I am definitely interested in going to bed with everybody and making love . . . P.S. Neal, write me a letter about sex. A.

Allen's attitude toward sex always managed to raise my Puritan hackles, and I suspect he knew it. It certainly pricked my romantic bubbles, but in other respects his thoughts were reassuring, and I felt accepted, thinking that if we all lived together, pressures could be siphoned off in small doses in a variety of ways. Deep in my heart I still yearned for a monogamous arrangement with Neal, but if it wasn't possible, perhaps this arrangement held possibilities hitherto unknown in conventional patterns. My ability to analyze it ended there.

Thirty-two

We hadn't heard from Jack directly since we had left him in Nogales, and I wondered if he was feeling remorse or if he was angry for some reason. The first week of June, however, we received a long reassuring letter:

I was very glad to see that letter you wrote Allen; he sent it for me to see. I had no idea my mail hadn't reached you (one letter to Tennessee and one to Frisco later) and no idea too you and Neal had stopped agreeing on an agree-basis . . . In your letter to Allen—how could I have enough of the Cassady clan? Including the children, hey? . . . If you and Neal (and I'll probably see you soon) really plan to make Mexico, then I'll be in on it with you—I'll have some sea money and more peace back home. We can all live down here in a house—sometimes I'll be either at sea or staying at home in Carolina or visiting Bill in Equador—Neal sometimes working in California (4 months) and the other 8 writing *The First Third* in his house in Mexico, with imminent advance—sounds logical and awright to me— don't want to force anybody.

As for discussing the emotional complexities of the matter, ahem, harrumph, egad, I really feel like Neal—incapable of dealing with such big abstract problems of love and mystery . . . There is an anxiety in you for Neal to love you in a certain way. What is that certain way ? . . . That certain way is lost in a tangle of shrouds if you ask me . . . Many's the time I wanted to hold your hand or kiss you, merely as acknowledgment that we were all in the car heading for the world unknown, but felt the jealousy- kick just as much as Neal and so played up to it and didn't do what I wanted . . . I don't think Neal was jealous, he just didn't know what we expected him to do, and we didn't either. I personally felt quite calm about the whole thing and still do except for qualms about how you feel, both of you—also, most cruelly, I am at your beck and call to come and go, in other words I accept loss and death, and if you offer me some of your life I'm very grateful but I know that nothing will come of it, of life, but death, so it really makes no difference to any of us what happens now and soon—Eternity is the only thing on my mind permanently, and you are a part of it.

And Oh, incidentally . . . I have already written a third of *Dr. Sax* in the past month in Mexico—in case I catch on like wildfire in New York with *On the Road*, I got another masterpiece ready for the press. I love you both and hope I don't bore you with my long long talks. Forward my mail. Kiss the grail—Please write—let me know what it was like in Tennessee and your plans for San Jose and the children, etc—with luck I'll be seeing you soon off an MCS ship. I'll ring the doorbell with dry martini mix and Shakespeare—'Ah, isn't it grr-and' like Henri Bleu (Bleup). Uncle Jack

He added a note to Neal and tidied up any possible loose ends to the various relationships, reiterating their brotherhood, that nothing had changed between them, they were 'well-nigh perfect friends' and nothing could affect 'our closeness and peace.'

His earlier letter finally caught up with us. In it he wrote that he had finished typing *On the Road*, and 'on Bill's advice, made Allen my agent; I suppose Allen may take it seriously and really go to work.'

When Allen received the manuscript of *On the Road*, he wrote us, 'Jack's book arrived and it is a holy mess—it's great all right but he did everything he could to fuck it up with a lot of meaningless bullshit I think,' and he continued with an analysis of everything he thought wrong with it:

. . . page after page of surrealist free association that doesn't make sense to anybody except to someone that has blown Jack. I don't think it can be published anywhere in its present state. I know this is an awful hangup for everyone concerned—he must be tired too—and that's how it stands I think. Your tape conversations were good reading; so I could hear what was happening out there—but he put it in entire and seemingly ununified so it just skips back and forth and touches on things momentarily and refers to events nowhere else in the book; and finally it appears to objective eye so diffuse and disorganized—which it is, on purpose—that it just *don't make*. Jack knows that too, I'll bet. Why is he tempting rejection and fate? Fucking spoiled child, like all of us, maybe, but goddam it, it ain't *right* to take on so paranoiac just to challenge and see how far you can go—when there's so much to say and live and do now, how hard it is albeit. Jack is an ignu and I'll bow down to him, but he done fuck up his writing money-wise, and also writing-wise. He was not experimenting and exploring in new deep form; he was purposely just screwing around as if anything he

187

did no matter what he did was OK, no bones attached. Not purposely, I guess, just drug out and driven to it and in a hole. I don't know what he'll say when I say this to him—he comes back to NY this week or next I think—and how he'll make out with all this shit to shovel around, I dunno. I will try to help but I feel so evil when I not *agree* in blindness. Well shit on this, you get the point.

Before learning of Allen's judgment, Jack was feeling good. He wrote that he'd 'finished *Dr. Sax*, a whole *tight* novel right here at Bill's . . .' He was ready to leave Mexico and travel to his mother's and thence to New York for a ship, and ended his letter with 'I sure wish I was with you right now Buddy, sharing a last glass of tokay and with that fine blonde kerouacass gal serving up hot pizza in the pie plate, goddam I miss you, tears just come to my eyes. I will see you soon in Frisco port let's pray.' He couldn't have heard Allen's reaction to his book at that point, but his anger toward publishers was fierce.

I am really getting fucked again by the publishing business: they just won't publish me any more, they're afraid of every chapter I write it seems—I'll pay them back someday . . . Carolyn your life would have been impossible with me—I'm very unlucky—and doomed to be robbed by all the cheap literateurs of my time . . .

The next word we got from Jack arrived two weeks later, a mysterious and enigmatic note. Had he heard of Allen's criticism? It sounded like a last farewell:

Just to let you know I'm leaving Mexico City and going to live, write and till my special soils in a small shack type made of dobe bricks in the country not far from here, in a valley—for practically and eventually nothing—don't know for how long—will be my headquarters. Won't write for a long time because want to sink into natural oblivion with myself, dog, indians, beautiful & sad indians & — Let my mail dust under a floorboard, see you on some spectral New Year's Eve. Love and dumb kisses . . . P.S. Eventually I want to go to Ecuador where the mangos, orchids & wives grow wild, no want, no phoney hassles, no anger and all that kind of shit ad infinitum. Any important messages for me send to Allen who will undoubtedly relay them telepathically and visit me on a burro.

Written along the side was 'XXX to you and children. Write that *First Third*—love C. Sentimentally. Old Zagg.' Neal and I didn't know what to make of it.

'Oh, he'll come out of it,' Neal sighed. 'He's just paranoid again—misunderstood. Old Zagg will sit in his mud hut and have himself a regular orgie with Miss Green—the bastard, why doesn't he send me some? Awrrgh. Fap.'

He strode to the window and stood gazing out—not at our backyard, I could tell, but at a Mexican valley warmed by a lazy sun where there were no bills, no pressures, just mangos and Miss Green.

Thirty-three

In August of 1952 I wistfully bid goodbye to the little house on Russian Hill where I had passed so many milestones and whose 'possibilities' had gone unfulfilled.

I surveyed the new potential of the huge house we'd found in San Jose fifty miles to the south. We were on the edge of the city—then aptly nicknamed 'Nowheresville'—but the lovely valley surrounding it was too vast to explore from afar, so we'd settled on this lucky find until we could learn more about the area and Neal could see how the new location would affect his work.

The one-story house had been part of an old estate, and had eight rooms of various sizes in a puzzling arrangement and high ceilings but, oddly enough, no fireplace. It was surrounded with neglected flowerbeds and set back far enough from the street to allow for a large front yard dotted with fruit and nut trees. Behind was a paved courtyard separating our big house from a smaller, newer one. Our decision to rent it had been finalized when we had met the young couple, Dick and Marie Forest, who lived in the smaller house behind. They had a boy about Jami's age and a baby girl, and their eagerness to help us move and to adjust to a new town was a taste of neighborliness in the old tradition.

The Forests had no notion of the kind of life their new neighbors had been living, but I confidently expected we would become as organized, peaceful and conventional as they—except, perhaps, in one respect. Neal had talked away my fears and planted some marijuana seeds in the flowerbeds, tucked behind the shrubs under the front porch, and in the vacant lot next door, hoping to eliminate constant searching and high prices. However, it would be a long time before the harvest. He was pleased the Forests were so 'square,' figuring they wouldn't know what the plants were when they saw them.

Every room in our house was covered in layers of old wallpaper, and I tried to get Neal to release some pent-up energy by scraping it off the walls of our bedroom. It was a much bigger job than it looked, but he attacked it furiously, fighting every inch, and once started it had to be finished. When the job was completed at last, he was proud of the result and of himself. I painted the walls a deep royal blue, the ceiling above the moulding white, made white tucked drapes out of old sheets and placed a white spread and yellow pillows on the bed. A red bulb in the overhead light turned the walls purple, the curtains, spread and ceiling pink, and the pillows orange. 'Psychedelic' we would have said if the word had been invented then. Instead, we called it our 'passion pit,' each of us projecting our own aspirations.

The change in location looked most promising for all of us. Neal enjoyed playing chess with Dick, a droll storyteller and a delight to the children. Neal seemed more settled and was able to spend more time at home. The freight runs began and ended in San Jose, whereas formerly he had had to 'deadhead' to and from San Francisco. I learned to forget how to read a timetable. Neal had gone to great lengths to teach me this complicated skill soon after he'd first been hired, but we had both come to regret it when I was able to figure out what time he *should* have come home.

Neal wanted to share this new house with Jack, plus which, Neal was out of tea. We had heard no more from Jack during our move, and assumed he'd gone off to his hut with the Indians. Neal decided to risk writing him at Bill's, fearing all along that Jack was angry with him for not being able to repay all of an old debt.

> Damn you for being in Mexico without me. Why in hell not give up the Indians to come back and tell me about them and to still earn about 2000 bucks on RR before the year's out? You can easily live in our big 9 room house here in sunny San Jose and ride about in my new station wagon.

He then apologized at length for not having any money (new station wagon to the contrary) saying, 'Sept. 26 this the first paycheck I'll have enough clear to even buy the 3 dozen light bulbs this house needs.' He understood that Jack was 'surely mad as hell' at him:

And rightly so, and I started letters and never sent them and I told Carolyn, who wants you back so desperately, to write you, and everything went to hell and I'm without even any help from Miss Green, and where the hell are you? I'll send you fare to get back here on, only hurry up or there won't be much RRing left . . . stay here until December then you'll have plenty to go east.

Before mailing the letter, we learned that Jack was in North Carolina with his mother, and I added a note saying I hoped he wasn't mad at us:

Neal and I still not making it without you. He says to tell you he'll join you in December, and you'll both go booming on the Florida East Coast Line. I shouldn't doubt it, and I'll be saying just what Cathy did the other night, 'Daddy and Jack both went off and left me.'

Suddenly the Southern Pacific came up with a new ruling that no new men over 30 would be hired. Jack had just turned 30 in March, so Neal rushed to write to him again and outlined in explicit detail not only how he could get around this ruling if he came immediately, but also how to travel on the trains at minimum expense—in such explicit detail, in fact, that Jack would have had to carry the letter in his hand all the way to be able to follow the complicated directions.

Jack agreed to come, but he left North Carolina before Neal's instructions arrived. The next word we received was a card from Denver. Neal went into a fit of expletives and dashed out to send Jack a telegram emphasizing the imminence of the hiring deadline. He even wired him $25.00 to prove the seriousness of the situation.

My spirits soared, my energy was electrified. Jack was coming back after only three months this time. Joyfully I hastened to make a room ready for him. We had brought the big plywood desktop from San Francisco, and it was reinstated in the bedroom next to ours. Although the room was nearer the rest of the household than had been his attic nook, it had French doors leading into a sunroom and thence to the front door.

Saturday afternoon Jack telephoned from San Francisco, and Neal told him to hop the 'Zipper,' the trainmen's nickname for the Zephyr, the fast through-freight to Los Angeles that stopped at San Jose. He said we'd meet him at the yard office. Neal had been called to work a freight to Watsonville, and I realized Jack and I would be alone this first night, and this thought, for the rest of the afternoon, caused a considerable lack of concentration on my household tasks.

I had to go along with Neal to meet the Zephyr, because Jack couldn't drive. The station wagon had broken down, but Neal now had a Model-A Ford to play with as well, and I enjoyed it too, once I got used to driving it in traffic. The night was inky black, and Neal parked near the far edge of the unpaved, weed-fringed parking lot next to the small wooden building that was the freight office. I stayed in the car while Neal went to check on his train. I could hear the Zephyr approaching. It screamed to a stop, clanging its bell and snorting steam that billowed orange and yellow in the lights from the office windows. Then, black-silhouetted against the engine's powerful shaft of white light, I saw two men coming toward me, Neal's lantern making crazy zig-zags as he pounded Jack on the back and punched him, boisterous and exuberant. Jack chuckled, trying to defend himself and looking shyly at the ground then sideways at Neal. When he saw me in the car he ran his fingers through his hair and shoved at his shirt-tail. I lit a cigarette to calm my nerves, trembling at the sight of the familiar hulk in the checkered shirt.

Jack climbed into the narrow back seat, dragging his sea bag with him, and Neal got into the driver's side. I was glad Neal had to wait awhile for his train and could carry the conversation. He asked Jack for details of his trip to California, lamenting the lost instructions, and then talked gaily about our house and how he anticipated showing Jack the sports they could see through the fence that divided our lot from the high school athletic field, 'and all the pretty high school girls, and cheerleaderesses, and—oops, ma, sorry.'

Jack giggled, and I smiled but said nothing, feeling Jack becoming increasingly attractive. Speech was even more difficult when our eyes met, and by the time Neal bounded off to catch his train the close air in the little car was dripping with desire. The darkness was warm and humid inside, and outside the fog wrapped a blanket around us.

'Let's don't go yet,' Jack said softly. 'Come back here.'

As we embraced, all the memories welled up within me, resurrected by his sweet smells, strengthened by his absence. In my happiness I had to smile, and broke away from his kiss.

'Honestly, Jack, I feel like a high school girl myself—necking in the back seat of a car, yet.'

Jack chuckled and groped for a poor-boy in his jacket pocket. After a few swallows apiece and distracted attempts at speech, he set the bottle on the shelf behind us and pulled me to him again. But when he attempted to change our positions his elbow struck the bottle, which flipped over and drenched us both. The spell broken, we laughingly tried to brush off the wine, but soon his ardor returned undampened. I was neither comfortable nor relaxed under these conditions, and when we were suddenly bathed in blinding light, we sprang apart, our breathing suspended. 'Oh, sorry—I was looking for—' The voice and light faded away in the fog.

As I swung the car around the back of the house and parked, Dick was climbing his front steps, having just checked our children. I waved and called my thanks before leading Jack into the house. We had told the Forests of Jack's impending visit, that he was a published author who had come to continue his writing and to work on the railroad with Neal. We had shown them *The Town and the City*, and they had been properly impressed. Nothing was said, of course, of our shared affections, and I hoped we could manage not to shock them.

We made a brief tip-toe tour of the house, Jack pleased with its age and even its unique layout—he and I shared a mutual interest in old houses. He had a bath while I made him a snack and poured the wine. He ate with relish; we lingered over our wine until our shyness subsided, and then flowed together to the magnet of his bed. His tenderness and appreciation made it almost impossible for me to leave him and return to my own bed, but that was my absolute rule, since often one of the girls came to me during the night.

In the morning they were awake long before Jack and could hardly keep still in their impatience to see him. Even so, they were both stricken with an attack of shyness. But when Jack sat down for breakfast and talked to them, they jostled each other to climb on his lap. He asked them to show him around outside, and nothing could have pleased them more. A child hanging on each hand, they set out, both of the girls talking at once. The first place Jack wanted to see was the high school ballfield. They had to go through the Forests' yard, and little Chris rushed out to join in the tour. As I watched them through the pantry window I mused on how content Jack always appeared with children. He relaxed into a naturalness that contrasted with the frequent discomfort he displayed with adults, male or female. With children he had nothing to prove, nothing to be that was more than himself.

Neal arrived in time for a celebration dinner of Jack's favorite pizza, after which we had the Forests over to meet him, and the Hinkles were invited to join us. They had moved to San Jose too, and had bought a tract house on the outskirts of town. Everyone was gay and agreeable, Dick and Neal swapping Paul Bunyon yarns, the rest of us an appreciative audience to their antics, which Jack, too, appeared to enjoy despite his shyness. What relief I felt to see Neal happy again.

The next day the serious business of getting Jack hired on the railroad was begun. He was fearful and resistant, but Neal prodded and coached, and after a day or so Jack was accepted and began his two weeks of student training trips. Every evening on his return home we had to cheer and encourage him anew. When training was over Jack signed on the extra-board, proud to be a 'genu-wine' brakie and to sport the same paraphernalia as Neal. Another celebration was called for.

Jack soon found he much preferred stories about railroads to the work itself. His physique and kinetic responses were more suited to running and dodging on a football field than to the swift and agile moves necessary for freight-car switching. Although we kept reassuring him he'd improve in time, his clumsiness was agony to him. He loved the earthy railroad men as characters, but his sensitivity and paranoia caused him to resent their practice of identifying men through nicknames, his becoming 'Keroway' which soon degenerated into 'Caraway Seed.' He was sure they all scorned and laughed at him. Neal, too, became more irritable, partially from sympathy for Jack, partially because he wanted to be proud of his friend, not listen to jokes at his expense, and partially (I suspected) because he didn't like Jack and me being alone together so much.

Once when Jack had a day off before he was called for a job, he asked me if the girls and I would like to go to San Francisco with him to visit our old haunts. The station wagon was running again, and we all set off in high spirits on an Indian summer day, the air heavy with the nostalgia inherent in autumn aromas. Our eager expectations were snuffed the minute we parked at Coit Tower. Cathy had to be taken to the emergency hospital and then straight home: she was diagnosed as having rheumatic fever, though it turned out to be osteomyelitis.

In spite of our abortive romantic excursion, Jack and I had lovely days at home, especially when Neal was off duty too. Our favorite pastimes enjoyed in San Francisco were revived. We read aloud, discussed books and authors, and usually recorded it all. (Having few tapes, which were expensive, we shortsightedly erased most of what we recorded.) The large, sparsely furnished dining room with the bay window had lots of space for the children to play while we three sat around the big round oak table. Neal juggled the fruit from the centerpiece, sending the girls scurrying under the table to retrieve those he'd drop. Sometimes Jack read to us from *Dr. Sax* in a great booming voice, spiced with W.C. Fields or Major Hoople imitations, while Neal, eyes sparkling above his grin, hissed 'Yeah . . . yeah . . . yeaahh' after nearly every sentence, especially when Jack made reference to sex, which would make Jack break off his serious tones and giggle. In turn, Neal liked reading Proust aloud, saying 'Listen to this, now. I want you to just listen to this—this is one paragraph, mind you just one paragraph . . .' and he'd read the intricate prose slowly and precisely, ignoring Jack's attempts to correct his French pronunciation. Other times we'd pass out our several copies of Shakespeare's plays, and each of us would take two or three parts, changing our voices to fit while Jack and Neal leaped about acting out their characters with exaggerated gestures.

And there were lovely evenings, too, when Jack and I were alone. We'd put the children to bed together, and he'd read them their stories, using all his range of voices. Jami was his special favorite still, and she'd fling her arms around his neck and give him big kisses on the cheeks, dissolving him into self-conscious mirth. Then we'd close their door and have our dinner in the big kitchen. Sometimes we were high and hilarious, other times sentimental and romantic.

One such night, when we had finished eating and I'd put our dishes in the sink, we sat dreamily sipping our wine in the flickering patterns of the candlelight, absorbing the music of blues and ballad, both of us silent and pensive. My mind was catching images drifting peacefully in the glowing atmosphere when Jack's voice broke the stillness like a great mellow gong, vibrating clear through me and reverberating in the air: '*God* . . . I love you.'

I looked at him to be sure I'd heard right and met his blue eyes, so intense and piercing I had to look down again, and I couldn't even smile, my breath caught somewhere. All I could manage was a whisper I didn't think he heard: 'I can't believe it.'

But he said, slow and steady, 'I could convince you.'

I tried to gather up my scattered wits to say something, but my eyes wouldn't move from the ruby light in my glass, and I could feel his hadn't wavered. All I could do was slide my hand along the table to his, but I still couldn't look at him. I closed my eyes and breathed deeply.

'Let's dance,' he said softly.

We floated close together, swaying, warm and blending—timeless. Soon I couldn't contain my joy in such a solemn mood. I broke away, filled our glasses and Jack loaded the phonograph with mambos. We danced and danced, abandoned to the music, sparks flying when we touched.

For years afterward, remembering this night, I'd think about Neal. Why could he and I no longer have these romantic, emotional love scenes? No one had been more deeply romantic than Neal in the beginning. Did this always cease with the advent of marriage? Did we know each other too well? Nevertheless, I never forgot Jack's magic words; they have warmed me ever since.

Other memories of those golden months drift by in small but vivid snatches: my sitting on Jack's bed rocking Johnny if he'd wake up crying, Jack propped on one elbow, patting Johnny too, talking to me about his mother, planning where we would meet. He'd read me her letters, and I'd insert comments in his letters to her.

Then there were afternoons when Jack would sit for hours experimenting with the tape recorder, singing both lyrics and 'scat,' accompanying himself on a tiny pair of bongos I'd given him for a joke. These tapes I listen to now and recall the long fall afternoons, fragrant with the smell of burning leaves, which reminded both of us of our beloved New England, and I relive the quiet pleasure of our being together.

Almost daily he'd go on walks with the girls, listening to their prattle, teaching them to make poems—walks that left their cheeks ruddy, their little fists clenched around precious scraggly flowers he'd helped them pick.

All this pleasure and my partial descriptions of it to Neal pleased him less and less. Jack was now more interested in Neal's family than in Neal, whose lonely brooding on long runs stoked his jealousy and resentment. Where was his old partner in crime? Where his excuse and sidekick for his own private desires? Then the chill of winter arrived and with it, the cold rains and the colds in the noses. When the railroad work slowed, the men were home together more often, and the feeling of confinement increased the restlessness and irritation in them both as they waited and waited for the calls that never came. There was nothing interesting to do in San Jose, and San Francisco was too far to go without a good excuse. It was evident that wanderlust was tugging at Neal again and the Mexican sun at Jack, and in me the seed of dread began to sprout.

Neal found the necessary reasons to drive the new car to San

Francisco more often as time went on, but he still couldn't persuade Jack to go with him or to cover up for him. For his part, Jack reverted to ranting and raving, growling and swearing at publishers, bitterly resenting his failure to be accepted and appreciated.

Nor was Jack blind to the cause of Neal's growing irascibility and resistance to his attempts to continue their former intellectual games. All Neal would talk to him about were his responsibilities and the expenses of the family. Jack got the message.

Telling me he thought maybe I should have one husband at a time, he insisted on moving to San Francisco and a skid-row hotel. Neal felt guilty but relieved and drove Jack to the city. Yet after less than a month, he persuaded Jack to return, establishing a better balance in all our affairs.

Thirty-four

———

In December the railroad laid off the men with the least amount of service, Jack among them. His paranoia ceased, and his mood brightened. He could turn his thoughts and plans again toward Mexico, sharing with me fondly remembered scenes. During one of these recitals he suddenly stopped and looked at me, a new thought forming. 'Carolyn! Why don't you come with me? Come visit me in Mexico. Please do.' He hugged me lifting me off the floor. 'You've never had a vacation from the kids—not since you married Neal. You really should, you know. You ought to get away from the children sometimes—it would do you both good. Just think of it!'

I did think of it, and at first the idea scared me. I was such a possessive mother and so opinionated about children, even though I knew the books said it was good for them to be without their mother sometimes. These thoughts spun in my head and then flipped over, and I played with the prospect of Mexico with Jack. The fear gave way to a tempting thrill of pleasure and suspense. Jack said he'd talk to Neal about it; we both knew that neither of us would consider it without his approval.

Neal's response was not exactly enthusiastic, but he said flatly, 'Great idea. Of course you should get away from the kids, Ma.'

In a way, I'd hoped he'd might say no. But after a few days of listening to Jack paint ever more enticing pictures of good times in Mexico with me, Neal began acting strangely. He would put things down too hard, he said very little, even being short with the children, and he was unusually distracted. When I'd try to ask what was troubling him, he'd look at me with the '*you* know what you've done' look of accusation that I, myself, had perfected, and if I got any answer at all it was a sarcastic one. Jack was faring no better—Neal wouldn't talk to him at all.

Jack and I conferred and decided to beard the lion. When we asked Neal if he'd changed his mind, if he really didn't want me to go or what else *was* the matter, he said, 'No, no, you must go, of course, I insist,' all the while looking the martyr.

It took me some time to sort it out, because I'd never thought I'd see Neal becoming this jealous because of me; it was quite different from his flash of possessiveness on account of Bud. It was an interesting phenomenon, and I watched him for a day or two more until his behavior verged on the farcical.

Jack, too, could not stand it any longer. He said, 'Hey, Neal, forget it, man. It's okay.'

I said, 'I won't go, Neal. I never wanted to without your blessing. We won't mention it again.'

We put on cheery faces and went back to normal. Then Neal became contrite; he was not as relieved by our surrender as we had expected.

We were all playing pinochle one evening, and I could tell Neal wasn't with it; there was something on his mind.

He got up to get a beer, then stood in the doorway and plunged. 'Tell you what, kiddies. I'll make you a deal.' He swooped into the chair beside me and took my hand, stroking it. 'You let me drive Jack to Mexico now—just so's I can get some tea, see? And when I get back, *you* go—stay as long as you like, an' I'll carry on here— everything will be fine, long as I have Miss Green. You see, darling, that way poor Jack won't have to hop those awful freights and sleep out in the cold and catch who knows what, and he'll get there twice as fast and in one piece, and I'll come right back, I promise, so you can go even sooner, right? See? Isn't that the *perfect* solution? Whaddya say?' He looked from me to Jack and back again.

I dodged the thought that I was being traded for marijuana and tried to be practical. 'Can we afford two trips that far?'

'Yes, certainly, my dear. It won't cost a thing—only the gas. I'll do nothing but drive down, pick up the stuff and drive straight back— less 'n' a week—nothing. The Gray Ghost is in great shape, she'll make it easy.'

Inwardly, I smiled. Practicality had nothing to do with it. Neal saw a chance and was rarin' to go.

'Yesss, well . . .' I stalled. 'I'll think about it.'

Think about it, I knew, was all I'd ever do. Then I got angry with myself when I realized what a slave I was. 'Why not, you schnook?' I raged inwardly. 'When are you ever going to get a chance to live like this? Other people do it all the time. What's to lose? You complain about being confined, and when you get a chance to break out, you won't take it?' It didn't work. I knew too well I could never leave the children and relax. It didn't fit into my idea of motherhood, I had lingering doubts about Neal's conduct, and it was a pretty serious disregard of my marriage vows. But privately I enjoyed the day dreams of Jack and me in that exotic locale. Oh, why was I so afraid of life?

I said nothing of my doubts to either man. It would have hurt Jack to reject his offer, and I was intrigued with the idea of Neal being a martyr because of me—wondering how serious this pose really was. Meanwhile, there was no use denying I felt good. So I thoughtfully agreed to the bargain. Neal forgot his misery and returned to his customary cheer when anticipating another 'road' adventure.

The morning of their departure arrived. Jack had packed only his sea bag again, leaving his manuscripts and books with us to be held until his return. Neal took very little over and above the essential two pairs of socks per day, a daily change of shorts, a toothbrush and a half-dozen handkerchiefs.

The early morning was cold and foggy, the children still asleep as the men stowed their gear in the car and returned to the house singly to say goodbye. Neal was first and in top form. Had it been an audition for a silent movie, he'd have swept the field. He wrapped me in his arms and kissed me long and desperately, then slowly backed away holding my hand in both of his, scanning my face with his tragic lovelorn look until, abruptly, he wheeled away and strode across the back porch, pausing only once at the door to look back and give his standard exit line: 'I'll be right back, darling.'

I remained standing by the kitchen table, trying to keep the appropriate expression on my face; there was another round to go, and this was all so strange. Jack was shy but less so than usual. He held me close a long time before he slid his cheek down mine to kiss me slowly, sweetly, then whispered in my ear, 'It'll only be a week or two at most. Please don't fail me, Carolyn. I'll fix a place for us, and Neal will hurry home, don't worry. It's just *au revoir* for now.' And with another brief tender kiss, he, too, backed slowly away, looking at me with eyes of love, and on the porch blew another kiss before heading down the outside steps.

I sat down, dazed. *Well!* Going back over the scene it struck me as funny, and I couldn't help laughing aloud, not least from the rare pleasure of being so flattered. I remained in a semi-dream state the rest of the day, going about my routines only half plugged in.

When I was able to think clearly again, I knew for sure I'd never go to Mexico, never leave the children. But I'd have to wait for Neal's return to find a way out and not lose the ground I'd gained. At least this trip of his left me with no anxieties, no sense of loss, and warmed by the feeling of being loved I was patient with the children, unharried and serene. What a blessed change.

A day or two later, I got an unusual letter from Neal, unusual in that it was so unnecessary in its reassurances, though this time they had more of a ring of truth:

Dear, dear wife Carolyn, Dolly:
Sitting in the gray ghost Nash in front of Bill Burroughs' house in which Jack and he are sleeping. I write by light of Brakielanternfreight-size. My heart is bleeding for you. From S.J. to Bakersfield—*first* stop for gas—my thoughts of you filled my mind so that I knew I was composing great love letters. Naturally, I came by lovely things to say to you—mostly it came out—I love *you*.

He briefly catalogued the rest of the journey, putting in 'I thought of you' at every turn, and ended with 'I have got to mail this now. Everything all O.K. Be home Sat. p.m.—leaving here Thurs. a.m. *This is Truth:* I have not and *will not* touch any kind of any ole female—I am with B.B. and Jack, talking only. Love, N.'

Saturday evening he spun into the driveway right on schedule, but he walked into the house like a condemned man, grim and silent. At first I didn't understand. He was tired? He hadn't scored? The car was ruined? He talked very little about the trip down, apart from a snide remark or two at Jack's expense and how he couldn't drive, 'couldn't even remember the clutch.' There was nothing he wished to relate about the trip back—'just drove.' Then what *was* the matter with him?

We sat next to each other drinking coffee, when impulsively he leaned over and put his head in my lap, squeezing the hand that lay there. I stroked his hair and said, 'What is it, dear?' but instead of answering me, he got up and walked into our bedroom. I followed and

202

blinked at what I saw: there he was, standing in the corner, his forehead actually against the wall. Ah ha! Now I got it—but I had to hurry out to stifle an impulse to laugh. So that was it: now that he'd had his part of the bargain he was campaigning to get out of keeping the other half—my half.

Maybe this would be my way out. For awhile I tried to play his game and pretend I didn't find anything unusual in his behavior. It was too fascinating to see what he'd do next.

Then a letter from Jack sent him into paroxysms of grief and tugged me in both directions:

Dear Neal & Carolyn:
I took a little dobe block up on Bill's roof, 2 rooms, lots of sun and old Indian women doing the wash. Will stay here awhile even though $12 a month is high rent. But perfect place to write, blast, think, fresh air, sun, moon, stars, the Roof of the City. All ready for your visit, Carolyn, I even bought Mexican pottery to brighten my 2 cells. Tonight I'm buying 3 dozen oysters for 35 cents equivalent (expensive) and frying them in butter, with imported Chianti for a chaser, and French bread. Every morning it's steak and eggs, which I buy for 30 cents and cook up . . . Now I'm completely alone on the roof. Now or never with a great new novel long anticipated from me in N.Y.—Day and night tomorrow to it . . . Carolyn, is you coming? Let me know—write—love to Cathy, Jami, Johnny and all. Love xxx Jack.

He added the clincher to me:

Just got your letter. Did Neal get home that night? . . . I am unbearably lonely in Mexico, I guess I'll never be satisfied with anything. Now that I have regained my regular love of life, of people, specifically of Neal—and you, after October's Darkness, the old human loneliness has come back to wash against my rock, ah me . . . please come visit me, Carolyn, my little pad is all ready . . . all the fresh air of the Indian plateau blows into it . . . Come on and get your vacation with me! We'll have wine, tea, oysters at midnight—we'll go dance the Mambo—XX J.

If only I could make this dream actually come true. If only it weren't so far and I could just *be* there, not have to traverse the miles between. But, ah, no, the idea of setting out alone on that journey was too much, and I couldn't watch Neal's apparent agony any more. Best to give up the game and get back to living. So I solemnly told Neal that, of course, I'd never leave him if he asked me not to. Nothing could have made me happier than to see him smile, his brow unfurrowed, the gloom dispelled.

'Now, how are we going to tell Jack without reawakening his paranoia?' I got out paper and pen to compose the 'Dear John.'

Neal snorted. '*Pah,* he'll get over it. Serves him right for stealing other men's wives.'

'You keep forgetting, dear heart, it was your idea in the first place.'

'How can you possibly say an untrue thing like that? Not a bit of it. *Harrummph.* Why would I ever do such a stupid thing?' And he stalked around me, waving his arms in mock seriousness like a Puritan preacher.

'Well, there was LuAnne . . .'

'I never did. You're mistaken, my dear . . . besides, altogether different—I gotta run. Tell the old boy to get his own girl.' He called back the last as he ran out to the car. I laughed and shook my head. But it had been Jack once again who had been the cement to bind our little family closer together. I sat a long time musing and smiling and looking forward to the Christmas I could plan in this big old house.

The mail arrived before I'd thought of what to say to Jack, and with it came a note from him making it unnecessary.

Dear Carolyn:
Please pardon me for running off to go home for Xmas—It looks like I did it on purpose, but it isn't. I love you and I love you for loving me, you— What we gonna do? I'll write, I'm hung up in the night. Don't pass up your vacations. Awful Jack Fool. How is Cathy Doll, Jami Doll and Johnny Doll? and Neal Doll, & you Doll? and me Doll? Nobody know.

Poor Jack. He just couldn't be alone for long. Everything had worked out for the best, and his mother would be happier, too.

Thirty-five

Neal showed his appreciation of my loyalty by giving us all a warm and bountiful Christmas, and his apparent contentment spread over us like an umbrella. I don't know if we were the sole reason or if he'd found compensatory pleasure in San Francisco, but my own happiness blocked any chance of suspicion. He was laid off the railroad on the first of the year, and although he was gone a good deal seeking other interim employment, he was home every evening for dinner.

We soon learned we had been wrong in assuming that Jack had found equivalent peace by his return to his mother. In the first week of January we got a letter from Allen, saying that Jack's mother, tired of the South and living in Caroline's family circle, had returned to Long Island, taking Jack with her.

Jack is back here. Have seen him not much though. He's at his mother's house hiding out, comes in to see his friends seldom—never except thru my arranging—Came in in time for New Year's, cried drunk & high in cab at dawn on way home. Couldn't tell why crying, except general recognition of the past and self back in N.Y.—older and (no?) wiser . . . and I feel there's some underlying battle somewhere lurking . . . Also he always all hung up on noise, noise, music bands, tea, excitement organizing—have feeling he doesn't respect presence of individual he's with (me) and is creating artificial excitement. He solitary and excited overly—won't talk—though of course knows, sees what I am thinking, and says, 'I want to see you and talk to you 4 times a year.' . . . I think his writing, except for preoccupation with self as subject is advancing greatly. Maybe right preoccupation but wrong lament lament lament for him. I keep thinking he has no adult society & marriage world to write about and keeps repeating lament for Mother. New book about 17 year old Mary Carney love affair . . .

A few days later we received Jack's version, generally more cheerful:

I have buried myself in writing-work in a concentrated crack at it before I give railroading further thought this year, my legs being bad, etc., and have two novels plus *Road, Sax* and *Town & City* underway . . .
　If you don't write that book about the Coast Division of the SP, I will. New Year is great, I like winter weather, storms, snow, long walks in overshoes . . . no girls, no money, just write and sleep; that's my life. I'm alright; no more talk of death, crap, no . . . But this is the way the world ends, everybody alone, that's good, that's how you started, remember? Everybody dead in the cemetery; husbands live with their wives; the 4:19's on time; Texas sheriffs wear stars, etc. . . . everybody's in his heaven, God made the world, I'm okay too and get hi once a night and still believe and still love you.

Neal and I read and sighed. Dear Jack—one minute it's the balmy warm exotic nights with the Indians in Mexico that make life idyllic, the next thing it's snow and storms. Before we had a chance to answer, he wrote again:

Dear Carolyn—Please let me know what's wrong that you don't write at all—are you gonna be mad at me because I'm not trying to steal you away from Neal?—or *take* you away—whatever—I should like to know how Jami is, and you—If you and Neal spend the rest of your lives fighting it'll only mean you were born to hate—Hey! . . . I find Mexican needment tea valuable in small quantities—like *you* say 'special events.' Ah, I hope you're well—Make me a pizza! Eat it for me! Mail me the recipe! Do something! Write!

He launched into rhapsodies describing John Clellon Holmes' new home in minute detail. John was a close friend whose book *Go*, in which Jack, Neal and Allen were characterized, had just been accepted by a publisher. Jack envied him both because of that and because of his house: 'Carolyn, like me you'd die seeing it—Big trees outside—sea fens and sea in back . . .' Neal and I agreed that if ever Jack were homesick, he was now—but for which and whose home?
　He continued to write frequently. In early spring I got a long,

rambling, tea-high letter written at dawn, Jack having 'been half awake all night thinking . . . that the Southern Pacific is picking up.' He fantasized about bringing his mother to live in a trailer in Milpitas, a scrubby little town at the foot of the Bay, and working the railroad, the story interrupted with, 'Yes, I will be your Valentine,' and then back to the fantasy. Then another sudden switch to

O, for krissakes Carolyn, I'm trying to say, also, please do send my birthday present [an ounce of marijuana] at once . . . and secondly, if railroad does call me, I think I will go for sure, and again, once more, I think I should live alone on my Frisco skid row or maybe better San Jose skid row . . . I don't want to interfere, let me be constant visitor instead of, and if not constant visitor, let Neal bring me to visit whenever he wants, if he doesn't want at all I am still in California on business of my own, and if there be horrible axe murder headlines I still have reason to defend my skull. I am not Ray Murphy but just as mad and no woman owns me not even you who should . . . I am all thru with life in that sense and starting on something new . . . And please can I say that boy do I wanna see my children tho, again . . . I do miss my walks with Jami and Cathy around the trees . . . In any case sweetheart good night. It's early in the morning and I must work all day and think of life well not just goof literary letters to other men's wives . . .

The next week brought another anxious plea: 'Lissen Neal, I realize I don't deserve your friendship anymore unless'n you forgive me, which I hope you will do, as you forgave me in October, etc.' He said if the Southern Pacific didn't call him soon, he'd go to Canada and work on the railroad there. 'I want to go back to my own people . . . the only thing is I'll miss seeing you and Carolyn and kiddies this spring . . .' Jack still didn't know *what* he wanted, it seemed to us. In spite of his backward look to our good times, I was not deceived into thinking it was me he wanted, or that he wished he were Neal in that respect. Both Jack and I knew marriage was not a solution for us, even had I been single; he knew he couldn't sit still long enough to shoulder the responsibilities, and as for me, I knew he was far too moody, too touchy and too wrapped up in himself.

Perhaps this self-consciousness was what caused him to write so well—locked up in the ivory tower of self, he could observe and report all the details of life outside. However his efforts to join in and partake of what he saw were generally disappointing, leaving him feeling threatened and thwarted. Perhaps that was one of the fascinations Neal held for him. He envied Neal's ability to make life happen, to be a principal in the action, not a bystander. And when Jack made love he did so with an air of apology. I felt that he never gave of himself completely; he preferred the woman to manage the event (so he could say, 'It wasn't *my* idea—or *my* fault'?). The success of our relationship was, I felt, due to my efforts to be alert to his moods and desires without imposing my own. I was allowed to share his observations, which I enjoyed, and he liked company—as long as it was sympathetic. I knew better than to express criticism or suspicion of his inner motives, an area where he was seldom objective. Neal was such a perfect listener to any and all of my ideas, I didn't need Jack for that, but I'd never known a man with such a tender heart, nor one so vulnerable. I wondered if he was ashamed of being gentle and compassionate. I knew sometimes he put on a show of bravado and coarseness, and it never failed to embarrass me—as in *On the Road*, where Sal Paradise was rarely the Jack I knew. The character seemed to me more based on Neal's behavior or on what Jack thought he was expected to be like. In Denver he used to brag to me about getting into fist fights if some guy cast aspersions on his toughness. I understood his dilemma, if that's what it was, since he'd been conditioned as I had by a society that believed 'real' men were just like that. I learned he had to be drunk to act so crudely, and perhaps that's why in later years he was rarely far from a bottle.

Neal failed to find a job right away, and by the third week of January 1953 our finances were in a near desperate state again. Then he heard there was work for him on the Southern Division as a 'boomer,' or freelance brakeman. He would be able to make up to $600 a month, really big money to us then. Neal burst in with the glad tidings and prepared to leave the next morning, 1 February. I accepted his decision sorrowfully, remembering the summer of 1948, but again the money was more important. The change in Neal since Jack had left had meant that the previous six weeks had been almost like a honeymoon, or the nearest we ever got to one. Now, when we were almost whole, here was another separation to endure. Sometimes a lurking thought told me our marriage would have been doomed without these separations.

We all bade lingering farewells, and Neal telephoned his safe arrival in Indio, just like a regular husband. Daily we wrote passionate love letters, saying all the things we'd wanted to in the past when my disapproving attitude had prevented us. He commented on my detailed descriptions of our domesticity and struggles without him, recitals which soon included complaints and whining, for now that we were so happy together, why did we have to be apart, and how I hated to be married yet alone.

He was to have been gone only two weeks, but when the second week ended, instead of Neal I got a dozen red roses and a Valentine card on which was written: 'Double the days that 14 are, and that's the day that I'll be thar.' Again, I was deeply touched by his unexpected sweetness.

In the midst of my self-pity came another letter from Jack, shot through with wistful nostalgia, making a hard knot form in my throat as I read:

Dear Carolyn:
I finally heard from you—thought you were really secretly peeved about Mexico . . . and you may be . . . But in a way it was better for Neal (I guess) . . . I really believe . . . your life and vacations is with him. Glad to hear Jami is 'more than ever,' I know what you mean, and she'll be . . . and is, great. Cathy is a sweet girl; don't underestimate her quiet little soul, honey. I miss my walks around the sidewalks with Cathy and Jami. I may suddenly come to California for RR, if they recall me, because I may need money . . . but I wouldn't stay at your house again, because the complications are too much, and Neal doesn't appreciate my awareness of everything, and 'felt sorry' for me, and I spend less money staying by myself in skid-row hotels . . . and I don't want to interfere any more with any corner of your hopes and hassles which is really all I've been doing, but only because you asked and the first year Neal asked . . . I told him I wanted to go to Mexico alone, in a bus, and pointed out that as long as he insisted he take me, it was HIS TRIP, not 'mine' . . . blah blahs of eternity . . . poor conniving Neal . . . nothing in the world I mind except the possibility that Neal secretly hates me for things he asked me to do and I did because I have always been led around by the nose and never minded neither . . . because I trusted him . . . because when I have something to do finally I do it.

In New York things are very exciting and too much so I want to leave . . . even William Faulkner is here running around having a big time, which he never did before . . . I told Viking Press they'd publish *Dr. Sax* if my name was Faulkner . . . they said they would publish it . . . 'at a loss' they predict, if I had another book that would make a gain . . . I do, and am typing it . . . no title but *great!* (My first Proustian love story.)

In Old Saybrook I saw a house for sale for $20,000; an aging colonial house still, that faded red-purple of New England, circa 1650. Beautiful stuff and all of its authentic antiques and going with a house and 20 ACRES TILLABLE LAND AND ANCIENT OLD HEAVY TREES AND across the fields, far, a little cemetery sinking, with faded dates and trees waving in the wind that blows from the sea a mile away . . . if I had money . . . not really . . . Do you want to take a vacation in Mexico still?

I'll meet you next week; I'm going for you know what . . . not really . . . next month . . .

Yes, Carolyn, I'm back on the old beam, but only in moderation and with control, like you always said.

All my best works will be swallowed, imitated, and, like Gertrude Stein, I'll just go to a dumpy grave and who cares . . . LOVE IS ALL THAT COUNTS. I'm glad you love Neal; he certainly loves you, remember that. Adios.

PS: I write you now instead of to Neal . . . is that what you secretly wanted to accomplish? I still suspect that. (Hor, hor hor)

But I loved you one day last fall so genuinely you'll never know . . . just feel . . . I loved you because you are great, and I'll always love you that way we loved, till graves soon sinking fields . . .

Neal was outshining himself in his letters, too:

Today I'm the loneliest yet; I mean lonely, alone and cut off from all but you, and it scares me; I realize how much I need you and how hopeless I am without you—and even with you. Will you hold my sad head and soothe the savage beast? Pathos and passion that twirl toward my heart each time I think of you, who is all there is, all five feet two, between me and the gallows death I dread . . . Songs mean so much to me. Will you sing to me in our bedroom that we depapered and painted? Love songs?

Why couldn't I find the fulfillment of my longings in one or the other of them, both or neither, for here I sat still alone. What good was it to be loved by two men if I couldn't have either? Reading letters from the two of them, I pondered their differences again. Jack always seemed to be straining to subdue his real feelings, whereas Neal welcomed the opportunity to verbalize his love in letters. He didn't seem to feel any action was required of him to uphold his avowals of love. Perhaps he wished he *could* believe in the intensity his words described. Jack had the feelings, Neal had the words; yet neither could bring that love—though directed at me—into my experience or join with mine in any sustained, constructive way.

I hung on for another two weeks, at the end of which:

Dear Baby: It's gone from bad to worse: hold onto yourself . . . THEY WON'T RELEASE ME! But they *must* before 13 March, cause that's when I have to be back on the Coast Division. So lookie here, it's really for the best . . .

And he desperately tried to convince me, outlining our need for the money, detailing his own loneliness, praising my help and planning all the household and garden tasks he was eager to engage in. 'I'm only sorry I'm not handy . . . and could make toys for the kids,' he wrote, followed by three or four pages of love. But my house of fortitude was built on sand, and it tumbled down around him.

Dear Neal:
Good thing that was such a sweet letter. This has been a blue weekend and a worse morning. I got up feeling like something had been put over on me again, but I'm fighting the impulse to believe it. Last night I got panicky and felt I just couldn't stand it another minute. Five years of the waiting, the last days of expecting you being the hardest . . . I go around keeping everything straightened, brushing my hair, dressing me and the kids to look pretty for Daddy and hearing every car all night within miles, even though I try not to listen. All for nothing . . . again and again. And now that everything is supposed to be right, and we're just about to *begin* . . . why can't we begin? Why can't we have it now?
The washing machine busted, and Johnny has a fever this a.m. So I guess the money you're making is what I should be blessing, and you for persevering instead of whining and complaining. That damn RR rules everything. I'm tired of playing second fiddle to that too. Now that you say you want me, where are you? I wasn't going to write at all to avoid saying all these things, but now that I've blabbed it all out, I can at least say I know you aren't to blame and are torn between all the demands I make on you and trying to do your best . . . it is THE best. I think you're terrific. Don't worry, I'll make it and not take it out on you any more.
Jack wrote a note asking you to write him a word about RR. He seems to be afraid the men don't like him, and he'll have a bad time or something. I don't get it. Such an affliction he has . . . what does he care what they think? Far as I can tell nobody thinks much about anybody.
. . . B. Goodman on radio playing 'My Guy's Come Back' . . . thought I'd be singing that too.

In spite of my efforts, my self-pity persisted:

Sunday is too awful . . . our peaceful living room . . . all rearranged, is fine for funnies and the concert and the almond tree almost thru blooming. I'm sick of telling you of things I enjoyed you are never here to share. We've had so *little* time 'together.' I fear again you've found other interests, and that's no good an attitude.
A big drunk just walked right in the front door. I'm still shaking. He said he wanted food. I gave him 50¢ cause I couldn't get him out. He grabbed Johnny and kissed him. Johnny screamed. The guy cried . . . (he has 3 of his own) I called the landlord for a lock. Think of all the times, especially nite I go to Forest's for hours. Wish I had a husband at such times . . . damn the money . . . if it means this. I guess I'm incorrigibly selfish. Do as you think best. I hope the call back will let you compromise. I'll *try* not to be bitter again . . .

Love, C.

211

Undaunted by my whining, Neal continued his cheer and encouragement. Although he gave me a factual account of his deadly hot days and cold lonely nights, he never complained. How did he manage it? I told him he should; it was part of my job to comfort him as well. But no, in fact, I never remember him complaining about anything that had to do with us. Even my selfish letters he'd answer with extravagant praise, seeing only good, and that spring I believed all Neal wrote—people can and must change, and with love all things seemed possible:

> . . . I'm carried away by yesterdays with you. I'm getting so that I can look at passing women without passion! Few attractive and those that do remind of you . . . just thought you'd like to know . . . I ain't spoke to anything resembling woman or female sorceressessess.
>
> I read Proust slowly and realized I really can write like he does. Of course he's better but I'm younger, and while less brilliant, still have a chance to learn how, with your help and patience. I'm terribly interested in life and wish you were here to share my musings and comments about living and dead things that pass so abstractly before me.

Not doubting his sincerity, and reveling in his reassurances, my magnanimity extended even to his sexual propensities—strange advice coming from me:

> Don't worry about your virtue—a splurge now and then might do you good. I'm not all that puritanical, and especially now I get my share and more. So trust your own character—you have a very good one and an indulgence or two, honestly accepted as such, won't make you an addict again necessarily. I believe in you more than ever; I am proud of you and I love you.

Neal replied in an equally unprecedented way:

> Your crass 'splurge now and then' horrifies me! Don't you go 'splurging'! I won't, cause I can't cause I love you and want you good and unsplurgie with anyone but me.
>
> When I get home we'll be in our rearranged bedroom and read again to each other all our love letters—all too few they are, so we'll make up for it by telling each other, mouth to ear, all the things we feel and all we want to say and have wanted to say forever. Just remember this: I have solved our sex problem. Don't forget to remind me to tell you about it when I get home.

Well, with that I did break my mournful mood and laughed.

Oh, those glorious reunions—this one far and away the best yet, fresh, unsullied, and the harvest of the words we'd been sowing all those weeks. I think Neal, too, thought a real change had occurred. But three weeks of this smug complacency was all we were allowed before we were presented with another challenge

Thirty-six

Late on the night of 10 April 1953, the telephone's shrill scream awakened me. The fear that overshadows all railroad wives had become reality: Neal had been hurt. He had been taken by ambulance from Millbrae to the Southern Pacific hospital in San Francisco. All I could learn was that the accident involved a leg, but he was alive and would recover.

I was shivering in my thin pajamas when I hung up the phone. Wrapping my robe around me I walked through the moonlit rooms, trying to subdue my quivering nerves and consider how this would affect us all. I had little to go on and must wait until morning for more information.

I left the children with Marie Forest and drove the fifty miles to the hospital. When I arrived, Neal was conscious but woozy and could remember few details of what had happened. He knew that he had been on top of a boxcar that had just been shunted onto a siding. He had been setting the brake when the car hit the bumper and Neal flew off, landing on the toe of his iron-toed boot so that the force of his fall tore the foot backwards, nearly severing it completely. Most of the bones in the foot and ankle were broken. The doctors had straightened it out and sewn it back on the best they could for now, and his leg hung in a huge cast and complex traction apparatus. He'd have to stay that way for about five weeks.

Neal was too groggy to talk for very long; he just held my hand and

214

tried to smile. (Nevertheless, he'd already had to dictate and sign a statement of what had happened.)

On my way home I faced the prospect of another long separation, of having to build our lives and habits alone once more. Well, this time I'd hang on to the thought that he'd be home *all* the time over the summer, even though inactive.

In a day or two I began to be bombarded by tales from other railroad men of how they had dealt with their accidents: how to file a claim, what to watch out for, how much money to expect from a damage settlement—no two stories alike, and the figures astronomical. It was all very bewildering, and nothing could be done just yet.

In another month the doctors completed all the operations possible for the time being, and Neal was strong enough to come home. He still had to remain lying or sitting down most of the time; the cast was too heavy for him to use his crutches for more than a few minutes, but he could at least get to most meals and to the bathroom. With great ceremony the children and I settled him on the living room couch, where he had an unobstructed view of most of the house as well as of the front yard and the street beyond. I overwhelmed him with books, magazines, newspapers and the radio, and he renewed his determination to work on his writing.

First, however, he answered Jack, who had received his call-back to the railroad, telling him to come out and check with the crew clerk. His attitude was cordial, if not as demanding as on former occasions. He told Jack quite matter-of-factly that he was to stay with us. I added no extra urging this time, not sure whether Jack's presence would help entertain Neal or would widen the rift with further jealousy.

In mid-May a welcome letter from Allen arrived, and I poured us each a cup of coffee and sat down to read it aloud. It was a long one, and we settled ourselves to relish it.

> . . . Then Jack told me a few days ago about your accident. I groaned when I read. But aren't you fortunate having wife and children around to care for you in pain and distress? Oh old father! What happened? (But not in T-hi incomprehensible detail) Are you getting compensation? Maybe you can read or improve your knowledge with the leisure. I'll bet you sit around blasting and coughing all day. Someday we will yet be of all one family. Now I'm on a new kick 2 weeks old, a very beautiful kick, which I invite you to share.

Allen had discovered Chinese painting and hence oriental philosophy. 'China is a bleak great blank in our intimate knowledge . . . Much of

215

the Buddhist writing you see is not interesting, vague, etc., because it has no context to us . . .' But through study of the art and dynasties '. . . you begin to see the vastitude and intelligence of the yellow men . . . I daily grow hungry on Orient . . .' He had been deeply impressed by a recording of Gandhi speaking. After describing it, Allen wrote: 'Well, anyway he mentions in his speech the great Teachers . . . Buddha, Christ and (of all people) Zoroaster, who the hell that is I don't know . . . Z in West is a vague magical name, somewhat of a seance joke.'

There was a knock on the back door, so I handed the letter to Neal so he could read the long Chinese poem Allen had included, and went to see who it was.

'Jack!' I gasped. 'Why, how did you get here? Why didn't you call?'

'I jes' thought I'd surprise you—but I ain't gonna stay.'

He looked shyly at me from under his brows, shuffling his feet. I was nervous, not knowing whether to embrace him or not, when Neal bellowed, 'Nonsense! Come in here and put your gear in your room.'

Jack chuckled, and I took his hand, leading him in to Neal. Jack shook his head when he saw Neal's cast, 'There's the old crip—my God, man, that thing's bigger'n you are. What some guys won't do to get outta work, hey?'

I went for more coffee while they bantered, then Jack and I settled down near Neal. Neal showed Jack the letter from Allen and said, 'What do you think of Allen's new oriental kick?'

'Oh, yeah—he's been filling my head full of it for weeks. Might be something in it—I dunno—I only read a little Buddhism, but I dig Gautama Buddha—don't know about the Zen stuff.'

'Hmmm. Well, ha, we'll have to find some books, Ma, and brush up on our own vague rememberings. Gotta keep track of ol' Allen.'

Jack stayed the weekend, but that was all. Whether by accident or design, he and I had few moments alone. There was a heavy aura of sadness about us, and his presence was even more engulfing in its tenderness and warmth, perhaps because I knew it couldn't last. He had made up his mind. He walked with the girls and talked to Neal, and Neal listened more attentively, tuning his own awareness to Jack's and reaffirming their brotherhood. Both Neal and I were concerned about Jack's next step, but he said he'd go find Al Sublette, the mulatto college student he had befriended on Russell Street, and probably stay in San Francisco. He would come visit us and we him. We all knew it was best, and it seemed we'd passed some sort of milestone in growing up, the kind that demands a sacrifice.

Jack's plan of living in San Francisco was at first thwarted, however, when he drew a two-week hold-down in San Luis. But that was followed by a local freight run between San Francisco and San Jose, which enabled him to return to the rundown Cameo Hotel. Once or twice he came to visit with Al Sublette, and he tried to be enthusiastic about writing his impressions of life around the hotel, of digging the bars and the music, but it was obvious he was not happy and was drinking more. The strain of having to rise very early every day plus his antagonism toward the conductor he served, whom he thought was unsympathetic towards his lack of expertise, finally got to him.

As suddenly as he had arrived, Jack was gone. Al came alone one weekend and told us he had felt that the railroad was too slow or something; he had gone home to New York and then shipped out. I spoke my thoughts aloud: 'He didn't even call to say goodbye.' To comfort me, Al said, 'Well, he was pretty drunk the night before he left. I guess he didn't know what to say—he'll write, I'm sure.'

He did write, but he didn't mail the letter for a week. And for Jack it was a brief and singularly uninformative letter; he was in nostalgic mood.

We are sailing in warm seas off the W. coast of Mexico, a great beautiful isolated island with a sand beach and huge mountains beyond, on our left—for all I know, one of the three Mary Isles, the Mexican penal colony. The sea smooth, sultry, tinted dawn clouds clouds at high noon—moveless shark fins sulking in the water—little sea birds—mad. Every day 350 miles further South, till Panama, then up between Yucatan and Cuba—to dull, dumb Mobile—then *out* east or west.

I have a new job, as a waiter in officer's saloon—very easy and cool . . . Ah, you ought to see those shrouded island mountains! And on the foremast a canvas lashed to top, so I keep imagining there is a shrouded sage of the Universe up there, blind, leading us thru the drooling tropical stars of night to a rendezvous of the unknown—ahead—like in Melville. This is no gray raw North Atlantic; these are the enchanted seas & typhoon seas—crazy—so write!—& keep me posted—I'll write too—Till later, Jack. P.S. Love and kisses to leetle ones—Tutte le strade conducono a Roma—all roads lead to Rome.

Jack had shown Al the advantages, especially financial, of a seaman's life, and when he too got a ship we received a letter 'enroute to Honolulu.' He had a job as a bellboy. 'Perhaps Neal would call this a "towel over the wrist" flunky job'—which was how Neal had described Jack's waiter job, with doubts about his tenacity—'but when you conduct yourself right you command respect.'

Jack was not resigned to conducting *him*self right. He soon rebeled at his 'flunky' status, as Neal had predicted, and with customary temper and paranoia jumped ship in Panama and returned to Richmond Hill and his mother, beloved Memere. Allen informed us of this, referring to Jack sadly as 'the thing from another world—of his own making, in which he'll allow only himself.'

In August I decided to write to Jack, concerned that he hadn't written. He answered at once:

But I did write you a big long letter about a month ago. I guess you never got it . . . I guess mail gets lost nowadays . . . tho it did flash paranoiacally across my mind that not only did Neal dispose of your copy of *Town & City* to remove taint of me from Cass household but also secretly solemnly coldly read my big gushletter and shamefaced tore it and never told you— and this may be very true considering his own flips of 1952 like when he hung phone up on me—actually I guess the letter just got lost or the FBI picked it off yr porch or it's in the deadletter office now.

This was extremely frustrating for me. I knew Neal wouldn't do such a thing—would he? No, not like him at all, and I'd not heard of any letters getting lost if they carried a return address. Any letter of Jack's was precious—not even so much for what he said but for how he said it. Well, here was one—

Be assured I not forget you at all. Here is what I wrote to you last night: 'Think of you all the time and as for back days of love they haunt me when I hear no more of them but solace me when they reach forward and ring again and are mentioned again—My position in geography is due to restlessness and ambition to see Samarkand and Ulan Bator not avoidance of sweet eternity there in San Jose—' See? Meanwhile problems continue and I have to decide what to do . . .

Neal now turned his attention to pressuring Allen to come for a visit, an idea Allen had toyed with for the previous six years. Neal used similar persuasions to those he'd used on Jack, and then,

Do your best in this, 'cause life so simple, good and easy here, that it's actually unreal seeming, like a joke or dream, no reason for worries, tho from old experience I try to, and all troubles of world like mirage one reads about only to keep abreast and pass time.

Allen replied that he came close to joining us after reading this letter, but he was still not ready. I was glad; Neal and I seemed to have reached another zenith of harmony, and I'd not had nearly enough.

Thirty-seven

No doubt a great deal of our peace was due to the fact that, as Neal pointed out, we had no financial hassles for once. The railroad had offered $1,800—a ridiculous sum according to other conductors, so we decided to take their advice and hire a famous local lawyer who specialized in cases against the Southern Pacific. He was a lively little Italian, brusque, out-spoken and confident. His crowning recommendation to Neal, however, was the fact that he owned eight Cadillacs and allowed Neal to drive one of them to the San Francisco courthouse. He warned us the suit would take several months (in fact, it was to take two years), but he would arrange for our support until the settlement was made.

While home the first month, Neal grew a goatee and shaved his head. It made him look heavier, tougher, not as boyish, and I had a new man to get used to. He spent his days reading, either newspapers and magazines or Céline and Dostoevsky. He'd listen to every ball game, guzzling coffee or beer, but when he was stronger he went outside with the children and watched them swing or play in the plastic pool. What endless patience he had with them; how I admired his reasonable approach and the calm, loving way he'd settle their disputes, with none of the anxiety that soured my supervision.

With no railroad calls to expect, a great treat now was the chance to go to drive-in movies. We could collapse the seat in the station wagon so that Neal with his cast could stretch out comfortably, propped up on pillows. The first time we went, however, I was mystified by the cashier's embarrassed double-take as I handed her the money. After parking I looked back at Neal and all became clear. He was lying on one side of the car, completely covered with a blanket so that none of his cast showed, as though waiting for me to join him.

'Neal, you nut! That looks terrible—what a set-up . . . everybody may suspect drive-ins are "passion pits," but that looks a tad too obvious.'

He laughed, getting a kick from the girl's shock, and uncovered the cast, warbling, 'I'm in the nude for luuuv . . .'

One morning soon after Neal's cast was removed and he could hobble about some, the children came running in, babbling together in terror. I ran to the front and saw fire engines everywhere. Two were parked in the empty lot next door, and a huge one was just swinging into our driveway. Marie came running from her house as fire fighters swarmed like ants over both our yards. We all calmed down when one of them explained they had to burn the dry grass and weeds in the lot next to us so as to create a fire break. They asked if we could help by hosing down the boundary fence and by helping to clear the area of anything that wouldn't burn.

Dick got out the hoses while Marie and I settled the children on their porch, where they could watch without danger; we gave them strict orders to stay put. Then I raced into our house to get Neal—not because we needed him, but because I knew he had planted marijuana in the lot.

'What'll we do, Neal? Will they recognize it? We'll deny it, right? Won't know what they're talking about, just like the Forests would do.' I was trying to help him into his pants. I'd rarely seen Neal so agitated.

'Great Caesar's ghost—we can't let them *burn* them! Come on, Ma, we gotta save the crops! Help me up.

This wasn't at all what I'd in mind, but I knew it was useless to argue. For months he'd been proudly watching the plants grow, and they were nearly ready for harvest. We agreed that I'd go over the fence and try to pull up the plants as I ostensibly searched for debris, then throw them back to him. While running the hose, he would act as clean-up man for anything Marie or I tossed over. Of course we didn't tell the Forests about these 'weeds,' and I must have put in a star performance of sweet innocence while surreptitiously yanking up a plant whenever I got the chance. All of them were firmly rooted in the dry ground, and it took me quite awhile. Neal was positively apoplectic. When at last it was over, I was suddenly stunned by the thought that perhaps the whole purpose of this project was to find out who would try to save those plants! I quickly blocked my rising panic and concentrated on looking dumb.

When the firemen began rolling up their hoses and everyone's attention was directed elsewhere, Neal grabbed his 'pile of brush' and hastily hobbled around to the other side of the house and out of sight. The Forests went inside to wash up, and I was glad to collect the children and go home.

Neal made a great thing out of the narrow escape—not ours, but the plants! He was overjoyed at our success, praised my heroism and gleefully showed me how he had hung the precious trophies upside down in the back of the coat closet behind the rack of winter clothes. (In spite of all this, the crop turned out to be almost worthless.)

Soon thereafter, the idyllic picture of our life that Neal had painted for Allen began to pall for him. He withdrew into himself and rarely participated in family life, smoked tea constantly and, mesmerized, lay for hours listening to the radio, especially to ball games. He moved his seat of operations to our bedroom, read less, slept more, increased his masturbation and spoke hardly a word to anyone except the children, with whom he always put on a show of normalcy. My own impatience and irritability grew as, every day, I had to clean up the sheets of newspapers and magazines littering the bedroom, failing to rouse his interest in any subject and receiving only monosyllabic answers.

Difficult for both of us was the continual postponement of the trial. I was eager to be able to plan. I wanted to know how much money to expect. Although the lawyer had sued for $75,000, I knew we'd get only a part of that, but how much? When I'd try to pin him down to a more realistic figure, he'd flair up at me, insisting we would get nothing less than the full amount. I still didn't dare believe it, and tried to avoid tempting daydreams.

At the beginning of Neal's treatment, the doctors had been positive he'd never walk again. By the time the first cast came off they thought he might be able to work, but limited service—passenger trains only. Neal decided otherwise—full reinstatement was his only goal. Every day he worked on stretching and loosening the rebuilt tendons, exercising, soaking, massaging.

During the fall, Allen and Jack also seemed to begin a gradual decline into the slough of despond. Although Allen's early letters were characterized by no more than his usual flux of restless frustrations, as winter approached his irritability and complaints increased.

> I was wrong not to have written since your last letter so long ago, so much more so since you invited me out—but the thing is, there is such a kind of confusion and hesitancy about life—moves in me that I kept putting off . . . Jack here is worried you don't answer his letter, thinks you've rejected him & wants word from you. If you talk to him straight whatever you think, he will accept, so do . . . I am handling Jack's books—so far successfully & *On the Road* will be published except for whatever slips there are between cups and lips. Otherwise, except for the romance of cocktails with his publishers, my worklife as copyboy is grubby . . . you should maybe write a novel of such fatal dissatisfaction—your own (what is yours? any? or are you redeemed by your early settling down? What would you have wanted to do ideally?)

My, how I wished Neal would put some thought into an answer to that one. How many times I had asked, and would continue to ask, that same question. Then Allen told us of a surprising action he'd taken:

> . . . I telegraphed Eisenhower last week: (it cost me $2.00) 'Rosenbergs are pathetic. Government will sordid. Execution obscene. America caught in crucifixion machine only barbarians want them burned. I say stop it before we fill our souls with deathhouse horror.' Didn't do no good.

This marked the first time we heard of Allen *doing* anything outright about his political complaints, and to us it was a drastic measure. We could not have imagined then what it was to lead to.

Thirty-eight

I'd had a fair dose of psychology in schools—psychoanalysis with Eric Fromm plus abnormal psychology at college, then post-graduate clinical psychology with the Army—so looking back I'm surprised that I never viewed Neal's extreme swings in mood and behaviour from that standpoint. It might have prepared me for them to some extent. Each downward plunge came as an inexplicable shock, and I continued to respond to him from a strictly personal angle—even after we received the results of his psychological tests, which neatly labeled him 'a sociopathic personality with schizophrenic and manic-depressive tendencies that could develop into psychosis.' It was all there. Neal read the diagnosis, looked grim, nodded but said nothing. All I did was try to soften and deny. In those, my still more naïve days, I didn't know there were hundreds, thousands of such individuals, far more destructive and dangerous than Neal, walking about everywhere, or that our society has little provision for helping either them or their victims. Since all the doctors did nothing beyond diagnosis, I assumed that all Neal needed was his will and my love.

In a letter, Jack strongly recommended we read Wilhelm Reich's *Function of the Orgasm*. Needless to say, the emphasis on sex as being absolutely necessary at all times appealed to Neal as a Gospel. Not so to me, but Jack's suggestion gave me an idea.

I hunted up all my psychology books: Freud, James, Fromm and Horney. There must be some answers to our repetitive problems, and

223

I couldn't believe the only explanation was our failure to share a mutual obsession with sex. Up until now Neal had been the target under fire but was it possible *I* might need some changing? So far, any alterations in my behaviour had been for simple self-preservation, not based on any change in my theories. Well, I'd tried everything else I knew . . .

Gathering to my bosom a journal and pens, I settled down each day when the children napped. I reviewed Horney's *Our Inner Conflicts* and was able to identify everyone I knew including myself, so I decided to give a concentrated effort to *Self Analysis*. Every day I faithfully recorded my attitudes, anxieties, flare-ups, dreams, etc. I thought I was pretty ruthless at picking myself apart. I probed and delved, and ended up months later with a notebook full of repetitious descriptions, all of which thoroughly condemned me.

The key to improvement, I learned, lay in the requirement that one must have a 'serious incentive to change.' If one failed, it was because one 'refused' to change: 'I can't' meant 'I won't.' I was positive I had that 'serious incentive,' but beyond that, what one actually had to *do* to change was elusive. Knowing was not enough for me, nor was intense desire; neither of these wielded more power than the old habitual reactions. Every negative action amounted to a 'neurotic trend,' and the more I called myself names, the more hopeless I felt.

During this time, adding grist to my mill and proving I'd accomplished nothing, Neal went to San Francisco more often on one pretext or other. The family routine disintegrated. I never knew when he'd be home, meals went to waste, nights were spent in tossing and turning, listening to every car, and if he did come home the relief was quickly dispelled by my compulsive need to freeze him out, fuming in helpless, sleepless despair as I listened to his swaggering snores.

One afternoon Al Sublette came to visit between ships, and I was glad to see a friend I knew to be sympathetic to me. Neal arrived soon after, bringing the Fergusons, a couple I'd heard him mention. Although I had to scavenge an unanticipated dinner, I felt encouraged by his desire to show off his wife and share his friends with me. As it turned out, Neal seduced the wife in front of both me and her husband, then took her out to our car.

To cap it all, when I expressed my shock to Al, instead of offering consolation he snapped impatiently, 'Look, Carolyn, I'd think you'd be *used* to it by now!'

I could not have been more stunned had he hit me, and I fled to my room. '*Used* to it . . . *used* to it' wouldn't settle in my mind. Why *wasn't* I used to it? *Should* one get used to such things? Then another cog went *click*. How could it be that here was I, a blob of shaking jelly, every sense and sensibility outraged, yet—behold—no one else was the least bit ruffled? How could an event so earth-shattering to me be of no consequence whatever to anyone else? The puzzle flitted around in my brain; no tangible answer came—then a faint glimmering of something, a tiny crack of light in the fortress wall, playing peek-a-boo in my mind.

When I woke the next morning, Neal had not returned from taking Al and the couple back to San Francisco, and I dragged through my routine with the children. The feeling that I'd had a close encounter with a revelation of some kind persisted, and it modified my behavior somewhat. I even abandoned my usual attitude of sanctimonious pain and mute silence when Neal returned late in the afternoon.

I had been trying to interest Neal in my attempts at analysis and hoped to encourage him to join me. Sometimes he had listened politely, at others he had been flip or indifferent. In the past, an incident like that of the previous evening would have caused me to force a separation. This time, however, I tried to get Neal to talk it over calmly, pointing out that something must be done. What did he think? Would he consider returning to therapy?

'Sure, baby.' He was cold, his eyes hard. 'Here, take a drag off this and cheer up.' And he handed me half a joint, the tip brilliant with lipstick.

My attempt at poise shattered like a glass hit by a high note, and my defeat seemed complete. This was not like Neal; usually he showed signs of remorse, asked forgiveness. But after a few days of silence, he, too, must have felt confused and hopeless, because he did go back to the clinic. Again, however, hard results were not forthcoming; we lived on day by day, in a closed circle of habit.

Although Neal still couldn't stand with his heel on the ground, he could wear shoes comfortably enough to get around with almost his customary speed. Much to our joy and relief he found a job on a parking lot. His hours dependable again, the family routine was re-established. He was once more his kind and considerate self, and he revived his correspondence with Jack and Allen, more anxious than ever for them to visit.

Neal wrote explaining that, when he was called back to the railroad

225

after the first of the year, Jack could take over the parking lot until he too, was called back, at which time Allen could take over. He had it worked out very neatly, and it appealed to Jack and Allen, too.

After all these years Allen suddenly decided the time had come to leave New York and start his pilgrimage west. He wanted the journey to be all-encompassing and considered it of great significance, and his excitement was contagious, mirroring our own joy. Special delivery letters from him arrived every other day, the first written before he had heard the parking lot plan.

> I am leaving New York inside of a month . . . I will take my time getting there as I plan a long *trip* across continent . . . Jack's novel rejected, I think for good . . . Bill's *sublime* work on South America will never see the light under the present structure of publishing in New York. I am sick of staying here and *must* leave . . . for every reason, especially that I want to go where it is sunny and the child I am can be happy. Carolyn: From the enclosed note you see what I want to do. I hope it will be welcome to you—I feel very well and full of vigor and have a whole load of projects both for living and writing—and depend very much in the immediate future on your welcome and Neal's . . . Jack (now in better mood) is casting around for plans and wants to know 1) If he can work anywhere . . . 2) Do you still love him? . . . I am excited and collecting maps. I will ship a trunkful of clothes and books ahead of me, and papers—you can open and read what you want. IS YOUR INVITATION STILL GOOD?

Then, being Allen, he explained every thought process and every step he would take in disentangling himself from New York, and the financial picture before, during and after. He planned an extensive itinerary: Florida, Cuba, Yucatan and Mexico, stopping to look at ruins and archeological digs, jungles, cities, and then up the West Coast to us.

Soon we heard from Jack himself:

> The parking lot job sounds like it's made to order for this old philosopher. With a *guarantee* from you or Neal that it is there and not a changeable by-the-time-I-get-there deal. I am ready to take off at the first possible moment, which is the day after Xmas, by bus, arriving around Dec. 29 and ready to work and glad to be with my 2 buddies again for another New Year's Eve. As you know, Ginsberg won't get to San Jose till Feb. at the earliest. He has made the astounding discovery that the New World had a 'Greece & Rome' of its own & you can get there by 2nd class bus . . . Ample thoughts for a parking lot & chance to avoid an Eastern winter, and see my little Jami.

We both answered him, approving his plan. Neal wrote:

226

The parking lot is all ready for you to take over . . . when you feel good and ready to handle it, i.e., know all monthly parkers, how to set up lot each day, various ways of knocking down for at least lunch money—then you keep job until spring rush, then give job to brother Ginsberg . . . Be careful, forget God (no such thing), forget being farmer (far too late or soon), say Hello to your mother for me, bring all your books, ideas of life and any amount of oolong tea you find to bolster stock at hand for New Year's Eve party . . .

Allen sent us a final note at the time of his departure with explicit instructions on what to do with mail, packages, trunks, etc. The day after Christmas, however, we received a letter from Jack. He had learned he wouldn't get paid for his Christmas mail job until the first week in January, so he couldn't leave. 'So, Neal, here's how to take advantage of this shortage of money, lateness, hiking, etc.' and he outlined every inch of travel, by way of Mexico for tea, and counted on Neal sending him railroad passes from Nogales on.

'Well,' Neal sighed, 'here we go again. I can't get the jerk passes, he knows that. Lord knows when he'll get here now.'

We knew it wouldn't be for another three weeks at best, so we calmed down and waited. Now I was the one who was restless. I'd been deeply discouraged by having to abandon my hopes for psychology, though I continued to toy with the idea of returning to psychoanalysis myself. Each time I thought of it, the expense and the time involved depressed me further, and I couldn't rouse the courage to act.

I also felt vaguely that this was not the missing piece of the puzzle. It seemed to me that what Neal and I lacked most was a common belief in a set of absolute values. We couldn't agree on an authority we both respected. His study of philosophy had demolished his faith in the Church, and I had never had any—the Bible was Greek to me. Neither of us could make sense of the orthodox view of God—the bearded old man of rewards and vengeance. I felt paralyzed and resentful that everyone wasn't handed a set of instructions at birth. My parents thought they had supplied one, and Neal's Church thought it had taught him the way. But our experiences proved that both of these were unreliable maps. Ah, what to do? Neal listened to my woes and tried to cheer me up, but he couldn't help himself, let alone me.

Part II

Thirty-nine

One evening soon after New Year, 1954, Neal came home earlier than usual and in a strange mood, as though some secret joy exhilarated him. He glowed with attentiveness toward the children, and throughout dinner, smiled irrepressibly at me, less talkative than usual. I braced myself, afraid to ask the reason. He played with the children quietly while I washed the dishes, and when he had my full attention, he sat me down, went into the bedroom and came back with a book which he ceremoniously placed in my lap.

'Now, my dear, here's a book you have *got* to read before you do another thing. It is fan-tas-tic. I found it on one of the car seats, and I read the whole thing today. No, now, don't worry — I'll take it back. In fact, the woman said I could borrow it for you. You'll never believe how amazing . . . not to mention the *timing* of finding it . . . you may say it's coincidence, but you'll know better when you read . . .'

'What is it about?' I asked as I picked it up. The title was *Many Mansions* by Gina Cerminara, and the jacket said she had a PhD in psychology.

'I couldn't possibly tell you — you'll see — now you just get started and leave the kiddies and everything else to me.'

I was certainly intrigued, and I opened the book at the first chapter, entitled 'The Magnificent Possibility.' All evening Neal was gentler, more thoughtful, and every now and then he'd look to see how far I'd read. Though he was serious, he didn't stop smiling, his eyes shining.

231

The book's content was chiefly a documentary about a man named Edgar Cayce, who went to sleep and answered questions, at first about people's health problems, but later about anything. The most exciting information concerned the purpose of life and involved the theory of reincarnation. Since the author was a psychologist, she approached the subject from that point of view, thus tying in with but vastly expanding on my own recent studies.

For me it was as though the door I had been pounding on and pushing against for so long suddenly swung open and let in a blast of refreshing air and light. At almost every paragraph I found myself thinking, 'Why yes, that makes sense.' Here, at last, was hope, real hope, altogether new hope. Here was a thrilling but logical explanation for all our troubles, and already I felt our conflicts were on the way to resolution.

The philosophy was all so positive: self-condemnation was a primary sin, not a virtue. Yes, of course, I could see it all so clearly now. All that emphasis on the *wrong* I had been doing (to say nothing of Neal)—going over and over the negative actions—could only produce more of the same. I attracted them, asked for them by keeping them constantly in mind. 'Mind is the builder,' said Cayce's source. 'Thoughts are things. The mind is as concrete as a post or a tree'—and it is in every cell of our bodies. I'd been raised, as most of us are, to consider such a positive attitude 'unrealistic,' as just a way of kidding ourselves. Be prepared for the worst, and you won't be disappointed—that had been the lesson.

Neal was delighted that I was receptive to the ideas that came through Cayce. Oddly enough, both of us had accepted his clairvoyance easily, and at last we'd found a measuring rod we could both accept. Far into the night we were of one mind, shining our new light into all our dark places. For the first time, too, we got a handle on religion; all the old, hollow terms were suddenly filled with meaning. A few flickering questions now and again told us we still had a lot to learn, and we couldn't wait. We felt as though all the things we'd supposed impossible for us *could* be ours if we wanted them enough. 'With God all things are possible.' 'God,' Cayce's informant explained, is an ever-present impartial force, a force like electricity which, with our free will, we can use either for good or ill. Reincarnation as a means for evolution made perfect sense to us, and Neal's compassionate heart was eased by the possibility that all the handicapped in the world were not being unfairly punished but were strong enough to learn from their afflictions and provide lessons for others.

Sometimes we'd be thinking silently, then one of us would come forward to share another insight. I asked Neal whether he remembered when Johnny was a baby and had 'disappeared' for that two weeks. 'Do you suppose he was having second thoughts about choosing us as parents?'

'Dunno—maybe. It was after that sickening—and our only—fight.' Here Neal reached over to hug and kiss me, pleading forgiveness. 'But he musta known we didn't mean it and came back.'

'Reincarnation has to be the explanation of why you and I are together—a more unlikely couple would be hard to find. That certainly makes me feel better. But what must I have done to you to deserve this life? Something awful!'

'On the other hand, it could be that I did something awful to you and you didn't forgive me, so now I have to do more stuff so you'll learn forgiveness. I can't make it up to you if you still hold a grudge, see?'

'Ah, yes, I never thought of it that way. Karma? An eye for an eye, a tooth for a tooth?'

'No, no—that's the Old Testament way—where some of us still are, to be sure, but in the New Testament, Jesus demonstrated how to "fulfill" the law through love—he added the vibration of Love. You don't have to pay for a mistake in kind if you can learn better otherwise—that's grace.'

'Well, it's a sure thing we can't get away from each other until we do understand what we did wrong. This must be the life that we chose to clear it up. You remember that every time I thought I could break away, either I'd get pregnant—even though it seemed impossible—or the Welfare would turn me down for no reason?'

'And why didn't you ever get pregnant before? And why didn't LuAnne by me, but first thing when she married Murphy?'

'Oh—and Cathy! What bliss to think there's some genuine reason to explain our strange hostility. I've felt this deep resentment and defiance since she was born . . . I wonder what it could be . . .'

We were convinced we had found *the* road to salvation, and we could hardly wait to enlighten our friends and relieve them as well. Much to our amazement, neither the Forests nor the Hinkles seemed impressed. Dick and Marie made jokes about it, not ridiculing our sincerity but unable to see anything very significant in our new vision. The Hinkles listened, but they felt their own views adequate. Neither quite liked the idea of reincarnation. We found it puzzling that people who shared so many points of view with us could be so at variance in regard to such basic human truths that seemed obvious to us. Well, surely Jack and Allen would embrace our exciting solution to life, and we looked forward to discussing it with them.

January was nearly gone and still no Jack. We had assured Jami he'd be here for her birthday on the 26th, and she was disappointed. The next day we got his letter—from New York:

> . . . All this time paralyzed and unable to write, torn between decisions sometimes changing by the hour, but now your letter settles my mind as to terms of action. Forgive the annoying habit I have of causing worrying delays with my bouts of indecision. Will explain when I see you. I've been deeply sunk in thought . . . Am leaving day after tomorrow, Jan. 29. Expect me on the 5 a.m. Zipper, no later than Feb. 5th. Neal, I'll learn the lot in one day, so hold on.

Meanwhile, we received our first 'book' of a letter from Allen, written from Mérida in the Yucatan, where he had gone by plane from 'horrid Havana and more horrid Miami Beach.' His experiences had been far from the common tourist fare. Then a postcard from Jack in Mississippi assured us he was finally on the way, and on 5 February he arrived. At least he had made it for Neal's birthday, his 28th.

To our sorrow, Jack, like our other friends, not only failed to grasp and support our Cayce revelations, but had also simultaneously discovered his own solution to life's problems: Buddhism. This he had been anticipating sharing with us! Neal tried to explain to Jack how the original Hindu and Buddhist ideas of reincarnation fitted into the Judeo-Christian tradition (evidence of which had been deleted from the Bible at the 11th Ecumenical Council), but Jack interrupted irritably, 'Naw—I don't believe in that stuff. I warn't no dawg!'

'No, man,' Neal hopped about as he always did when excited and trying to make a point, 'that's not reincarnation, that's *transmigration* —a dumb mix-up of perverted Hinduism. You can't come back as an animal—you've evolved past that—you are a soul! What you don't understand is that man has evolved on this planet through *all* the kingdoms: mineral, vegetable, animal—consuming and incorporating the one before, each nourishing the one above, yet we're composed of them all. And we have to go on evolving beyond the human, as some have already. I, and some others I know, ahem, still have problems with the animal part—but you have to evolve spiritually first, then the physical form follows. It's so beautifully simple, see?'

'Animals are living sentient beings, m'boy. Don't you speak of them in that tone. And don't let me catch you swatting any more flies, y'hear?' Jack was bellowing; he hadn't absorbed a word.

Neal put on a demeanor of utmost patience. 'Certainly they are—so are plants and minerals—the Life Force in them and in us is the same force—but the *soul*, man—the individual, unique *soul*. Most animals have group souls, but you *are* a soul, you just *occupy* a body. The identity you've built from dozens of lives or experiences in this solar system . . . on different dimensions, even, making it or blowing it . . . "What you sow, you reap." "God is not mocked." ' And Neal stood with his forefinger raised, gazing upward.

'Bah! All life is suffering and pain. The cause is *desire!*'—Jack emphasized the word sinisterly—'and the way of salvation is the Eightfold Path. The world is illusion, emptiness . . . nothingness. Nuthin' means nuthin', period.' He sank back in his chair scowling.

It would appear we had a schism. Each of us found it hard to understand and difficult to accept. Up to now, we had all felt so close in every way. As the weeks went by we tried with extra concern to listen to each other's views, to understand and yet to sway, in a vain attempt to mend the rift. Instead, in the end, we had to concede sadly that in the realm of theory we marched to different drums. This made it seem even more miraculous that Neal and I, rather than Jack and Neal, had agreed so readily in the first place.

Neal and I still had to learn to accept, however, that this new basis for agreement would not transform our lives overnight. The deep grooves worn by our habitual emotions and attitudes were not re-routed by intellectual enlightenment. The daily frustrations continued. An entry in my journal a few days after Jack's arrival reads:

Jack here, and Neal and I edgy again. Neal is amorous but willing to disparage each of us in the other's eyes. I'm moody and resentful more. Got mad at Neal for lying about the Fergusons again, and because he put up the big nude poster in Jack's room, not thinking of the children first. I don't want Jack to hear us fight as of old, yet think it hard for him to watch us being loving. Neal has been better in some ways, though, and Jack is helping Neal to sidestep me again, probably to reinforce the shaky friendship. Maybe it's not good to have this three-way play against each other, because we want each other and each resents the third.

It was going to take a lot of work and much greater understanding for our new insights to become of practical use to us. At least, however, it was a beginning, and neither Neal nor I doubted the potential, nor could we choose but to go on with it.

Meanwhile tensions grew with Jack. This time he was the one isolated from the magic circle. Also, he was not learning to handle the parking lot in the swift way demanded by Neal, and the railroad had not yet called him back. When Jack attempted to extend more warmth to me, Neal cooled. Jack couldn't play this game for long, and soon the private grumblings of the two men rumbled like dormant volcanos, every now and then bursting forth with little spurts of fire. Once more Neal vented his irritation in oblique cracks about Jack's presence as a freeloader on the family, again forgetting it had been his own idea, and Jack's hypersensitivity and paranoia reacted instantly to an exaggerated degree. One night at dinner Neal referred to the pork chops *he* had provided, and Jack got up from the table, vowing he would go out the very next day and buy himself a hot-plate, put it in his room, buy his own food and eat alone henceforth.

I watched and listened in melancholy disbelief, as I'd done in October of '52, still no closer to finding ways to help. They, too, fought against the trend, one day sentimental brothers, the next snarling pups.

The break finally came over a disagreement in the division of a batch of tea, and Jack decided to go home. We tried to persuade him to stay and wait for Allen, suggesting that a fourth person might square the triangle, but he would neither be deterred nor comforted. He left a week before my birthday near the end of April and a few days later we got a note:

> Hey. Please send my mail on, I finally got home in one piece, quite starved and the better for it; hunger makes you angry; anger makes you understand yourself, etc. Ha. I hope you got yr money by now, whatever it is, and all yr ideas about karma come true; personally I don't believe in karma; and just found out I'd made a dreadful mistake thinking Emptiness had preceded the Now World; a big mistake; it's not that the world is 'empty' but, that you say about it, it neither Is, or, IS NOT, but merely a manifestation of mind, the reflection of the moon on a lake; so the next porkchop you eat, remember, it's merely a porkchop reflected off water, and your hunger, and you the hungerer, Narcissus you—but for purposes of this world, I say let the wine and porkchops flow anything to put us asleep, or put ME asleep leastways Who me? Who you? Who you ever be who ever I be send what ever is Someone may try to tell me something, maybe, and I want to see.

Not only did he not begin with a salutation of love, he signed it only 'J.' A small postscript said, 'How unreal.'

Neal sighed and tossed the letter back to me after he'd read it. 'Well, I *personally* think the crux of brother Jack's trouble is that wish to just go to sleep—that's where he's *really* at.'

' "To sleep, perchance to dream," ' I added sadly.

Forty

If Neal hadn't made a habit of reading every printed word in the newspapers, he would have missed the almost hidden advertisement for a series of lectures by Edgar Cayce's son, Hugh Lynn, to be held under the auspices of the recently formed A.R.E., the organization founded to preserve the 'readings.'

After the discovery of *Many Mansions*, this was the second catalyst to the profound changes that were taking place in our lives. 'When the chela is ready, the guru appears' say the Buddhists.

We embarked on our quest for knowledge and spiritual growth with this conference and our subsequent counseling with Hugh Lynn and his associate, Elsie Sechrist, both during their annual programs in San Jose and by post. In addition, we joined the A.R.E. and for many years were nourished monthly by the readings and other publications. We joined a number of study groups and worked hard to master the alien activities of prayer and meditation, now revealed to hold a previously unsuspected meaning and power.

Before, neither of us had considered investigations into realms of knowledge other than the physical sciences and philosophy. Now new and complex worlds opened before us that took a good deal of sorting and evaluating. Along the way we learned the awesome power of the mind. Later on I took one of the courses in mind-control myself and saw it as a revelation, until the final exam convinced me I was not ready to handle that force to that degree.

Luckily Neal and I accepted and rejected the same information, on the whole. Some of it we considered possible and were inclined to believe, some we were undecided about, and some we rejected. These categories were to shift and change continually for the rest of our lives. For us, the object was always to find a concept that was of practical use in our daily existence—it was far too tempting to be swept into phantasmagorical realms that served no immediate purpose. The first great joyous revelation had been that life—all life—is purposeful. That we believed wholeheartedly. One had to keep asking, 'But what is that knowledge *for*? What use will that power be put to?' Even Cayce's source had said it was not enough to be 'good;' one had to be good *for* something.

Allen's trunks and books had arrived, and we stored them in the room Jack had vacated. Another long letter told us that Allen had met a legendary woman who had grown up in the Palenque area and owned a huge cocoa plantation where he was staying, and he wasn't sure when he would leave. He was immersed in the delights of the jungle and developing a new self-image with a goatee and 'moustachio,' long hair, heavy shoes: 'ride horses, go fishing at nite in streams with natives giggling with *focos* [flashlights] & long stick with prongs to catch crawfishes size of lobsters.' He had found a set of drums, and played 'several hours daily, mostly very soft listening, and when a file of Indians ride in thru the trails from Aqua Azul eden-like little town in hills an hour ride away, I break out in african reverberations which can be heard for miles around.'

In his bizarre paradise Allen had also been introduced to the possibilities inherent in meditation and the contemplative life, via a book called *The Cloud of Unknowing*.

. . . Time spent here has been mainly contemplative of this fixed idea, and I had one day of excited agitation, thinking I should go be a monk, but no need to do that, can develop anywhere and such agitations are passing. What hung me on *Cloud of Un*. was the lovely and obviously true idea that a contemplative doesn't have to do anything but what he feels like, sit and think or walk and think, don't worry about work, life, money, no hangups, his job is to have no job but the unknown Abstraction and its sensations & his love of it.

'Ha, yaah,' Neal laughed, 'that sounds like every man's wish fulfilled.'

Then Allen wrote, 'Forgive me not answering your letter about

238

spiritualism sooner,' and we bristled—'spiritualism' we understood to mean communication with the dead via seances and mediums, which we couldn't accept, feeling that Edgar Cayce's clairvoyance was in another vein altogether. But Allen did say 'that Neal is religious is a great piece of news: I always wondered what he would be like with some overpowering Awful thought humbling his soul to saintliness.'

After a lengthy letter written the first week of April 1954, we didn't hear from Allen for over a month. We became uneasy and I wrote to Jack, thinking he might have heard something. He answered at once:

> . . . he may be on purpose being silent and mysterious, bet you $10 that's what it is. There's no danger in Mexico so much. Besides, I think Allen is already back in New York, hiding, I saw him on the corner the other night; I was very drunk, yelled out 'Allen!' He was standing in beat coat, tanned, tangled-haired, mad looking, and just stared back at me like flipped Village intellectual . . . I wouldn't be surprised if it was Allen. I wouldn't be surprised too if he'd gone mad finally, like his mother, I expect that someday, definitely.

Jack was with his mother at his sister's home in North Carolina. He still sounded bitter and angry for the most part, but said he was glad to hear from us:

> . . . I see all the mistakes I made, all the mistakes you and Neal made, I recognize once more as on that brilliant, radiant sympathetic, sinless original night when I arrived remember on the freight train and we drank beer and argued the dharma, realize once more, we're all the same, we three, and for us to fight is as silly as can be. Everybody is the same; I never hit a girl but I might have done in previous lives. But now I don't think I'll ever return to California, so won't see you for ages, unless some crazy ride in cars is proposed by someone around here . . .

If nothing else is sure in this world, I thought, one can always count on Jack's ambiguity. He sent pages of single-spaced typing, extolling Buddhist doctrine and criticizing Cayce, whose teachings he misunderstood. He had been collecting railroad unemployment, but decided not to bother:

> . . . and in my deep mind, I see no reason to even say anything and for that matter to even collect said checks and no reason to live because life is not worth living . . . yet you've got to get your food every day at least and worry about your close ones—compassion. But now let me tell you how I think now. If, for instance, you and I do meet some day in the future, it won't be you, or I, but someone like you, and someone like me drawn

239

together for the same reasons. I think that's what Buddha means when he says 'I was that deer' or 'I was that prince countless kalpas ago,' he means as we'd say, for instance, in *Brother Karamazov* I am Alyosha and you are Katerina Ivanovna . . . assigning roles . . . The greatest things you've told me devolved from the times you spoke of Horney and said in effect, 'There is no need to grasp or reject, but take what's given you,' then you can live, do anything you want, so long as you don't grab, or turn down, anything, but understand it, you said in Horney sense something, my sense is: a dream, relax from the dream . . . Let me know about the little ones who know that God is Pooh-Bear and that the rainbow went in the water . . . May be vajra raja enlightening diamond radiate beams upon your house and remember to have a big spacy backyard for old Jack who may yet pitch a shack back yonder and grow latelife beans and grapevine . . . All my love, Jack

If I had said anything like that derived from Horney, I couldn't remember it. Poor Jack, he seemed to be grasping all right, but for oblivion.

Forty-one

Earlier in March 1954, the date for the trial had finally arrived—eleven months after Neal's accident. The trial lasted for days, and when I was requested to attend with the children to add weight to our plea, I was appalled at the performance which everyone else seemed to accept as usual court behavior. It appeared to me to be no more than a sparring match between the two lawyers as they attempted to influence the jury by discrediting each other. By the time they had quibbled, hashed and re-hashed the accident, no one had any idea what had really happened, including Neal, who was now so confused he contradicted his original statement.

His recovery did seem a miracle, and the Southern Pacific doctors, in describing the injury, turned out to be the best witnesses for our case. Neal himself, however, was so determined not to be handicapped that he refused to limp, and our lawyer exclaimed, 'Jesus, Neal, that's the least you could do!'

In the end we were awarded about one third of the original estimate, and when the lawyer had subtracted his fee and our expenses we received $16,000. It was tax-free, and we felt rich. We were told it would take a little while to get the check (and it did—two months), but it was over at last, and now Neal could return to work on the railroad.

So we turned our attention to the piles of mail and incessant telephone calls that resulted from the publicity in the papers—

exaggerated out of all proportion—about our settlement. Like a pack of hounds, dozens of people had their own ideas as to what we should do with the money, an unpleasant consequence of our good fortune. In May the check arrived, and this and the Cayce books kept our relationship on an even keel.

Then we got a letter addressed in Allen's familiar scrawl. It was another adventure-packed chronicle. He said he was okay; he had been at Xbalba—'pronounced—dig sound—Chivalva'—for a month, penniless, so he hadn't been able to get to town to send word. '. . . What unluck Jack is gone; I delayed too long . . . but it will be sweet to see you at the end.'

Upon Allen's arrival in San Jose I was extremely nervous in his presence, despite our correspondence. Seven years had elapsed since I'd seen him, and I still feared he didn't really like me. He looked much the same; more mature perhaps, but he had shaved his goatee, so he still had the same eager and youthful appearance, and very soon he put me completely at ease.

He arrived in the early afternoon and hastily stowed his gear, eager to open his trunk and show us the goodies we'd been waiting for him to present. He had notebooks full of poetry and photographs of everyone in New York, and he had brought me some masks and figurines carved from a soft white wood, and two colorful woven bags from the Yucatan and Guatamala. There was so much he wanted to tell and talk about, he hardly knew where to begin. When the children got up from their naps he turned his attention to them, to the house and yard, and asked us about Jack and ourselves. I got ready to go to the store, but he jumped up and stopped me.

'No, now wait. I'll show you I am the world's most perfect guest. Just you let me take care of all that. We'll have one of my culinary masterpieces,' and he asked Neal if he'd lead him to the local food emporium.

He was as good as his word, operating in the kitchen like a master chef and producing a delicious meal. Afterward, though he protested, I insisted he go talk to Neal and leave the dishes to me; even then he hung about, helping me clear the table, until I promised he could do the dishes the next day but *not* on his first night with Neal.

When the children had been bathed and read to and tucked into bed, I joined Neal and Allen in the living room. We demanded to know all about the plantation, the ruins and the mysterious mountain he'd written about.

'Yeah, and what about that broad in the jungle, hey?' Neal insinuated with eyebrow action à *la* Groucho Marx, puffing his cigarette like a cigar.

Allen grinned at him, then became serious and told his strange and exotic tale. 'And,' he said, 'I took a lot of pictures—you'll have to tell me how to get them developed. I'll remember more when I get them back. Now then, tomorrow, if it's all right with you, I want to sort my manuscripts . . . you still have the tape recorder? Good. I'd like very much to do some recording—read my poems aloud, you know. I've never *heard* them—great kicks—poetry is supposed to be *spoken*, you know.' He rubbed his hands together in anticipation, grinning, his black eyes sparkling.

Neal was busier on the railroad now, and Allen and I spent a lot of time together. Sometimes he wrote or recorded, and unless he asked me to listen, which he often did, I'd leave him alone and keep the children from disturbing him. Part of every day he spent with them and with me, and he was more considerate, aware, patient and kind than anyone I'd ever known besides Neal. He filled each day with a variety of enthusiasms, always stimulating and amusing, and like me he enjoyed sharing; I was never bored or lonely. Once in awhile we'd go to a movie in the evening; it was almost like having a 'date' again, and afterwards we'd sit at a café counter drinking cokes and bringing our superior critical intellects to bear on every facet of the film we'd seen.

Although I had only a hazy idea of the marketplace, I was hoping we could build our own home now, and I'd drawn detailed plans for it. Every time I'd get the urge to hunt for a lot, Allen would come along and tramp all over, as intently involved as if it were part of his own dream, too.

When Neal was home, we'd bombard Allen with our new interest in Cayce, and he would listen respectfully. Like our other friends, he wasn't convinced that it would solve all the world's problems, but he didn't bring us down. And like Jack he didn't like the idea of having to come back again and again: 'This life is enough—all I can stand, and anyway, I'd probably just sit around and do nothing if I thought it was a never-ending process. Why try?' Neal gave him a lengthy explanation of soul evolution as the catalyst for physical, but Allen was not sold, and again like Jack was unable to separate the Christian metaphysic from the theological dogma.

One evening Allen accompanied me to a lecture on hypnotism and trance. Neither of us was too impressed; somehow the speaker made me uncomfortable. When it was over and we were outside, I was approached by an investment broker who had made a bid for our settlement money and who had revealed an interest in Cayce, thereby securing an afternoon with Neal. I introduced him to Allen, but the man wanted to talk to me: 'Listen . . . that hypnotist could really help Neal. Let me make an appointment for him . . . the man's a Kahuna . . . you know, the ancient Hawaiian high priests—or he was in his last life and remembers all of it now . . . there aren't very many of them left.' He hardly paused for breath, but from the fanatical way he spoke, the flesh was crawling on my back. I thanked him for the offer but said I'd have to talk it over with Neal. He invited Allen and me to the hypnotist's home in Sunnyvale, and out of curiosity Allen agreed to go. Once there, we became no more enthusiastic than we had been before. Everyone was more interested in such occult phenomena as pendulums and ouija boards than in a philosophy to live by. We extricated ourselves as soon as possible, and discussed the affair on the way home; we'd had something of a lark, but we both felt those were muddy waters one should be wary of. When we related our adventure to Neal, he was glad to forgo the 'cure.'

We often talked of Jack, and I had written to let him know we were all thinking of him and wishing he were with us. He answered:

> . . . Just got your nice little letter and welcomed it dearly. I just sent Allen (and Neal) a huge letter in a big manila envelope and it should get there about the same time as this. So this will be YOUR letter and they have theirs. Incidentally, don't get mad at me for anything in their letter, re: gals, etc. After reading the Diamond Sutra . . . it seems I've been loosening my grip on Virtue and being just a common good old pot . . . I want to go back to California this September if Allen is still there and my God if Burroughs goes there I'm sure to come on the fly. Wouldn't it be wonderful for Neal, Allen, Bill and me and you to be all together talking at night; Bill and me with our wine, Allen with his upheld index finger, Neal with his oolong, and you with your pizza pies . . . and wine. I want to work on the SP for another crack, for poetical reasons now . . . I know you'll be mad at me for suggesting to him that he take a trip in his red and black boat [our new Rambler station wagon] but God, what's a red n black boat for, and a driver like Neal and lonesome American roads? Well, get mad, you've gotten mad befo . . . Get an old farmhouse in the valley please— You never 'irritate' me, as you say. You are a golden angel and I'll always love you as I have and will. Everybody write me at length! Tell Jami I said 'Hello, Jami!!!' Where's Al Sublette?

At least he didn't seem to resent not being with us; he said Buddha had convinced him that none of us was real anyway—only 'ripples,' as Einstein had proved 'mathematically'!

Forty-two

Appreciating Allen's company as I did, and knowing that his prime reason for being with us was to see Neal, I did my best to make myself scarce whenever Neal was home and able to spend some time with Allen. Although Neal liked to take Allen off to San Francisco to show him his kicks, he also enjoyed reading Allen's poems and having intellectual discussions as they had had in the past.

Allen had hesitated to show me a notebook full of love poems to Neal, but I thought them beautiful and felt no threat, trusting what he had written some years before about having overcome his sexual desire for Neal. I knew 'The Green Automobile' was a poem about their earlier love, and I knew how much it meant to Allen. When he could count on using the tape recorder undisturbed, he'd record himself reading it, and he must have done so a dozen times. He and Neal got high occasionally and made tapes of Allen's new drumming techniques with Neal on the recorder, thereby catching up somewhat with the joys Jack and Neal had described in San Francisco.

As the perfect guest, Allen got along well with the Forests, and we saw a lot of the Hinkles, once or twice having funny, wild card parties together. Allen had come to dislike clothing, and although he was discreet when anyone was around, if he were sufficiently high and it would embarrass no one, he'd doff the lot—usually after dark, and with the house lights off. One hot night after I'd consumed quite a bit of wine, he persuaded me to join him. It was extremely difficult for me to shed my self-consciousness, and truthfully I am always more comfortable with some bodily wrapping, but my curiosity got the better of me again, and I finally gave in. We lay about a foot or two apart on the rug in the living room like a couple of innocent children, enjoying the sensual soft breeze that floated through the French doors and windows open to the starry summer night, the moonlight laying cool white banners across the floor. Allen bellowed poem after poem to infinity, and I found myself relaxing in the safety of being with a man intent only on his own body, not mine.

Allen must have been with us about six weeks when one afternoon our idyllic life came to a shattering end. Neal and Allen had been in the latter's room for some time. I had a question to ask Neal, so I tapped on the door as a matter of courtesy and, not waiting for an answer, opened it and walked in. The question stuck in my throat at what I saw before me. The force of the shock nearly knocked my head off, or so it felt. I backed out and shut the door, my insides turning sickening cartwheels. In that brief instant the picture registered *in toto*. Allen had lifted his head toward me quizzically, but I was gone — to tremble, pace, cry to heaven, wring my hands and fight down the revulsion that threatened to turn me inside out.

By the time they'd put on their pants and come out, I was sitting miserably on the edge of the couch, staring at the floor and trying to figure myself out. Neal went into the bathroom, but Allen calmly sat down in the armchair opposite me. It was my move.

'Allen . . . I just don't know what to say . . . I'm so *sorry*. I just don't really understand myself. You know I don't have any prejudice . . . well, you see, it's no different than if you were a *woman* guest in our home . . . you understand? I'd be pretty shook if I found her . . . well . . . I know you love Neal, but I thought you'd resolved the sex part . . . I mean . . . Oh, I don't know. I'm just afraid I couldn't stand it. I just want you to leave.'

'That's okay. I understand.' He sighed and said no more. I felt terrible. After all our lovely times together. I must appear a proper bigoted bitch, I thought, but I couldn't seem to help it.

'I'll be glad to pay your way anywhere you want to go, Allen. I'll help all I can, but you will have to go . . . as soon as possible.'

I just wanted to go on saying 'I'm sorry, I'm sorry' but the knowledge was too strong, and I knew it was useless for me even to try. I'd be frightened, jealous, suspicious all the time.

When Neal had to appear at last, he said nothing at all. Later, alone together, I said, 'How *could* you? Right here in our home?' It was my standard response, and a question that never received an answer. The only possible answer was one I wouldn't want to face. Feeling stupid and miserable I went on with my duties during the next day or so while Allen solemnly considered where to go, being himself gently compliant and sad. He had an uncle in Riverside, a city southeast of Los Angeles, and he thought about visiting him, but it wouldn't be a permanent solution. In the end he decided on San Francisco, and I was disappointed, knowing how handy that would be for Neal when he wanted to get away from me. I'd provided him with the perfect alternative. But I could hardly make any more demands on Allen, and my heart sank. I wanted to cry, watching him pack up his treasures, his books, notebooks and clothes. What a rotten ending. What was the matter with me? How could I get such a violent reaction to something I'd accepted long ago? I had always championed homosexuals—in fact, I was forever pointing out that so many great men of history with superior creative talents had been homosexual, and how much they had enriched our world. But, of course, that wasn't it.

The next week I drove Allen to the city, where he could visit old friends and make inquiries about Berkeley and the University of California. On the way I apologized and begged his pardon a dozen different ways. He was kind and understanding, but I wondered what inner turmoils he was surmounting. As he got out of the car, he kissed me, told me not to worry and said he'd keep in touch. I drove home in a lonely blue funk, trying to forgive myself. If only he and Neal had been more careful or gone somewhere else . . . this time I would rather have been deceived if it had meant our good times could continue.

I didn't expect Neal to be mad at me, and he wasn't. Seeing me so distressed, he took my part, apologized, maligned himself and begged my forgiveness.

Once more I turned to Jack, hoping to find some comfort from the absent friend. I poured out the whole story, condemning myself and feeling sure Jack would think me far too prudish. However, true to his good-hearted nature, he didn't let me down and answered immediately:

Dear Car—Just a note to send right on and reassure you that I'm not mad bout your throwing Allen out, in fact, I expected it—or that is, not surprised at all. You threw me out once, remember? 1949 summer? . . . Poor Neal needs love more than anybody else, try to give it to him . . . Don't worry about Allen—Allen and Neal are old buddies and hit the road together and seen visions together; don't be harsh with our Prophets, Miss Virago—as for me—'It's not my line,' as Céline said in Africa . . . Really surprised to hear you say you pray—but it's always the women end up

247

praying—my mother prays—I fly into a rage at the mere suggestion that I pray . . .

He continued his lengthy consolation far beyond my expectations. He said that Allen hadn't written anything about the incident; Jack didn't think his anger would be anything other than standard criticism of American puritanical, matriarchal, etc. repression and squareness, 'like I can hear him and Bill talking about it already.' He wrote that Bill prided himself on being disliked intensely by all his friends' women, including both of Jack's wives and his mother and thousands of his college friends' mothers and girlfriends, and that Lucien's wife had thrown him out, so I would be added to the standard wild stories about the adventures of the generation and 'the time Carolyn got mad'—'but don't stay mad, be glad . . . Allen is alright. If he has eyes for what he had eyes for, that I am not responsible for, till I speak to him; but I'm sure it's the wrong thing to do . . . Tell Allen to be Myshkin to Neal's Rogozin, not Edouard to Neal's poor Bernard.'

Jack rambled on about the railroad and about what he was writing—a science-fiction book—as well as his expectation of finishing before the New Year the

grand *On the Road*, the plot of which I been workin on since 1948—all the long W.C. Fields road—with all of us fictionalized . . . Why do I write like this? Seems like one time I heard you say the phrase 'write yourself to death' to Neal, and I thought then, paranoiacally, you were warning him against following my example just to make good as a writer. Well, I do feel like I'm writing myself to death . . .

He also covered his latest Buddhist visions, his ups and downs emotionally, but he kept coming back to my problem, and then related Neal's mind to Buddhist concepts.

As usual, I read the letter aloud to Neal. Putting it down, I said, 'Well, at least it's good he's still excited about writing new works . . . but I still think Cayce could help him more in his search for "What to do?" '

Neal sighed. 'Yeah, if he'd only listen—he'd understand if he wanted to. But no, he's hung up on all his long names and sweet silence.' Here, I thought, might be a clue to why Jack was so drawn to Buddhism and Neal to metaphysics. He felt a need for a demonstrable means of change here and now, whereas Jack, weaver of words, was enthralled by the colorful tapestry in the Sutras, and perhaps also their remoteness took him out of this world. Yet I couldn't see how it

248

was helping him avoid pain and suffering, although it probably added a dimension to his imagination. He was the dreamer, the be-er, the Yin, Neal the do-er, the Yang. It may have had something to do with their attraction to one another. At any rate, Jack's compassion always helped to relieve my suffering, if only temporarily.

Forty-three

In August of 1954 all anxieties were displaced by my discovery of a house near Los Gatos, about ten miles southwest of San Jose at the foot of the ever-green Santa Cruz mountains and twenty miles from the ocean. The house was on a short dead-end street in the middle of prune orchards, with only a few scattered neighbors, yet only a mile from Los Gatos village. There was even a small swimming pool set in the flower-filled patio, and through the picture window in the living room we could gaze across the lawn to the beautiful green and bronze mountain that rose beyond the orchard and the eucalyptus trees across the road. Behind the house stretched a third of an acre, still supporting a few prune trees. I fell in love with the place on sight, my only worry being its ten-mile distance from the S.P. yard office and depot, but Neal scoffed at such trivia, welcoming the challenge.

Of course the first expenditure of the settlement money had been to buy the 'black and red boat' Jack had mentioned, but this time for cash. We had sent Diana $1,000, and now we split the rest of the money between investments and the down-payment on the house. We hadn't found the old farmhouse Jack had wanted (much as I'd have loved that, too), but as usual Jack's dreams were incompatible with Neal's job. I felt at home at last; Neal had never had a home, and I thought the joys of owning and maintaining his own might overcome his restlessness. I was sure it would work wonders for my disposition as well.

As soon as I'd found the house, even before we could move in, I'd hurried to write to Jack about it. He answered:

> . . . I wish you could send me a complete description of your new house, of location, how big the yard, how much it cost, etc. Los Gatos is well known in New York among the friends at Columbia I had, many of them had lived there, and I'm sure Katherine Windsor had an estate at Los Gatos — strangely, in my novel of last summer about the colored girl, I used Los Gatos as the place where we weekended. Tell me about the house. Tell me about the kids.

Writing back, I described the property in the minute detail he liked, suggesting it might be John Steinbeck he had heard owned a home near Los Gatos. Then it struck me like a thunderbolt that I had completely forgotten to consider a place for Jack to stay! There was no guest room. I felt like a traitor, but Neal soothed me by suggesting maybe we could find — or Jack could — an inexpensive house-trailer to put in the back yard. 'He'd like that even better.'

We now had our first television set, and it was fun to watch almost anything with Neal — he was interested in so many subjects. He enjoyed my favorites such as *Omnibus* and *The Play of the Week*, British movies and documentaries, but he enlarged my field with the faith healer Oral Roberts and other shows I'd never have thought to watch. During the week the whole family gathered for *Our Miss Brooks*, *Car 54*, *Ensign O'Toole*, *I Love Lucy*, *My Little Margie*, *Leave It to Beaver*, and any suitable documentaries before the children's bedtime. Sports events I generally left to Neal. When he was alone he switched channels continually, taking in the full gamut of broadcasts all at once, a practice I found disconcerting but amusing. And late on Sunday nights he loved to watch the girls on *Roller Derby*; at first I thought we'd have to move the set out of the bedroom, but after he'd gentled me into watching, I found it fascinating in its absurdity and a great treat to lie in bed with Neal and laugh at the hysterical shenanigans of our favorite girls. We still had our exciting discussions far into the night, now fired with new fuel by our studies of the occult world.

To decorate our walls I painted portraits of the children, and from then on I had occasional commissions from surrounding families or their friends. I entered the girls in the Los Gatos ballet school, and by the end of that year I had become responsible for the costumes for their bi-annual productions. My life and sense of usefulness blossomed and I became less picky about trivial matters with the children. Neal's erratic schedule gave him time with them after school, to play ball or cavort in the pool. He showed keen interest in the girls' dance lessons, and frequently amused us with his attempts to achieve one of his idiosyncratic ambitions, trying to hold onto one foot and jump over it with the other. If the children weren't home he slept or bathed, the latter becoming a source of wonder to us all. He'd lie in the bathtub reading a magazine, adding more hot water from time to time by turning on the faucet with his toes; but when the tub was full he'd be too cold to wash so would have to go to the other bathroom to take a shower to get clean.

That first year may have held some of Neal's happiest times, as well as mine. He was proud of his home, and although not accustomed to looking after one as the men in my family had been, he tried to help out to the best of his ability. He enjoyed planting trees and shrubs, but when it came to carpentry he was inept, and his rage and self-condemnation were unmerciful if he bungled a job. There still remains a fence post bristling with a dozen or so nails, when two or three were all that were needed. So I learned not to ask more than I felt he could handle competently; to see his pride and self-esteem bloom was a pleasure worth the sacrifice.

Neal was popular with everyone in the Cayce study groups, and no one guessed his past. I'd always found him perfectly capable of mingling with any social 'class.' At home, we adopted religious practices, long familiar but never understood until now, such as grace before meals, and bedtime prayers. For the latter Neal would sit on Johnny's bed after the stories were read, the girls on either side and I on the floor leaning against his knees, all of us touching. We'd say the Lord's Prayer aloud together, following Cayce's explanation of its relationship to the endocrine glands and chakras.

Often Neal would answer a query from one of the children with a long, excited discourse on the Cayce revelations. Many times he'd become carried away in his zeal, and I doubted they were understanding a tenth of what he said, but his interest, attention and concern for them registered deeply — and perhaps some of the message was assimilated subliminally. Once or twice Johnny startled us by adding comments that were beyond what Neal had been saying, and it gave us an eerie feeling; in later years we came to believe that two of the children were more evolved than we and had come to us to help us along. 'You get to Heaven leaning on the arm of someone you have helped,' said Cayce. At least Neal didn't talk to the children about ectoplasm or materializations or amortizing or astral planes.

When he and I settled down to our adult evenings together, our feelings toward each other had invariably been lifted and cemented. Even on those occasions when I might be nursing some complaint against him and he was feeling rotten, we would not allow our emotional strain to interfere with the children's bedtime ritual of reverence and excitement. A truce was always established until we could be alone and the doors firmly closed to the back of the house.

Another factor may have contributed to Neal's apparent contentment. As I had feared, with Allen in San Francisco, he had an anchor at that end of the line. He had enough seniority now to keep a regular passenger run, which often meant taking a commuter train from San Jose to San Francisco in the early morning and having all day free in the city before bringing another train back in the evening—a perfect job for Neal. He made new friends with artists, poets and would-bes, and it was difficult to assess where his primary allegiance lay. His home life was an oasis of strength and contributed to a self-image of respectability which reassured him, but that made it even easier for him to indulge in his personal proclivities at the other end of the line. The double life was convenient and fairly well balanced as to time, and only rarely did the two conflict. However, less troubled now by guilt, Neal began to relax the boundaries, forgetting that my hopes remained fixed on a conventional family.

Another source of increasing anxiety was the change wrought in Neal's personality when he was high on marijuana, and he used it at home more and more. I resented him for not being himself, the difference being strong enough to make me worry lest the children notice. By now, he'd been using marijuana for so long that it was extremely hard for him to stop, and often when he'd try he'd be so irritable and edgy with me, I felt like withdrawing my objections.

Allen was living in a hotel with a new love, Peter Orlovsky, and Neal became part of their group of friends, even beginning to return to San Francisco in the evenings to be with them. He told me about some of their activities, sticking to the safe subjects such as their intense literary and artistic discussions or his talk in favor of Cayce, which earned him the nickname 'The Preacher.' One day when I was in San Francisco, Neal took me to see a huge mural which Bob LaVigne was painting. In the center of the painting was the image of a seated red-haired nude, a girl named Natalie Jackson. Neal introduced me to Bob but not to the model; nor did he tell me she and he had fallen deeply in love.

Judging only from what I knew, Neal's pleasures sounded innocent enough, but his secrecy and evasion increased after he had met Natalie, as did his time away from home. Weekends became our only reliable time together. My suspicions mounted, and they were often far from pleasant; small wonder Neal preferred the other end of the line. He made one thought-provoking statement: 'Why should I want to come home to that long face?' Our only remaining close points of contact were our monthly metaphysical discussions when the Cayce material arrived, and time spent with the children, but my delight at such times only seemed to emphasize their rarity.

By myself I studied and tried to learn meditation and positive prayer. Tiny revelations and successes began to occur, although they sounded ridiculous in the telling, but insignificant though the results may have appeared they were tangible evidence and nourished my fragile faith, helping me keep up my efforts.

I began to dread Neal's comings and goings and the need I felt to complain of his neglect. 'Loving indifference' was the ideal attitude according to Cayce, and although I liked it better than the 'detachment' of Buddhism and understood it better than the 'choiceless awareness' of Krishnamurti, I couldn't see how I could ever achieve it. The deeper and symbolic meanings of the Bible were being revealed to us, and gradually we developed what is called 'practicing the presence'—that is, a constant awareness of a higher, ever-present power. Phrases from the Bible or Cayce, some symbolizing natural 'laws', would pop into our heads when relevant to some incident in our daily lives. Whereas once we had squirmed at such quotes we found now a sort of game that delighted us. For instance, I recalled noticing that when Neal came home, no matter when, the children always greeted him with open arms and were happy just to see him, not asking where he'd been or what he'd been doing. This time 'Be as a little child' came to mind. But I still didn't know how to function without taking on the mother-warden role. Cayce said the three dimensions were Time, Space and Patience. Well, patience was a virtue I had a lot of opportunities to cultivate.

To make matters worse, Neal received a long letter from Jack, sent to the yard office, and seeing nothing to hide he left it for me to read. Jack seemed to want to return to their former close relationship, which I could understand, but his motive made me feel even more abandoned. He began: 'Dear Buddy: Please don't go thinking "Here's old shittypants Kerouac again coming on with the buddy-buddy talk now that he's been away from me long enough to have gotten over his latest imaginary peeve," etc.' Then he described things he'd been doing which were particularly enjoyable to Neal, and continued:

> . . . so you see what kicks we could have if you were here . . . that's why I'm writing this letter, buddy, and mailing it to you to your railroad so Carolyn won't see it, tho there's nothing to hide from her, it's just that I want to write to YOU now without having someone read over your shoulder even tho it be your sweet protective Carolyn. The point of my letter is, I want you and I to be big buddies anyhow; in thinking about Reincarnation and Cayceism, I'm not too sure that maybe you aren't my brother Gerard reborn. Sometimes I explain it to myself that way, what is all the holy feeling I have for holy Neal, maybe he's my brother at that . . . It was you first said we were Blood brothers, remember? . . . I approve of your Cayceism interest, I have the same interest in Edgar Cayce I think he's great and I think you're the greatest . . . Please believe me, Neal, we got a long life ahead of us, I'm on good terms with your wife because I actually do love her, and your children are like as if they were mine—and I'm not queer—and I'm happy for you when you make it, like Willie Mays for his brother Monte Irvin just now. I understand all your vices because I have them myself; I don't agree at all that you're crazy, as the Rorschach says, because they had one about me, too—in the Navy . . . you, the greatest writer in America, crazy? So was Whitman, so was Thoreau, so was Poe . . . Man for you to stop writing, for you to say 'I quit' is ridiculous—Never mind what Carolyn says about sex-writing being 'dirt', instead of art—of course she knows it's art, it's new art—but I don't want to start new fights . . . Ah, Neal, listen to your buddy, your older brother, and do what he says: write on, don't stop, in secret even, don't tell C. maybe, scribble , type it up, or I'll type it up for you—consider too, that our friendship and brotherhood has really been a literary association, djever think that? . . . Boy, I won't bother you with 'nothin means nothin ' no more; that nothin means nothin is the saddest thing I know, and you know how sad I am all the time—But rather than cling to that ridiculously obvious truth, I'd rather, at the age of fifty, be going out to get groceries with you, sitting in the front seat of the car, with the kids in back (kids'll be grown up!??) looking at you waiting for whatever you got to say next—my name Shadow.

He declared he'd dedicate himself to enormous artistic labors, whether it brought 'riches or nothin—it's the work itself I want,' and he planned to spend part of the time with his mother and sister, part of his time in Mexico City, and part of it staying with us or in our yard, 'buying my share of groceries from now on.' Then, 'In closing I want you to remember the night we met in a crummy in Watsonville and you said 'We don't talk any more' with tears in your eyes—Forgive me, O Neal, for everything that I done wrong. Holy Angels bless you. Jack.'

My heart, too, cried for lost Jack, and the letter didn't exactly soothe my emotional condition. Along with feeling sympathy for him, I agreed with his belief in Neal, who was not writing at all any more, not even letters. We'd both lost him.

The next week I got a letter, too; perhaps Jack felt guilty. He wrote:

What has happened to us two pen pals? On my side of the fence it seems that, after I'd written to Neal telling him to send me his scribblings and I'd type them even if they were pornographic, I conceived the idea that you were displeased, tho I still say, whatever Neal writes is great because he has as much talent as James Joyce or any other great Irishman writing in the English language . . . Apparently something has happened and everybody has changed . . . my face has changed and I scowl all the time; a smirch of displeasure is printed right on it. I fly off the handle at the drop of a hat.

Obviously Neal had not answered Jack's letter, probably in part because he feared that if he revealed secrets to Jack, I'd hear about them, too. He continued:

. . . Ah, Carolyn, there would be a lot to talk about. Any kind of nonsense. I plan to go to Frisco and sleep on Allen's couch and meet the characters this summer, after a month or two in the Mexican Desert; at that time, I most certainly intend to drop in on you and the kids . . . I feel like Cézanne, tranquil, lonely, profound, sad as I go to the woods to write & meditate. Thoughts of you often—hope all is all right.

It helped a little to hear from him that he still felt kindly toward me, but I knew now there was no permanent relief to be had from that quarter, and I was much too anxious to work things out with Neal anyway. My answer must have conveyed some of these feelings, for his next letter was resigned and sad. He hadn't got the money he'd expected to fund his trip to California, and wrote that although the only good thing that would come of it would have been seeing me and the kids, even then he was afraid that he wouldn't measure up now to their former feelings for him,

based and built on past kiddy glees with tape and wine in the living room and good times when Neal respected me. Nah, and all I would want to do is grab you . . . and I don't think you'd like that any more and even if you did it wouldn't be right but all wrong and Neal included, ah, it's a mess, I'd better leave things as they are . . . Well, enough of this gray talk. Your letter was well received, I detected in it a new note of assurance, aloofness, self-dependence. I'm sure you'll handle everything and everything is

256

alright. [If he only had known . . .] . . . Oh, well we could talk all night and have a good time and eat pizza and drink wine and by God we will when I get travelin money. Meanwhile, sweetie, be cool, be blessed, be relaxed, like roses in the rain here I see out my window right now . . .

His loneliness only intensified my own. I missed him more than ever now, missed someone to talk to who was kind; yet I knew it could never be the same as before. In my misery and confusion I turned to Elsie Sechrist and wrote her for personal advice; but never at these times was I able to express the extent of my pain, always thinking it sounded so melodramatic, and my early training had taught me to make light of private woes to others.

Cayce had said that no one meets a circumstance he hasn't the power to overcome—if he will. This was welcome news, but then he also said, 'The stronger you are, the tougher the tests.'

Forty-four

My worst fears were realized when I came across two notes in the pocket of a pair of Neal's jeans which I was about to wash. One had been written to him by Natalie Jackson, the girl in Bob LaVigne's painting, and the other was from Neal to her. Trembling, I read hers first:

Dear N. 11:10 p.m.—We're stimulated by pleasurable unexpected surprises, ie, I love you more now, but better. In the everyday . . . I know your body—It's a mystery to me. I half forget about you then your body surprises mine . . . I know every inch, mole, blemish, hair, scar, pore yet don't think of them really (except maybe a tenderness for a favorite or outstanding one) until I see them again—then the flash of memories, and how probably felt with my hands or touched and sensed and tasted all the feelings and your reactions to touch and the different tastes of the various parts of your body yet it excites me more than someone or something that is as yet unexplored to me. I love you. N. At 5 a.m. this sounds like a label on a bottle of English lice killer or care and treatment of scabies. Is best over absinthe.

I needed nothing more graphic to define their relationship, but to leave me no doubts at all the notes were wrapped around some snapshots of Neal and Natalie cavorting with Allen and Peter on a sunny street in the City, Neal and Natalie entwined or Neal joyously clutching her in a variety of suggestive poses. His own half-finished note to her supplied the capstone to my grief:

258

How does one begin? Especially after so long our moment was too brief (as this train is too fast, the roadbed too rough, my penmanship too poor for good writing) yet my memory dwelling on those sweet brown eyes pouring out into me for that instant—a need matching my own intensity . . . I dreamed of you last night . . . Among other things, including verification of validity of authentic vibration between us, as opposed to simple sex hunger, actually similar level of Mind—I met your San Jose girlfriend in the train yard and suggested I take her to you just so I could see you again. That was the main part of the dream, the desire to find you again . . . I believe it quite possible, but rare, to feel a perfect lover, one with whom you are one because each match, as radio stations attuned perhaps . . .

That was all there was, and it was more than enough for me. I never considered that this might simply be more of the old rhetoric he'd written to me and to countless others over the years. I believed every searing word just as I'd believed all his love letters to me.

Neal found me red-eyed from weeping, the incriminating evidence laid out on the dresser. I was too beaten to yell at him, but I asked him if he wanted a divorce now that he'd found someone so completely compatible. I was hurt all the more because I'd thought him incapable of such sentiments in regard to sex, and I assumed his words matched his actions, even though they rarely did with me. He said he didn't want a divorce, and I tried to understand. 'But Neal—I just can't take anymore, *please*. You don't love me at all, what could be more obvious? Why on earth must we stay married? This is no marriage.'

He answered with the usual sympathy and comfort and an intense effort to explain Natalie away, insisting she was no threat to *our* relationship.

'What "relationship"?' I asked, and got only 'Now, darling . . .' in reply.

I wrote again to Elsie Sechrist, and she replied with a very long and thoughtful letter; but the essence of her answer was that 'God will make the separation' if a spiritual state is endangered. Otherwise, love and patience would overcome. She stressed the need for constant prayer and meditation, recommended that I read Starr Daily's book *Release* and said she and Hugh Lynn would see us soon to talk things over.

I still felt trapped, and I strained against the bars, but I trusted Elsie's judgment and believed her advice. That 'something' within me still overruled my reason, and I was becoming more convinced by my studies that there are no such things as accidents, no coincidences.

Sadly, I handed the letter to Neal when he was next home. He read it with great concentration, eager to comply with its suggestions.

We read *Release*, as well as other books by Starr Daily, and Elsie was right: they were inspiring. It was hard for us to accept that there could be a repetition in modern times of St. Paul's conversion, but Starr's similar experience in prison was a convincing example, and Neal desperately hoped he'd be next. He was particularly impressed because Starr had been far more depraved in his youth than Neal had, and far more cruel.

The Cayce conference and our interviews had taken place in the spring, but by summer no improvement was evident. In other areas, I could acknowledge effects from my meditation and prayer, but in the matter of my relationship with Neal, our grooves were too deeply etched; we were both too impatient, too easily discouraged.

Hugh Lynn had told me that all I had to do was 'keep still' but I was not convinced that this advice met my particular needs. Although I felt he had completely missed the point, it was strange how his words continued to pop into my mind whenever I was self-righteously reminding Neal of his accumulating crimes, words that were irksome, like a persistent fly. How could anyone 'keep still' in the face of Neal's actions? Was he to think me a blind fool? Still, each time I'd begin my complaints Hugh Lynn's solution came into my mind, and I'd bite my tongue and try; I was never successful for more than twenty minutes at a time.

Neal was gone more and more, my life a lonely round of housework and children, my sanity saved only by their need of me and the lovely environment surrounding me. Doing the dishes, I'd survey the hills beyond the village with their pattern of vineyards tended by the Jesuits, and higher up the firetrails scarring the serene and constant bulk of mountain. Every spare moment I'd search the readings for comfort and stamina, trying to resign myself to Elsie's dictum that 'God would make the separation.'

To a certain extent He did, through Neal, but not a way I'd have chosen. Neal announced he wanted to move to the city and share an apartment with Allen and Peter. The reason he gave was that the railroad was so busy it would be easier for him, since he had to spend so much time in San Francisco between trains—one of his weaker attempts. Allen and Peter, my foot . . . Natalie! But there was nothing I could do. On 10 May I awoke alone in bed, a note on the bedside table:

Dear Ma: I hate myself, and you know it. But I looked long and hard at my son last night, & I fully realize my responsibilities, plus I am in full fear of my failings that once a man starts down he never comes back— never.

N.

My heart chilled at his ominous tone. Did he intend to stop trying? One of his favorite Cayce dictums was 'You haven't failed yet.'

I dragged on, clutching at the edge of the plateau I'd reached with Elsie and the conference. I took up the gauntlet and leaned into 'long-suffering,' not divorce. Neal came home every two weeks on payday.

One constant thorn was that I knew so little about Natalie and the nature of my competition. The only clue came from the Hinkles, to whose home Neal had taken Natalie once or twice. Helen thought her 'strange' and 'weird': 'She just sat there, not saying a word, staring into space—catatonic, I'd say—' and Helen shuddered and made a face. Why would Neal be so enamored of that? Al said she was well known on the 'Beach' for certain oral sexual practices, and that made more sense, but the notes I'd read suggested a much deeper bond.

One weekend Neal appeared with another man, stayed a few minutes, and then left alone. I realized at once that this was an effort to salve his conscience by offering a substitute; in his own mind, I'm sure he thought he was doing me a kindness.

Pat was the man's name. He was a tall, muscular Adonis, bronzed and blond and as unlike Neal in every way as anyone could be. I was not receptive to the arrangement; I wanted to tell Neal I'd choose my own friends, thank you. But I would have been delighted to fall in love with someone who could replace Neal in my heart, so I made no immediate objections. Pat came down from San Francisco every Sunday thereafter, and although it was a change in my routine, he was little company. On first arriving he'd spend an hour or two cleaning and polishing his Austin-Healy. Then he'd take the portable radio and a beach towel out by the pool to swim and lie in the sun. The facilities were obviously the chief attraction. He was good about playing with the children in and around the pool, and it made Sunday dinner more fun for them, but it made me sick when he'd make a big deal out of the fact that one of them, through a slip of the tongue, called him 'Daddy.'

Forty-five

We hadn't heard from Jack all summer, but then I received a note from Mexico:

> . . . Want you to know I'll be passing thru Los Gatos in a week or two on my way to Allen's cottage in Berkeley, where I will wait for word from you, by note or via Neal—whatever you see fit to convey—My silence has been intentional, awkward and naturally, often I think of you—don't want to cause pain on any side—In yr. communications with me, tell the truth, that is, don't gild anything for my benefit. I have no male ego to speak of any more. Whatever the case may be, I will come peek at you and kiddies & new house anyhow, but didn't want to take you by surprise, because the element of surprise is no factor—Our mutual silence has been good. God bless you & little family.

Depressing on two counts. In the first place, what did he mean by 'tell the truth'? Did he think I'd stopped caring and might pretend? Because I hadn't written? I hadn't written because I was afraid I'd do nothing but complain about Neal and Natalie, which I knew would pain him and embarrass me. Damn. Well, he'd be coming, and I could straighten that out.

The second jolt was to learn that Allen had been living not in San Francisco, but in Berkeley.

I told Neal of Jack's impending visit and he met Jack at the yard office in San Jose and drove him home for dinner—his favorite one, of course. I presumed Neal had brought him up to date on Natalie and their activities in the City on the way over.

What with all the water under the bridge—or, should I say, women under Neal—we didn't exactly recapture the bright hopes of our former relationship, but if we were older and sadder, there was a mellowness born of loneliness and endurance, and perhaps a deeper longing and a warmer empathy between Jack and me.

When the children were finally quieted down and put to bed and Jack had been duly impressed with our prayer ritual, we moved the television set into the living room. We hadn't shared TV before, and it would keep us away from discussing personal pitfalls. But none of us could stop talking for long, and Neal played his channel-switching game with his usual running critique on commericals, situations comedies and musical variety shows alike, and Jack added his own highlights.

Jack had brought tea from Mexico and produced it now, spreading it out on a newspaper on his lap to manicure it and pour it into the familiar Sir Walter Raleigh tobacco can that Neal provided. Neal remained in action, hopping back and forth from the TV and stopping only to exclaim over the tight, curly leaves of Jack's supply and urging him to hurry.

I was sitting across the room opposite the window when I saw a car turn into our driveway; I supposed it was just someone turning around. But no, it came on further and parked. Then I saw the flashing red lights.

'My God, Neal—it's the cops!' I ran to the window just as the uniformed sheriff opened the car door. Terror shot us into action. I sprang to turn out the lamp, while Jack scooped the tea and newspaper behind his back, turning his full attention to the TV. Neal sat in my chair, also apparently totally engrossed.

I answered the door, trembling from head to foot. The officer stepped into the dark entryway and asked for Neal Cassady.

Neal jumped to his feet, all eagerness to please. 'Yes, sir—what can I do for you?'

I knew I should turn on a light, but not being sure how well Jack had concealed the tea, I didn't, and the officer turned on his flashlight, shining it around the room. I held my breath. Jack was still absorbed in the TV, and I joined him.

'I'm sorry to disturb you,' the officer was saying to Neal, 'but when you came by the office this afternoon to pay the traffic fines, we made a mistake. Instead of $200, it should have been $260—we need another sixty dollars.'

Neal sprinted to our bedroom, calling back, 'Uh, dear, where's the checkbook?' I jumped up and went into the bedroom and he returned to the living room and chatted casually with the officer while I wrote out the check, my hand shaking.

When the car finally backed out of the driveway and zoomed off into the night, I felt weak from relief—and considerably sobered. Not so Jack and Neal; they were light-headed and giddy at the narrow escape, retrieving the tea from its hiding place and carefully seeking out every fallen crumb while giggling and chortling at having put one over on the cop. The episode had frightened me, but also the revelation of the amount of money we had lost on citations dampened my mood.

When Neal left for work the next morning, he said he'd try and get Allen to come back with him that evening to go with us to hear the Bishop. This was Bishop Romano, a slight, handsome young Swiss who had been ordained in the Liberal Catholic Church, a small sect that accepted reincarnation and the universality of all religious doctrines. Father Romano favored the teachings of Sri Aurobindo, the Indian sage, which seemed somewhat incongruous when he was attired in the black and purple robes of the Roman Church. An additional curiosity was that his sermons were supposely delivered by a higher being for whom the Bishop served as a 'channel' (the new term for a medium). Neither Neal nor I had experienced this phenomenon before, and it made us even more in awe of him as well as a bit nervous. During services, his face was smooth, almost glowing, his eyes large and luminous; afterward, when shaking hands with him at the door, I saw that his complexion was actually sallow and sickly.

Jack elected to spend the day with me, but we could rarely talk seriously for any length of time; the children kept him too busy exploring the neighborhood, showing him all their 'forts' and favorite climbing trees, and in return Jack taught them how to compose haikus. In the afternoon he swam with them, frightening me but impressing them with his jack-knife dives off the end of the pool into four feet of water.

We had heard that the Bishop sometimes went to people's houses after the meetings, and when Neal arrived home he promised to ask him over after tonight's service. The Bishop accepted our invitation;

Neal had already arranged for Allen, Peter and Pat to join us but unfortunately they couldn't get here in time for the service. I was panic-stricken at having so many guests to prepare for, especially as they included the awesome personage of the Bishop, but I supposed he would like tea—the liquid kind—and I had plenty of that. Jack had his wine and hoped the Bishop would join him; I was worried that Jack had had too much already. He had also declined to come to the service—our whole idea had been for them all to hear this remarkable man and witness his transformation.

Allen, Peter and Pat had already arrived when we returned home, and I barely had time to put on the kettle and inspect the living room before the Bishop's car drove in. I felt anything but the competent hostess, lacking an upbringing that made one at ease with the clergy, and I was further unsettled when I opened the door to not only the Bishop but two middle-aged ladies as well. The Bishop introduced them as his mother and his aunt. Struggling for poise, I didn't note their appearance in detail; my only impression was that Dickens would have loved them.

Our furniture was make-shift and sparse, but we recruited some chairs from the patio. The two ladies sat together on the couch, and Jack sat on the floor beside the Bishop, cuddling his bottle that no one cared to share. He leaned back against the bookcase, his eyes closed, and quoted a few passages from the Diamond Sutra.

The Bishop took it from there, expanding and commenting as though it were as familiar a topic as the weather, whereupon Jack leaned against the Bishop's knee, lifted his face and declared, 'I love you,' then sank back and took another swallow. The Bishop smiled; the rest of us pretended not to notice.

Neal paced about at the opposite end of the room, searching his mind, I knew, for relevant examples from Cayce, but he was still somewhat shy in the presence of a real 'preacher.' The two women gave me the strange feeling that they had presented us with a magic doll; they never took their eyes off the Bishop, and they never spoke.

I slipped out to prepare the tea, and then heard that Neal had found an opening to present *his* favorite sage. The Bishop was equally at home with this approach and brought his comments down to earth accordingly, but he went on to explain that the harmony needed to develop the new age must come from an understanding of both Eastern and Western thought. Like Sri Aurobindo and Yogananda, he stressed the compatability of the Eastern teachings with those of Jesus.

Allen had so far said nothing. I had expected the closest rapport to come from him, he being the best informed among us on Eastern philosophy, and I wondered if he were feeling his ego challenged by this ethereal young man. Whatever the case, he did not introduce the Gita or Sri Krishna into the discussion; there was another topic on his mind. He helped me pass out the tea cups and then marched over to the couch and squeezed himself in between the two ladies. 'Now then,' he fairly yelled, 'what about sex?'

I suppose I should have been grateful he didn't remove his clothes, but the effect was much the same. Even Neal fidgeted and looked at his feet. Jack giggled, 'Allen!'; Pat's prominent jaw dropped; and Peter looked blank, as did the ladies. Allen grinned, his black eyes peering at the Bishop, but the latter spoke seriously, without batting an eye: 'Well, of course, sex is a vitally important aspect of the whole—the governing Life Force that must be understood for what it is and properly directed. The Adam-man uses this force, the Kundalini, to create new bodies for his own sensual pleasure, but when he rises to the Christ-man, he uses it to create ideas that materialize in benefits for mankind while evolving his own consciousness onward. A very powerful force, indeed. We are probably more familiar with it in its destructive power when it is misdirected in a negative, sexual way.' I said a silent 'Amen' to that.

With this variety of nuts and with Jack's intermittent 'I love you's, to the Bishop, I was heartily glad when the ladies broke their silence by indicating decisively to their charge that it was time to go. When the trio had departed, we all breathed again, and mirthful reflection took over. We reconstructed the evening with hilarious 'might-have-been's, though I felt quite enough *had* been. Jack's chuckle grew into a hearty laugh with 'God, Allen—you and your "Now what about sex," ' and he rolled over on the floor holding his stomach. Allen shrugged and grinned: 'I was only trying to liven things up a bit. Those two gargoyles loved it. I nearly put a hand on each knee— they'd have loved that, too.' Neal chortled at the idea, but his reverence for the Bishop and the subjects we had been discussing kept him from expanding it further.

Neal had neatly arranged his own return to the city for the night, using Allen and Peter as his excuse. Pat, he said, was going to visit friends further down the coast, so he *had* to take them back to Berkeley.

Jack and I had not anticipated being alone together, and it was like an unexpected gift. We fairly smothered each other with released

266

longing, grasping and clutching and hanging on for dear life, pouring into each other our pent-up affection and sorrow. Now there was no one else to worry about, no nervousness, and we outdid all the doomed lovers of fame for all we were worth. We never really slept, so afraid were we to miss a minute of being together, we only dozed now and then, clinging to each other's warmth and our hopeless dreams.

A little before dawn he took his sleeping bag and went outside so the children wouldn't find him in my bed.

Next morning when I got up, Jack was basking in the sun on the patio, but he came in when he heard me in the kitchen.

'Have some orange juice, Jack. Coffee'll be ready in a minute. Did you sleep at all?'

'Yeah, sure—that is, once I got settled. I started out here on the patio, but Cayce [our cocker spaniel] kept licking my face. So I moved way out beyond the fence to that lone prune tree. Beautiful unobstructed view of the stars—and so quiet! You should sleep out there allatime . . . only . . . what's the smell?'

'Oh, dear. We don't have sewers here. I'm afraid that's the septic tank. But if you put a house-trailer back far enough . . .'

'That's what I'm gonna do, soon as I sell a book.'

When I had fed the children and they'd left for school, I gave Jack a pamphlet by Sri Aurobindo to read while I did the breakfast dishes. He read it carefully, making notes in the margins and occasionally reading passages aloud to me. His interest was gratifying; I'd missed Neal in that role for quite a long time. Soon I joined him outside and we sat on the grass by the pool. He had a hangover from the wine and brought a beer to sip.

'The man's right, you know. Self-surrender is the key. You ought to surrender to Neal.'

'Whatever do you mean, "surrender"? Do what he wants— anything at all? Oh, come now, Jack—"This above all, to thine own self be true." Unless you mean surrender my personal ego, my attachment. I agree with that, all right, and I am trying, but it's such a foreign concept from all that's traditional.'

We continued a long, intense discussion, our first on our developing ideas. Jack's mind didn't like logical analysis; he preferred ethereal mystical imagery and intuition, so whether we achieved more understanding of the issues, I can't say. I tried to bring him back to practical application: 'And all my fussing at Neal is really because I want him to be *mine*—want him to love me *more*.'

'Neal does love you,' said Jack.

'Oh, I suppose so, in his way. Starr Daily said something I'd never realized before. He said people love to the very best of their ability at any given time, and that is all you can expect. Love can't be demanded, so it's useless for me to demand that Neal love me the way I love him—he's giving it his best shot right now. Dante said love's like a mirror—the more given out, the more is reflected back, and thus it expands. I have to admit I'm not giving out much at the moment.' I thought about these sobering thoughts, then sighed and sing-songed, 'Cayce says if you wanna be loved, be lovely.'

'And you are, and I love you.'

'Dear Jack. I am better at loving *you* the right way. But then, I know I could never possess you, so I don't demand more love from you— and you and I haven't made great vows to each other. Yet we both believe in marriage—how odd. You and I believe vows are to be kept, Neal that they're to be broken—yet it's he and I who are married. Well, both of you do very well in loving me "indifferently," I must say.'

'Neal gets pretty possessive when he thinks he might lose you.'

'Any of his women, actually—you should know. It all comes back to ego, I suppose—self. It's hard to get ourselves out of the way.'

'I just read that in the Aurobindo book—only he was talking about standing aside and watching your machinery work. That's also the basis of spontaneous prose and poetry: you don't say *I* do; it's the gunas that work—aspects of God. That's why publishers have no business telling writers how or what to write.'

' "Let go and let God," ' I quoted. We leaned close against each other, silent in thought, watching the white puffy clouds rearrange their shapes in the vivid blue above us.

'If only Neal could break the tea habit and replace it with meditation. He knows there are no shortcuts. What a powerhouse he would be.'

'Yeah, I try and tell him, too, but he don't listen to me no more. Anyway, he's got to be active—always running. You gotta go off by yourself. That's what I'm going to do—find a mountain top and sit alone and meditate. But Neal, aw, that's the way he is, woman. Just you do what he wants and know he's great.' Jack turned on his side, his head propped on his hand, his eyes closed, scowling. A lock of hair fell down, and when I brushed it back, the scowl cleared and he laughed softly. Then jumping up he reached for my hands and pulled me to my feet. 'Come on, let's get some wine.'

We got as far as the french doors when we heard the front door slam, and Neal flashed past us, calling back, 'Come along, children, hurry up, we're going to the track. Can't miss the first race.' Jack burst into hearty laughter now—this was the Neal he loved—and he went inside to the kitchen to get his wine, while I followed Neal into our bedroom where he was changing his socks.

'The what? What did you say?'

'The track, baby, racetrack—Bay Meadows. You'll love it. C'mon.' Jack came out of the kitchen and nodded to me. 'Ever seen a horse race?'

'Only in the movies. But how come, Neal? I didn't know you liked horse racing.'

'Never used to. But this is different.' He hitched his jeans and swiped at his hair, ricochetting from bathroom to me. 'I don't go to see the races, y'understand . . . uh . . . ah . . . well, you see, I've come upon this marvelous secret system, yass, yass' and he adopted his W.C. Fields accent, grinning at Jack. 'Uh, hunh, m'dear . . . don't say a word. I know what you're thinking, but this one really works. I'll show you—prove it to you. Now, leave a note for the kiddies and tell them where we're going. We'll be back for dinner—hurry up, now, or we'll miss the first race.' In the wake of Jack's advice, I let go and did what Neal asked.

On the way to Bay Meadows Neal briefly explained his 'system.' You simply bet the third-choice horse, the theory being that the first and second choices were often over-rated, but the third choice was likely to be just as good, and by the law of averages it had been proven to be so—the third choices won frequently and consistently, and the odds were better. The trick, of course, was to bet enough money each time to cover any previous losses. Neal began with two dollars, and the system usually hit before he lost very much, thereby getting all his losses back plus the winnings. He had been doing this for a month or so (I groaned) and had begun to keep records by checking the race results daily in the paper. So far, the longest period of loss was eleven consecutive races. Well, no, he hadn't had the capital to cover that . . . 'But think, if I *had*! Honestly, darling, think of it. Now, in time, you see, I'll have other guys covering all the tracks in the country—all the races! But it has to be done scientifically—no getting interested in the horses, no listening to tips from touts. It's hard work, not fun.'

'Well, I guess I've heard everything now. I'd never have believed you'd become a gambler!'

'No, no, of course I'm *not*, my dear. This isn't gambling. I just told you—it's scientific. Just a job. You have to keep your ears shut and just watch the tote board until the very last instant, then run for the window and bet the third choice. Then wait for the next race. That's why nobody does it, dig? It's too tough.'

Not wanting to bring him down any further with my doubts, I rode the rest of the way to the track in silence, while Neal rattled off the latest statistics to Jack. I could tell Jack wasn't altogether convinced either, and Neal was putting even more conviction into selling his theory to him.

At the track, after Jack had shown me the paddocks, the tote board and the betting windows, I stayed in my seat while they ran back and forth. I found the people fascinating but the races quite different from the movie versions where the suspense was built by dragging out each race so that it seemed to last at least half an hour. At the track the race was over in a flash, but the time in between them seemed interminable.

Neal didn't win that afternoon, and he was thoughtful and quiet on the way home. Directly after dinner he left again for San Francisco, this time taking Jack with him.

One morning a few weeks after our day at the races, I received a telephone call from the banker in Cupertino who had set up our investment funds. Neal and I had felt unusually lucky, since our initial investment of $5,000 had doubled in value in just one year, so I greeted the gentleman warmly.

'Mrs. Cassady? I'm sorry to bother you again, but when you and your husband were in the other day to withdraw your money, I forgot one paper for you to sign.' My mind went blank.

'You what? Oh, you must have the wrong Cassady.' I laughed. 'I haven't been in your bank since last year . . .'

I expected Neal home that night. In my condition, I felt it was safer to leave him a note, not start talking—I thought of Hugh Lynn's 'keep still' and knew the written word was just as wrong, but I considered it a tiny bit of progress. I wrote it out several times, and when I was satisfied that it was as unemotional as I could manage, I left it by the bed:

Dear Neal:
In case I'm too sleepy to keep you awake tonight, I'll talk at you by this less painful method. What did we say about getting greater tests as we grow stronger? It sure happens fast. The good Lord decided I should know about your deal in Cupertino, too. I keep wondering why, but am going on

270

the assumption it's to give me an 'opportunity' to overcome rather than one to get even. Poor guy, when he called I said, no, we hadn't gone East nor had my mother died. I really thought he had the wrong Cassady. Anyway, when he persisted, I had to admit ignorance of the deal (clever boy, why must you make things so complicated?). He wanted to sell the stock immediately and swear out a warrant for Natalie's arrest. I therefore gathered the children from their schools and dashed over there to countersign the whole thing and told him to hold it. He assured me he'd be standing by if I ever wanted to bring the guilty party to justice. I tried to explain that you thrive on punishment, so nothing to do but try something different, and hope the horses come in. No wonder your parties are so renowned, wow! By the way, is the identification card of mine she used something I'd miss? She did very well, I must say, but could use a bit more practice on the C's.

Like you say, I ain't dead yet.

Guess I've said all I can keep from. Wake me if I won today. C.

It took every ounce of grit I had not to let fly all the vindictiveness I felt. I'd never have believed he'd go so far. Not being able to sleep, I spent the night working on myself, repeating every affirmation and Christian principle I could remember, even when I heard him come in, read the note, and slide into bed and to sleep. Still I hung on, keeping my mouth shut but filling my head in constant rote: 'Bless those who despitefully use you,' 'Resist not evil,' 'Judge not that ye be not judged,' 'Love your enemies,' 'Vengeance is mine, saith the Lord,' etc., etc. At last I could accept it in a fatalistic way. After all, I told myself, it was really *his* money to begin with. We were no worse off than if he'd never had the accident—better: we still had the house.

Next morning Neal was overcome with contrition and remorse, both for getting caught and for the act itself. My note (and my closed mouth) seemed to have helped that much, anyway. He, too, was amazed at his action in retrospect, but he'd been so sure that he'd win back the money in no time and replace it, and no one would be any the wiser, only richer. He had planned to show me proudly that the system worked, and that we were set for life. Instead, he had not been able to follow his own advice; he had listened to touts and tips, missed races, and in close to a month lost nearly all of the $10,000.

'Neal, what dumbfounds me—aside from the idea that you can get something for nothing—is that you always manage to get caught. You slip up on some little thing every time. Like the night Jack was here, and the sheriff came. Do you suppose subconsciously you demand to be punished? You're always dropping clues about for me to find, like Natalie's notes. I don't even have to be a nosy wife.'

He pondered. 'It sure looks that way.'

'Well, *I* don't want to punish you. Get somebody else to be your warden or mother—go to confession. It's a role I detest, though I've played it to the hilt, I admit.'

I didn't give up the role overnight, but to be able to see some improvement in my behavior and feel the blessed relief when I succeeded in my efforts made the struggle worthwhile. Besides, the relationship was more workable now; we could talk about it more objectively, even lovingly, instead of throwing up a wall of emotions between us and battering against it uselessly. In these years I still lost my patience both with Neal and the children, and we often skirted the crater of despair, but with our growing knowledge of life's principles and purpose there was a place to turn to, a direction to follow, and we'd already learned that when we managed to act on the theory, it never failed to work.

Forty-six

On 1 December, I sent the children off to school and sat down with a cup of coffee and the morning paper. On page two was a headline: 'WOMAN FIGHTS OFF RESCUE, LEAPS 3 STORIES TO DEATH.' I don't usually pursue that sort of news, but this item included one of those compelling photographs of a building with a dotted line superimposed from roof to sidewalk. As my eye followed the arrow, it ended at a car—a car just like Neal's. The familiar sickening wave of fear made my hands tremble so I could hardly read the article:

> An unidentified woman about 35 years old slashed her throat on a roof top at 1041 Franklin Street yesterday, then kicked free from the grip of a husky policeman and jumped to her death from a third-story fire escape.
> Wearing only a bathrobe and T-shirt, she stood poised outside the railing of the narrow fire escape walkway as Officer O'Rourke lunged through a window to grab her. 'All I could do was dive through and grab,' he said. 'I got a grip on one arm and her robe just as she tried to kick loose. But I couldn't hold her. All at once I was just holding the robe, and she had fallen.' His partner said she might have slashed herself with fragments from a broken skylight.

Could it be Natalie? Why would I think that? It could be anyone's Packard, and I thought Neal had said Natalie was only 24. I must be imagining—dramatizing. But the apprehension lingered.

An hour later, Neal telephoned me. 'Carolyn . . . Natalie . . . Natalie's dead.'

'I saw the paper, Neal. I'm so sorry. Do you want to come home for a while?' He didn't hesitate. 'Oh, could I?'

'Of course, Neal. This is your home still, like it or not.' Did I have to add that? 'I know you loved her. It must be awful for you.'

Later that evening he dragged into the house looking gray and gaunt. I'd never seen him so unhinged and defenseless. I poured him a cup of coffee, and he slumped into a chair. I got the feeling he wanted to talk, but it was hard for him to discuss her with me, after denying her for so long. Maybe if I sounded matter-of-fact, he could too. 'I saw your car in the photograph. Where were you?'

'I was asleep, see? She got up and went out. I'd no idea, but when I heard the sirens, I thought of you and the kids getting involved and just grabbed my stuff and ran out the back way.'

'I certainly thank you for that! What made her do it? Was it suicide, do you think?' I hated to suggest it, but that might explain some of his misery. He'd become convinced by the Cayce readings that suicide was the worst possible offense against yourself and God.

Neal groaned. 'I don't know. Partially—no, I don't want to believe that—but she had become completely paranoid the past couple of weeks. She had an obsession about cops. Part of it was feeling so guilty about forging your signature—she's been agonizing ever since—and she did that for me. I kept telling her it was all right and that you weren't mad, but it didn't help. She got so bad, she talked about nothing but sin and guilt and how we were going to be arrested for our sins. Last week she tried to cut her wrists, but with a dull knife, and I told her all about suicide and not to think of it again. I thought she was better—in fact, she was her old self last night, and we'd talked a long time. I'll never know if she really cut her throat on purpose. One paper said she fell on the skylight and could have done it that way. And she didn't actually *jump*—she was so afraid of the cop, when he grabbed for her she must have backed up and off . . .' He stared blankly into space.

'But look, Neal, maybe it was an out for her, do you think? Maybe it was a chance for her to change her course—start over. She seemed to have boxed herself in. It could be a merciful release, couldn't it?' Neal brightened a trifle. 'Yeah, I suppose it really is better for her. She was insane—I couldn't help her.'

The next day Neal moved his things back home. He was considerably sobered with grief. He had loved her very much, and now she had become something of a martyr in his eyes, verging on sainthood, I feared. But I was grateful he'd not been implicated and had thought of his family. By the next day, the papers were still saying that the body had not been identified, and we thought it would be safe for Neal to do it and get the poor girl settled. That grim task set him back some more. LuAnne told me later that he had called her. She met him at the depot and he held on to her hands and talked it all out again. He had sounded, she said, as though it had impressed upon him his own downward path toward destruction. Violence and death he had been successful in avoiding until now. He felt the incident represented a powerful warning or punishment. For my part, I felt God had 'made a separation.' I resolved to work even harder to make Neal happy, now that this obstacle had been removed.

During this time, Jack had been visiting in San Francisco and Berkeley, meeting Allen's new friends such as Gary Snyder, with whom he'd spent a couple of months climbing mountains in the Sierras and enjoying Zen practices. Jack had known Natalie only slightly and had been frightened by her insanity. His Buddhist therapy of no use, he fled southward, planning to camp out in Mexico. On his way back to North Carolina for Christmas, he stopped to see us for a few days. It was cold and wet, and we made fires all afternoon and evening, sitting on the floor, drinking wine and talking. On the evenings Neal was home, we'd bring in the TV. The atmosphere was cozy and genial, but I was aware that Jack persisted in feeling that in this house he was an outsider. He had to sleep on the couch, and the house was all too open; there was no private room where he could shut the door to nap or write, and now he couldn't escape by staying outside. I know he didn't intend to, but he gave the impression that we'd done this on purpose, and he spoke more often of his homelessness.

Neal's obsession with the races continued to grow, and now he insisted that he had to continue the system in order to atone for the guilt of having lost our savings and for Natalie's death. He turned a deaf ear to reason. Every evening he spent an hour studying the newspaper race results, calculating every race and noting exact scores with hieroglyphics in the margins. Then, folding the sheet meticulously with the chart uppermost, he'd place it carefully, in order, in a beer carton and replace the carton on the closet shelf. I'd sigh as I watched the cartons accumulate, wishing all that mental genius and concentration were being directed toward some more constructive end. Jack agreed but said little.

The week before Christmas, Jack left to hitchhike South, and he looked forlorn and lonely starting off in the cold, gray fog. I received a welcome postcard when he reached North Carolina, 'just to let you know I got home safe . . .' He had hopped freight trains and hitched rides, having big nights with truck drivers, '. . . and so it was all the way from sultry Mexican bars to Christmas farmlands of Ohio, one ride, and I came home. Please let me know specifically how Neal made out the day he played (Monday) and the day I was sposed to play for him (Tuesday) just so I can check karma that wd. have befell me—Happy New Year—xxx Jack.'

On Christmas Day, Allen, Peter, and Peter's brother, Lafcadio, came to share our feast. They were the most gratifying of guests to cook for: I watched a twenty-pound turkey melt away as though by time-lapse photography. I wondered how frequently they ate. But we had a jolly time, Allen always so helpful and considerate, and Peter, too. We all liked Peter. He had craggy features, but his eyes were warm, his manner gentle and quiet, yet alert and intelligent. He spoke only when he had something to say. I couldn't imagine him being as boisterous as I knew Allen could be at times—even on the night of the Bishop's visit, he'd been so quiet I'd hardly known he was there. Maybe he was Allen's straight man, I thought then, though I learned my error in years to come.

Jack responded to my news:

God, it seems to me Allen G. wanted to clean out your icebox like a vacuum cleaner, bringing that monstrous Lafcadio, who, as I understand, wants to weigh 300 lbs. before June. But I see you had a Merry Xmas. Mine was weird, I was alone, my mother suddenly was called to her stepmother's funeral . . . and I was alone realizing shit I shoulda waited and had Xmas with you and besides, to make it worse, and prove you're right again, Malcolm Cowley came to the Bay area with my *On the Road* under his arm all ready to do the final re-touching on ms. before publication and I wasn't there . . . All I had to do was relax and bide my time by the fireplace with my golden chalice port and read the Cayce pamphlets and light fires and play catch with Neal in the yard. Well, all for later . . .

Forty-seven

In January of 1956 an event took place that surprised and delighted us: a book entitled *The Search for Bridey Murphy* was published, and it caused a furor because it supported the evidence for reincarnation. To us it was perplexing that this book should receive so much attention, rather than a book such as *Many Mansions* written by a modern scientist. Through our own reading on the subject we had discovered extensive literature from every century which was already available but ignored by the standard-setters of the day. But of course we were delighted that people in all walks of life were suddenly talking about Bridey Murphy and reincarnation. Neal jumped for joy. 'See? See? Cayce was right! He said that between 1958 and 1998 there would be a renewed wave of interest in spiritual matters throughout the world!' And so it would seem.

Two months later an article by Morey Bernstein, author of *Bridey*, appeared in *True* magazine. He stated that he had originally been fascinated by the work of Edgar Cayce, but had known that no one would listen if he wrote about him and so had decided to do some experimenting on his own. Now he could acknowledge the debt to Cayce. Apparently Bernstein had pushed the right button at the right time, for from then on we witnessed an astonishingly rapid heightening of interest in the spiritual and occult, and in the next decade we were to accept as commonplace events that would have been considered miracles in our youth.

Jack had heard the news, too, and he wrote at once. He gave a detailed account of all the previous lives he had remembered while meditating under his backyard tree (as Buddha had done under the Bo tree). Shakespeare and Balzac were prominent memories, he declared.

> . . . All this thinking caused by sudden realization Cayce must be right, and Bridey Murphy excitement, which has carried over to my sister, and she and I want you to send us Cayce's literature address at Atlantic Beach so we can send for literature, my sister especially het up now on Astrology.

Neal and I were excited at first—could it be that Jack might come around? But no, we finally had to accept the fact that he would stick to Buddhism; it provided him with an instant remedy for any painful situation that challenged him. It seemed to us a cop-out, not a way to grow and overcome, and this began to be a barrier to our closeness. And the more Jack drank, the more he repeated Buddhist phrases, allowing no 'communication on a human level,' to use his words.

Jack had also been investigating Oral Roberts. 'Did you know Oral Roberts is a Cherokeen Indian? A real old-fashioned witchdoctor's what he is . . . he has great compassionate heart. I don't disbelieve him.' He went on to say he himself had healed his mother of a cough by hypnotizing himself to find out what was wrong with her and having a vision.

> The next day her cough subsided, stopped all together . . . and my INTUITION was verified by the doctor . . . This doesn't surprise me, and I'm not going to get excited about it, but just ease my way into it, as a channel of God, and whenever someone's sick I'll try again . . . This, together with my recent letter about 'Shakespeare-reincarnation' must make you think that I'm really crazy, and actually, I am way out this spring . . .

Sickness, Jack believed, was an opportunity for punishing one's self, and he thought his phlebitis resulted from his cruelties in football. My own realization was that these Catholic-reared boys simply could not lose the idea of 'punishment.'

Then casually Jack mentioned,

> I wrote a new Novel, from New Years Day to the 16th of January, *Visions of Gerard*, a beautiful poem of death and I'm almost finished typing it now and will send it to the publishers who don't care anyway. But it's a beaut, my best . . . real cracky teeth closing down on great awful final statements about the grave and all. Enuf to make Shakespeare raise an eyebrow

Neal (left) and Jack, 1952.

Neal with John Allen and Jami, 1952

Jack, Cathy and Neal, 1952.

Carolyn Cassady

A cartoon drawn by Jack to amuse the children in about 1953.

BEGINNING TODAY
DOCTOR SAX
and
The Deception of the
Sea Shroud
—JK

BROOKLYN WATERFRONT
Midnight!

FROM OUT OF A SUNKEN OLD TUGBOAT

IT RISES !!

HIGH ATOP A TELEPHONE POLE
IT EXAMINES BROOKLYN...

NEXT DAY
AT BROAD NOON, ON BOROUGH HALL,
NEATLY ATTIRED AND WITH BRIEFCASE,
the Sea Shroud walks

Jack (l) and Neal in San Jose, 1952.

With Neal and son John Allen, summer 1955.

(L. to R.) Peter Orlovsky, Allen Ginsberg, Natalie Jackson and Neal, San Francisco, 1956

Portrait of Allen Ginsberg
by the author, 1954.

Colour pencil drawing

Allen Ginsberg in
Yukatan, 1953.

I took this photograph in 1959 to send to Neal in San Quentin. My unhappy expression was designed to make an impression on his jailers, though the emotion was real enough.

Neal in heaven – a car and a girl, any time any place. (Actually with Anne Murphy, 1960).

Neal, Los Gatos, 1960 –
after a hard day at the
tire recapping shop.

Neal "hammer-flipping", with the Merry
Pranksters' bus, 1966 or '67.

Neal, near the end.

Destination "Further". The Merry Pranksters' bus on Ken Kesey's ranch in Oregon, July 1988.

In the next letter was more good news:

Joy of joys, I made arrangements with Viking Press to come out and finish my manuscript work with Cowley at Stanford University , . the time has come to get that thing on the presses, it's the original daddy of the rock 'n' roll books. Also, I'm pretty well now homeless.

Next came even better news, and Jack was exuberant:

O boy, O boy, O here I go, I got the offer for the job watching fires on top of the mountains in the Cascade country in Northwest . . . and I told the Forest Ranger I hoped he'd take me back next year, and the next, and all my life. It will be my life work, in my hut there, and city apartment in Mex. City, and in transit twice a year I can knock on yore door and pester you for a meal, a few weeks at a crack with my charming tired presence and roaring fires and priceless comments at television and if you want a camping trip to the Sierra with the kids we can do it whenever you're ready. Know just the place, just the trail, just the beautiful lake.

I looked up from the letter to Neal. 'Well, Jack actually followed through and got that Ranger job. I thought he was just wishing again. Do you think he'll really like it?'

'Hell no, he'll hate it. That guy's lonesome in a crowd. He doesn't like his own company that much. Imagine him completely alone. He'll go mad from boredom. Pah.'

As if to prove how much Jack needed someone to talk to, I got another letter within the week, a long rambling one full of possible incarnations and Buddhist prayers. '. . . It's a crucial moment but a JOYOUS moment in my life. I feel great new happiness coming on . . . See you soon sweet friend.'

When Jack did come to California, I saw him seldom. He was busy with his editor Malcolm Cowley and with catching up on Allen, who had improved his lot and his art and had been traveling through the Northwest reading poetry and lecturing at colleges. Jack renewed his Berkeley friendships and tried to show some interest in Neal by going to the races with him and grumbling about the system. Then he said goodbye to everyone and the world and went off to his mountain-top.

The solitude affected him just as we had predicted. Although there were moments he cherished, he nearly went mad with loneliness and boredom, and he knew he'd never go back. He was further disillusioned at having to face this truth about himself.

When Jack next came to see us, he was worn out from partying in

San Francisco and depressed from his revelation on the mountain, so as Neal wasn't home he asked me to drive him through the redwood forests in the Santa Cruz mountains, hoping to find a secluded spot to set up camp and try again but, this time, not so far from friends. It was a gray, damp day, but I packed a lunch and we stopped in Saratoga to buy wine, then headed up the winding road.

Jack had started out gloomy and resentful, but when I told him — and I had to repeat it several times — that it was unlawful to light fires in these mountains except at designated campsites, his disillusion was compounded. On and on he ranted about 'progress' and 'civilization' and the interference of bureaucracy in private lives. It was useless to argue with him, so after a stab or two at more cheerful conversation, I gave up and subsided into noises of agreement. Then he growled, 'Well, hell, there's no use going any farther, then. Drive up that dirt road and we'll have lunch.'

The sun had begun to peep through the fog, and golden shafts filtered through the trees to steam the ground. I loved the varied smells of these wooded hills, and tried to get Jack to forget his woes and join me in a jolly picnic in a tiny clearing beside a redwood grove, where the ground was covered with soft brown leaves warmed by the sun. He tried to be more cheerful, but fell to reminiscing about us and became glum again. Then, when we'd finished eating, he stretched out on the ground saying 'C'mon' and pulled me down beside him, and I knew he wanted to make love. In spite of the picnic, the sunshine and the wine, his having sung the blues all morning and dwelled on his rootlessness made it difficult for me to dissolve the lump in my throat and feel interested in sex. His own mood and the daylight made him too shy to make the first move, and I pretended I didn't read his signals.

When we got home, Jack built his fire in the fireplace and I poured him some more wine, so by the time Neal came home for dinner he was happy once more and ready to indulge in an evening of Neal's brand of television watching. He slept outside again, lugging his great pack that had so intrigued the children, and in the morning accompanied Neal on his train back to San Francisco.

Gregory Corso was there. He and Jack and Neal had gone to the races together and joined other friends in parties. However, Jack was unhappy that Neal and Gregory didn't get along as well as Jack had hoped, so he asked if he might bring Gregory to our house for the weekend. Saturday afternoon the three went to the track, but Gregory wouldn't follow Neal's instructions on how to bet, which didn't help bring them any closer. As it happened, Gregory would have won, but since he broke even he remained neutral and Neal disgruntled. Neal won, however, so at least he was in good enough spirits to be patient with Gregory. They rode to San Jose on Neal's train, and he drove them home in time for dinner.

Gregory made me nervous. He wore a perpetual scowl and he didn't talk sense. Actually he didn't talk—he'd just suddenly blurt out or shout some sentence I couldn't connect with anything. So I tried to shrink into the background for fear I'd antagonize him further. After dinner, with everyone somewhat ill at ease, we watched Neal and television, all of us sitting on our low bed in the dark bedroom with Neal perched on the edge ready to pilot the machine from channel to channel. Gregory didn't understand the game and bellowed, 'How can I see the show?' but Neal explained that since you always know what's going to happen next, this way you could watch all the shows. Jack added: 'It's all one show!'

Next day, no greater rapport developed between Neal and Gregory. I saw that Neal couldn't talk to him any better than I could; we didn't know how to penetrate Gregory's brooding façade. Both Neal and I withdrew in the face of disapproval and discontent, and Gregory seemed disgusted with everything and everybody. So Neal went on doing what he would normally: reading newspapers and magazines while lying on the bed watching television and answering any queries put to him by the children, Jack or me; he was perfectly capable of taking in all this stimuli at once and sorting it. This time he was watching a sports event, so he didn't change the channels. Meanwhile, Gregory wandered around restlessly. He didn't even seem to want the big breakfast of bacon and eggs that I had prepared; he just pushed and picked at it, scowling. Jack took the children for their expected walk, and shortly after lunch Neal announced we should all come watch Oral Roberts, a regular ritual for Neal.

'You don't *believe* all that crap, man?' Gregory was more disgusted than ever.

'Just watch. He's great!' Neal said and leaned forward avidly taking in every word, muttering 'Yaay, yeah' every few seconds and bowing his head when they prayed. Although the Baptist terminology didn't mean much to me personally, I like Roberts' sincerity and joy which was unusual in the orthodox denominations, and he didn't preach hellfire and damnation like some.

Jack and I obliged Neal for a while, and then left Gregory to growl at him while we sat in the living room.

'Well, Jack, after five years, *On the Road* is finally going to be published. When will it actually come out?'

'Yep—they said May or June, but now I suppose in the fall. Maybe then I'll at least have enough money to bring Ma out here. We'll find something near enough so we can all see each other often, visit back and forth, hey? We'll have big Sunday feeds—chats across the fence? A real home at last. 'Course I'll still travel and go to Mexico now and then, but to have a place to come *back* to . . . and if you're near enough and don't mind, I'll feel better when I'm gone, knowing you're lookin' out for her.'

Although I said how much I'd like that and how much happier we'd all be, and really meant it, I never counted on his prophecies any more. He'd made so many thousands of plans that never materialized. I was tired of disappointments, and I hadn't forgotten all our grand expectations through the years of sharing a big old house together somewhere. I'd really thought that was going to happen. Why couldn't these men stick to anything? They still wanted the same ultimate ends, but they didn't persevere, couldn't sacrifice a small thing for a bigger dream, couldn't keep their eye on the ball—they just scattered their energies fruitlessly. Jack and I couldn't discuss religion anymore, either. We'd each found our 'path,' and he was no longer seeking—he didn't feel the need I felt to test my new, tender beliefs. He knew all the answers he cared to.

That evening I fed the children first and put them to bed, then served the rest of us buffet-style in the living room by the fire with wine and candles, hoping to mellow Gregory a bit. Neal tried to please him, too, by challenging him to a game of chess while Jack helped me with the dishes. Then, since Gregory and Neal couldn't converse, it was back to the TV. This time Neal let us stay with a movie; the three of us always loved watching movies together and were entirely compatible in our tastes and criticisms. About halfway through, Jack heard a noise and went to see what it was. He let out a mock shriek when he opened the front door to Allen, Peter and a girl who had come to get Gregory. They looked in at us to say hello, then Jack took them out to the patio, whereupon Peter instantly shed his clothes and dived into the icy pool.

In the morning there was only time for a brief kiss goodbye before Neal took Jack to the yard office to begin another trek to Mexico.

Later that summer, Gregory, then in Amsterdam, wrote to Neal apologizing for his actions that weekend:

... You, my friend, did offer me a fortune by placing my bets on your choice. I did not follow you—I was an ass—but reason I did not follow you was because I felt that you inspired in me a shot at what number illumed before me. The number lost. I lost. I will never forget the loss. Not that I lost 30 dollars, but that I lost your power that you so kindly bestowed upon me. I now ask you to forgive me and give me another chance.

He was expecting 20,000 francs and would take it to the races and bet any way Neal said until he told him to stop. He would tell everyone else to do so as well.

You will be a millionaire in no time because you deserve to be—what I learn from Jack & Allen and my short life with you is that you are wonderful human being—As I write this letter I am happy to remember that you were kind to me and liked me—the mad no brakes car ride—the track—your home and television—your suddenly transformed actions when you were in your RR garb—your love of women—your sad face— our great conversation in McCorkles shack when I first realized your mind—I love you—Gregory.

Like most of us, I thought, Gregory had hidden resources of goodness, and I regretted my condemnation.

Forty-eight

That spring we attended the Cayce lectures as usual and had our private counselling with Elsie Sechrist and Hugh Lynn. In the summer we went to a conference where the featured speaker was Starr Daily, the ex-convict whose books had so inspired us.

Starr Daily was dynamic, a rugged, no-bullshit ex-con with blazing blue eyes in a tanned face beneath a shock of gray hair. Neal had high hopes that this perfect father figure would give him the answers which had eluded him thus far. He was confident Daily had been 'sent' to help him unify his fragmented behavior and conflicting drives.

But when the time came, Starr, like Hugh Lynn, could only tell Neal to pull *himself* together and use the faculties within himself. Poor Neal, there was no magic spell—just DIY. Said Starr, 'You have just as much of the Spirit of God within you as Jesus had, you know. Now get with it, boy, pray like the very devil and discipline yourself on a daily basis. Keep the light glowing. It will take time. You didn't get those lousy habits in a day, and you won't get rid of 'em in a hurry either, but don't fight yourself—*revere* the life that's in you, for that life is God, and rebellion is irreverence. Start with that. Keep that thought. You take the first step and God will rush in to help. You must choose.'

However, Neal could not surrender his feelings of guilt and unworthiness; his prayers were the apologies and supplications, not of a God-filled vessel affirming his divinity but of a miserable worm. His

284

continued losses at the track reminded him constantly of his failure and he became ever more desperate.

In my efforts to change the pattern of his thinking, I found myself virtually insisting we didn't need any money—a strange situation, when it was all we could do to scrounge a living from hand to mouth. It was such a bizarre fixation for Neal to have, too; he'd never been acquisitive, and everybody knew he either gave money away or spent it on others, yet here he was obsessed with the need to make a fortune. And for no special purpose other than to expiate his guilt. He even confessed to me that he had been considering faking another accident. I was horrified and begged him not to think about such an idea.

I shuddered and he smiled at my outburst. 'I know,' he said sadly. 'Don't worry, baby, I realize the karma I'd be asking for.'

Imagine my reaction, then, when only a few weeks later I got the dreaded phone call for the second time. Neal had had an accident and injured a foot, was back in the S.P. hospital, and I'd get no details until morning. I replaced the receiver and stumbled back to bed to sit in dazed disbelief and fear. Now I feared for his sanity, to say nothing of the dire results which would surely follow such a deliberate deception and the flaunting of what he knew to be right. All night my mind swam round and round in a whirlpool of dread. I felt suddenly isolated, called upon to handle alone a situation that I couldn't face, to humor a sick mind, never knowing where it would lead him next. Fitful sleep came only when I remembered the decree that you never get more than you can handle.

Next morning I was torn between rushing to find out more and fearing to see him, but when I hesitatingly approached his hospital bed, Neal was smiling knowingly and fairly fell out of bed in his eagerness to reach for me.

'Wait—I know what you're thinking—' he silenced my forming question '—No, darling, I did *not* do it on purpose. But isn't it fantastic? I had that *thought*, right? Wow—talk about instant karma— Wait till you hear how it happened! You'll never believe! Sit down now and listen.' He was chortling with awe and delight at what he saw as a perfect 'demonstration.'

'I was facing the car,' he said, 'hanging onto the handhold by the passenger car steps, you know, ready to drop off when we'd slowed enough, and like a dummy I let my foot off the step. I forgot about the metal mile-posts beside the track. Now, can you imagine me doing that? Don't I know every little thing about getting off a train? Haven't I practiced till it's second nature? Now, honestly, darling, do I ever make that kind of mistake? *But I did*—and my foot hit that thin metal marker. It sliced it neatly—right through my shoe—we musta been going about thirty miles an hour.'

I winced and looked over at the enormous white cradle holding his right leg from the knee to his toes. Seeing my look, he said, 'No—now get *this*, baby—not one bone was hit—not one! Just flesh. Now is that possible? *And*, it's the *other* foot! I'd be a gonner for sure if it had been the same one as before, right? But wait . . .' His grin broadened. He was relishing his tale and my absorption in it '. . . On top of all that, I can't collect one red cent! We were just *barely* beyond the yard limits, and I was *off duty*. How about that?' he asked in a hushed voice. 'Isn't that the most fantastically, perfectly clear and precise demonstration lesson? *God is not mocked*! Wheweeeew.' He sank back on the pillow and gazed upward in wonder.

I almost collapsed with relief. Not only had he committed no crime, he wasn't insane either. Best yet, he'd seen proof that a power beyond his own will could affect his life. Even if he wasn't sure God loved him, he marveled at His shrewdness and appreciated His mercy. (It didn't seem like a good time to try to convince him that the power he had just witnessed came from nowhere other than himself; instead of lifting him up to view his own Spirit, it would have diminished his respect for God.)

During this time, Allen was preparing to move on. He'd been in the Bay area nearly three years, and could now justify his existence as a 'poet without a job'; he'd even made some money. So at last Allen was not the 'sick blank' he had once feared. He planned to return East and then reach out still further by invading Europe.

Jack was in Mexico, and Allen, Peter Orlovsky and Gregory Corso made a detour to visit him there. But Gregory was again soon grumbling. He disliked the shabby living arrangements and insisted on moving into a posh hotel. In the end he gave up altogether and took a plane out, while the other three found a share-the-ride deal and drove across the wintry USA. Once in New York, Jack and Allen wrote a letter together, their mood high:

> Here's Allen and Jack writing you a letter on a nice typewriter in a big yellow airy apartment on 15th street and 6th avenue with a Hi Fi set, Chinese mattings . . . Picasso, big cats . . . Jack has a pretty girl who clings to him constantly so he has taken refuge in R's apartment to type novels for which there is a constant demand and from thousands of publishers clamoring over the telephone for our stories & poems . . . Please send

immediately one huge metaphysical manuscript to circulate among the fairy editors of Manhattan. How is your foot? . . . How is sweet Carolyn? God has forgiven her (tell her) so how can I not? (says Allen) . . . Please tell her to forgive me for that night in her house. The money you owe me, since you are sick you can have it for keeps . . . but in half a year when we are starving to death in Europe . . . I will write you big demanding desperate letters, please do not let us starve to death, please, otherwise the money is yours . . .

Jack added a paragraph of his own:

I am now going to Europe with Allen, to see ole Bill in Tangiers, and write in sunny Spain, and April in Paris, . . . read *Finnegan's Wake* in Dublin Library and visit Céline (got his address) and if I make a lot of money within next five years I will get a Mercedes-Benz and drive right up your driveway and give you the key, but don't wreck my new fenders . . . Will write to you from Europe . . . Allen says he loves you, and that goes for me too . . . he says forever & ever & always will & will be your husband in Paradise (he says) . . . and as soon as back from Europe he'll come court you again, he says . . . I don't know what to say to Neal, says I . . .

In February of 1957, Jack left to go directly to Tangiers and await Allen and Peter at Bill Burroughs'. In spite of his promise to write, we got only postcards. Neal and I did so hope that he might be inspired to write books less preoccupied with himself, but from what we learned and read after his trip he had taken himself along and home was where his heart remained.

Some time prior to this, Allen had read a poem called *Howl* at the Six Gallery in San Francisco and whipped his audience into a frenzy. In the audience had been Lawrence Ferlinghetti, who had arranged to publish the poem in a limited edition including other poems as well. The edition had sold out, though receiving little attention from anyone other than those already familiar with the poetry readings. However, when a new batch was printed in England and shipped to the City Lights Bookstore in the spring of 1957, the U.S. Customs seized the books as obscene literature. Both Ferlinghetti and his clerk were arrested.

The hearing opened in August and the 'Beat Generation' was launched. The furor kept the papers selling until 3 October, when a decision was reached in favor of Ferlinghetti.

Neal got to look in on the proceedings frequently when he was between trains. In his passenger train uniform, doubtless no one in the crowded courtroom full of North Beach bohemians suspected that he was the 'N.C, secret hero of these poems,' as Allen wrote in the dedication.

Indicative of how unknown both the poetry and the poet were before the trial, one newspaper columnist at the outset made a casual note of the seizure of the books, spelling Allen's name wrong and giving the book's title as *How*, 'a sort of do-it-yourself thing, I guess.' But it wasn't long before the national magazines picked it up, and the success of *Howl* was assured.

Since Allen was in Europe, I carefully clipped every word written about the case which crossed my path, so he would be able to reconstruct his rocket-trip to fame. By the time I saw him again it was all ancient history, and he was far beyond the launching pad.

Before the arrests had been made, we received a letter from Allen with his foreseen plea for money. Here was Allen scrounging for sustenance, unaware that the spinning wheel of fate had picked up his thread and was rapidly converting it to gold.

Just before leaving Tangiers for Paris, Jack finally wrote us a long letter giving a brief summary of life among the Arabs, raising Neal's temperature with '. . . you should see Morocco and all North Africa to believe it, imagine a whole culture of t-smokers—and those lil ole Arab gals with veils, that charge 3 bucks & pant and puff boy—(no disrespect meant to Ma, who'll read this (Maw) but wow what goils)—unluckily am low in funds and just look mostly—' Then he got to his principal concern, the familiar refrain: 'Well, Neal, I have a proposition now to make to you. My mother and I wanta move lock stock & bullshit to California once for all . . .' He would give Neal a week's wages for me and his expenses if he'd come move them, '. . . where, within days I find good cheap pad like in Berkeley or even Telegraph Hill and move in and there we are at last with our permanent homes next to each other . . .' He said he didn't want to move his mother back to New York because 'I feel like I'm finished with that old frosty fagtown . . .'

> . . . give me your decision on this, write to me here at this Tangier address, soon as you can, if you're too incapable, have Carolyn write the letter . . . I'm sure Carolyn will be glad to hear that I want to move my home out there; we'll have occasional big family sprees in Chinatown, etc. and sometimes you bring kiddies to my mother's house for big Sunday dinners, etc. Also you can use my bedroom for inbetween railroad naps, any time day or night . . . Anyway, my mother says in her letter, quote, 'It's a good idea to ask *Neal*, I'd rather he would come and help us.' . . . So please write soon, don't put it off, besides you never never answer my letters anymore

. . . *On the Road* coming out in the fall, I sure do hope no one recognizes you too much in that opus—all been carefully culled for libelious or unpleasant touches . . . might be best seller and we all get rich on third choice. My love to Carolyn and kiddies . . .

He wrote postscripts on all the flaps of the fold-up airmail letter, one being to me: 'Dear Carolyn, I'm praying now that I'll finally make it to my true home—J. XXX.' But the trip was never made. Neal had been promoted to conductor and, between regular runs, was frantically busy—at the track, playing his role at home, and involved with more women in the City. I wondered, too, if maybe this trip hadn't appealed to him as much as former ones because it was all planned out—there was no element of suspense or conflict.

Jack returned to Florida soon after Ferlinghetti's trial, swooped up his mother, arranged to have her furniture shipped, took her on a long bus ride through part of Mexico, and then settled with her in Berkeley—all unbeknown to me. Thus it came as quite a surprise to get a postcard from Jack, mailed in—Berkeley!

Am home here with my Maw, for good. Couldn't find you, Neal, on Beach or any news about you—What's the matter?—Drop in or drop me a line, we now neighbors—Did you get my telegram from N.Y.? Whatever the case, I understand. Carolyn, hope to see you soon.

Neal and I looked at each other. Telegram? What did he 'understand'? Jack's paranoia was sprouting again.

Neal hunted him up, taking LuAnne, Al Hinkle and the Fergusons to Berkeley, though I knew nothing about the visit until Neal brought home a copy of *On the Road* and said he'd seen Jack. I assumed that soon arrangements would be made for all of us to get together and for me to meet Memere, a long-awaited pleasure. The next thing I heard, however, was that Jack had left Berkeley and gone back East because his mother was unhappy. 'But he never brought her down here—or contacted me at all! She might have liked Los Gatos better. Why didn't he?' But Neal was unable to explain it. I was very hurt. It was an episode never unraveled between Jack and me, and years later I was further dismayed to read in *Desolation Angels* that I had been mad at him and 'refused' to see his mother.

On the Road was in the bookstores in September, and about a month after Jack left Berkeley, we received a frenzied letter to Neal:

. . . Come on, you old sonumbitch and get on that typewriter and write me your first letter in 5 years, if not to me, who?—My mother and I rode 4 days and 4 nights on the bus to Florida and got a $45 a month pad a week later, then I went to NY for publication of my book & everything exploded—To the point where for instance Warner Bros. wanted to buy *On the Road* for 110,000 dollars with me playing part of Sal Paradise and my agent turned it down because it wasn't enough money or something—Everybody asking me 'WHO will play Dean Moriarty?' and I say 'He will himself if he wants to,' so boy maybe truly you can become movie star with luck (tho my girl Joyce says not to wish that fate on you).

He went on to describe, act by act, a play he'd written. The story was about the same people and scenes he'd been living among when last in Los Gatos and San Francisco. But it was turned down, and only a hint of the last act ever surfaced, becoming the basis for the amateur film *Pull My Daisy*, which was vaguely related to the evening the Bishop came for tea.

Jack was being besieged by magazines for stories and had already sold three.

Appeared on TV, John Wingate's *Nightbeat* before 40 million viewers and talked about God monstrously . . . BWay producers bring beautiful models sit on edge of my (girl's) bed, ugh, wanted to make it so much with so many . . . Everything happened and I was wondering: what has all this done to you, are people bugging you & chasing you in Frisco?

He described frantic wild parties, he was 'drunk alatime,' had now switched from wine to whiskey 'which, by the way, is much easier than wine—all the time wondering "What is Neal thinking?" . . .' And on and on with great dreams of the future, of coming to stay with us '. . . with money to burn on groceries, kicks, etc. . . . Now come on, Neal, reason I didn't see much of you in Frisco this last time was shortness of money—no other reason—so write and let's get on the ball here, HIBALL.'

The high spirits soon sank. Although some of the reviews of *On the Road* were favorable, Jack had not anticipated the bitter attacks. He took them all personally, and they cast him into a new hell; every word of derision and sarcasm slashed his tender heart and fed his paranoia. He sought oblivion all the more in Mexico, Buddha and drink, the last two at hopeless cross-purposes.

Neal and I, too, were surprised at the ferocity and cruelty of many of the reviewers. They were like angry dogs threatened by a wolf. We took them almost personally ourselves, for Jack's sake—and all so soon after rejoicing with him over his changed luck.

Typical of the violent reaction against the activities and sensibilities of Jack and his followers was a piece by Art Cohn in the *San Francisco Chronicle*. The title of his article was 'Sick Little Bums,' and it ended with:

This, then is the new religion, the Jehovah of the Beaten handed down from his Mount: Thou shalt kill for the sake of killing. Thou shalt defile all flesh, including your own. Thou shalt deny thy birthright and resign from the human race. Thou shalt contribute nothing to the world except scorn. Thou shalt destroy the innocent. Thou shalt make a mockery of morality, justice, law, common fairness and, most of all, love. Thou shalt dishonor thy father and mother and curse them for giving thee birth.
Amen, you pathetic, self-pitying, degenerate bums, amen!

There were many, many more 'reviews' along the same lines, and we grieved for Jack.

When Neal brought home the advance copy Jack had given him in Berkeley, I was far enough removed from the events it described to be able to read it through, and I was as curious as everyone else to know how Neal felt about it. He said he enjoyed Jack's descriptions of what they'd done together and got a kick out of reminiscing by reading it, but the glorification of his antics in print also made him uneasy. He wasn't proud of this side of his nature; he had tried very hard to overcome it. And the review in *Time* magazine hit too close to home:

. . . In contemporary terms, Moriarty seems close to a prison psychosis that is a variety of the Ganser Syndrome. Its symptoms, as described by one psychiatrist, sound like a playback from Kerouac's novel: 'The patient exaggerates his mood and his feelings; he "lets himself go" and gets himself into highly emotional states. He is uncooperative, refuses to answer questions or obey orders . . . At other times he will thrash about wildly. His talk may be disjointed and difficult to follow.' The significant thing about sufferers from the Ganser Syndrome is that they are not really mad—they only seem to be.

It hurt Neal deeply to find himself exposed as that kind of nut. 'And why don't they ever look at my work record? "Uncooperative"? "Not answer questions"? "Not obey orders"? Hunh.'

I wanted to fly to the defense of both men, but there was no way, and besides, here was another test of 'Bless those who despitefully use you.'

Forty-nine

The process of growth is almost imperceptible at times—'Grow as a tree grows,' said the Buddha. Three years elapsed before I was able to score a solid win by applying Hugh Lynn's curt and decisive command to 'keep still.' My efforts before had been consciously willed, and perhaps had failed precisely because I had been trying to 'fight one force with another.' This time there was no conscious effort on my part, more a weary rebellion against the usual conditioned response.

The day in question remains in my memory as a vivid manifestation of the laws we'd read and heard over and over again.

The winter was one of the wettest we'd had in years, and freight work was slowing down, so that the men with more seniority were able to 'bump' Neal from his regular runs more often. One morning after the children had gone, he came home to announce—or try to announce, after he'd beaten about the bush a good deal—that he wanted to . . . um . . . go to . . . uh . . . Mexico, 'just for a short trip, understand—I'll be right back.' My adrenaline surged through its well-worn channels, but suddenly the thought came to me that I was *tired* of feeling this way. It was a strange sensation, rather like sky diving, I imagine, floating in emptiness with no bearings, or like suddenly walking off a cliff.

I said nothing and continued making the bed. Neal, taken aback by my unusual silence, continued speaking in his own defense, just as though I had responded with the familiar objections. In a moment I began to feel the change in me, the relief at not reacting negatively. I was in control. I could tell I now had the advantage, and I kept on keeping still, though I also had to keep busy. I walked past Neal into the bathroom and began to brush my hair.

He followed. 'So? How about it?' The mystery made him nervous and irritable.

I sighed wearily. 'Neal, you know as well as I what the situation is here. I don't have to tell you about our finances. What is there for me to say?'

Was I really saying this so calmly? I spoke without emotion or bitterness. He couldn't figure me out—after nearly ten years of a constant pattern? And neither of us knew the rules to this new game.

He then stamped around the house, slamming the refrigerator door and working himself into a fury, while I held my breath. He came back to me. 'Damn it, Carolyn, why not? I'll only be gone a few days. It won't cost that much. I've been working solid all year; I gave up going to get Jack. A man deserves a vacation, doesn't he? What the hell!'

This was my cue to say 'What about me? Don't I ever get a vacation?' etc. But now I had no desire to say it, and I continued to straighten the house, somewhat anxiously, not knowing what was supposed to happen next. Neal noisily poured himself a cup of coffee, but again turned to me in his frustration.

Then for the first time ever he actuallly made critical remarks about me, but they were aimed at my former responses, not at my present stance. It was all I could do not to lash back in defense, but I didn't look at him and hastily loaded the washing machine, hanging on for dear life. Then I caught on to what he was trying to do, even if unconsciously.

'That won't work, Neal.' I was still calm! 'You're just trying to make me mad so I'll throw you out again. If I tell you to get out as before, then you can skip off with a clear conscience, right? And then come humbly back and beg my forgiveness. Forget it. I won't make your decision for you this time. It's entirely up to you.'

With every statement my insides seemed to expand and become lighter, knots untying in slow motion. With this came an unfamiliar sense of power. . . . or something . . . it was all so new. I wanted to tell Neal about it, but the game wasn't over yet. Part of me still felt defeat and sorrow at his desire to go, but the stronger sensation was one of resignation—with a trace of triumph. Neal could see what I said made sense and he dropped his defenses; but now he was at a loss as to how to proceed.

He sulked to his closet and began banging hangers and shoes around. I assumed he was packing; I'd never doubted his decision would be to go. When he came out, however, he had changed into his old clothes. And just as though there'd been no discussion whatever, he pleasantly inquired, 'Did you say once you wanted that stump removed from the front yard?'

'Why . . . yes, I did . . . several times, dear.' What now?

'Better give it a go then, I guess.' Gruffly he marched out the front door. When I looked out the front window, there he was with a shovel and a pick-axe digging away with a vengeance in the cold fog, his frustration flung at the wet ground through his flying pick. I gazed in wonder and admiration, smiling all over. It was then I realized I had done no more than follow Hugh Lynn's advice—and it had worked! He had understood all along.

The next time I looked, Neal had completed a deep trench around the stump, backed the big old Packard within a few feet of it, and was trying to attach a chain to both—a chain that looked suspiciously like the dog's leash. Could it possibly be strong enough? Misgivings rose within me, but I brushed them aside. 'He'll find out. Don't interfere.' Soon I heard the motor of the Packard racing and grinding. I went to the window again to watch the extraction. The Packard was spraying grass and mud high into the air as it ground itself into the lawn, halfway up the hubcaps. Then the chain snapped. As Neal jumped from the car, I hastily retreated. I didn't doubt he could get the car out with boards or something, but I knew the setback would anger him.

In another minute or two I checked his progress. I could hardly believe my eyes. Anger, indeed, had obviously distorted his reason, for there he was, backing the Rambler station wagon into position on the lawn to tow the Packard! This I couldn't watch. I retreated back into Johnny's room and became very busy, bracing myself for the inevitable explosion. I could hear the second car churning, then silence.

To my surprise, Neal came into the house slowly, quietly, not slamming the door, and walked back to where I was. He dropped onto the bed, defeated but humble.

'What is it, honey?' (As if I didn't know.)

'Well, it just shows you. I should have gone. I just blew everything, that's all . . . everything.'

294

'Oh? How's that?' I went into the living room to look. Sure enough, there were both cars deeply embedded in the green turf, the stump secure. It was all I could do not to laugh; Mack Sennett would have loved it. But at that moment I didn't think Neal would share in my amusement. So I hung on and rallied round. 'Oh well, no good lamenting. Tell you what, maybe the 3-A could get them out with their tow truck. Shall I call them?' Neal opened up like a sunflower. He never could get accustomed to these available services.

In a matter of minutes, the tow truck not only dislodged both cars but extracted the stump as a bonus. The day was won. Happily, Neal filled in the hole and the ruts with earth. I reassured him that the grass would repair itself, and by the time the children came home from school he was glowing and serene, proud of his contribution to his home, and I heaped on the gratitude.

For the rest of the afternoon Neal sat on the couch in the family room, the children clustered around him, and right before my skeptical eyes he created intricate toys out of toothpicks and string. He was patient and skillful, emanating warmth and his special sparkling humor. Here was the man I'd married, the same man who'd spent another afternoon stringing tiny glass beads on silver wire to make a spider's web.

He continued to give of his best through dinner and the bedtime rituals. When the children were tucked in, we returned to our room, and I thanked him for giving us all such a lovely day. 'You know what it makes me think of, Neal? That saying, that the greater the negative impulse overcome, the greater is the positive energy released in the opposite direction, like the kick from a gun. Remember? Maybe because you overcame your desire to go to Mexico, you set the law in motion and automatically released all that creative energy in its place. You were certainly a blessing to us. Don't you feel good, too?'

'Yeah . . . sure. You're right, of course.' He didn't take up the discussion eagerly in his customary way, and I wondered why not. Then he went into the bathroom for a long time, and my uneasiness returned. When he came out he opened his closet and stared into it. I sensed his restlessness but pretended to study the *TV Guide*. 'Anything in particular you'd like to watch tonight?'

'Well . . . actually, sweetheart . . .' He sat down close to me on the bed. 'You know, there is a Cayce lecture in town tonight, and I thought I'd go hear it . . . uh . . . would you like to go, too?'

From his manner, I knew what my answer had to be. 'No, not tonight, thanks.' My high spirits began to sink.

'Well, then . . . I really do think I should run down to Mexico . . . you see, I promised Doug . . .' I needed to hear no more and dashed for the bathroom, shutting the door with one hand and my mouth with the other. So it had all been for nothing. No, I couldn't believe 'nothing'; but why didn't the cure last? Why, once you caught on, couldn't it be permanent? (It was to be many more years before I understood that, once you think you've got it, the tests begin.)

When I'd composed myself and revived the show of resignation, I returned to the *TV Guide*. He, meanwhile, was throwing socks and shorts into his suitcase. He closed it and came over to hug me, back to the original script. 'Now, darling, don't you fret. *If* I go, I'll be home no later than a week. First I'll go to the lecture, and maybe afterward I won't want to go. I'll take these clothes just in case—no sense "doubling back," eh? Heh, heh.' He winked and grinned, wobbling his eyebrows. I was not amused and had reverted to my stony resistance.

When the front door closed behind him, I let loose the tears. I knew, even if he pretended he didn't, what his decision would be. What was the use of anything—of even learning to keep my mouth shut? What difference did it make? When I was all cried out and nearly asleep, I was frightened awake by a noise like a door sneakily opened and closed. I froze in terror. But who should softly tip-toe in but Neal. The miracle was complete, in spite of my limited faith.

We didn't want to let it go just yet by going to sleep so, cuddling together, Neal told me about the lecture. 'Actually, you see, today we both did what the lecture was about: crucifixion. By "crucifying" our selfish desires, we were lifted up—"resurrected," see? . . . into "heaven," hunh, baby?'

One evening in early February, after the children were in bed and I had taken some mending into our bedroom, Neal came in and sat on the bed—and fidgeted. Ever since he'd come home from work he'd been behaving as he did when there was something on his mind which he was debating whether to tell me about, and I was bracing myself for whatever it was—a serious matter judging by his tone and appearance.

He took a deep breath. 'Carolyn, there's something I think I should tell you.' He'd been much more open and communicative with me since Natalie's death and our twenty-four hours in 'heaven.' 'You see, I was at a sort of party this afternoon at the Fergusons' pad in

North Beach. When I left to get my train, a couple of guys said they'd drive me to the depot. When we got there, I offered them a couple of joints in return, went to my locker and brought them three. Then on my way home it hit me: something told me they were narcs. I'm positive now they were.'

I didn't know what to say; I'd no idea what it meant. 'Do you mean you think they'll do something? What?'

'That's just it. I think it was a trap. You see, a couple of months ago some other guys asked me to buy them some tea. They gave me forty dollars, and I said I'd try. I was sure they were agents, so I took the forty dollars to the track . . . which of course let them know *I* knew. Now, somehow, I think it's all connected. Damn.'

Up to that point, my experience with law enforcement agents in our society had been limited to receiving a parking ticket or two, and I still considered them public servants and protectors of peace. I'd supported them over Neal's traffic citations, only vaguely irritated that their methods didn't seem to deter him from continued infractions.

My ignorance left me unable to offer solace or practical suggestions to Neal. I wasn't as affected as he was simply because I didn't know the consequences, whereas he did. As the weeks went by and nothing happened, Neal relaxed and I forgot about the matter, figuring either he had been mistaken or his guilt was insignificant, my trust in the authorities intact.

Gradually, however, a bizarre change began taking place in Neal. He became hard, cocky, swaggering, sharp and cynical. We were less and less in rapport. He'd answer my questions or comments with a smart retort or callous remark, obviously not 'with' me at all. I couldn't figure him out, and my apprehension grew. When I talked to Helen and Al about it, they admitted they had noticed it, too, and were concerned. They'd never heard him be boastful or smart-alecky before. Helen felt sometimes that he was afraid of something — something physical. 'It's almost as though he's afraid for his *life*,' she said, puzzled. Al looked serious and shook his head sadly. 'He's really asking for it this time' was all he'd say. The only thing I could do was grit my teeth and get through my encounters with the new, boorish Neal as best I could.

One chill, foggy morning in the first week in April, I was clearing the breakfast table when the doorbell rang. At seven-thirty? Probably some neighbor, I thought. I opened the door to find two men dressed in hats and topcoats, and as they asked politely for Neal Cassady they snapped open and shut what I presumed were IDs. I didn't see anything identifiable, but I'd seen enough movies to know what the gesture meant.

I left them to go call Neal, my heart pounding with dread, but they followed right behind me into the bedroom where Neal was beginning to dress. 'You're Neal Cassady? We have a warrant for your arrest. You'll have to come along with us.' Those hackneyed lines are familiar from theatrics, but their impact is utterly different in reality. At first I didn't remember Neal's story from February. I knew he was on a three-year probation for a 60-day suspended sentence for traffic violations, so my first thought hooked into that. But when I heard the words 'San Francisco,' I knew it was more serious. My shock and disbelief brought on a storm of stupidity. Seeing those two stony monsters standing at the open bathroom door, I hurled words at their backs.

'How is it possible that you people can walk in unannounced, and snatch a man away from his home, his family, his job—just like that? How can you do it? How do you support your own families by destroying another's? How can you sleep nights?' Oh, I was a tiger, and a pitiful one. Suddenly I was afraid I'd go too far, and they'd take me, too—why not? They didn't care.

Neal, on the other hand, said not a word, just continued shaving carefully. But I was sure his mind was racing. He was not allowed to close the door, the men hovering, watching his every move. Each time I'd realize what was in their minds, the horrible purpose of their maneuvers stung me anew. And I also saw that they were afraid of *him*. How could I have watched this sort of thing acted out in movies and not realized the baseness of it?

I couldn't watch any more; the tears began to flow, and I fled to the living room to wring my hands and choke back the tears of rage. When the men came out, I flung myself on Neal for one electric kiss, no words possible.

Through the window I saw them walk to the waiting police car, and the final hideous sight was branded on my memory forever: the man I loved, the father of my children, a man I knew to be gentle and kind, shackled in steel chains and being hauled off by other men as though he were a dangerous beast. 'He's a *man*,' I wanted to scream, 'a son of God, whether you *like* him or not.' How was this possible? He looked so forlorn, humble and defenseless. Neal, Neal—no one could be so evil as to deserve such humiliation. I sobbed and moaned, but it was only the beginning. How blind to it all I had been.

298

I repeated all the affirmations, but at this moment they weren't enough, my faith was too young. Now what to do? I wandered around, shifting between pity for Neal, for myself and the kids, and rage at the law. I sat and stared, wandered through the house some more, sat and cried When I had reached dead ends in every line of speculation and my emotions were numb, I did what I always did when something unusual happened: drove over to Helen and Al's.

By the time the children came home from school, I had achieved an appearance of stability. Not having the faintest idea of how best to tell them about their father, I said nothing. Each time I looked at them and thought of having to do it, I felt it would be equivalent to telling them there was a live, fire-breathing dragon in the closet and expecting them to believe it. In my efforts at normality, I almost convinced myself it was all a bad dream—only to awaken when I'd bid the children goodnight, the painful scene having left its aura with Neal's clothes still lying around the bedroom.

In the morning, Helen telephoned as soon as the children had gone. The *San Jose Mercury-News* had a short article on the second page which she read to me. Boy, that reporter had been busy working on his 'story' and no doubt on a promotion, too. He wrote that he had talked to the San Francisco police, the S.P. officials and to some of Neal's fellow trainmen. Since no facts were known to any but the police, the resulting piece was colorful guesswork from beginning to end, the whole made as sensational as possible with no concern whatever for the truth. Even Neal's name was spelled wrong—but not wrong enough, worse luck, and we knew the story would be believed as it was printed. According to the reporter, Neal was part of a gang of marijuana smugglers; he was supposed to be the one who could bring in large quantities from Mexico on the S.P. trains. (No one had informed the reporter that Neal's trains didn't even go to Los Angeles, much less to Mexico.)

Hanging up the phone, I shook with that special chill which these blows produce.

I was startled by the doorbell. On the stoop stood a short, dark-haired man. He spoke quickly. 'I'm Sam Hanson from the *Los Gatos Times-Observer*. I wondered if I might ask you a few questions. I . . .'

I cut him off fiercely. 'I'm sorry, you'll have to find some other way to sell your papers besides my personal tragedy.' The damning false words of the San Jose paper still ringing in my ears, I vented my fury willingly on this member of the press, but he hurried on before I could slam the door.

'That's just it, Mrs. Cassady. We saw the item in the *Mercury*, and we have to print something . . . I thought it might help if we got the true story and were able to do it in some other way.'

I stared at him, mortified by my outburst, and meekly asked him to come in.

He stayed and talked, or rather listened, for at least an hour, while I, still a jumble of nerves and confusion, tried to reconstruct some sense of our life that would mean something to other people. I don't know what I told him—too much, I feared after he'd gone—or was it too little? For hours after, I remembered things I hadn't explained properly.

That evening I hung around the front of the house to be sure I'd get the paper before one of the children. When I opened it, I got quite a surprise. The whole bottom half of the front page, plus two columns on the second, were devoted to our plight. Sam Hanson had told me that he had recently left the *Mercury* because he disagreed with their policies, and had been writing special-interest columns for our local paper, but this was about four times the space usually given to his output. It was a different subject in every way. Since 'dope' in any context was the most heinous of human degradations in the eyes of the general public, the success of selling a sympathetic story to an upper middle-class community would seem highly unlikely. I was amazed at his and the newspaper's courage.

In the article he did his best to play down the drug angle, stating truthfully that nothing was yet certain. He emphasized Neal's ten years of steady service with the railroad and my community volunteer activities as a Brownie Scout leader and fund-raiser for various charities, my four years of designing for the ballet school and my painting. The variety of these activities had brought me into contact with a large number of residents in the Los Gatos and Saratoga area, and now I didn't know whether to be glad or sorry for that. My immediate neighbors were professional or business people, highly respectable. The article's last sentence read: 'Let's show Mrs. Cassady she lives in a community that can and will help.'

Later that evening Helen came over to read the article and to comfort me, and she suddenly got the idea we should search the house for tea, in case the authorities beat us to it. Such an idea would never have occurred to me. In one of Neal's shoes we found an envelope containing five rolled joints. Helen made a fire at once and threw them on. To my astonishment, I found myself feeling like a traitor to Neal, knowing how hard to come by the joints had been and how much they meant to him. Inwardly I felt as he would have, watching those five sticks glow red. I almost cried out to save them, but stopped short, appalled at myself, considering the price I was paying for the brothers of those babies.

I still couldn't bring myself to tell the children. What do you tell children aged nine, eight and six? However, I knew that the next day I'd have to think of something; everyone would have read the article, and I didn't want them to hear the news first from some other child on the school bus. But at breakfast I failed again, deciding to drive them to school and pray; if I told them before school, they'd be no good at their lessons, and I didn't want them to stay, miserable, at home.

When I picked them up that afternoon, Cathy came out to the car with tears streaming from her eyes. She climbed in the back seat, and I turned around, holding out my hand. 'Cathy, dear, I'm so sorry . . .'

'It's nothing, Mom. I think I must have a cold. My eyes and nose started running last period.' Relief flooded in, but the scare was enough to ignite my courage. So after dinner I told them as serenely and undramatically as possible that their father had been arrested and would be gone for awhile.

'What for?'

'We're not sure yet . . . Oh, don't worry—he hasn't hurt anyone or stolen anything—you all know he couldn't do that. It is just something to do with cigarettes—a kind that aren't considered legal.' When my voice broke, Jami started to cry, and Cathy and Johnny stared into space, bewildered. What were they thinking? All I could add was 'Everything will be all right, you mustn't think about it. I only hope you don't have a bad time at school. If you do—anything— please let me know and call me at any time.' And again I tried to continue our usual routine and talk cheerfully of other things.

After I had left the children at school the next day, I learned that Sam Hanson had succeeded beyond belief, and for the rest of the week I was kept at a constant trot between the telephone and the front door. Old friends, casual acquaintances, total strangers, teachers from school and Sunday school, past and present, friends of friends, brakemen and conductors—hordes poured in and out of the house while others called on the phone to wish us well and offer help of every kind. Cards and notes arrived by the dozen, each one containing money and blessings; there was even one with $2.00 from the local 'hermit,' whom I'd never even seen.

Some of the visitors arrived in startling combinations: rough train men with their colorful if earthy language told bawdy stories in the presence of neighborhood mothers or Christian Science Sunday school teachers, and my lack of poise was keenly felt. All levels of society seemed destined to meet in my living room, harmonized by their magnanimous purpose. They all appeared so hungry to *give*, as though starved for an opportunity. And since I was also being given a good exercise in receiving, something I'd always found far more difficult than giving, I was blessed even more than they suspected.

And almost everyone, it seemed, had a skeleton in his or her closet, and evidently welcomed a chance to air it, hoping thereby to comfort me. I was somewhat uneasy lest, in future, they'd hold these confessions against me.

Along with good wishes and encouragement came not only cash but groceries, so many in fact that I had to hurry and stash them out of sight in the garage before each new arrival in case they would think their own gift superfluous or unappreciated.

There was a third stage of what to me was a genuine miracle. I continued driving the children to school throughout the following week and remained braced for a call from one of them. None came. When I questioned them as to whether any child had been curious or cruel, they all shook their heads. Mystified, I asked a neighbor what she thought. 'Well, I don't know about anyone else,' she replied, 'but we burned our papers the minute we read them, and our children know nothing about it.' I've had no more humbling experience than the realization that almost the entire population of the surrounding area must have shared a single thought that night. Not once were any of the children accosted at school—nor later even, during the two years Neal was gone.

Fifty

———

Al Hinkle drove me to see Neal in the San Francisco City Jail where he was being held pending indictment by the grand jury. How could I have lived so long, I wondered, without any knowledge that such places existed? Details didn't register, so shocking was the total picture to my stunned senses. I remember only the impression of hard, cold bars, from the floor to ceiling, in tiers, behind which shadowy figures paced or cowered or slumped, all sound echoing and reverberating hollowly. The officers were brusque, rude and tense. The somber atmosphere was oppressive, heavy-laden with hostility.

They had Neal's name spelled wrong, and I was furious. Now why would that small detail antagonize me so? I guess it was because his true identity was of no importance to them; he was just a disagreeable thing they had to deal with.

At long last I was able to see Neal; I had been made to wait an hour. Visitors and prisoners were herded along opposite sides of a long counter with a double barrier of glass and steel mesh, divided into sections about two feet wide. Here we stood, elbow to elbow with the person on either side, and tried to establish some kind of personal communication through a speaker system, everyone wailing and trying to out-shout the others in an effort to hear and be heard.

Neal looked cheerful, and his talking eyes were at their best. 'Don't worry, baby. Carolyn, hear me? Everything's cool. Terrible place, I know, but God is with me. I'm way above it all, believe me. I feel great, not antagonistic. I'll tell you all about it later, just don't fret, Mommie, promise?' He gave me the name of the public defender assigned to him, a Mr. Nicco, and told me where to find him. 'Don't get another lawyer—this guy is terrific, all I'll need.'

A week later Helen went with me to see Mr. Nicco. My hopes rose when I met him. He was sharp, dynamic and wonderfully understanding. He felt sure Neal's chances were good and asked about our situation at home. Much encouraged, Helen and I were walking to the stairs that led down to the street when, hearing footsteps clattering down the flight above us, we paused to look up. I reached for the handrail, close to a good old-fashioned swoon. It was Neal! He was bounding down the steps two at a time, a big grin on his face. He caught up with us, put his arms about us both and pulled us down the remaining steps.

'Neal, wait, wait' I gasped. 'What are you doing out?'

'Ha, *ha*—I'm free! The grand jury couldn't find enough evidence. They just laughed at the charges! I *told* you, didn't I? Hunh? Didn't I? Ha, ha—where's the car? Come on, *let's go home!*'

What a rollicking ride that was. We stopped at the depot for Neal to sign on the extra board and sailed gleefully home, the world alive and spinning once again.

When the children came home from school and found him, they fell all over him, and we pampered him the rest of the day and evening, dedicated to dissolving the traumatic impressions of the previous week. Our bedtime prayers were highly charged and filled with thanksgiving that night.

Afterward he and I lay close together on the bed and talked. He was dumbfounded by the article in the paper and the community's response. 'And—oh, Neal—I'm so proud of your own attitude. See what a difference it can make? It's true—it's how you *react* to a situation that determines its effect on you. You had a choice, right? By choosing not to let *them* dictate your feelings, the situation couldn't really affect you.'

'Right on, love—but listen, that's not all. Wait till I tell you. Why, do you know I did the most amazing thing? You saw those cells? God, are they awful! The toilet's right out in the middle of it, you know—no seat on it, of course . . .' I interrupted to ask why. 'Why, my dear— terrible weapon! I suppose they figure you could bash in somebody's head. God knows—it's how they think. Anyway, I was in one with three other guys—yeah, three—one was an addict on withdrawal, sick as hell, but the other two started fighting—a huge spade and a

Mexican, and, believe it or not, before I even thought, I stepped right in between them and stopped the fight! Gad, when I sat down I nearly passed out. Only then did I think what I'd just risked—they could have killed me on the spot. But it was an instant reaction instigated by my peaceful state of mind, dig? Beautiful.'

'But why did they arrest you, if there was so little evidence?'

'Yeah—well, I found out. These two detectives, see, kept bugging me. They wanted me to tell them everybody I knew who smoked marijuana and where they got it. Guess they'd seen me around enough and thought I knew most. I wouldn't tell them anything. They took me in a private room and got madder and madder. "Cooperation," baby—that's the key word around there. "If you'll just *cooperate* now, Mr. Cassady . . . " They hit you in the stomach 'cause it doesn't show . . .'

'Aggghh, Neal, no-o-o-o,' I wailed and put my hand over his mouth. He kissed and held it. 'Yeah, hunh, well, when they'd wasted their week, they were really p.o.'d and said, "We'll see you in San Quentin, Cassady, if it's the last thing we do." Ha, the bastards! Yes, sir, my dear, that was a terrific warning and example to me. I know now. I'm free of that crap forever, hear me?' He grabbed my shoulders and shook me, his teeth clenched in determination.

'Oh yes, do I ever hear you.'

But Anslinger's boys on the narcotics squad were not so easily diverted from their vow. The following morning the doorbell summoned me once again and I was faced with a second pair of vultures. My night of renewal gave me confidence. 'You must be mistaken,' I smiled sweetly. 'He was released for lack of evidence yesterday.'

'Sorry, ma'am, we have a new warrant. He'll have to come with us.'

This time I simply sat down in complete bewilderment, letting the principals play out the second performance without me. Only this time, Neal was angry—no, furious. He didn't accompany them humbly as before, but strode out ahead of them, his head high, muttering curses under his breath. A new wave of forboding swept over me. Now what?

One thing was sure: I couldn't tell the children again. It had been so wonderful to have him back, the dark cloud dispelled. So, trusting the good people around us, I told them Neal had been called for a hold-down north of San Francisco and would not be home for quite a long time, but that he'd write. Not all this at once, of course, because I hoped he'd get out as before, and I tried to be vague enough not to propagate a big lie for them to discover later. They accepted my explanation readily. It was one time when I was grateful for the railroad and the children's familiarity with its erratic schedule.

My faith in the community was justified, and unbelievable as it sounds, the children learned nothing of Neal's incarceration until they were in their teens.

Next day I hurried to San Francisco, eager to learn the reason for Neal's re-arrest. The filthy jail was the same, but Neal was not. He was seething with defiant anger, practically twitching all over with the effort to control his fury and his language. Any attempt to remind him of the lesson in attitude he'd learned the first time was futile. He was deaf to my pleas. All he knew at present was that, at midnight the night before, the two detectives had demanded a special session of the grand jury and had trumped up new evidence and witnesses. He'd find out more and write to me.

When I returned home, I immediately sat down to write to him, hoping to find a way to reverse his attitude. I stuffed in as many quotes from Cayce as possible. Two agonizing days later I received his reply:

> Henceforth, restrict your letters to two pages, one side only . . . I've read all of *Science and Health* . . . by Eddy. She has something, not enuf in toto, tho; reread all New Testament, refreshing as usual. Am now finishing all the Bible, without pronouncing the names, of course. Have attended all available church services: confession, mass, Protestant and 1 negro fundamentalist. Say numerous rosaries daily and have memorized 7 gifts of Holy Ghosts, 12 fruits of same, prayers for Dead, sick, unity, confidence, adoration, love, life, Angelus, various litanies, various arts, 10 commandments, 11 mysteries, etc.—so I'm well up in Spirit, highest *ever*; only Grace beats Karma, etc. However, ahem, uh & gulp: *Please save* form charts, most important. Mostly disturbed about John. Pray constantly. Even believe can now father him correctly and girls too. Bless them . . .

It seemed to me that Neal was avidly filling his mind with as much rote as possible to prevent his anger from surfacing. He wasn't giving it much thought; his attitude remained the same. Outwitting the detectives was his prime concern. He had read the transcript of the grand jury hearing and was confident he could do it. From the transcript he learned that everything stemmed from the $40.00 given him by the agents to buy marijuana, but they had neither a receipt nor the marijuana.

Bail was set at $12,000, but Neal was going to court to try to get it lowered. He said the District Attorney had made 'wild claims . . .

which clearly showed that the D.A. had "facts" (his exact words in court) from some newspaper source.' These 'facts' had been taken word for word from the *San Jose Mercury-News*. 'All this to show the judge I'm dangerous outside.'

I marvelled at the amount of bail, as did Helen when I called her. It sounded far more serious than was warranted by the comparative triviality of the 'crime.' 'Neal says it's to keep him off the streets. What does that mean?' Helen asked Al.

'Yeah, see,' he explained, 'that means since Neal knows the identity of the narcs, he can blow their cover, tell his friends, and they'd lose their jobs.'

'Humph,' chimed in Helen, 'tough-titty—what about *Neal*'s job? Jesus. But Carolyn, will you get the property bond on the house?'

'Gee, Helen, I don't know what to do. How can I do that? It's all we've got, and no income—and how can I hire a lawyer? It cost us $7,000 for the S.P. trial—where would I get the money? Unless I lose the house, and I just can't do that. If I could trust Neal's word better, it would be okay, but you remember how oddly he was behaving before all this? Can you imagine him ever actually surrendering willingly, once free?'

'Frankly, no. That would be hard to believe—he hates them so, and has vowed so often never to go back to jail. I don't know, gal. I'm glad I'm not in your shoes.'

So I sweated and strained and weighed and balanced, trying to make a decision on whether to use the house as security for bail. One thing I didn't know at this time was that the Fergusons had also been arrested with Neal, so I missed completely the significance of his emphasis on a jury trial—he meant one for him alone. Nor did I know that the entire cast had been changed and Neal assigned a different public defender—all of them in cahoots, said Neal later—so I was still counting on Mr. Nicco to step forward and iron things out.

Beyond these immediate considerations, my ignorance also extended to the function of the courts. I assumed they were there for the sole purpose of administering righteous judgment, impartial justice, and were ruled over by men of the highest integrity—all that myth we learn at school. I didn't feel qualified to guess whether a Higher justice was operating here. Even if Neal were innocent of *this* charge—and I had some misgivings—how many crimes had he already gotten away with, undetected by man's laws? Did I have a right to interfere, and if so, how much? Was it all just part of Neal's need for punishment? A karmic debt? What a rotten responsibility, I moaned.

Al had found out that the S.P. wanted no part of Neal ever again. Neither Al nor I shared Neal's confidence that he could talk them into taking him back, nor were they about to come to his defense now. They said they didn't care if the newspaper story were true or not; the mere fact that the railroad had been implicated in print was enough. With no possibility of money from that quarter, with multiple debts already past due, and with no income in sight, I could not bring myself to risk losing the house.

I wrote to Mr. Nicco, and he told me that another public defender had been assigned to Neal, but that in his opinion Neal should be free in about three weeks. Ah, here was the answer to my prayers.

When I told Neal I couldn't bring myself to risk losing the house, he wouldn't believe it. At first he just repeated his requests, mildly ridiculing my objections. When he realized I was in earnest, he became frantic, and his only pitiful means of persuasion lay in writing. He had been transferred to the county facility at San Bruno and told me not to visit.

I flinched at his letters, but still read them avidly, hoping he could find a reasonable way out for me. But his final desperate attempts to reach me only made matters worse:

... Carolyn, I'll never forgive you. How can you be so blithely demented? *What* are you afraid of and where is the risk? *Calm* yourself & *face* it simply: I show for court and house is *safe*, period. Do you *really* fear I'll run away? No? Then what's wrong? ... I assure you all problems will be quite solved during my bail-procured freedom by a method necessarily unrevealed, as it involves the *big* money. If you hesitate because the P.D. said 'only three more weeks,' I *know* he is incorrect by *months* ... Remember, *now* is your *only* hope to avert the deep sorrow you'll forever have in knowing it was you *alone* who prevented us having $100,000 & that by your *absurd* fear that I'd run off with our precious house! ... But aside from this *concrete* 100 thousand is the *fact* I can successfully handle this case only if I get out *now*. Please 'know' that McNamara [Neal's new public defender] is *not* Nicco & Superior Court is also something else, so, believe me, without *instant* bail, I'm Quentin bound. The one silver lining, when *that* happens, is that the state will grant you an uncontested divorce for only 1 dollar ...

He then said that if I wouldn't put up the house I should call LuAnne, Al, Al's uncle or anyone who would, after which he chattily veered off to describe the books he'd been reading as though nothing else were on his mind, before venting his spleen again in one final, vitriolic paragraph.

Every word stung me to tears, but now I feared for his sanity. Could he seriously think that I'd believe he could suddenly raise such a sum—legally—if he had not done so long ago? A much smaller sum might have caused me to hesitate, but that outlandish claim—had he lost all reason? I debated with myself over and over again, and I didn't altogether agree with those who kept saying 'He should have thought of that before breaking the law.' I could never willingly contribute to penning up anyone in such an inhuman place—but with three little children dependent on me, I could not risk what little security they had. As it was, my naïvety caused me to assume a debt of guilt I am still paying off.

No further word came from Neal. I accepted his rejection sorrowfully, but if he were as innocent as he believed, I counted on the trial to prove it. I hardly left the house as I waited for a call from Mr. McNamara, who no doubt would want to talk to me before the trial; any day he would call, and I waited for him or Neal to tell me the trial date.

Fifty-one

The next communication I received from Neal was a full month later—and the trial was over. The wounds of his rejection and my own self-doubts were reopened when I realized he hadn't wanted me to be there, and they were salted now by his bitter acceptance of the fate from which I had refused to save him:

> Dear Wife:
> Your husband, tho still imperfectly contrite, does freely forgive you for his now being a felon whose recent conviction by jury could so easily have been averted by bail and separate trial . . . You may be paradoxically consoled that thru your refusal, I'll hand back most of those 10 bad years you've endured, since on *first* conviction, the law prescribes 5 to life on each of my 2 counts . . . understand that this sentence is quite mandatory for those who go to jury . . .

He held out one frail hope: I was to write to Judge Walter Carpanetti pleading on his behalf and get anyone else I could find to do so, too.

> Enclose good snapshot of kids (dog?) and plead a minimum sentence . . . I repeat, for all else has failed now, your letter is my one last chance to escape the pen and subsequent parole for the rest of my ruined life . . . get these mailed immediately as I get sentenced next week.
> . . . Flatly unpersuasive . . . so seemingly bitter and beyond hope . . . as this final letter is . . . there is yet a further glimmer of unlikable insight for

310

it to report: I *desperately* need to see you. *Not* to berate, belittle or bewail, but to speak . . . about our future. This Saturday, then—my last here—let kiddies play in park across from building while you go in . . . as soon as possible after 1 p.m. Thanks.

. . . 'Beat' is even in Catholic pamphlets now; poor Sublette, I pray every hour now, have for weeks; it's wonderful. If wasn't for kids would *enjoy* prison, just what I need. Don't miss sex, driving or freedom, but must confess still hanker terribly for candy bars and cigarettes. *Please* forgive my last two brutal letters; they were obviously meant to snap you out of your folly in time, but they failed, alas, just as your attempts to awaken me before it was too late . . . Be strong, patient, peaceful. I love *you*. Neal

Given this second chance, I shot into instant action. I wrote the judge two single-spaced pages of the best arguments, *sans* bitterness, I could. I didn't want him to think we believed in getting away with anything, I just asked for a realistic choice of correction that would benefit Neal and society the most. Five years in prison could only produce one hardened criminal and three possible delinquents, besides a whole family for the State to support. It wasn't as though Neal were dangerous. I still trusted the lawyer and the courts.

In his letter, Neal had mentioned Al Sublette, referring to another tragedy that had splashed across the papers just before the trial. Al had been living with a girl for over a year when he decided to break off with her—'We're dying together,' he'd told me—and had taken an apartment on the other side of town. Late one night she had tried to go to him, but in the alley beside Al's apartment she was raped and murdered by a seaman. The latter was now in jail with Neal and said he had not known he had killed the girl. According to him, when Al refused to open his door to the girl she had enticed the passing seaman and led him to the alley. There she had disrobed, folding her clothes carefully over the wire fence (as they were found by the police) and offering him her bottle of whiskey. The seaman said he had only attempted to curb her irrational screaming; she was a cripple, an alcoholic and a wreck of a human being, and it probably took very little to extinguish her dim light.

Al had become involved in the mess, not only emotionally, since he blamed himself for her death, but publicly, too, the whole sensationalized scandal annihilating his will and turning him, too, into a hopeless alcoholic.

On the day Neal was to be sentenced, Helen and I hurried to the Superior Court, and in the hallway outside the courtroom Mr. McNamara bore down upon us.

311

'Oh, Mrs. Cassady, I'm so glad to see you. I'd like to ask you some questions.'

I cut him off sharply. 'Don't you think it's a trifle late for that? Why haven't you contacted me before?' I swept him a scathing glance.

'Well, you see . . . since we haven't actually any proof of your husband's guilt . . . let me see . . .' and he began shuffling nervously through his papers.

'Then what is he doing *here*?' I retorted, and was so angry and close to tears that I turned on my heel and Helen and I bolted for the courtroom, where I faithfully expected to see our revered democratic system in action.

The judge duly honored and seated, about a dozen men were herded in, shackled in pairs by their wrists, the whole looking like a scene from *Les Misérables*. Neal's partner was none other than the seaman, the fearsome murderer of Al Sublette's girl, but he appeared more like a weak and terrified rabbit. His sentence was postponed, and even though we were sure he hadn't a chance, we were grateful not to have to witness his fate.

The man sentenced just before Neal had been apprehended with a car full of marijuana and had accepted money from an agent for its sale. He was treated with respect bordering on the friendly. Later we learned he had 'cooperated' and implicated several other people. He was sentenced to one count of five years to life.

The proceedings were carried out quite casually, with more boredom than the awesome solemnity I had grown accustomed to seeing on the big screen. The judge spoke softly, it was difficult to hear him, but he seemed serious and concerned enough, so my hopes rose. I wondered if he'd ever received my letter. Neal was called, and I leaned forward to hear. He stood straight, his manner respectful, answering calmly when spoken to. The judge read off the data concluded at the trial, but he spoke fast and so softly I was only able to catch a little. But we did hear one incredible statement. Neal had denied ever having smoked marijuana, and now when the judge asked him again, Neal repeated his denial. Helen and I looked at each other in dismay. What could he be thinking?

The judge said, 'In that case, I must assume your connection with marijuana is as a dealer.' Mr. McNamara lunged from his sideline in a vain attempt to interrupt. The judge ignored him and began berating Neal, his voice rising and his color mounting until he was practically screaming insults at Neal about his 'double life,' despicable character and lack of cooperation with the law. Aha. That was the bit that really irked the judge. There stood Neal, his head bowed, poised, cool and respectful, and there screeched this man who believed himself worthy to judge his fellow man, absolutely hysterical with vindictive rage.

McNamara went close to the judge, practically pawing at his gown. 'But your honor—we haven't any *proof!*' he shouted over and over to get Carpanetti's attention.

When the latter ceased ranting, he heard McNamara, stopped to look at him briefly, then turned back to Neal with 'Yes, well, *I don't care!* I'm sorry for his wife and children, but I don't like his *attitude!*' And with no hesitation he sentenced Neal to two counts of five years to life in a penitentiary, both sentences to run concurrently.

Neal didn't flinch, but sat down quietly to be reshackled. I came apart and clutched the bench with all my strength to keep from racing down the aisle to tell the judge what I thought of him and his administration of justice. When I could take no more, I ran outside to tremble against the stair-rail until Helen joined me, saying 'Jesus, what a farce.' Then McNamara came bustling over, but I didn't dare speak to him, only glared. He stammered and mumbled something about making a motion for a new trial, but I knew he was only trying to save face, so we walked away from him, saying '*Do* that!' without any hope that he would. It was obvious that the two narcotics agents had triumphed; they could ply their trade with no further threat from Neal. It was all like something out of *Alice in Wonderland*.

In my disillusionment, Neal looked even more the martyr to me. No one knew his weaknesses better than I, but now I was proud of his integrity in sticking to his own principles, especially in the face of the judge's display of passion and prejudice. Not once did it occur to Neal to try and save his own skin by 'cooperating' and implicating someone else, good citizenship to the contrary. That Higher justice that Neal and I had come to believe in was now all I could turn to for solace.

Ironically, Neal began serving his sentence on Independence Day, 1958, for what I believed would be five or more years. I'd not yet learned that sentences don't mean what they say. 'Five years' means two, and 'life' means seven years with innumerable variations. The whole thing is an intricate game; one should definitely study the rules and get a score-card before participating.

Before investigating how prisoners' families were supposed to survive, I wrote Jack and Allen, and, of course, they answered with sympathy, distress, questions, suggestions and encouragement. As a bonus, I received an unexpected note from Gregory Corso, which I cherished. He explained first his behavior when visiting us, then ended with:

> ... This is hard to say, yet I feel I have made the earthly journey that is miles and miles of vision and sorrow and awakening to say: Neal's walk in life has always been pyloned by roses; and if a great old sick rose blocks his walk, he'd certainly not sidestep. That's what is so true and lovely in the man. When you see him please tell him for me that I well know that all things render themselves; I never knew this before, because when I used to come upon that obstructive rose I'd not sidestep, yet would I continue on, venture on, but stand there and complain; well, I learned enough this last year in Europe to dispense with the complaints; how absurd I realized to complain that which is life. I hope this makes sense. I want it to, because I am very unhappy about what has happened to Neal. I'm almost apt to say, Poor God and not Poor Neal. My love ...

My only other consolation lay in the fact that Neal's letters were so full of religious fervor. Desperately I hoped the higher power had intervened—that this might possibly be an enforced monastic interlude for Neal that could help him, as he insisted was the case.

Neal was sent first to a medical facility at Vacaville where prisoners underwent psychological studies, supposedly to discover the best method for their correction. As far as we ever learned this aim remained in the realm of theory only, but Vacaville was a more humane institution than most, and he stayed there in comparable decency for several months.

Over a week passed before I heard from him. This letter was actually the sixth attempt he'd made to reach me, but the previous five had been returned to him for a variety of rule infractions or what the censor considered 'double-talk.' He recapped each of these earlier letters in detail—yet *this* one had been allowed! The humor of it dispelled my anxiety. He went on to say I was not to try any more ways of releasing him or getting him a new trial:

> There is absolutely nothing—unfortunately for you & children—that can get me out before finishing ⅓—20 months—of my minimum sentence. You see, all first time 5-to-lifers, no matter the charge, go before the 3-man prison board in *18 months* and *then* get their time set ... & this is usually 2½ in, 2½ out on parole; despite this more or less standard policy, God's Grace crowning our humble efforts, I'm still sure of being home to start our 'Easter of New Beginnings' at least by the exact date in 1960.

I studied all he said again and again, but like Alice, all I could think was 'curiouser and curiouser'. It doesn't please me now to have learned that had I but known it then, a private lawyer would almost certainly have had Neal out in sixty days for only a misdemeanor. Ignorance then was definitely not bliss.

He went on to say he'd begun seriously composing prayers of his own and was memorizing the names of all the popes to help 'hasten my growth as well as all mankind. To better emulate these leaders, I am memorizing their names & add a new one each day to the prayer, i.e. today's Pope—the 21st in order. (I began July 1st) is St. Cornelius, who reigned from 251–263 . . .' This wasn't at all what I have envisaged as his monastic life—ah, but what did I know? I was grateful for his explanation of the rules, and the knowledge that at least he wouldn't be away five whole years.

Neal wrote each week when he could, often practicing word games and imitations of Proust's endless sentences. When I mentioned Neal's religious ardor, he saw beneath my casual comments an anxiety that he might be overdoing it somewhat, and, in his usual way, he brought it right to the surface in clear, precisely analytical terms. Then,

One last bit on the religion 'kick' (& indeed it is this, whether in or out, it's really the only 'kick' left, true?). I read that Postulant in Cistercian monastery spends 90 days at least as such; this corresponds to my 3 months in SF jail; 2 years as novice, equaling my term inside pen, 3 years under 'simple vows,' my period of outside parole. So just as they take 5 years in all before finally accepted, I'll be completely discharged & accepted back into society only after a similar passage of time. Interesting what?

By the by, *On the Road* is in library here & Doug Ferguson . . . bewails that it's always checked out, so he still hasn't read it, as I wish no one would, frankly . . .

In most of his letters Neal managed to maintain an objective, sarcastic or satirical tone—with one eye on the censors—when describing his conditions. It was my penance to visit him, and it was always a torment for me, whether or not Neal was hostile.

Nothing could be more depressing than the prisons themselves. Vacaville wasn't as bad as San Quentin was to prove, and provided a reasonably gentle introduction to the system. The grounds were not as formidable, the building less of a fortress. Still, the two-way mirrors and the order, which I continually forgot, to 'keep your hands on the table' were humiliating. The 'don't touch' policy was the cruelest of all. The only benefit I could imagine from these encounters would

315

have been just to hold each other and sop up by osmosis what we both really needed.

Vacaville wasn't deliberately degrading to the inmates; there were psychological games to play as well as a balanced physical life. Soon after he was settled in, Neal wrote: ' . . . I look out cell window and watch trains meeting and passing a half mile away and within few 100 yards there daily comes creeping a local freight over Sacramento Northern branch line; ho hum, let 'em work; I'm on vacation.' In the same cheerful way he described the physical and mental tests he'd taken and excelled in:

. . . Took gym test today, ran 250 yards back & forth in 53 seconds, chin-ups 15, sit-ups 37—all in the 'very good' category. Took 900 question quiz on attitude and comprehension; then spelling, I.Q., mechanical apt. scholastic, math, vocab., voc. skills, etc. Now all tests over & am in 2 week doz.-person 'Group Behavior Adjustment' class. Our ball team (tell Johnny I'm a Giant, too, just like on his cap) won 2 of last 3 and now in second place in league. Each Sat. go to confession to receive on Sun. the Holy Euchurist from fine German priest here. Gained 10 lbs! Feeling increasingly purged of old desires, especially of flesh.

Neal hoped to be transferred to Soledad, 'where the kissing facilities are better,' but I suspected it was because Soledad was beyond visiting range. As in the armed services, I suppose, the place you request is the only one you may be sure you won't see, and so Neal was sent to San Quentin, and I received a poignant account of the transfer:

Dearest Dear Carolyn, Wonder Wife:
Even as they were striking my leg irons, that had, along with two sidearmed officers, locked door, barred windows & snow-white pajamas worn—minus the half-expected bright red or yellow bullseye on back—most adequately subdued any wild urge to disembark during the short bus ride from Vacaville, I began experiencing generation of a not inconsiderable self-pity, soon to become, while procedure progressed, almost overpowering by virtue of those repeated shocks every new dismal view bordering sheer disbelief administered in separate but accumulative blows to my so-sorry-for-myself sharpened conception as, now buffeted from both within and without into a bewildering numbness, I at last encountered, when first stumbling across the 'Big Yard'—as the 'cons' call it—in that characteristic state it seems to engender, a paradoxical one of hazelike concentration, the main source of what gloomy emanations my all-too-sympathetic mood had rendered it recipient; that physical wall each convict's despair-ridden tension made to exist inside the, high and wide though they be, far weaker stone walls of this infamous old—1859 is

316

chisled atop the façade of one still used building—prison, at which, accompanying 23 more, I finally arrived last week . . .

In the bunk above his was a 'thug who'd escaped 8 times . . . Truly, I've never seen nor is there elsewhere in this noble country concentrated . . . such an assorted assemblage of absolutely pitiful misfits as are the 5,042 felons—latest count, which Radio KROW announced on 6 p.m. news as largest number here since 1942.'

San Quentin, whether viewed from inside or out, left no doubt as to its purpose. It was an ugly eruption on a jut of land beside the bay, a barren blemish in the otherwise lush landscape. In what seemed a desperate attempt at camouflage, exquisite rose bushes closely lined the concrete walk from the gatehouse to the small entrance—turned away sideways as though hiding in shame. Wooden steps led to the door, and inside were more steps to a small, dingy waiting room containing old, hacked benches as rigid as pews, hard, cold and crowded with the pitiful collection of family and friends: old and young mothers, girlfriends, brothers, babies and every age of child and a smattering of old fathers. Beside the steps was a low counter where, if the officer happened to be there, you gave the name and number of the inmate you wished to see. After checking a file, the officer handed you a 'chit.' You then waited, and waited, and waited. I spent as long as three hours expecting 'Cassidy' to bark from the loudspeaker. I tried to time my visits so that Neal would miss work, not a meal, but sometimes, he explained, they had 'forgotten' to tell him I was there!

When the welcome name was called, you went up four or five more steps through the formidable steel door attended by an armed guard, who took your chit and allowed you to sit at one of the tables in the huge echoing room. The windows were high and heavily barred, the burly guards stood about the cracked ancient walls bristling with armaments. Another thick steel door opened to a windowless passageway that curved down to some lower depth from which the inmates emerged.

One day, when I was trying to talk to Neal, an alarm suddenly set all the guards to nervous activity, their hands hovering near their pistols, their eyes full of fear. My heart jumped at this display and I turned to Neal for an explanation. He looked back over his shoulder just as a small, frail black man came up the ramp of the huge passageway, armed guards on either side of him. As he drew nearer, the guards in our room leaped to slam shut with reverberating clangs the two steel doors. 'Probably a death-row inmate come to see his lawyer,' Neal suggested. 'There's a private room just outside there.'

Neal was quite used to all this; I was not. 'What a fantastic performance! That defenseless little man half the size of those guards—not to mention the guns. What do they suppose he could possibly do to *them*? You'd think he was a wild boar!'

'Yeah, well, they like being dramatic—you know how it is.'

I was learning how it was, and I'd wonder all the way home each time *why* it was and what could be done about it; no good could come of it in any way that I could see.

Neal wrote lovely letters to the children on their birthdays, and at Christmas and Easter. He'd tell them the history of the Mother Goose rhymes and the origins of different words, and he'd correct the grammar in their letters to him, and tell them some of the things he had done at their age. Most ironic, to me, were his lectures on behavior, emphasizing 'obedience' and 'truth'; and when John reached seven, 'the age of reason,' Neal outlined for him at length the difference between 'right' and 'wrong.' I sighed and remembered Cayce's proclamation that 'knowledge not used is sin.' When I received letters from Neal to the children, I cut off the top two inches containing his number and the name of his famous residence; on the back of this strip would be a note for me.

Instead of being taught a useful trade, Neal was put to work sweeping the floor of the textile mill:

> To overcome eardrum-bursting racket made by the cotton textile mill's 4 million dollars worth of 1745 RPM, 68 × 72" hi-speed looms, whose constantly collecting flug is my weary job to sweep all day from beside & beneath, I, thus, noisely assured safeguard from eavesdropping, deadening surfaced thought to equate the deafness, incessantly shout into that accompanying roar every prayer known, & since saying them hurriedly, it takes just one hour to complete their entirety, each minute, after the first 60, finds me repeating the very one said on that very moment last hour. Don't demurmer, it at least eliminates clockwatching.

On our first anniversary apart, he tried to convey to me the conditions under which he existed in his 4½ × 7½ × 9½-foot cell:

> . . . To get some better idea of what lying so encaged is like you might put car mattress in the bathtub, thereby making it softer & if not as long, at least much cleaner than is my bug-ridden bunk; bring your 200 lb. friend, Edna, or the more negatively aggressive Pam, then lock the door, & after

318

dragging 11 rowdy kids into our bedroom to parallel the 1,100 noisy ones housed in this particular cell block (of course you must remove the toilet seat, towel racks, cabinets—anything other than a small mirror & 4½″ shelf) remaining almost motionless so as not to inadvertently irritate armed robber Edna, ponder past mistakes, present agonies and future defeats in the light of whatever insights your thus-disturbed condition allows.

We learned with great disappointment and wonder that Neal was not allowed to receive letters or even pamphlets from Hugh Lynn Cayce; the best we could do was for me to pass his messages on. (Only after Neal's release did I learn he had been allowed to communicate only with women, LuAnne and other lovers among them. I preferred not to ponder the policy.)

In spite of Neal's generally loving letters, his resentment against me for not having furnished his bail lay like a coiled serpent in his heart, and every so often he was unable to prevent its striking out. As time passed, I grew to sense its constant presence, and although I desperately wished to believe in his rebirth, I dared not rely on it completely, his hate affected me so strongly. The first indication of its continued vitality came as a sudden blow, in a note to me on top of one of the children's letters exactly one year after his sentencing. It was at the time when we were getting people to put in a good word for him to the Adult Authority prior to their setting his time. He wrote: '. . . now's the time, probably too late already in fact, of course all this means as little or less than did my bail so maybe better forget such help . . . and just go ahead and spend a buck to do that which I advised a year ago . . .' In other words, he was telling me to get a divorce.

The next letter bore a humble apology and a long dirge about how much my love for him had dwindled, as evinced, he said, by the few letters I'd written and fewer visits I'd made. Then he immediately justified my actions, taking the blame himself for not having written and for asking me not to visit.

. . . yet there is no gainsaying my love for you, much as I thrash & flail to dismiss it because can't face that I'm its slave . . . The kiddies, about whom I dream practically every night, badly need a father—and not a weak-willed one handicapping them with an 'ex-convict' tag that can snatch him away again whenever a parole officer wishes . . . It took all the strength I had to advise you to spend that buck for final freedom from being a felon's mate, with all the lonely fears . . . etc. that being married to one, esp. one mad enuf to have messed with marijuana, forces down your

319

throat . . . I want you to accept [happiness] without guilt or worry about
me . . . Don't write or visit. Not worth the trouble nor even necessary. I
love you too much to need them now. Really, and besides, the frustration
of daily expecting to see or hear from you is fatal to peace of mind. All love,
always. N.

I wondered how much real satisfaction this tormenting me afforded
him—love and hate so entwined, pushing me away, hauling me back.
I'd have done anything he asked now, visited as often as he wished,
even though the few visits I did make were invariably traumatic and I
drove home in tears. The sight of me roused the serpent; his forked
tongue lashed out. As usual, Neal was fully aware of his actions, and,
as usual, felt apologies would change their effect. After one such
encounter, he wrote:

> . . . Well, here it is, the letter you KNEW would come—Oh, yes you did,
> even as you drove away in tears (figurative ones only I pray), even as you
> left in bewilderment hurt & with a certain wonderment & sense of
> hopelessness at the utter, at least seemingly, futility of our 'visit,' your
> intuition told you deep down, that whether today, next week or . . . next
> month, you would get a letter from me like the one I now extend . . . did
> we really sit there, thumbnailing table scratches & staring at wall-spots,
> your loving, humble efforts to reach me stymied by my stiff-necked
> adolescent gawk? I shall speak of that one word which constantly rose in
> answer to that question . . . WHY? WHY? . . . namely, 'resentment' . . .
> O.K., I said, O.K., so I resent her; WHY?

There followed a detailed account of everything I'd ever done as a
homemaker and mother, besides 'countless other tasks above and
beyond,' all listed and counted. There was no lack of humor or drama
in this tale, and when I thought he had finished, he wrote, '. . . I will
at last get down to the business at hand: an analysis of resentment
with examples of how I've taken it out on you, titled WHAT IS
RESENTMENT?, subtitled, "I'm not angry, but just look what
you've done to me?" ' And so he did, filling a page now with every
possible critical insight into himself. I hoped it was purging for him,
but I doubted it, even though I appreciated the effort.

Fifty-two

During this time, confusion vied with bewilderment on the home front. Cayce said, 'Why worry when you can pray?' but I had not yet learned the difference between real prayer and the accepted practise of supplication to God and concentrated worry, so worry I did.

It was up to me to find a means of survival. Through friends who knew about such things, I was led to the Welfare Department. Their program provided 'emergency rations' while they considered your case. These rations took two months to arrive and were pitifully inadequate, but my stocked garage kept us going. After another two months my application for aid was refused. I'd long ago given up trying to fathom their reasoning. After a further two months of pulling strings I was finally awarded Aid to Needy Children, or ANC. The parent and his or her obligations were ignored; the monthly sum for the four of us was $184.50. Our house payment alone came to $105, so we had $79.50 to cover all other expenses. To compensate, we were issued 'surplus' food in the form of butter, cheese, dry milk and occasional vegetables. Then there was always corn meal. Although I never mastered the art of making tortillas, many was the time that cornmeal mush saved the day. (Later, the policy of issuing these surpluses to welfare recipients was discontinued on the grounds of 'lack of interest.' It never occurred to the welfare people that the dispensary was ten to fifteen miles from most of those eligible, few of whom owned cars, and that no bus service existed.)

During the six months before we received any aid, I was kept busy worrying about the debts we already owed. Aside from the mortgage and utility regulars, there were scattered charges for children's clothes and a few installments on appliances. I wrote or called everyone concerned, and performed the disagreeable task of explaining my lack of funds while assuring them they would all be paid in time. To make matters worse, I learned via notifications of missed payments that Neal had taken out three loans unknown to me, totalling close to $800 in all. One company agreed to wait, one wrote the debt off, and the third said 'tough' and sent the sheriff to collect my car. When I asked how I could earn the money to repay him without a car, he said that was my problem, and then informed me it would cost $10 to take the car to storage and $5 per *day* as long as it remained there. More and more the nightmare of nonsense closed in.

Grace was still mine, however, in the form of the ballet master's father, a former loan-company owner. He paid off Neal's loans, chastised the lenders, collected my car and gave me an interest-free loan to be repaid when I could manage it. Many of the townspeople also tried to assist by commissioning me to paint portraits. This income saved us from foreclosure.

My first welfare check in September—I'd been without income since March—looked enormous, but the $79.50 didn't go very far. Along with it I got a new social worker, who was to review the whole situation and re-evaluate my needs. I had heard that he was an ex-Baptist minister, and I looked forward to stimulating discussions on religion. After his initial visit, he reported that I had a car and a 'swimming pool' and resented my surplus butter; I lost both him and the aid.

Neal heard the news in the following manner:

. . . The following quote, in its entirety, is of a message last night laid on my cell bars: 'We have been informed by the Santa Clara County Welfare Agency that your dependants (Cassidy-A-47667) are no longer receiving welfare assistance. Your name (Cassidy-A-47667) will now be removed from the restricted commissary list by the Finance Officer.' What in the world is happening? What does this mean? . . . Now suddenly this terrible blow—'Your family is cut off without a cent—sleep well, spend you sentence time constructively, obey the rules, rehabilitate . . .'

He went on to condemn the agencies, but blamed himself most and wallowed in guilt and remorse. He ended sadly with 'I can do nothing . . . for today I enter the hospital to lead worried immobility until

December 8 or so . . . Chin up, dear heart . . . Cathy Crosby to star in *Beat Generation* by MGM. Imagine a "beat" Crosby, revolting what? . . .'

I was allowed to visit Neal in the infirmary where we were left alone and permitted to touch, but I came home in tears again, this time for him. His operation had been for hemorrhoids, and because he carried a card stamped 'DU' (not 'Denver University,' he informed me, but 'Drug User'), he had been forbidden an anesthetic. This senseless sadism and his stoic acceptance drew tears of rage at our helplessness.

At home I returned to the battle with the welfare to get the aid reinstated. This time they dispatched their head man to deal with me. He had a reputation to uphold and boasted that he had been 99 percent successful in getting lone mothers to go to work. I was his latest target, a challenge I welcomed. Again I countered with simple logic—it made no sense for me to go to work and pay a stranger the exact same money to stay with *my* kids. We went round and round, with me upholding *their* policies as stated in their pamphlets, with which I agreed. Although he had to concede several points, he was not distracted from his goal.

Now I was required to take a whole battery of aptitude and psychological tests to see what jobs I was fitted for, and as I expected the results showed I'd be good at work that would have made me a basket case in a week. When I discussed all this with my social worker, he got another idea. Social workers had to have college degrees. I had such a degree. So now he made me sign up for the social work exam.

I rather hoped I'd flunk it, but I passed and then had to have an interview with a board of five examiners. This was carried out in an empty amphitheater, much like an inquisition, and had I wanted the job, I'd have been too frozen with fright to make a decent case for myself. After a few questions about my background, the answers to which they held in their hands already, the critical question occurred to one of them: 'I see you're a recipient of ANC. Would this experience have a bearing on your attitude toward the work?' My answer was swift: 'You bet it would!' My name was placed at the bottom of the list, never to rise.

My social worker shifted his attack; now he tried to convince me that I should divorce Neal. He reported with some enthusiasm that divorced women had a better chance in the marketplace. I didn't hesitate to let him know how shocked I was at such a suggestion from someone who was supposed to be holding families together in times of crisis. He finally retired from the field and my aid was reinstated.

Another blow came soon after, however. Misunderstanding the rules, I had not realized that any money earned could not be used to clear up old debts but instead would be subtracted from the monthly allotment. I had honestly reported my portrait earnings, long since spent, and the bitter truth was made known to me when my December check totaled $13.00.

What to do about Christmas? What to tell the children when there wasn't one? But my anxiety was misplaced. Instead, I had more difficulty explaining to them the ever-increasing flood of gifts from strangers, some of them expensive items such as watches, with sad tags attached saying 'BOY—aged 7,' etc. which had to be yanked off. We were on the 'needy' list of every organization going, and something of a bandwagon cause. My concern now was how we would ever be able to live up to *this* Christmas in future!

Outside the pressures I became involved in more theater projects. My friend Margaret, an authority on Old West traveling shows, founded a company called 'The Wagon Stagers' and hired me as costume and makeup designer. A perfect setting was found for these authentic melodramas in a replica of an early town enclosed in a high stockade. The stage was a flat-bed wagon flanked on either side by 'Calistogas' which served as dressing rooms. The audience sat on benches under the stars, and a campfire under a huge pot of coffee sent authentic aromas through the summer air. Cowboys whistled and yelled as the can-can dancers arrived in the nick of time, squealing and hooting atop the stage coach, and at the intermission these hands staged a gunfight. For me the long drive and the lovely evenings in the country were a soothing balm, so long had I been immersed in our depressing affairs. The children often came with me, sometimes included in the 'Oleo' acts following the play, and the museum, the town and the horses were an exciting change for them.

When our first successful summer was over, I was offered another job with the drama club at the University of Santa Clara, an all-male Jesuit school. I was in my element discussing religion and the arts with the young men well versed in logic. They didn't scoff at my weird ideas but were often amused at the metaphysical claims I put forward in opposition to their dogma. They treated me like a queen—and not a queen mother either, even though until then I'd felt ancient at 36.

Naturally I wrote to Neal about my new pursuits and friends, anticipating sharing them with him. He approved the Catholic connection but answered bluntly when it came to my new friends—noting that they were chiefly male, and stressing 'don't you think if I wanted more friends, I could make them from among the 5,000-odd miserable wretches in here? I've seen enough people to last a lifetime . . .' His response was at such cross purposes to my intent, I suspected he resented my freedom in spite of all my efforts to the contrary.

Also at this time two incidents occurred which I did so wish I could have shared with him and which a few years earlier would have spooked me considerably. Both involved Jami's apparently miraculous ability to 'heal' herself—first, an injured foot, and then a severe case of flu.

When I reported these concrete, visible demonstrations of the 'super' natural with some excitement to Neal, he didn't respond as I'd anticipated, and I could only conclude he didn't really believe me or felt left out again. I had hoped the experiences would have strengthened his faith, as they had mine. He must have thought about them some, however, because I received a confession of renewed self-appraisal soon after:

> I've found that all my metaphysical reading and thinking cannot create that understanding so desperately sought in order to *Believe*. Rather it is vice versa: I must believe to achieve understanding . . . but faith fails and virtue vanishes, what then? Patience, I guess, for, small as it is, that's all I've got left.

Throughout this time, another new realization dawned: I became aware that, for the first time in ten years, I knew where Neal was and what he was doing; I wasn't constantly on the defensive, constantly braced for the next shock or pain. I cannot deny that this gave me indescribable relief.

As Allen and Jack had requested, I wrote to them occasionally to keep them posted on Neal. I received a long and amusing letter from Peter and Allen in New York, Peter full of sympathy for our plight and Allen revealing new plans. He was coming to read at the University of California and the San Francisco Poetry Center and hoped to find a way to help Neal:

> . . . don't know if I'm considered officially a Nice Person out there or Juvenile Delinquent but with Professorial address it ought to be OK. See if you can get Neal to fill out forms for me to visit . . . and write if possible.
> Reporter from the *NY Post* doing sympathetic 12-part literary story on 'Beat writing' been interviewing me and W.C. Williams & going out to

Calif this week to see Gary Snyder, Ferlinghetti, poets there, etc. will probably look you up . . . I assume anyway he's sympathetic within the limitations of journalism. See him if you wish or not. He might eventually, if his story is sincere enough, be able to help—he sees Neal as sort of a martyr, given bad deal by Wicked Opinion, Law. Reporter's name is Al Aronowitz.

. . . Finishing new book of poems, main long poem about my mother 50 pages long & higher and wilder than *Howl* . . .

A few weeks later I heard from Jack, the first letter in a long time:

No, the prison authorities rejected my application to correspond with Neal, also Allen's. They are cruel in every possible way. Imagine that guy getting off with parole after murdering Al's girl . . . and poor Neal with his pockets full of innocent loco weed that grows wild in Texas and getting an indefinite term . . . Do you mind if I say this in my next *Escapade Magazine* column, or shouldn't I mention Neal's name? . . . Let me know how much you need for the typewriter and I'll send the check. The money will represent my debt to Neal for all the porkchop suppers we had over the years in your dear sweet kiddie kitchen, remember? (And all the pizzas.) I don't want you and Neal to think my book had anything to do with his arrest . . . If anything, if all the *On the Road* fans all over the world knew what had happened to 'Dean' they would all be writing protesting letters to SQ about it . . . But, O my book, *On the Road*, isn't it a paean to Neal? I hope you think so.

. . .When and if I ever come to Frisco, I'd like to see you again and have more pizza and wine. You'll find me jaded, compared to last time. Too much adultation is worse than non-reception, I see now, except on the economic level. 'Too much adulation' means also the disgusting abuse from critics which has caused my family in Lowell to announce, for instance, that I have disgraced the name of Kerouac, when all the time the disgrace emanates from critics and press.

Ah, it's all sad, like I said, like you said, like Neal knew. I shall certainly go to Heaven kneeling. I desire to remain in solitude, says Milarepa, because much talk is of no avail. So you won't see much of me unless I get a solitary cabin somewhere in Calif. But I think of your sweetness and tranquility the same as ever . . . The other day I paid my income tax and had a $30 deficit in the bank! So you see, I'm not rich at all and I'm not lying to you. But I got a check today that enables me to get that typewriter for the Preacher, as I call Neal now, too. I think the latter part of your lives will be prophetically blissful, so don't despair . . .

When Allen came to San Francisco, he took care of the typewriter himself and then came to see me over the weekend. He had finished *Kaddish*, the long poem, now much celebrated about his mother, and he read it aloud to me. I was so moved I held the genuine conviction that it was a masterpiece.

Then I received a postcard from Jack on three consecutive days. The first read: '. . . Allen taking care of everything, I just sent him check. He also told me the wonderful news that it is feasible that N. can be out in the fall . . . I'll do my part . . .' I couldn't explain why he'd sent the check to Allen instead of me, nor where he'd gotten the idea that Neal could be released. The second card read:

'Friends & Neighbors—Thanks for card. You want me to mail you a Book of Dreams?—worth 2.50—got ten of em to give away—Hope I can get to California but big snakes in the night are crawling toward me for my huge fortune (including snake Uncle Sam) (ex-wife) (relatives) (etc.) (ugh)— the 'Promise of America' is clearly crooks. Optimistic Jack.'

He didn't send the book. The third card said only: 'I Love You.'

After Allen had left the area, Al Aronowitz came to interview the members of the 'Beat' movement on the coast. He went to San Quentin and was allowed to tape a conversation with Neal, whose reaction was not favorable: '. . . Had a 3-hour interview with Pagan Reporter, no rapport. Everytime I began to go into the spiritual reality, he forced return to physical one, ugh, when will they leave us alone?'

A few days later, Aronowitz called to ask if he could talk to me, and I agreed. Maybe I could get in some licks where Neal had failed. Al was a stocky, dark-haired man about our age. I saw what Neal meant when I, too, tried to explain some of our spiritual changes. He didn't seem to comprehend a word of it, so completely fixed was his mind on the physical–social level. I felt as though I were speaking in tongues. He did try, but we talked in circles and afterward I wondered if anything had been accomplished. He was personable and pleasant enough, and if I stayed in his groove, we got along all right.

A day or so later he called me again and asked if I'd go with him to Big Sur to try and find Henry Miller. Miller had once made some sympathetic comments on Jack's work, and Al thought it would be a boon to his series to include the eminent writer. I could hardly refuse such an intriguing assignment. It was a lovely sunny day, and my spirits were ever recharged by a ride through the pine- and redwood-studded mountains to the coast, the rolling truck farms of Watsonville and the rugged cliffs of Big Sur. Our conversation eased without the formality of the tape recorder, and it was fun to talk with someone from New York again. Al had all that big city's tensions I'd forgotten people lived with; life was a laborious and depressing rat-race. But he'd done some fascinating articles, and to me, his life sounded full of glamor and excitement. I was spellbound.

After finding the identifying mailbox, we drove several miles before reaching the Miller property itself. Finally we parked the car and walked up some stepping stones to the crest of a small hill, below which lay a picturesque Spanish-style adobe house and patio. To our left was a long shed-like building. On the patio we were met by a pretty girl with shoulder-length black hair, but I had difficulty keeping my eyes from wandering to her lower half. Beneath a loose, low-cut blouse, she wore nothing but light blue ballet tights—she might as well have been walking around in her underwear. With her was a handsome, swarthy young man.

The girl, whom I assumed to be the latest Mrs. Miller, told us Henry was busy writing in the adjacent building and was not to be disturbed, 'but he should be out soon. You may wait in the house, if you'd like.' We walked across the patio and the tiled floor of the spacious living room and sat down in adjacent rattan chairs. The girl and her companion sat across the room near the fireplace, remaining intent on their own intimate conversation and making no move to include us in it. I began to feel they shared the same room with us only so as to prevent our swiping the silver. At least an hour passed, and Al and I were on the verge of abandoning our quest when the girl said it was nearly time for Mr. Miller to emerge. We returned to the patio to watch for him, admiring the painted plaques and other artefacts decorating the walls, which, Mrs. Miller explained, had been done by the children.

Like a burst of sunlight, Henry Miller suddenly opened the door of his writing shed and bounded toward us down the steps. Quickly, Al informed him of his mission, and even more quickly Henry said he was sorry, but he couldn't give us an interview because this was the time he always played ping-pong with his children, and he considered it a sacred obligation. We saw no children, but we could hardly object. Then he courteously walked us to the road where our car was parked, and in that five or ten minutes gave us a sparkling and erudite lecture on literature. He was only mildly interested in Jack's spontaneous prose style, saying, 'That sort of thing works only in relationship to the mind behind it—if the mind is of genius, good, if not, trash.' But he gave a rundown of the history of literature in relation to spontaneity from the Greeks onward, the likes of which I'd never heard; I only wished the tape recorder had been running. His comments were particularly rewarding to me since I'd never been able to get past page one of anything he'd written. This charming, cultured, genial gentleman didn't fit my preconceived image at all, and I was pleased about that.

When I saw Al's series of articles, I thought them remarkably well written, and they showed a sincere effort to understand men who lived lives so different from his own. Even if he himself missed the essence of the spiritual search, he'd done a good job in repeating some of what we'd said. Jack's reaction was: 'The Aronowitz series is frightening and yet I get the feeling it did a lot of good . . . the best part was Neal's dialogue about 'pineal fire,' etc. Big Cayce, Aurobindo mysticisms suddenly appearing on the page.'

Fifty-three

When Neal's time was officially set and we knew he'd be released in June 1960—if not a couple of months earlier—I began to try to find him work, a prerequisite for parole. We had expected he'd learn a useful trade during the two years in prison, and he had been taking as many courses as he could. He had begun with psychology but switched to music, and then when he had learned to read music and was about to be issued with an instrument, 'the order . . . finally came through . . . yes, music school and cotton phlug are now forever in my prison past, for from here on out—(it's a three-year course at minimum) I shall be learning the printing trade.' I couldn't understand such lack of organization. He'd wasted a whole year in the textile mill, and now when he was about to begin a course that might provide a livelihood on the outside, it would require too much time to complete, and so would be wasted effort yet again.

I had already asked everyone I knew for job suggestions, but most were unfeasible because of Neal's record and the fact that he was unbondable. I remembered Starr Daily explaining the hopelessness of expecting your debt to society ever to be paid by prison terms; the punishment never ends.

Although no marketable skill was to result from it, Neal's favorite course in prison was Comparative Religion, taught by 'Gavin' Arthur. At the time of our first meeting, Gavin was 59 years old, but the longer I knew him, the longer those years seemed to stretch in order to accommodate the vast number of experiences he had had and the people he had known. He had fought in the Irish Rebellion with a price on his head, and in the Spanish Civil War. Names of the famous and infamous peppered every conversation, yet he felt no need to impress, and each person was regarded with equal respect. No field of endeavor, no social class and no section of the globe was excluded. Consequently his company was always inspiring, his zest for life contagious. Gavin had nothing left of his father's millions through his mother's divorce and partly through his own second wife. A series of worldwide adventures and poor investments accounted for the rest. He now earned a meager livelihood by casting horoscopes and teaching. He had become famous in the 1930s as a San Francisco 'character'—the grandson of a President of the United States selling newspapers on a Market Street corner! But he never gave one the impression of being poor in any sense of the word. His bearing was always that of an elegant, cultured gentleman. He was tall and graceful, fine-boned and slender, his features of classic proportions, barring a short nose. His skin was smooth and clear and wrinkle-free. His fine brown hair was turning gray when we met, and during the twelve years of our friendship he always groomed it in the current style—long, short, bearded or shaven. Gradually, too, his mode of dress changed from immaculately tailored shirts and slacks to the colorful garb of the oncoming generations. His dark brown eyes twinkled with good humor and kindness, flashing sparks only if someone was rude or ill mannered in his home—his remarkable tolerance ended there.

Gavin's lodgings were always on the verge of condemnation and destruction by the city, and he would be forced to seek others—always in an equally doomed building. Moving was a Herculean feat. 'How I wish I were a Shiva instead of a Vishnu,' he wailed at these times. His students and friends helped out by decorating the decrepit structures with imaginative paintings or astrological schematics. But on first entering Gavin's rooms, these were not half so awesome as the walls, which were covered from the top of the orange-crate bookcases to the high ceilings with overlapping pictures, photographs of the famous in every field—Gavin on the knee of Ernest Hemingway, or chatting with Greta Garbo, for example—amid cut-up pictures of every imaginable subject: earthly, celestial, sacred or profane. The corner of only one room was always orderly and consistent—the 'President's Corner.' Here were signed photographs of all the Presidents since his grandfather's day, plus those of dignitaries and monarchs who had been among their friends, and personal souvenirs such as his grandfather's cigar clipper and his father's branding iron from his Texas ranch. Flanking the photographs were 80 loose-leafed notebooks packed with their letters. Other bookcases contained Gavin's extensive library, and yet more were filled with the 6,000 horoscopes he had done to date, all filed in colorful notebooks identified by characters from every known alphabet in the world.

Gavin came to appreciate me because I had stuck to Neal and thought first of keeping the family together in spite of Neal's infidelities, unlike Gavin's own mother, who had divorced his father. Neal himself loved him dearly, but from prison he wrote satirically:

Last Sunday 'Uncle Gavin' Arthur, grandson of our 21st President, who, Republican though he was, could hardly have been more conservative than is Gavin underneath all his Occult Astrology, failed to show (again, for the third time in six weeks) to teach our class in Comparative Religion and Philosophy, about three dozen regularly in attendance, on account of a death in his group at the Global House, which he bought by selling newspapers on Market Street for ten years; so again it was my pleasurable duty to instruct the boys in Caycehood—a task they always urge upon me whenever our respected and illustrious Leader, who knows literally everyone important in the Metaphysical and other fields (his talks range from descriptions of taking Yoga enemas with the great Gurdjieff to making horoscopes for Mrs. Winter's old crony, Dr. Blanche Baker, and Lottie von Stral (who he now suspects is losing her psychic power because of using it exclusively to get money to keep her husband, the Baron, who's dying of cancer, alive despite his oft-repeated desire to go). Our Leader either oversleeps or runs out of gas, as he did on two times previous . . .

Neal had not told me how he had first met Gavin, but Gavin filled me in when he called to collect data for the horoscopes he wished to construct for us. In the course of the conversation, Gavin gave me his impressions of Neal and recalled how he had first heard of him:

'I had read *On the Road*, of course, and I was driving Gary Snyder down to visit the Onslow-Fords near Carmel. Gordon Onslow-Ford is an English painter who paints far-out things and wrote a book about "instant" painting. He and his wife Jacqueline admired Gary Snyder's poetry and were going to give him a letter of introduction to a sculptor in Japan. So I said, "Gary, I know you're the hero of *Dharma Bums* but do you happen to know the hero of *On the Road*?"

And Gary said, "Oh, yes, indeed, I do. He's one of my best friends," and then he grinned and slapped me on the knee and said, "And *you* are going to meet him at ten o'clock tomorrow morning.'

'Well, I was absolutely flabbergasted! How could he know such a thing as that?

'With a sly grin, Gary said, "Didn't you tell me you are opening a class in comparative religion at ten o'clock tomorrow morning at San Quentin?" and I said, "Yes, but what has that got to do with it?" So then Gary told me that Neal was in "Q" for exchanging a joint of marijuana for a ride, and "He'll be the first one to sign up for your class—you'll see!"

' "Well," I said, "will I recognize him? I've never even seen a picture of him," and Gary said, "Oh, you'll know him all right, don't worry about that." He was sort of chortling about it, you know, pleased with himself. So I went to class the next day and looked up at the sea of faces—there were about sixty cons who took my class—and there was one face that was really *shining*.

'There was something about Neal when he wasn't taking dope that was absolutely angelic. I could easily recognize him out of all those sixty faces. And, sure enough, when the talk was over, he shouldered his way down, you know, with that impetuosity of his, and said, "Mr. Arthur, you read my name as Neal Cassady but you might know me better as Dean Moriarty."

' "Oh, yes," I said, "your friend Gary Snyder told me you'd be the first to sign up for this class."

' "I was, *I was!*" He was so enthusiastic, like a jack-in-the-box, so delighted that Gary would know that. Really, his enthusiasm was just—just breathtaking. I loved him the *moment* I saw him.

'Then, from time to time, I would bring guest speakers to the class. One day I invited Varda.' Yanko Varda was a prominent Greek artist who lived on an 'ark' in Sausalito Bay, and Gavin had him speak to his class on the Greek Orthodox religion. 'After the class, Varda turned to me and said, "I suppose you know you have a saint in your class. He has a halo around him." ' Varda believed in auras and, according to Gavin, sometimes painted halos around his subjects. Neal was the 'saint' he had espied.

'After that,' continued Gavin, 'Onslow-Ford came one time, too. He's a great friend of Braque and Picasso and so on, and he, too, was very much impressed with Neal's shining. But the visitor that topped them all was Allen Ginsberg. One day Neal said to me, "Allen's in town. Do bring him to class. You really should have him."

'And I said, "Do you think for one minute the authorities would allow the author of *Howl* to come to San Quentin as a guest speaker? You're *mad*."

' "No," said Neal, "I doubt if they've ever heard of him, and if you can get the chaplains to okay it, I'm sure you can do it." I doubted it, but I did broach the subject at lunch the next day, and the various chaplains said they'd love to meet Ginsberg and would see what they could do.

'Well, in a few days they called me to say the pass was going to be all right. So I called the place where Allen was staying, but they said he was visiting Margaret Mead's husband for the day, so I left word for Allen to call me the minute he got in, no matter the time. He took me at my word and called—it must have been nearly three in the morning—and I told him Neal wanted him to speak to my class and that I felt it would be very appropriate because it was Mother's Day, and I understood he had just written a poem about his mother. Allen said, "Oh, I'd love to do that, and it would give me a chance to talk to Neal without all those bars." And so it was arranged.

'I picked Allen up on the morning of the class, and being very sleepy I didn't notice he was wearing jeans—no free man is allowed into the prison in jeans, as that's what the cons wear. We got to the West Gate where I go in, and the guard said, "I'm sorry, Mr. Arthur, but we cannot allow your guest to come in wearing those blue jeans."

' "Oh, dear," I said, "it's all scheduled, and well—call Chaplain Eshelman and ask if he could lend us a pair of trousers and bring them to the gate, would you please?" He did so, but Chaplain Eshelman is much taller than Allen, so Allen had to roll up the pantlegs three times. When we were walking through the "Garden Beautiful" on the way to the class, I overheard one of the cons say to another, "Who do you suppose Mr. Arthur is going to bring as his guest next time? Last week it was a Yogi in orange robes, and this week it's Charlie Chaplin himself."

'So Allen stood before them, and to my amazement all three chaplains were there to hear him, all sitting together in a row. I felt so downed—they wouldn't do that for *me*—but Allen got up and stared at those sixty cons, including Neal, through those thick spectacles that made him look like a black goldfish looking out of a goldfish bowl, and he did what is ab-so-*lu*-tely *de rigueur*—impossible to do if you are a free man—he used the most frightful four-letter words in describing his recent accomplishments with the Navy. And, well, I just wanted to *die*—literally, I wanted the ground to open up and swallow me—because, I thought—I *knew*—that Allen and I were going to be incarcerated in San Quentin for years and years and years!'

'What do you mean,' I asked with my usual naïvety, ' "accomplishments with the Navy"? The Merchant Marine?'

'No, no, my dear—*sailors* you know, *sexual* exploits! But then, I

334

suddenly realized that all sixty cons were cheering. You couldn't hear yourself *think*. And I finally dared to look up, and there were all three chaplains—Catholic, Protestant and Jew—up on their feet cheering and stamping. Well! I knew then that everything would be all right.'

'Were there guards in the classroom?'

'Yes, certainly. That's just it. Amazing!' And Gavin shook his head chuckling to himself.

After that episode, Neal wrote to Jack, through me, urging him to come to speak to the class, too:

Dear Bro. Jackson: . . . On the night of the 20th, Herr Beat Brendan Behan Balzac better not guzzle too much wine, because the next *9 a.m.* you'll be following the lead of G. Snyder and A. Ginsberg—ask him about the scene—by addressing our class studying COMPARATIVE RELIGIONS; in which forum-style, anything from the BIG TABLE—in the Chapel library here, thanks to Allen & pastor from Texas—on up is religiously compared with life, as guessed at by we two dozen students so separated from it—tho the room, indeed the entire building, would be overpacked to fire hazard proportion if I dared let out that YOU were coming, why, they'd stampede, honestly. I'm sick of overhearing your nigh-notorious name being always mispronounced in 'Big Yard' conversations EVERY Day . . .

Jack came to California at the end of November—I heard of his arrival via the grapevine because he didn't call me. Also around then, *Life* magazine had published a story on the 'Beats,' including a squib about Neal being in prison. My family took *Life* and read it from cover to cover, so I was truly worried they'd find out where Neal was; I hadn't told them—that would have been way too much for them to accept. I wrote Neal about this anxiety and also for a report on Jack. He answered:

. . . No, I didn't see Jack; yes, I did see that *Life*—rushed to me the a.m. it arrived by the local Herb Caen of our newspaper, who, for the upcoming 'Bastille-by-the-Bay' column wanted permission to do a vignette on the exiled 'Prime Minister' of the 'Beatnuts,' etc.; bah, bum bunk like the rest of it all, pure puke. Sorry about your folks and the possibility of their hearing via Luce's lousy rag . . .

The following week he passed on information he'd received in a letter from Jack sent via Gavin:

Uncle is bringing the famed Alan Watts over next Saturday to make up for the defection of Kerouac, who, as he said in a long letter . . . met uncle and

335

was set to come here until 3 parties the night before caused the drunkenness I predicted in the postcard to him the month preceding.

Jack had given plenty of excuses: 'nervous exhaustion,' 'H'wood TV appearances,' 'didn't dare visit Carolyn in my condition,' and countless parties at famous addresses. He wrote:

> . . . Isn't it strange how all the best writers always get together? Like you, me, Allen, etc., but in the past it didn't constitute a Federal case what stimulant they used, even Coleridge & Dequincey . . . I had a great trip crossing country back to my mother—who sends you respects—in motels nightly, eating good meals daily; not like old days with you On the Road . . .

I agreed with Neal that Jack's situation was a sad one, and likely to get worse. It already had, in fact; I heard from Gavin that Jack had been called on stage at the San Francisco Film Festival where the film *Pull My Daisy* was being shown, and that he had been so drunk he had fallen down twice. Gavin had tried to set up his appearance at San Quentin for the next day, but Jack was too hungover. My heart ached for him.

As I contemplated Neal's release I was less and less inclined to return to the life of deception and suspicion I'd known with him, to which prospect was now added a real fear of his resentment toward me and the bitterness he felt toward the law.

One day the Hinkles called and proposed a bold plan. They wanted to go abroad and suggested I join them. They had saved some money, and thought I might have enough equity in the house to enable us to work out a feasible financial arrangement, with their help. It was a wild idea, but the more I thought about it the more appealing it became.

We chose Scotland, a country with traditions dear to us all, and which we figured would be inexpensive; the schools were said to be the best in the world, and we wouldn't have problems with language. (We completely overlooked our antipathy to cold, damp climates.) The whole scheme was obviously quite unrealistic, but it served as a sustaining dream for the last year of Neal's absence. We studied maps, saturated ourselves with history and travel articles and taught our children the currency. We wrote to schools and generally researched everything as thoroughly as possible.

When we'd worked out the initial details, I set upon the task of justifying this move to Neal without revealing my fears concerning his

336

behavior. I suggested he could use the time of his parole to find himself and to test his conviction that a family was what he really wanted. If our experiment worked, he could join us when his parole was up and start a new life himself; if not, we would return, everyone more confident of their true desires. My first attempt to sell Neal on the idea in late July 1959 did not bring the response I had hoped for. His letter was resentful and filled with self-pity; again he asked me not to visit or write.

I answered him by reaffirming that my greatest desire, which had never changed, was for him to be my one and only husband and all the rest that implied, and his next two letters were apologetic and positive. Although I wished desperately to believe in his 'devotion,' my resolve often wavered, and now that I had growing children to consider, I didn't feel confident in my ability to handle my own tensions as well as theirs. I even wrote to Hugh Lynn Cayce for advice and got it: 'Part of the difficulty has been your willingness in many directions giving way to him and constantly retreating when he failed to live up to his part of the bargain.' Well, that was true enough. So it was strictly up to me.

Then I couldn't make a visit Neal had requested—the car had broken down—and Neal's response tipped the scales in the direction of leaving: '. . . Rather than being sorry, I was quite relieved you couldn't make it up here Friday, pimples on the proboscis pushing pride until preventing any desire to be seen; so I'm glad the car isn't fixed, that visits have pretty well vanished like hope itself.' He treated me to a long sarcastic tirade because the promised photos of the kids had not arrived, either, and in a postscript he asked what I'd do with the dog when we went to Scotland: '. . . I'm sure it's too risky for him to go, because if he ever fell overboard, he'd not get bailed-out either.'

The Christmas season depressed him even more, understandably:

Hugh Lynn hep smart injun, for you and I are definitely going in opposite directions—especially in the social sphere; you toward people, me away. My idea of marriage?—a Karmic Kutup. What I want you to become?— free of me . . . I want to work myself to death, seriously, a kind of legitimate suicide; why? well, not being loving, cheerful, etc., and not being able to stand people or the world, about the only service left that I can perform is supporting you all . . . [Hugh Lynn had told Neal that suicide was out of the question—he would never be allowed so easy a solution—for he had come to face his past and face it he must.] Please don't write any more for I simply CAN'T reply kindly, sorry and—all my sour grapes, Neal, the REAL heel . . .

On the reverse of the page he apologized again and wrote sense, but I didn't overlook the fact that he allowed the first letter to reach me. He also included a bitter, sarcastic attack on Jack and other alcoholic poets.

I had asked him to be specific about his views and about his own plans for the period of our absence. He replied that he intended to ask his father to live with him while he worked two jobs, saved his money and waited for us or, if we didn't come back, until his parole was over. He reiterated his loathing of all people, including two fans who had written him letters.

> . . . I keep thinking I should swallow my own yearnings and step out of the picture entirely, so please feel absolutely free in shopping for a Scottish mate while you're there—and since you're the only woman I've ever known with any real class, you ought to find several attractive bargains— otherwise—but who can see beyond mid-61? . . . and frankly, I'm SICK of looking forward, esp. with all this uncertainty concerning us; perhaps, I keep thinking, if you weren't leaving so damn quick I might be able to make you happy . . .

He indulged in more negative suppositions about not being released, jobs not being available, and resentment against my leaving. My emotions rose and fell as I read every innuendo in his changing moods; I could easily sense what he was holding back—and that was what I feared. If only I could believe he was being truly sincere. What could I do and where could I turn? At that time, I felt I could only run. Past efforts to be of help to him had always failed.

Neal told me that occasionally parole dates were advanced a few months if there were sufficient reason, so I sat down to plead my case in a letter to the board. I told them of my prearranged plans to leave the country on 1 July, and explained that since Neal's release date was June, it would give us very little time together. This time was important, I wrote, because I was undecided as to whether or not he was psychologically fit to take over family responsibilities again; I referred to their own and other tests that had indicated he was pre-psychotic already:

> No one knows what degree of stress would turn the tide and cause this affliction to develop into violence and/or psychosis . . . I am vitally concerned with observing his behavior under as little strain as possible to help me judge if the family can remain united without danger to the children and if his prognosis appears good . . .

338

I pleaded for Neal to be released a few months early.

Al Hinkle had been trying throughout the year to soften the attitude of the Southern Pacific superintendent, without success. The retribution for Neal's 'crime' did seem unnecessarily severe, and I knew his bitterness rose in direct proportion, fanning out to include the world and life in general. Even though most people still said. 'He should have thought of that,' and I agreed, I knew he didn't deserve such harsh treatment; all he'd learned from it was to hate, a new handicap he'd previously been without.

Easter of 1960 came and went, and we had no 'new beginnings' as we'd hoped. My appeal was turned down. Then I received a notification of parole requirements, and my plans for Scotland were brought to a sudden halt—one of the prerequisites for release was that the prisoner had a home to go to as well as a job. Well, there it was. We would stay home, of course.

Somehow, in my heart, I'd always known we'd never go, even though I already had the steamship tickets. Helen and Al planned to go anyway, but they would tour, not settle down. I wondered if I could get along without them.

Neal was resigned to the change of plan, and to lessen the disappointment for the children he suggested we take a shorter trip to visit my family in Michigan, where a family reunion had been planned for July at our Glen Lake cottage. If we agreed, Neal would then have some free time to re-evaluate his life on his own. His initial reaction to the news that I had abandoned the Scotland move had not been as exuberant as I had expected, and I asked if he were disappointed himself. '. . . No, I'm NOT disappointed, on the contrary, my heart sings to know—YOU'RE NOT LEAVING! Hip, hip hurray!!' But he added, 'Besides, my tensions always spoil my intentions even here, so who knows to what depth my dreadful desires might plunge if I were free of you and the children for a year or more?' Now, what did he mean by that switch? I didn't dare think about it.

From now on our letters were full of only one plan: what to do on his release. His spirits had risen and stayed fairly consistent once the actual date was in view:

> . . . Here is the way things shape up now . . . giving a tentative schedule for your approval: Arriving between 9:30 and 10 on the morning of my exit, you drive me to see Mr. McKinnon in the S.P. building on Market St.; after my appeal—it should be some time before we know if it succeeded . . . we drive home in time for me to take Johnny to the Cub meeting . . . fix Cathy's scientific models and help Jami with her

homework. Early the next morning (like the fade-out of a Hollywood movie, I skip describing *that* night, leaving it to your and the censor's imagination, ahem) take a bus to S.J. and report to parole agent, after which . . . look for a job, unless you've already found me one, of course . . .

I had. One tire company agreed to risk hiring a convicted felon.

. . . we'll save money, sell house and go to Europe in summer of 1963 when my parole has expired and more important, when kids are old enuf to appreciate it & without their psyches getting all fouled up in the process, right? . . . THANKING GOD you're not going . . .

I approved of every word—if only I could believe it would happen as he said. Now I hoped he could go with us to Michigan, but when I inquired about such a trip, I learned he would have to have written permission from every state we passed through. There wasn't time for such nonsense.

Neal's mood skyrocketed as the time drew near, and I exerted my best efforts to calm my fears and earn his forgiveness. He wisely asked:

. . . just what the heck am I to tell the kids when they ask where I've been for 787 days and nights? Try and remember exactly what lies you've told them, so I can make up some to match (sickening, what?) . . . (Just felt a BIG surge of love for you, realizing afresh how gamely you've struggled thru all these years without money or help not to mention affection, understanding or concern; all the things you crave, which your EX-dope *will* DELIVER till his time for the grave—only, as Cayce said was best, it's to be cremation, *promise*?
. . . Put buttermilk & sour cream on dinner menu (but no figs), add more later, all can think of now is what I don't want (beans, etc.); let's buy matching rings BEFORE you go East, OK?

Strange Neal should mention death, I thought, just when we had something pleasant to think about and communicate. Then misfortune struck—this time it was our dog, Cayce, who received an injury to his spine and had to be put to sleep. I hated to have to tell Neal, especially at this time. He was always so sentimental about our animals, and many had been the time I'd been jealous of the affection he lavished on them. He had written of Cayce so often and was so looking forward to seeing him. His reply to the news (parts of which I read to the children) made us all break down once more:

. . . So Cayce is dead; well, at least he had company in both his hour and manner of his release from misery, for he must have gone at about the same time that we here last had an animal 'put to sleep'—seriously,

340

though (Ha! if THAT isn't serious, what is?), we HAVE had our last dog, since the pain of losing one IS too great, the self-recrimination for having failed there, too, in some way is too great. I can see poor old Cayce, third in our line but first hound in our hearts, dragging himself home, lying at your feet and wagging his 'tail cut short and his ears cut long' only gently, being dazed, in shock; how sad it must have been to watch the way he shook. Then his immobile ordeal under Cathy's bed, a nighttime of worry on your part, and, no doubt, wonderment on his; finally, his Calvary, the mighty, loyal, unshaken submission to your hurting-to-help will as you 'shooshed' him into the car—THERE is love'for you!

When I learned the date of Neal's release, I wrote briefly to Jack. He answered,

. . . I hadn't written to you for the simple reason that someone told me you were leaving Neal when he got out—Allen and Aronowitz apparently thought that—but now I see from your tone you intend to stick to old Neal—because I had thought 'If C. leaves Neal she won't be wanting to hear from *me*'—I think Neal loves you very much and always will and I'm glad you're going to stick together—I can't picture anything grayer than the thought of Neal in one part of the world, alone, and you in another, alone, lacking your intimate conversation between each other, which, as you remember from the last visit I made, even Gregory Corso couldn't interrupt—

By the way, in another forthcoming novel [*Desolation Angels*], about 1961–2 I guess, you'll laugh to read about Neal and I at the races, etc., the Bishop, etc. I hope you and Neal embark on a new road of love and wisdom now, stop fighting, realize each other and work out your karmas—My karma's pretty heavy as I'm loaded down with sicknesses now, a smashed elbow from drunken night, phlebitis in feets, hurting hands (neuritis), wow, and newspapermen hovering around my door for what I got to say about Ferlinghetti's poem on Christ—All I could possibly say is that I have written about Jesus in my own way but you can guess how it would emerge all twisted in the papers so I say nothing . . . It was nice to hear from you, my darling blonde aristocratic Carolyn, and my next great moment will be when once again you and Neal and I sit in front of the fireplace with wine and the Television and laugh—I'll be seeing you when I come to Calif. again—Show this letter to Neal when he comes out, tell him I love him, and by the way in the Italian *Life* magazine is a big picture of him calling him '*El Santo*' . . . but anyway happiness from now on for you two mystical greats . . .

It was so like a summation, I hoped it wasn't an ending.
Then the day finally arrived: 3 June 1960.

Fifty-four

The highway was crowded with holiday traffic, and as I drove onto the dusty narrow road to the prison for the last time, my dress was sticking to my back from the heat of the car and from my nerves. I had only just pulled into a parking space when I looked toward the gatehouse and saw Neal striding briskly toward me and freedom. His face told me immediately that, released from an undeserved hell, one's joy can be eclipsed by resentment. Otherwise, his appearance was not very different, even though he was dressed in his prison-issued clothes. (I had asked him if I was to bring anything for him to wear, and he had answered, 'Do you think they send us out naked?')

He jumped into the car and would indulge in only a brief embrace, warm but awkward, before urging me to get him away as fast as possible. I'd expected we'd jabber like jaybirds, but little conversation passed between us on the drive back to the city. My mind was spinning with thoughts, questions, fears and impressions too numerous to grasp in this unprecedented situation. I tried to imagine what was going through *his* mind that he couldn't express, but there was no way I could guess.

As he had requested, for an all-out effort at a new start, we drove straight to North Beach and a little jewelry shop that sold the original and artistic designs of Peter Macchierini, which I had often admired. There we chose matching gold rings, sculpted in uneven fluid circlets, his thicker and heavier than mine. We put them on each other's

342

fingers, but not at all as I had rehearsed the scene; we were too self-conscious in front of the proprietor to do more than squeeze hands and smile at each other.

Neal had told me that Gavin had insisted we visit him at Global House for lunch, and I was delighted, not only for this manner of celebration, but because the company of a third party might help normalize our emotions.

First, however, Neal said he had to deliver a message to someone from a fellow inmate, and he directed me to drive a few blocks down Columbus Avenue. I parked the car and waited while he dashed across the street and disappeared around a corner. He must have been gone close to an hour, and my discomfort in the heat inside the car was exacerbated by my wandering thoughts. Reviewing the incident later, I suspected Neal had been with a lover.

When he returned, he seemed better able to concentrate his attention toward me and home, and his manner was more relaxed. His good humor surfaced as he led me by the hand and bounded up the broad steps of Global House. A young man admitted us to a sunny white-wainscoted, plant-filled room where a table was set for three. Gavin joined us, and after a warm welcome to Neal, we were served a delicious lunch of seafood salad and wine, waited upon by the young men who lived and studied at Global House. After lunch Neal and I wandered hand in hand throughout the rooms, surveying their testimony to Gavin's rich and unusual life.

The first week or so of Neal's return was all joy and gladness, much clinging together and becoming reacquainted. He began work in the San Jose tire shop, drawing the night shift as the newest employee, but he said he preferred that. We all appreciated having him around during the day, and he'd get up early for breakfast to see more of the children.

Strange how an absence can make you forget the personal habits and mannerisms of someone you've lived with for so long. For two years I hadn't had to pick up endless matchbooks with the covers torn off—a habit Neal had acquired early on to keep his women from knowing where he'd been or whose telephone number he'd scribbled on the flap. Back, too, was the litter of magazines and newspapers beside the bed, the abundant handkerchiefs for his problem nose, and the ritual of his feet that required an ever-ready supply of clean socks. It didn't matter to him that his job was rough and dirty; he still paid careful attention to grooming, patting and fussing with his hair and warning me not to muss it when he kissed me goodbye. It was his hands that took the worst beating, and I was sorry to see them grow thick and calloused with ground-in grease and rubber; I tried to get him to leave his new wedding ring at home, but he wouldn't take it off. The one idiosyncracy I always welcomed was his appreciation of food. Our 'garbage disposal' was back: Neal cleaned up all leftovers as though they were special treats, and dove into every meal as though it were a banquet.

By the second or third week it was as though he'd never been gone. He was making special efforts to be considerate and affectionate and live up to his extravagant prison-letter vows, and he succeeded enough to allay my fears. Since he was not allowed to leave the county, and the race tracks were all elsewhere, he was obliged to follow his 'system' only on paper. He insisted he wanted nothing to do with his former acquaintances, and in spite of his previous antagonism, he was gracious to my new friends and with some developed lasting relationships. With these good people looking out for Neal, my mind was more at ease when the children and I took off for Michigan.

My sister met us at the airport alone, and during the twenty-mile drive to the lake, I asked her the burning question: 'Did the folks see in that *Life* magazine about Neal being in prison?'

'Oh, my yes, they certainly did.'

'Then why didn't they say anything all this time?'

'You know them. It's not a subject they're likely to discuss.'

Neither my parents nor my oldest brother and his wife showed any difference in attitude toward me or the children, but the next morning when I found my mother alone on the beach I told her how sorry I was to have been the cause of yet more sorrow. I asked her if there were any details she'd care to have explained, either about Neal's arrest or about how we had managed without him.

Her face was grim, her hands trembling as she snapped, 'Is it true?'

'Yes, but . . .'

'That's all I want to know,' and she hurried away to her own cottage next door. I had so hoped I would be able to tell her how good everyone had been to us, how unjustified Neal's punishment had been, but there was nothing to do but drop the subject altogether.

Only one other time near the end of our three-week stay did I make an effort to explain that Neal wasn't all bad. Again she shook with fury and fumed, 'It would have been far, far better for them if he had knocked every one of those children in the head!' Did she mean, rather than disgrace them so? It was no use; we were worlds apart in our

344

personal beliefs, farther than I'd thought possible for members of the same family.

We had a good time despite these drawbacks; it was a great pleasure to share my childhood wonders with my own children, even though the area had changed so much I no longer cared to return for long. The family didn't take their grudges out on the children, and as long as I didn't mention Neal, they were kind to me.

Near the end of July 1960, we heard that Jack had returned to San Francisco; I wondered if we'd see him. Neal showed no particular interest, and since he was restricted to our county it only made him grim to remember the past binges that had led to his present state.

So I was surprised one dark evening to hear a loud scuffling and banging on the patio door and to see Jack stagger in, surrounded by a motley group of men. He was drunk and bellowing, but I greeted him warmly and put my hands on his shoulders, intending to kiss him hello. He shoved me away roughly with some rude remark, and I backed up, mortified, thinking how odd my behavior must look to the assembled strangers.

These were sorted out as Lew Welch, a poet originally from Reno but more recently from Reed College in Oregon; Paul Smith, a friend of Lew's who played bass fiddle and sang; and a roustabout who had come to San Francisco in advance of his employers, Barnum & Bailey's circus—I don't know where they found him, and I never learned his name. I eventually discovered that the visit was a spur-of-the-moment whim of Jack's to see Neal and introduce him to Lew, as usual wishing to share people he liked with his 'brother.'

I telephoned Neal at the tire shop; he couldn't talk long, with all types of tires to time in their cooking processes, so he suggested everyone come to the shop and talk or watch him work after the boss left around midnight—he wouldn't finish work himself until 2 a.m. Meanwhile, I asked if they were hungry. After Jack had patted his pocket and embarrassed us by complaining loudly to me that people were only interested in him for his traveler's checks, he nevertheless insisted on buying a dinner 'to go' that they could bring to the house. There were few suitable places in Los Gatos, but I called a nearby Italian restaurant and they agreed to prepare a specialty to take out.

The men were gone so long I feared the worst, and I was nearly right. When they returned, Lew, Jack and Paul tried to tell me about the chaos they'd created at the restaurant, but they were laughing so hard from the recollection, I'm not sure I know yet what happened.

The restaurant was as 'square' as was possible, and the clientele quite elegantly so. In had walked this startling group. Jack in his checked lumberjack shirt, sagging rumpled jeans and hiking boots, his hair wild and falling into his half-closed eyes; he was obviously drunk. Then there was Lew with thick, straight red hair, also rather unruly, and wide, bright, piercing blue eyes, slight of frame but wiry, and although clean enough, dressed in well-worn jeans, tennis shoes and a casual knit shirt. Paul Smith was the personification of a Roman athlete, and even though his appearance was rather the opposite of Jack's, he was nonetheless equally out of place. His golden hair was full and wavy and blended into a short beard; his eyes were gold as well, almost yellow, and he wore no shirt or shoes. His smooth muscular chest and arms were tanned an even deeper gold than his hair, and with his only visible garment being a pair of beige slacks, he was conspicuous as a tonal image of golden youth, a vision almost too clean, healthy and gleaming to be real. The fourth member, the silent roustabout, was of medium height, thickset, and wore a red-and-white-striped T-shirt, taut against his bulging muscles, with short curls over his forehead that reminded me of our white-faced cattle at home.

I thought afterward that they should have told the management they were actors from some local play, rather than trying to impress the staff with Jack's fame and the reliability of his check. Understandably, no one had ever heard of him. (At this particular time in our lives, our own name was also useless as a character reference.) Perhaps the decision to trust them had been eventually taken as the only way of removing their noisy and colorful presence from the dining room, where Jack had been earnestly engaged in an attempt to seduce a waitress.

While they had been gone, I had built a fire and set the table. The food turned out to be superb, and soon the chagrin caused by Jack's rebuff left me. They all made a game of honoring me, the sole woman among such attentive and attractive males. Lew Welch was a great delight. He spoke with mock seriousness, a flicker of a smile or a glint of glee sparkling in his eyes to reveal that his intelligent and erudite patter was often in essence satirical. I was particularly impressed with his sharp insights, his quick wit and poetic imagery, though the occasional earthy expression was added for spice . . . or to shock me. Jack tried to keep up with him, but too soon he was capable only of unintelligible roars and grumbles. Paul said little, just sat smiling at me or hovering, his eyes waxing and waning, now shining gold, now

346

shaded bronze; a disturbing attraction had ignited between us. The roustabout never spoke.

When someone noticed it was nearly one o'clock, they all scrambled into Lew's jeep 'Willie' and rattled away to see Neal. I could imagine that scene well enough. I'd seen the tire shop, a pre fabricated aluminum structure all open to the street in the middle of San Jose, with a radio blaring Country & Western music over the din of the re-capping machinery, and Neal's slamming and thudding of the huge truck tires from the stacks to the floor, he looking like a creature from the deep in his goggles and grime.

While they were gone, I did the dishes, straightened the living room and dug out blankets and pillows until I heard the roar of the two cars spinning into the drive. Lew was an acclaimed driver, like Neal, so no doubt some fearful competition had taken place on the way home. Neal was shattered, and the others exhausted from alcohol, tea and each other. Bed was all anyone wanted now.

Next morning everyone slept late. Jack came inside as I was making coffee. Now that he was sober, he seemed pathetically glad to see me, and I was relieved he seemed to have forgotten our initial encounter. He asked me to come out to the patio where we could talk alone. Once again we sat on the grass in the sun. He was full of clinging nostalgia, as though he somehow knew we would never get back to the simple pleasures and sweet dreams we'd anticipated ten years before. No longer did he make staunch vows to stop drinking; he knew he was being slowly pulled down into the quagmire, and his will was too weak to resist. His tormented eyes foretold the future, his face like that of a character from Poe. The usual solutions blinked on and off in my mind, but I knew now they were useless — the shame and isolation he felt deep within were too powerful to be uprooted by overworked admonitions. All I could do was sigh and wonder at the sense of it all.

'I know now my Buddhism is no help,' he said, 'and why Buddha forbade alcohol . . . but I just *can't* stop. Thinking of those critics and the rubbish I've gone through with publishers starts filling my mind, and I reach for the bottle . . .'

'But these past three weeks you've been at Big Sur . . . didn't it help at all?'

'Naw, you know how it is. It was all right at first, then I got bored. Why is that? Why can't I be content?'

Lew came bounding out the door in some hilarious charade concerning 'Aunt Harriet,' his equivalent to Mrs. Grundy, and the scene exploded into slapstick shenanigans between Jack and Lew

347

until my stomach ached from laughing. The roustabout had to get back to sign in with the circus, and Lew wanted to see his girl, so they were eager to return to the city. First, however, Jack needed more wine, so I rode with Lew and Jack in 'Willie' to direct them to the nearest liquor store. All the way they kept up a fast and witty dialogue, replaying a mythical baseball game that did nothing to ease my stomach pain. Returning home they collected Paul and the roustabout and said goodbye to Neal, who was still in bed.

The following Friday night when Neal came home from work, he told me he had been laid off. The boss had financial difficulties and had to let some men go. It was time for the house payment. Over my objections, Neal thought it would be all right to ask Jack for a loan, so the next morning he telephoned him in San Francisco. Jack welcomed the chance, having so often told us his elaborate plans for supporting us all, and said he'd get Lew to drive him down with the money.

This time two jeeps appeared in the driveway. Lew and Paul were in 'Willie,' and Lawrence Ferlinghetti had driven Jack, Philip Whalen and Victor Wong in another. Victor was the artist son of a prominent Chinatown family, and he delighted me with multi-colored pen drawings as I sat beside him on the floor. I liked Phil Whalen very much, too, although I was unfamiliar with his poetry, and he certainly didn't look like a poet—a professor maybe, being rather stocky, tweedy and pipe-smoking. He struck me as an extremely kind and gentle person, quiet yet openly friendly, and definitely not 'beat.' His presence was reassuring, as was Ferlinghetti's.

Since Neal had no work to go to, and since they were all on their way to the cabin in Big Sur, they mock-pleaded with 'Ma' to let him go off with the boys for the weekend. This time I was glad for Neal to have a respite, a time to get out to the wilds, and in company I approved. I forgot about the ban on his leaving the county, and so did he. He was overjoyed and, through his kisses, gushed promises to hunt for another job 'first thing on Monday.'

Sunday evening Jack and Paul stayed on at the cabin while Lew drove Neal home and Lawrence drove Phil and Victor back to the city. Lew stayed with us to rest for a few hours. Neal turned on the television to await the news, and Lew lay down on the big low bed while I sat on the end. No sooner were we settled than Neal said he was out of cigarettes and asked Lew if he could make a run in 'Willie.'

Lew was serious now, no longer the comedian, and the time we spent in Neal's absence was awkward and tense. He gave the impression that I should be trying to seduce him or offering myself for a quickie while my husband was away, and I tried to pretend to be absorbed in the television until I heard Neal return and could relax and be myself again. I left them together, but I overheard bits of Lew's remarks to Neal which sounded as though he were commiserating with Neal for being married to such a frigid and unresponsive female. I regretted his censure, if so it was, not because I thought him particularly mistaken, but because I liked him so much and wished for his approval. But if leaping into bed with every available male was a prerequisite to his friendship, we would never be friends.

Fifty-five

On Monday morning Neal went to the Los Gatos Tire Company on the recommendation of a friend, and those wonderful men agreed to hire him, even though they weren't particularly short-handed. It was a great relief. He would be close to home, and his hours were the regular day-shift, so we could live a more normal life again. As usual, Neal astounded everyone with his speed and efficiency. Employers, employees and customers stood by and watched him in unabashed awe. But when he came home so physically exhausted, I feared he was using this manual labor to work out much of his bitterness, like a penitent flagellating himself. How I wished he could find an occupation that would employ his remarkable mind. No hope for that now that he was a convicted felon; even more doors were closed to him, and his faith in himself was even less likely to bloom. All I could do to help was to try and keep our home life as peaceful as possible, and most evenings after his bath he'd take a beer and float around in the pool in one of the huge innertubes he'd brought home.

Our Rambler wagon was finally in bad enough shape for even Neal to admit it was useless. We hated to let it go; it had served us long and well . . . and it was paid for. But now that Neal had a driver's license again, he was anxious to use it, and the first chance we got after his return to work, we hunted for another car. To our joy we found a jeep, just like Lew Welch's 'Willie,' only maroon instead of blue, and we got a good deal with our trade-in.

To check out the jeep we decided that, Friday after work, we'd surprise Jack in Big Sur and show it off. I made a picnic supper for us to eat on the way, and the children and I sat on a mattress on the floor in the back, which was low enough for us not to be aware of the cliff-hanging roads of Big Sur. Neal's driving terrified me enough on straight flat roads, and I seldom went anywhere with him anymore, but this trip had been too good to turn down. When we turned off the highway onto the dirt trail that led down to the cabin, I looked out once and only once. The road was chipped out from the hillside at a downward slant—one lane and no guard rails.

'Sure hope we don't meet a loggin' rig, Ma,' Neal cheerily yelled back to me, not watching the road ahead, ' 'cause I'd have to back up all the way to the highway to let him pass.' I moaned, and prayed.

At last we reached the cabin, and Neal lustily knocked on the door. Before there was a response, he flung it open. Inside, I could see nothing but darkness and the dim flicker of a fire; the brightness of the sun had weakened my vision. A second later we heard Jack roar, and he bounded toward us, laughing. 'My God! It's a band of *angels* . . . with St. Michael at their head!' He couldn't get over our unexpected appearance. He had been sitting in the dark room, and the sudden burst of sunlight with all the blond heads shining in it kept him exclaiming for many minutes, and he referred to it ever after.

The cabin consisted of one large room. Jack noticed me taking it all in. 'Yessir, Ferlinghetti built this in four days, Carolyn. Imagine that, *four days*! There's no bathroom, but we use a beautiful outhouse out back, and Lawrence and I have taken care to put a can of water and some soap out there, so you needn't worry about that. We'll teach these heathen yet about proper bawthroom hygiene . . . like us French have always known forever, right?' This feature of the accommodations intrigued the children who, never having seen a real outhouse, had to run out and investigate.

On one side of the room were some folding cots against the wall, and on the other I could now see a small table and chairs. Paul Smith had stood up from his seat near the hearth and now greeted us, quiet and smiling. At the table sat a pretty dark-haired girl in tight jeans holding a small child, and beside her sat a slim young man with black curls framing a handsome face. We were introduced to Mike McClure and his wife, Joanna. Mike had been discussing a poem with Jack, and Neal was now asked to read it for his comments. Both Jack and Neal expressed extravagant praise and approval, and when they'd finished, they handed it to me.

The title was the first jolt: 'Fuck Ode.' I read about halfway down the page before embarrassment and revulsion prevented me from reading farther, and I hoped no one would notice. Luckily no one was anxious for my opinion. I looked sideways at the lovely delicate girl and her cherubic child and wondered how she felt about her husband describing in such relentless and gross detail sexual acts between them that to me would be cherished as personal and private. Was *that* what sex meant to him? To *her*? It seemed to me that anybody could describe sex realistically like that, and was it 'poetry' because the lines were chopped up? Well, I was biased, no doubt.

Neal and Jack took the children to get the car (which had been left at a gate down the trail), the McClures went ahead to the beach where we would join them later, and I was left alone with Paul. He was such a pleasure to look at; I would have liked to have painted him. His every movement was harmonious and graceful, and he was such a perfect 'specimen' that it was all I could do not to touch him as one would a piece of sculpture. But I knew it would be like putting a match to tinder; together we created that aura of magnetism that made conversation halting. So it was a relief to hear the rattle and bang of the jeep as Neal backed it up to the porch. He and Jack stomped up the steps, and it was evident even before I saw his bloodshot eyes that Neal had indulged in marijuana. He headed off with the children, following a stream toward the beach. Jack grabbed my hand and pulled me to the door, quite purposely away from Paul. 'Come on, Ma, I'll show you my meditation cove.' Paul merely smiled and ran ahead to catch up with the children.

Jack and I ambled slowly beside the stream; he was telling me small incidents and observations from his previous stay there, and I was sopping up the smells and sights of the sun-dappled woods. The stream opened out and spread itself over a clean, sandy beach in a broad, secluded cove far below overhanging rocks and cliffs. High overhead was the thin ribbon of a silver bridge, and I shuddered when Neal, ahead of us, pointed out the remains of a car lying upside down, rusted and mute, on the nearby rocks.

Jack led me around a jut of rock, away from the others. We sat in the warm sand in a snug little cove while the reddening sun slid into the water and stained it and the surf a brilliant pink.

'Did you do any writing while you were here?' I asked.

'Only poetry. I wrote a great poem to the sea . . . "Cherson! Cherson! Shoo . . . shaw . . . shirsh . . . Go on die salt light, you billion

352

yeared rock knocker . . ." Like that, see? But I haven't been able to write much else since all this awful attention—everybody at me.'

'Do you still carry those little notebooks everywhere?'

'Naw . . . I forget . . .'

'I have an old one of yours, did you know? You left it at the house one time. I've kept it, hoping you'll write more stories like that . . . more like you. I'm sorry, Jack, but a lot of *On the Road* and *The Subterraneans* . . . they just don't sound like the Jack I know. Are you really that rough and vulgar when I'm not around? That much interested in sex?'

Jack interrupted, laughing, 'Hey, lemme tell you a funny thing about that! When Neal and I went to the hot springs with the boys last week, he and I were the only guys there who wouldn't take off our shorts. I thought at the time, "Ha, the big 'Road' heroes!" ' He shook his head and chuckled.

Then he looked at me suddenly, seriously, and pulled me to him and kissed me in a desperate sort of way. We lay back against the rock, my head on his arm, and watched the sky cool and the stars pop out one by one.

I became too chilly to sit any longer, and the tide was creeping up, so we searched our way back to the cabin, clinging to each other in the now dark woods.

The hot coffee by the fire was welcome. I sat down in a low-slung canvas chair on one side of the hearth, Jack in a chair opposite, and Paul folded himself cross-legged on the floor beside me, leaning his back against my chair. Neal went to lie down on a cot by the far wall, while the children found some cards and sat at the table to play. Mike and Joanna announced they were going back to sleep on the beach.

Paul began to sing softly. Absentmindedly, my hand wandered through his hair from time to time, as one would stroke a pet. Everything seemed settled and cozy. Then, little by little, Jack began to fidget, now and then grumbling or spitting out a remark I would either ignore or try to answer without acknowledging his tone. I couldn't figure out what was eating him until he got up and fiercely threw a piece of wood at the fire, bursting out with, 'My God, Paul, haven't you got any consideration for Neal, man. How can you be so unfeeling?' And he smashed another piece of wood against the first.

Paul stopped singing abruptly, and I tried not to laugh. 'Neal?' I said quietly. 'If you look closely, Jack, you'll see he's so concerned he's fast asleep.' But Jack growled and stamped over to the kitchen area to look for wine. There was none. He hesitated, then went over to Neal.

'Hey, Neal, Neal? Come on, man, drive me into town for some wine, okay?' He was gruff and angry. Neal stirred and sat up, good natured as always, even when suddenly awakened. I spoke up. 'You men said you wanted to build a big bonfire on the beach, remember?'

'Yeah, well . . . you and *Paul* do that while we're gone, and we'll join you later. Come on, Neal.'

'Right,' said Neal and got up, calling to the children to come along if they liked, and everyone scrambled into the jeep and rumbled away.

Paul and I put on sweaters, collected matches and paper, and walked back to the beach with a flashlight. The waves were now lapping and shushing among the rocks, and smoothing the sand in a glassy reflection of the moonlight. I'd rarely seen a night on the ocean without fog, but tonight the stars hung over us so glittering and close everything looked almost artificial, like a ballroom dome. We stood close together for warmth for a minute while absorbing the wonder, but when Paul's hands began the restless seeking of the male, I hastened to our stated purpose: the fire. It kept him busy until it was lighted and roaring. We looked about for the McClures, but they were nowhere in view, so we sat by the fire back to back, hugging our knees, and Paul sang until there was only a bed of coals. Neal and Jack never appeared. I became anxious about the children, and we hurried to bury the fire and trudge back through the cold woods.

The jeep was parked beside the porch, and inside it I saw the children snug and asleep. Jack was a lump in his sleeping bag on the porch, and inside the cabin Neal slept on a cot. I was relieved, but also disappointed and a little angry that they had left me with Paul. I climbed in with Neal and the smoky aroma in the stuffy room soon put me to sleep.

Next morning Jack and Neal were grouchy and furtive, and I was annoyed. When we were alone, I tackled Jack: 'Why didn't you come back to the beach? We had that big fire going, and all for nothing.' My tone was petulant, but his was harsh and accusing. 'Neal thought you and Paul wanted to be alone.'

'Oh, *Neal* did! That's just dandy. He might consult me once in awhile instead of pushing me off on any male who happens to look interested. Why doesn't he *protect* me from wolves, not *encourage* them?' I meant him to know my protest included him, too, but my outburst served only to brighten his mood, though he was still suspicious.

When Paul returned, Jack stopped him outside on the porch, and I hurried to fix breakfast for the children. In a few moments Jack came in all smiles again; Paul had banished his fears, but his having doubted me didn't improve my disposition. As for Neal, he didn't care enough even to ask; he just assumed what he wished to . . . another act of 'sharing,' I supposed . . . which now looked to me more like cowardice.

After a late breakfast, we all climbed into our respective jeeps. I had to be back for a Wagon Stagers performance, and despite my disappointment in Jack, I was excited about sharing my new enthusiasm with him. Not since Denver had he participated in my theatrical activities. Neal had already accompanied me several times and had applauded with generous approval and real enjoyment, so I expected him to support my stance toward Jack. But it was too late, the timing all wrong.

Jack had his jug of wine and, after some beer en route, was well on the way to his now daily intoxicated condition. At one point we stopped at a roadside café, and I hoped Jack would sober up. Instead, he refused to eat, and Neal seemed intent on maintaining his aloofness toward me. Then a siren wailed and a fire engine came screaming into the parking lot. The children came running to me out of breath to report that our car was on fire!

Fortunately the fire was out by the time we got there. It had been mostly smoke, anyway, caused by a smoldering cigarette in the mattress. Jack had been sitting on the tail-gate with his jug, so the finger of suspicion was pointed at him, but no one voiced the accusation.

By the time we arrived at Old Town, Jack had reached the stage of singing with half-closed eyes, so all I could hope for from him was that he'd be subdued. I went off to get passes for them, and when I returned Jack was standing in the center of the stage barking something at the owner of the stockade, Frank Dean, in an exaggerated Western twang. I cringed and made signs of chagrin to Frank behind Jack's back, and then ran to bring Neal to the rescue. He and the children collected Jack and took him on a tour of the town, as I ducked into the men's dressing room, now quite late for work.

The actors were all good friends and kidded me about Jack's behavior as I applied their makeup and beards, and I knew they sympathized with me but were also disappointed now that it looked unlikely they would get to talk to the great writer. As each one finished dressing, he'd go out and report back to me on what Jack was up to. In a way I was glad I couldn't see for myself. The children had taken him to the old saloon, and on seeing the piano, Jack had pounced on it and started banging out great dissonant chords while bellowing tuneless Western songs, his behavior still smacking largely of mockery. The audience was beginning to straggle in, and Frank asked Jack not to play the piano and disturb the other saloon guests. Jack became defensive and defiant and, in his most obnoxious way, yelled back at Frank about his 'rights as a customer.' Frank had something of a temper, and now he ordered Jack off the premises.

Neal had taken advantage of my absence to go back to the car and smoke more tea, and now Jack strode angrily out to join him, growling, swearing and grumbling. When this was reported to me, I hurried out the back gate and around to the car, sick with disappointment and fury. 'Is it that I demand so damn much of you guys that just *one* time in all these years you couldn't manage to do me the courtesy to even *act* interested in something I care about? Oh no, everybody's supposed to fall all over *you* two . . . just give, give, give to you . . . but *you* . . . oh, to hell with it . . .' I had to stop to stem the tears, and Neal looked sheepish.

'Uh . . . maybe you could get a ride home with somebody? Don't you think I'd better take old Jack away?' — then he allowed a note of sarcasm and ridicule to enter his tone — 'so's we won't bother you or embarrass you further, my dear?'

I was hurt and disgusted. I slammed the car door and ran back through the gate. I glanced back to see the tires spin in the dirt, and then the jeep swept out of the driveway in a cloud of dust. So now they'd managed to have their time alone together.

'Huh, you deserve each other. Good riddance,' I said aloud.

Now I was even more grateful for Paul and his warm adoration. On the drive home, he told me how much he'd enjoyed the evening; it had struck him as a sort of celebration, he said, for the next day was his birthday. 'Your birthday? Why, Paul, why didn't you tell us sooner? How old will you be?' I expected him to say 25 or 26. 'Seventeen,' he said shyly. Seventeen! *Seventeen*?

Neal didn't return with the car the next day, so Paul was stranded at our house. Without the excitement of Neal and Jack around, the rose color began to fade from his glasses. I could see it, even if he couldn't yet, and I had known from the start that it was inevitable. To ease his growing restlessness and keep us occupied, I painted an oil portrait of him, and that evening friends of his from Palo Alto came to take us to dinner. In the morning Neal still had not returned, so Paul set out to hitch-hike down the coast. The next I heard of him was in a letter from Gavin some months later:

> ... had a wonderful Xmas lunch at my nephew's mother's and a fine bearded friend of yours was there among the 20 — Paul Smith and his red-headed chick. We talked much of you and Neal and came to complete agreement. *You* are the saint. But Neal, in spite of the fact he has never realized that it is inevitable that one horse (or car) can run faster than another — remains one of the great human beings that we have ever known — a kind of *wunderkind*, as the Germans put it. If we didn't love him so much we wouldn't worry so about the seeming inevitability of his going back to the Big House ...

When Neal returned he blamed his absence on Jack, of course, and told me that he'd taken Jack to see a girl named Jackie, one of his own former lovers. It occurred to me that the meeting might have been behind the whole fiasco at the Wagon Stagers performance, consciously or unconsciously. Neal was telling me about it to prove to me he was through with Jackie, and I clutched at the reassurance, even though I knew it proved nothing. I understood also that, legalities notwithstanding, his confinement to our county was at an end — and my peace of mind with it.

The following Friday evening Jack and Lew appeared again at the door, this time accompanied by Lew's girl, Lenore Kandell. Jack had been drinking but was still coherent. Conversation centered on their plans for the coming week at Big Sur, and I wondered why the threesome? As with errant schoolboys, the truth leaked out — Jackie and her child were outside in the car.

I was horrified. 'Now really, Jack, how could you leave her out there in the freezing cold? What's the matter with you? Bring her in at once!'

'Are you sure it's all right?' Jack actually looked fearful.

'Of *course* it's all right! What are you thinking of?'

'Oh, oh —' Lew sing-songed 'bring on the saucer of cream!'

I was flabbergasted. 'You guys are nuts! Or do you watch too many soap operas — or what? You "innovators" — you "new age prophets" — you "rebels from Victoriana"! Are you really suggesting Jackie and I are going to tear each other's hair out in some jealous rage?'

But now Jack had gone out, and sheepishly he returned with Jackie. I asked her to sit down, inquired about her child, who was asleep under blankets in the car, and we had an ordinary conversation about children and motherhood like two normal adult women.

Jack was sitting opposite me on the couch and now began sending me unmistakable soulful looks and suggestive remarks and invitations. This irritated me even more. I did my best to ignore him and my own inward sobs of regret, and to keep my attention on the pitiful mother-in-the-middle, Jackie. Then Neal started going into the agony-act of jealousy I'd seen so many times before—pacing, growling, breathing hard, humphing, glaring—the same syndrome I'd first seen in my Denver hotel room—only this time it was for Jackie's benefit, not mine. It was all so insane.

Lew became bored and eager to be on his way. At the door Jack said to me, 'Now Neal's mad at me because of Jackie. I can tell—but it was *his* idea!'

'No, no, Jack—*that*'s not the reason for his behavior—oh, never mind, run along—it isn't *you* he's angry with . . .'

How depressing the whole episode was, but at least it eliminated my need to condemn Neal. Jackie was punishing him for me—and he had asked for it again.

Little did I know that that was the last time I would ever see Jack.

Many months later I got a letter, the first of many that I received throughout the remaining years of his life, all of which continued to tell of his never-to-be-fulfilled wish to return.

. . . Not writing because I dreamed of you last night, and *quel* dream! but I was planning for weeks to write and explain my months-long silence. I in fact wrote you a big letter from Mexico City saying 'How about me coming up to Los Gatos?' but I tore it up because the Mexican fiasco made me wonder I might get all hung up in Frisco again instead of just at home with you and Neal. So came home. But that too was favorable in the stars because after 6 weeks at home . . . boom, I just finished my new novel, *Big Sur*, about the summer 1960 you remember. In it as a matter of fact I sort of answer your letter of last summer. You know, that old idea about you and me meeting in Nirvana later at which time Neal will be perfect, etc., you remember. Anyway, pretty romantic. I just want you to know that I cherished your letter, and I cherish you, in that special way you'll realize when you read the book . . . like when we walked down the Big Sur path to the sea, you and I talking as of yore, and Neal and his new magenta (?) jeepster . . . and the kids, and McClure, and then that awful night I brought Jackie to your house. So ashamed of that I never came back for my old shirt you'd sewn for me so sweetly . . . but you never were even mad.

Anyway at this time, naturally, having just written a book in which you figure (and don't worry, you come off just like you are, which is moral and clean) (as a contrast to all the big lewd Lew Welches and Jacks and Paul Smiths whoopee) you're so on my mind I wish you'd write . . . I hope you appreciate the fact that I feel, well, shamed? awful? shitty? for writing about everybody as they are. I always make an effort to clean up the mess by changing names, times, places, circumstances. But in years from now no one will see a 'mess' there, just people, just Karma . . . And in this case, of you and me, the soft and gentle Karma that ain't even started. (Wow, that dream last night.) But Carolyn forgive me also for intruding on your gentle home life and for all I know you've got something new to absorb you but just write me letter on typewriter like old days. I'd like to come out Calif. right soon. Sigh, pain in the ass jack. In fact, wait a minute, I ain't finished.

He recapped more events of that July in 1960—'. . . and that funny evening I got thrown out of the Hiss the Villain play?'— and told of how he had described me and the children and our home in *Big Sur*:

. . . but there's that undercurrent of strange muted romance between us. So please don't get mad. What I'm really worried (about somebody's getting mad) is Jackie; I come right out and say she bores me whereas you (Evelyn) never do . . . but I'd like to tell you all about it when I see you— At least one of these days we'll have one of our old quiet religious arguments by the fireplace as Neal sits there playing self-chess saying, 'Hm, yass, got ya dirty pawn' . . . 'You old Queen . . .'

Jack wrote several more letters about his work on *Big Sur*. It evidently excited him a good deal, and when I read it, I thought it had been a turning point in his writing in that he was more objective about himself without sacrificing his true emotions—although he still wasn't writing anything very intimate about our relationship, as he seemed to think he had. I understood his reticence; after all, I was the wife of his friend, a woman with children, all of whom would grow up to read the books.

Part III

Fifty-six

Neal's resolve to stay home and avoid his former acquaintances was short-lived. After the Jackie episodes I had to face the fact that he was reverting to old habits in spite of his continued expressions to the contrary. His resentment toward me flared occasionally, revealing its still-present power, and often I wished we had gone to Scotland.

The first infraction was going 'only to the track' on Saturday afternoons, but this time away soon extended into Saturday nights, and gradually more nights were added.

Sometimes we went together to visit John Gourley, an engineer I'd met in Neal's absence, and we often took the children to play in John's gym or with his elaborate racing-car set. John was an agreeable sort with myriad interests, and Neal soon began using this apparently innocent friendship as a springboard for clandestine affairs — John's home becoming a place in which to write letters to girls, a cover for runs to the city (in John's car) and a place to indulge in tea, methadone or Benzedrine. I accompanied him less and less, and the last time we went to John's together, I happened to run across an interview in a *Holiday* magazine in which Neal was quoted as saying that Natalie had been 'his only true love.'

I had not known of the interview, and reading these words in a national magazine stabbed me with a pain as intense as any I'd ever felt. All the old burning jealousy was alive and well. I had flunked the test. And I had worked so hard every day; my progress had been slow but, I thought, steady. Neal had been changing, too, had grown calmer, less defensive and more open, even telling me his feelings and fears. Now the article not only signalled my failure in 'loving indifference,' but also prompted an about-face of my own. Formerly I had insisted that knowing the truth gave one a choice; now I firmly adopted the motto 'What you don't know won't hurt you.'

As my attitudes and responses slowly changed from possessiveness to detachment, I tried to work on the 'loving' part of the formula and reviewed Neal's good qualities instead of concentrating on those I disliked. Thinking back on our first months together I was ashamed at how completely I'd buried my recognition of his many unusual virtues. Why, I wondered, did I feel it my duty to keep him informed of his *vices*? After all, everyone really knows within himself when he is doing something right or wrong; it isn't anyone else's business. This exercise allowed me to love Neal more, but in quite a different way, and in exchange for these tiny triumphs I traded in my original dream—the dream I'd fought so long to hold; the reason, I believed, for my living. I knew only greater pain would come from hanging on to a lost cause, and I also knew better than to forfeit the peace of mind I'd attained. It was an isolated and lonely peace at first. The bridge between Neal and me had fallen, and I looked at him now from the opposite bank, a gulf between us. Was this 'loving indifference'?

For the next two years I fluctuated, sometimes managing positive reactions, sometimes falling back, ego-wounded and resentful, even though I was better now at concealing my feelings. Our home life together was peaceful, but there wasn't a great deal of it, and I didn't know how much this was related to Neal's bitterness against me or was merely a continuation of his former need to spread himself thinly. He wanted and appreciated a home and family, but he wanted everything else as well—his 'cake and eat it, too'.

As he became more entangled, I became less so. My theater activities still kept me busy designing and sewing, but they were diminishing. The ballet school had added an annual *Nutcracker* to its regular spring production, but once the first production was finished, only a few new costumes were required each year, and now I costumed only one or two plays a year for the University. The Wagon Stagers had succumbed to the inevitable result of 'democracy' in the theater: disagreement, factions and failure. I had a brief period as artistic director for a newly formed opera company, but I escaped after only one opera was produced and just before the company went bankrupt. By 1963 I had left behind my efforts toward a career; I gave up teaching classes in makeup and made only occasional costumes for ballets or individual performers.

During the first two years of Neal's three-year parole, the Santa Clara students still came to the house for parties and were often there when Neal came home in the early hours. He would cheerfully join the group sitting on the floor around the stone coffee table, making me feel less the abandoned wife, and the young men welcomed him, knowing a little of his reputation, although few, if any, had read Jack's books. How charming Neal could be. I'd watch him as he entered the discussions on philosophy, listening and nodding with earnestness, not asserting himself in any overbearing way, yet keeping up his end brilliantly, to everyone's greater enjoyment. At such times the sharp pang of my lost dream would thicken my throat with longing for what might have been.

One such night, the boys had all begun to filter out of the house to go home, when my niece, who was staying with us, drove in with Hoyt Axton in tow. She had attended his performance in San Francisco and invited him home. Much to her surprise, he had accepted. Of course, everyone filed right back into the house, and the remainder of the night and a great part of the morning were delightful. Neal played the gracious host, and Hoyt was completely at ease, insisting on playing his guitar and singing between conversation, food and wine. As the sun rose and the students left, he and Neal were having discussions of quite a different sort from those we'd all indulged in earlier—or so I gathered when I overheard Hoyt saying to Neal, 'Well, I'm an *ass* man, myself.'

Neal's pay was far below his previous railroad standard even without the gambling losses, and our debts continued to rise, periodic refinancing of the house or loans from friends saving our skins from time to time. I decided to go back to work. In this way, I thought I could perhaps gradually lose my dependence on Neal financially, as I was doing emotionally.

I began on the switchboard of a local newspaper but was soon drafted into display advertising. It brought in little income, but it helped, and my only object now was to wait out the children's growth and keep a roof over their heads.

The beautiful setting of the house continued to sustain my spirit and my sanity, and not a day went by when I wasn't grateful for it. It was worth even Neal's resentment, for I didn't really believe I'd have gained him in exchange for bail. Sometimes as I looked out at the ever-changing colors of the hills behind the orchard, our youthful expectations of life and the plans we'd all made would parade through my mind, and I'd trace the fates of the three protagonists. Was there any hope for Jack or Neal?

Allen, on the other hand, was going his own way and doing well. At least he was happy doing what he liked. We heard from him seldom, but when we did, we knew we were still in his thoughts as he was in ours. At the end of 1960 we received a wildly scrawled letter from New York:

> Merry Xmas . . . Forgive my silence . . . I will write you. Peter and I were at Harvard last week eating synthetic mushrooms . . . very high. *The Revolution Has Begun* . . . Stop giving your authority to Christ & the Void & the Imagination . . . *You are it,* now, the *God* . . . I will have babies . . . all's well . . . we're starting a plot to get everyone in power in America high— Hurrah!—I flipped my lid last week at Harvard & rushed out stark naked to telephone Jack and wake him up—he's always wanting to die—I stopped vomiting up the Universe last week. My book *Kaddish* (all Death Death Death) (hymns) done and will be out in a few months. How are you? and Caroline & the Babies? I love you in Life's sweet July. What kind of money work you doing? Why don't you write again to communicate the holy news to the world? . . . you are *needed*—stop hiding your light in a bushel. I'll sit down & write you a long gossipy letter soon as I can . . . Always, always, always . . .

He and Peter took off again for Europe soon after, and we only got postcards until they arrived in India, when Allen wrote:

> . . . When'd I last write? I forgot . . . Met some weird saints on streets, but no guru. We (Peter here too) know a lot of people, poets & businessmen; go around on streets in indian clothes & I got long black hair down to shoulders & a beard & Peter long blond hair, we sure look looney. But everybody here also looks looney so we pass unnoticed more than if we were in slacks & U.S. hair . . .

About the only close tie that Neal and I had left was to read Jack and Allen's letters together, and it was one reason I welcomed them more than ever. Yet they were arriving far less often now. Jack wrote only two or three times a year, and occasionally we'd get two in a row, each beginning, 'Lately I've been writing letters without remembering . . .' and he'd repeat the news he'd sent in the first one. He was still seeking a home, always planning to come see us, and steadily lamenting and drinking his life away. Once in awhile he'd try to reach Neal directly again, but without much hope:

. . . You don't have to answer this letter, I just feel like talking to you . . . Well, anyway, I wanted to tell you what happened here. The ex-wife got remarried to an Arab; he laid her up to 2 twins, but a year ago she walked out on him saying she couldn't stand him and came to NY with his twins and the daughter to sue me. Saying in the papers I made $50,000 a year. Thinks she's a bigtime suer. I not only never made 50 G's a year but don't have 50 or 25 or 10 g's in my poke. But with all the bullshit thats bein written about me I can foresee a Judge getting wise. If I couldn't make these ridiculous payments, I'd have to go to jail, like Sir Walter Raleigh and yourself . . . When I sobered up last summer I realized Jackie could also put me thru the racks if she wanted to (tho I doubt she's mean). A man can't even get laid any more. Best to cut it off, brother . . . When I see you again sometime I'll be wanting you to lecture Cayce to me. I want to know about him and what he said. I remember a few things . . .

Neal snorted at this point. 'Ha, what could he remember? He never listened and never will, bah.' I said nothing, knowing how painful to him was Jack's decline into alcoholism, the picture of his own father forever before him.

For a long time we got no such chatty letters, only notes accompanying a few fan letters for Dean Moriarty—for example:

. . . Never mind Xmas cards . . . how about a little note . . . I'm sending you these letters to show you what they think of you (the nuts of America I guess) Also a poem . . . I know you are bugged by all types of horseshit but there you are—None of it is native to me either . . . I give your address to nobody. See you this summer. Tell Carolyn to write me if you can't, Hey, Carolyn, Write.

Sometimes the fans would ferret out Neal's address for themselves: 'We are assuming that you are the Neal Cassady as immortalized in Jack Kerouac's *On the Road* as Dean Moriarty and *Big Sur* as Cody Pomeray . . .' The fan letters made Neal flinch with guilt, and he didn't answer them.

When I felt lonely and needed to talk to someone who understood Neal, I'd write to Jack, and his letters served to keep me together and on the right path, few and far between though they were. He had written he was going to Europe, then wrote:

No, didn't go to E . . . long story I'll tell you sometime in front of fireplace . . . N has a DUTY to God and Mankind, too, which is to WRITE, otherwise me'n St. Michael's got him all lined up for a breadline in Purgatory altho St. Michael's already looking leery at ME (Because I can't write anymore myself . . .)

Once I wrote in October and didn't receive any answer until the following January. Then the next summer I poured out my woes again, and he responded in October in kind:

> . . . I'm so sick and tired of being insulted by critics I've just about decided not to publish any more, except for already-written *Visions of Gerard* and *Desolation Angels* . . . When Neal buries himself in TV, don't worry, he's studying the culture, I also do it, football games, long dray-mas, everything it's every bit important. Also newspapers; all about committees for respectable cheating . . . Neal shld never leave you and kids, he can have his freedom right the way he's doing now. Ask him for a future weekend in the City . . . also big meal in Chinatown and a show. He'll do it . . . and when I gets there, yes, I'll talk at your Santa Clara because I AM a Jesuit—tell them . . . Have courage angels . . .

Well, I wasn't particularly happy with Neal's 'freedom right the way he's doing now,' and it amused me that Jack didn't realize that the kind of outing he proposed would be great with him but not possible with Neal.

I'd long since lost track of how many times Jack had moved his mother from New York to Florida and back. I thought they'd just gone to Florida when he wrote:

> . . . I can't stand this Florida subdivision one more minute . . . found a swell house which I bought in Northport . . . a new gem which is a great pad like yours, modern ranchito . . . *Big Sur* was to me a little pwfiddly, light, now I'm going to knock out the horrible tragedy 'Vanity of Duluoz' . . . and this will be much better . . . Come May, I come see you— (TRULY, just wait and see) . . .

Wait I did; see I did not.

Early in the fall of 1962 a Cayce conference was to be held at Asilomar, a conference facility in our favorite vacation spot of Pacific Grove. Neal encouraged me to take the children for the week. I had a few qualms but in the end decided to trust his insistence that he could handle things at home.

We rented a cabin in pine woods close to the conference grounds and the beach. Each morning I walked to Asilomar to attend Elsie Sechrist's class on meditation, and the children managed for themselves, swimming in the pool, beachcombing, climbing dunes or reading.

Late Sunday afternoon we drove home, sunburned, sandy and refreshed, and entered the house to a macabre version of Goldilocks

368

and the Three Bears. The living room gave no particular clues, but my bedroom, Johnny's room and the patio provided a number of sickening jolts. My bed was stripped, the blankets in a heap on the floor. I found the missing sheets stuffed hastily into the washing machine and splotched with blood. But in Johnny's room was the worst shock . John Gourley had given Neal the extravagant race-car set that had been the star attraction in his own home, and Neal in turn had presented it to Johnny with ceremonious loving glee. Our son cherished it not only for itself, but because it was a gift from Neal, and he cared for it as he had never cared for any other toy. Now Johnny stood in his doorway, struck dumb: it looked as though a tornado had swept through the room. The bed was a mess, his books and papers scattered all over, and the race track was a twisted tangle of metal. Some cars had been tossed here and there in the room, some were found in the girls' room, and one was at the bottom of the pool. The patio was in a similar condition. In addition to the toy car, the pool contained sticks, stones, tools, dishes and silverware.

It was obvious that an unsupervised child had had a lot of time on its hands. Only then did I remember the occasion when a man at the tire shop had confused me with another woman and inquired about my son of 2 or 3 years old. Ah, so. This woman and her son must have been Neal's weekend guests.

My supposed progress in 'loving indifference' vanished in a flash of fury. All the worst of the old emotions flooded over me, plus some new ones I'd never known existed. When Neal's devilry hit at the children, my maternal instincts blotted out all else. How could he? How *could* he! What thoughts were in Johnny's 11-year-old mind, I never knew. Naturally, I said as little as possible to the children, but I could not conceal my displeasure and pain.

That night when the children were asleep and the house in order again, I sat in the living room in the dark and looked out on the lush moon-washed lawn and the shadowy, stately eucalyptus swaying in the distance below the towering hill. 'All answers come from within.' I tried to match the peaceful scene by silencing my crowding thoughts and raging emotions, but it was no use. Self-pity returned as strong as ever. I reviewed my life to this point. Why this consistent failure at permanence? Why were the two men I cared most about of no use to me and rapidly disintegrating, while nothing I did was of any help? And now my efforts to overcome my own weaknesses were apparently a flop as well. What was it all for? Where was I going? Little flickers of positive thoughts tried to muscle in, but I denied them space. I could think of only two words to describe myself: ineffective and ineffectual. A total loss.

The next day I wrote a long agonized letter to Elsie, but it was never mailed. I knew already what her answer would be: 'God will make the separation.' I could no longer accept that. Even if I were wrong, I just didn't want to take it any more. Besides, another problem had become increasingly evident since Neal's return from prison: the children were living under a double standard—Neal's permissiveness and my discipline. I had a sneaking suspicion his way might be best, but I was too insecure to try it, and I wouldn't have known how to begin.

When Neal returned, I made little effort to conceal my disgust. The whole state of affairs had progressed beyond my power to cope. Grimly, I told Neal it was time for a divorce. In the year and a half since his return from San Quentin I had several times mentioned the disparity between his theories while there and his subsequent practice, as well as my growing desire to set him free from the drudgery of supporting a family, if that wasn't what he wanted. He had steadfastly refused to discuss it. This time, however, there was a new wrinkle.

One of my advertising accounts with the newspaper was the owner of a local music store. George was twelve years older than I but witty and good company, a professional musician and, he assured me, financially secure. He could hardly have been more the opposite of Neal, nor offered a life farther removed from the one I was thoroughly tired of. He was popular, even President of a local civic club. To further his wooing, George had arranged for Johnny to have music lessons and had 'loaned' us a piano. He knew I was unhappy with Neal, and when he began to pressure me to marry him, I wondered if he were God's agent, heaven-sent.

Reluctantly, Neal agreed to the divorce, only, he said, because he could see that George could do so much more for the children. We made the decision a year before his parole was up, but I told him I'd wait for his freedom before filing suit.

I wrote to tell Jack, suddenly realizing this would probably mean the end of his friendship as well. It gave me pause to think. I was the one breaking up the old gang, as it were, but on the other hand I hadn't much hope for Jack, either, and was determined to put all of the past behind me.

Jack answered sadly, assuming it was all because of money:

Well, Carolyn, I'm quite confused by everything that's going on, but I'm not there to judge, judge what Neal himself really wants, or whatever, but I do know it's a sad plan that you both may regret when years later, all your economic wants becoming satisfied and showing themselves for what they are, transitory arrangements, you starts missin' each other's souls. Hey? . . . Ah well, the Old Counselor is signing off, and him not even sure if he can manage his own affairs for the next 24 hours . . . Have faith in St. Mary, both of you, because she's human like us. Write again soon. I'm retired from NY scenes now and quite energetic and busy happy writer and will answer your every letter . . .

He offered me advice on raising the girls and Johnny, and all around the margins added notes to Neal about how positive he was that the 'system' wouldn't work, pleading with him to give it up.

Four days before the end of Neal's parole, I went to court. This time it was all very simple and went smoothly, and good old Helen once again agreed to be my witness. Now we had a year to wait before I could marry George. Neal behaved as though I'd been to the dentist or the like, and made no plans, at least none that he confided to me. I called the children together to try to explain what it meant and felt a worse traitor than ever. As usual they understood, as far as I could tell; many of their friends' parents were divorced. Still, not wanting to rock their boat too suddenly, I didn't urge Neal to pack up and depart, even though for a long time it was difficult to look at him without remembering that devastating weekend. Now I'd done what most aggrieved wives do—retaliated with divorce—and it brought little consolation. I had already stopped all sex between us many months before. To my surprise, he had taken it calmly. Only occasionally did he snarl at me about it; he knew he had small justification, considering his other outlets.

As soon as his parole was over in the summer of 1963, he not surprisingly expressed his freedom by blasting off on a cross-country trip. This time he took new friends; they were unknown to me, something I was grateful for when I read Jack's description of their visit to him:

Dear Carolyn—
By now Neal must be home. If he'd come to see me by himself, he could have stayed in my mother's house indefinitely. But he had those rude people with him, one of whom reached without invitation into my pantry and icebox for *the* most expensive delicacies, the other put his feet on the kitchen table after eating and even threw bread around while eating to show what a great independent hipster he was. I disliked him very much,

and had the D.T. shakes anyway . . . But Neal, alone with me for 5 minutes, was as sweet and gentle and polite and intelligent and interesting as ever he was with me or anyone else he's ever liked . . . As you see I've grown older and bored with the world. Good luck with your new marriage, which is probably for the best after all, seeing as how Neal keeps taking such chances as on the last run . . . But my thoughts, believe it or not, occur daily about you and Neal, from habit, and from unchanged affection in *Thou*. All those hanger-onners, *NO!* Pay no attention to drunken letters I wrote last Spring. Enough. I haven't touched a drink since Neal left.

Kinda funny, I thought wryly—not so long ago it was Jack with all the 'hanger-onners,' and now it was Neal.

Fifty-seven

During the time I had been considering the divorce, a Cayce enthusiast had told me of a woman, Dr. Neva Dell Hunter, who served as a channel for a 'seventh-plane teacher.' A doctor of psychology, Dr. Hunter had once when near death had a vision and had given over her life to serve this teacher, a 'Dr. Ralph Gordon,' who had a job to do on earth and needed an instrument. To support his teaching tasks, he gave past-life readings as detailed as Cayce's, issued through Dr. Hunter when she was in a state of trance.

I could hardly wait to tell Neal, and he was soon even more eager than I to have a reading. (Had it not been for the Bishop's example of 'channeling', and our listening to several recorded readings, I would have been too apprehensive to participate in anything so 'supernatural.') In due course we were approved for individual appointments.

After Neal had had his first reading he came home red-eyed and grim, and although it was nearly eleven o'clock, he insisted I listen to the tape. We settled on the bed and started the reel. Neal lay back with his eyes closed, and soon his face was glistening with tears. For ninety minutes I sat transfixed, frequently horrified and often moved to tears myself. At the end of the recital of six lives, Dr. Gordon asked Neal if he had any questions. I heard Neal's voice on the tape, sobbing so he could hardly answer: 'I think you've covered everything.'

Such tragic lives as these were not usually revealed, but Dr. Gordon considered Neal strong enough to take them and likely to benefit from the knowing. Extremely abbreviated, the readings were as follows.

In the first recounted life, as a Bedouin prince, Neal learned the art of deception and was obsessed with revenge. His own son finally stabbed him to death; left in the street to be cursed by all, he heard and absorbed these denouncements and thereby learned there is no 'death.' Here were planted the seeds of his later self-loathing, his deep sense of guilt and his fearlessness, all of which were to be compounded in subsequent lives.

The next life explored was awesome in its evil. Having been publicly castrated for rape, Neal changed his name, abandoned his family and amassed a fortune, thereby proving he could be a success even without his 'manhood.' Again he was obsessed with 'getting even.' As the king of vice in Babylon he promoted as many degrading activities as possible, the more extreme the better. There were many continuities we could glean from this life, among them his lack of interest in money, and many women could testify to his unconscious need to 'get even.' Then as now, he loved his children but had to watch them grow up from afar.

In a Chinese incarnation he sowed the seeds of drug dependency as an opium addict. He added masochism to his sadistic bent by becoming a fakir who reveled in throwing himself on beds of spikes. He had killed his brother, and as his mind weakened he was beset by hallucinations of the brother rising from the ground. Afflicted with syphilis, he 'allowed' himself to drown. In the present, Neal shied away from water; his attempts at compassionate aid had been rejected by a father and many others and, as a child, he had withstood torture by a brother.

Any lives one might have lived in the presence of Jesus were always revealed because of their benign spiritual effects. Neal's encounter was again dramatic and extreme, that short life echoing his avid search for knowledge and deep feelings of unworthiness.

In a life with me as his wife, he became a religious fanatic—many would say he still was—and I drowned in a pool which Neal had filled with sheep's blood and demanded I enter. His daughters were sworn to silence. One of them was Cathy, for whom in this life he had a special affection; not so she for him.

In the last life given at this session, only one incident was described, but that one was enough. The same son, John, whom Neal adored, had died before his eyes, chopped to bits by the knife-blades Neal had attached to the wheels of their Assyrian racing chariots. Neal had often told me of his aversion to knives: 'I never even wanted a pocket knife like all the other boys.'

A year later Neal had a 'spiritual attributes' reading, the first having been concerned with physical and emotional influences. This one was like a long mystical prayer, the antithesis of the first. Only three of the lives were touched upon. Dr. Gordon had instructed Neva Dell to listen to this account for her own education, and she wept at the beauty of it, saying that never before, in over 5,000 readings, had she heard Dr. Gordon speak in such a way.

Whether or not these tales were true, I hardly think any writer of fiction could have imagined lives of such extreme depravity. In some ways I felt I knew these six men, and Neal himself felt a very deep emotional kinship, convinced of the readings' authenticity. We both believed 'all things are possible.' We did not feel it was necessary for anyone to know their past lives in order to live this one properly, any more than it was necessary to believe in reincarnation, but together these two readings formed a portrait that was at once inspiring and chillingly faithful to Neal's own condemnation of himself.

I can point to no concrete evidence that Neal derived any tangible benefit from this knowledge, and Dr. Gordon had not offered an optimistic prognosis, stressing that Neal's body was already so unbalanced chemically he would have to be extremely careful what he put into it—'but the conquering light of your own soul will bring you back . . .' The tapes meant a great deal to Neal, and he insisted on carrying them everywhere.

My own readings were far more banal, even the spiritual one merely giving lines which related to whatever talents I possess. The greatest blessing was a possible explanation of the hostility which existed between Cathy and me, lifting a cloud of guilt that had oppressed me since her second year. There was a life, too, that offered clues to my relationship with Jack.

I did not feel the one previous life shared by Neal and me could completely explain our present relationship, yet, having taken my life then, it was possible that this time he had sacrificed himself to some extent for my benefit. Apparently the extremes of trauma I experienced at his hands were necessary for me to change my ingrained attitudes, hence our inability to separate entirely. In the end, I was even able to understand Neal's innocent and reasonable viewpoint in regard to his first trip and my warped 'righteous' indignation. There is no such thing.

And, pertinent or not, Neal was born under the sign of Aquarius, ruled by Uranus—the planet associated with the shattering of static forms so that new ones may emerge.

By this time Jack had taken to telephoning me more often than writing. I was excited to tell him of our romantic mutual life together in the past, but he was in his usual drunken state. I got as far as telling him he had been a son of King David, which I thought would please him, when he interrupted by bellowing, 'I WAS JESUS CHRIST!'

'Uh—yes, Jack, come on . . .' Obviously this was not the time to discuss it. He went on: 'Jesus was really a Frenchman, you know—a Norman!'

'I see.'

'Yes, he was! You know how the twelve tribes of Israel scattered throughout northern Europe and all that? Even Cayce said one of 'em built Stonehenge—Neal told me—well, Jesus was a Gaul, see? But the Church changed all that, kept it a big secret, and I come from the same place—Brittany. So you see . . .' I let him rave on.

Neal had moved out piecemeal before making his trip East, and although he and I were under a certain amount of emotional stress, I hoped it was not noticeable to the children. A great relief for me, and certainly for the neighbors, was the disappearance of the five broken-down cars from the driveway. All of them had been dearly beloved, even though none ran. Neal had been ever-hopeful he'd meet a mechanic he could con into fixing them. The catalyst had been not a nagging wife but the city fathers, who asked if we were running an unlicensed repair service. Neal even made $15.00 a piece on them, so was content. When we added up, we discovered Neal had gone through eighteen cars in less than two years.

The only other noticeable change in our lives was that Neal was around more often than before. Typical perversity. Just like a shadow, I figured: chase it and it runs away, turn your back and you can't get rid of it.

I had left the newspaper a month after the interlocutory decree was granted, and took a job 'for a year' in a doctors' office until I could marry George. Then one day George disappeared. He left the store, the town, me—and vanished.

I was more relieved than I would admit, and felt more sure than ever that George had been 'sent' to serve as my escape from Neal. When Neal learned the news, his reaction was 'Great! Now I can move back in.' I held out, though not without a struggle, saying,

'Look, Neal, all you do is come here to rest and regain your strength—and it's my strength you sap, leaving me nowhere, neither fish nor fowl, neither married nor single. Please, Neal no more.' I hoped that, once away from a solid home life, he would choose to respect it. Then his job lost its purpose and he quit, cutting his only other lifeline.

For awhile he was determined to pull himself together according to Dr. Gordon's suggestion. Allen was in San Francisco again, and Neal stayed with him, vowing to set up a daily schedule of writing, '. . . if I don't go to Mexico.' I encouraged him all I could, holding out the promise that if he could just show me he was capable of self-control, I'd gladly welcome him back.

It was far too late. He increased his use of 'speed' and marijuana, and took anything else available. In despair I'd watch him swallow pills he'd 'found'—not knowing what they were—and in the next four short years I saw him pursue death with every breath of life.

Was I to blame? Should I have given him what little support a home and job could offer? I sweated and strained, but I'll never know the answer; I only knew I couldn't cope with teenagers and Neal, too.

Neal had already expanded his circle of friends and admirers by the spring of 1961, and he rapidly made up for time lost in prison by seducing a number of girls simultaneously. How well I remembered my own earlier feelings of trust and happiness when, after his death, I read their letters to him. He was still casting the same spells.

My first encounter with Anne Murphy, the woman of the critical weekend, was over the phone, when one day a tearful voice asked if I knew where Neal was. In trying to get to him in Los Gatos she had become confused and had taken a number of wrong buses. Then she had fallen asleep, and now she didn't know where she was. I didn't ask her name, but located Neal and sent him off to find her. She was so dumbfounded that I not only hadn't become angry with her but had been willing to help her that she has been devoted to me from that day on.

Neal had come home several times, sleeping alone on the couch, before I found out that on these occasions Anne remained in the car at the end of the street. He was still trying to deny the existence of any other woman. When he confessed, I was horrified, but he insisted that Anne wouldn't have it any other way. I couldn't stand it, nonetheless, and demanded he bring her in. Her hair was reddish-blonde and stringy and she looked thin and unhealthy, but she could have been quite pretty, I thought. I learned she was intelligent and a good artist. With me she was always meek and sweet, if a little too humble; I could never picture the banshee Neal sometimes made her out to be. She proved to be a measure of my own progress in that it gradually dawned on me that I had passed some exams after all. I had vanquished the green-eyed monster! It was a heavenly relief.

Anne was to become Neal's *chela* as well as tormentor for the next eight years and was ever-present in the foreground or background, always expecting to marry Neal when our divorce was final. Like LuAnne, she and Neal were too much alike; she couldn't leave men alone nor he women, yet both could feel bitterly jealous and the emotional battles that ensued would have split most couples much earlier in the game.

I was surprised to learn that Neal was in and out of jail at this time. His driver's license had been revoked soon after his parole had ended because of his never-ending citations, and when his friends were unable to pay his fines, he'd spend a week or more in one or another county jail. He no longer seemed to care, but at least time spent in jail was time away from drugs and other temptations.

Fifty-eight

One weekend soon after returning from India, Allen, Peter and Peter's brother Julius came to visit. Neal and Anne also managed to join us. Allen had bought a Volkswagen bus, and they showed us excitedly how well it served as a home. They brought groceries and Allen cooked another of his gourmet dinners, while Peter insisted on doing the dishes.

I asked Neal about Julius. He sat wherever he was told, gazing into space, and never spoke. Neal explained that he had entered a catatonic state at around the age of 19; he was now about 30, and had to be told to do everything: 'Sit down, Julie . . . Pick up your cup . . . Put your cup down.' He wasn't dangerous to others, but he had to be watched constantly. One night he'd started out the door in San Francisco and just continued walking. Peter had found him nearly thirty miles away, doggedly plodding on. (Neal claimed he himself had once given Julie some LSD, whereupon he had talked and behaved normally, but the story was never confirmed by anyone else.)

Allen, Peter and Julius spent the night in the van, and Neal made Anne happy by sharing a bed with her. I thought he'd come a long way from denying her existence, and I decided that he must at last have acknowledged our divorce. I had forgotten that legal maneuvers were meaningless to Neal.

The next afternoon Allen, Peter and Julius all went back to the city, backing out of the drive to the clang of finger cymbals and with voices raised in Hari to Lord Krishna, while I filmed the departure.

The next evening Jack telephoned. He was well on his way to oblivion, but I was excited. 'Oh, Jack, how I wish you'd been here last night! We could have had a reunion—even Neal was here.' Jack had asked for Neal as he always did, and as always I had answered, 'You know, Jack, Neal doesn't live here anymore.'

Now he said, 'Who was that answered the phone?' then bellowed, 'By God, I'll *kill* him—got my machete right here!'

'Jack, *Jack*, wait,' I tried to out-yell him. 'That was *John*.'

'John? John who? Who the hell does he think . . . coming into Neal's home . . . I'm gonna come out there and . . .'

'Jack, stop—it's Johnny, you know, our son?'

'The hell it is—Johnny's a kid—I know Johnny's voice, that warn't no kid . . .'

'No, not any more. He's 14 now and five feet eight.' Jack was silent a minute, then said more quietly, 'Yeah?' Another silence. It had indeed been a long time. He still sounded a bit doubtful. 'Yeah? You sure?'

'Come on, Jack, you know there wouldn't be anybody else here. I'd tell you if I planned to marry again.'

'Listen—wait—gotta get another drink—just wait right there—don't go 'way.' I could hear him rustling about and a refrigerator door open, then a howl. He came back to the phone.

'God damn it—somebody's stole my whiskey—'sgone.'

'Oh? Who'd do a thing like that?' I hated trying to think up things to say to him when he was in this state.

'My Maw—damned ol' alcoholic . . .'

'Jack! Shame! Now cut it out.'

'Saaaay, listen you . . . d'ya know what I'd do if I were there right now? Hunh? I'd take you an' . . .' I stopped my ears. I'd heard it before, and coming from Jack it made me sicker than it would ordinarily. He was yelling. When I dared to listen again, he'd begun to wind down. 'An' marriage, hunh—I won't marry you as long as Neal's alive. We gotta wait till the halls of Nirvana, like I said in *Big Sur*. You're Neal's wife, an' you better not come aknockin' at ma doh, lessen you got that death certificate in your han', y'heah?' He'd fall back on a Southern accent only at such drunken times. Later, I was unable to read *Pic*, remembering.

By the time he called again I had received the copy of *Big Sur* he'd promised, and this time he was almost sober. I thanked him for the book, '. . . And I really like it, Jack. Seems to me you wrote more honestly this time . . .'

'Yeah, I guess—but listen, I've been to Paris since I last talked to you—to Brittany, looking up my family name and all. Then I got drunk and messed up again and just came home.' He sounded completely defeated. Then he brightened. 'But listen, Carolyn, I went to the little church of St. Louis en l'Ile—on the island in the Seine. That's the name of the church in Lowell where I was baptised, remember? And I've always wanted to see the original, like I used to tell you when we sat in Washington Square. Anyway, it was—well, wonderful—a rainy, misty night, see? And I come in out of the rain to the warm glowing candle-lighted chapel with its ancient statues and stained glass, and there's these guys in red coats blowing long brass horns and an organ playing softly. I sat down in a pew and took off my old battered hat that I wear in the rain, and I was holding it in my lap, upside down, you know—so the rain would drip off—and I'm sitting there spellbound, when a family comes up the aisle and the woman leans over and drops twenty centimes—four cents!—into my hat!'

I didn't know what to say. A stab of pity shot through me. His voice was close to breaking. Then he said softly, 'Think of that.' He was quiet, thinking of it. The mood passed. 'My Maw said I shoulda put the money in the poor box, and I shoulda. I didn't think of it, I was so stricken.'

That was to be our last sober conversation and, soon after, I received the last serious letter as well:

I'm not at all capable of living up to your knowledge but understand you perfectly and always did know nothing stood between you and me but your husband, my friend, and I know you will have faith in me for at least that. The other business about how I've turned into an orating drunken 'author' is all true—but I'm fighting against it *now*. It has been forced upon me really by thousands of interrupting maniacs from here to Sweden—(if only you knew how it's managed)—It's managed blindly and with no real ill-intent by numberless interlopers who, for instance, would not let you and me sit talking religion by the fireplace for a minute, or could I have an oldtime day alone with Neal? No. Eugene Burdick was right, saying 'the circle is closing in' on me, Allen, Neal, etc. We should, we will stop it—You, Carolyn, are only woman in the world I can really talk to without having subject changed, or love with—Don't worry, I'll do my best for you, dear heart sweet lady, lover—(Going to Mexico to think alone now, then Fall in Calif.) (or Winter) Be peaceful with me. See you. XXX Jack

Although he telephoned often after that and wrote a few postcards, he was never really 'with me' again. The more he called and the less he wrote, the more I began to see it was a voluntary plunge into the void.

There were periods now when Neal wouldn't turn up for a couple of months, and I'd become worried about him. During one of these long absences, when I was about to leave for work one morning, a car swerved into the driveway with two Highway Patrol cars in hot pursuit, lights flashing, sirens blaring. That sickening sensation which I had thought I was free of forever surged through me again. Shaking, I mustered all the grit I could manage and walked calmly out of the house, locking the door for the first time since we'd bought it.

As I approached the melee, a couple of the officers were closing in on Neal as he emerged from his car. Inside I could see several shaggy heads, but I didn't want to find out what it was all about, and I was irritated that the Highway Patrol cars had been deliberately parked so as to block my drive. With some impatience, I accosted an officer. 'Could someone move one of those cars? I have to go to work.' He agreed courteously, and one of the cars was swiftly backed out of my way. To the other officer I said, 'I'd appreciate any speed you can manage in dispatching your duty. This sort of thing doesn't make me too popular with my neighbors.' He couldn't have been more polite and concerned. To Neal I simply said, 'I'll be home for lunch.'

As I typed routine reports at the office and calmed down, I wondered what was transpiring in my front yard. Then an odd idea flashed across my mind. Neal had had to hurry to try to out-distance the police. Was it possible he had originally planned to arrive *after* I had left for work? Did he do this often, when neither I nor the children were home? A chill went through me. Would I ever wise up? Well, this time I had locked the door, thank God.

On my lunch hour I rushed home, braced. Neal's car was still in the driveway. At the door I fumbled with the key; then I heard voices and found the door was unlocked. I hardly recognized my own living room; it had been completely rearranged and disarranged, and four or five scruffy, hairy creatures sat on the floor or were draped over the furniture. I turned away to close the door and stifle my rising indignation. When I could, I asked, 'Where's Neal?' Someone answered, 'The cops took him with them. He told us to wait here.'

'How did you get in?'

'We found a window we could open.'

382

So much for my locked door. I went into my bedroom to think. It, too, was a shambles, bedclothes and pillows strewn about. I retreated to the kitchen and my anger rose like mercury in a thermometer as I cleared up the remnants of the feast they had helped themselves to, and put pans, glasses and dishes to soak in the sink. By now I was so furious, I had to make another dash for the bedroom and hold my head, trying desperately to remember some Christian affirmations. In cases like this I'd read it sometimes helped to ask oneself, 'What would Jesus do?' He had said if anyone took your shirt, give him your coat, too. But *Jesus,* dear Jesus, give 'em an inch and they take a mile! Go the extra mile? How about not casting pearls before swine? That's the one! Besides, my lunch hour was fast disappearing—along with my spiritual progress.

Still making a superhuman effort to remain serene, I went back to the kitchen and sat on the stool behind the counter that opened into the living room. Keeping my tone even, I said, 'I'm very sorry, but I'll have to ask you all to leave. This is my home, not Neal's.' My ire began to rise again, and I had to measure my words slowly. 'I have a job and go to work every day, not because I like it, but because I want what it provides, like this house, a car and food. I don't expect anyone else's labor to furnish it for me. If you are genuinely in need, or if you allow me the opportunity to *give* to you, I might give you all I have, but if you simply take what I've worked for and take me for granted as well . . .' I couldn't go on, and I felt rotten, which made me resent them and Neal all the more.

Sheepishly, they began to collect their scattered goods. One girl came over to me and said reverently, 'May I shake your hand?' I couldn't tell if she were mocking me, and I had no idea what she meant by it. At least she surprised me so much that I shut up, and when I closed the door behind them I released my pent-up anger by putting the house back in order.

When I next saw Neal I insisted that such an episode never be repeated. 'Don't make *me* call the police, Neal,' I threatened. I knew I never could, but did he?

Gavin was having his own problems with Neal at the other end of the line. He had hoped to be something of a magus to Neal on his release from prison and had offered him the use of his home. But Neal had taken advantage of the offer and ignored the counsel. After one of Neal's visits, Gavin wrote to him:

Dear Neal—(No longer Saint Neal!) . . . You see, the ruthless way you carry out whatever impluse your *desire body* may have makes one realize what a complete slave you really are. You talk glibly about Cayce and all that spiritual stuff, but make no effort to become master of yourself. You and I had an agreement, and about half the time you lived up to it. I very much wanted to rescue you from that shadowy underworld of racing touts and junkies—& loved you so much that I was willing to go far out on a limb to do so. Love to all from your very sad friend and would-be comrade, Gavin.

By Christmas 1965, the situation had deteriorated badly, and Gavin's card to me bore a dismal message: 'Neal was here for a week, but I finally had to ask them to leave, as chaos was taking over.'

Neal might have been wearing out his welcome with his old friends, but he was still capable of making new ones. One of these was the publisher of a literary magazine in Palo Alto, the writer Gordon Lish. Neal often visited his home, alone or with Anne and, in exchange for their hospitality, gave of himself, charming Gordon's wife and children and endearing himself to them forever. Also in Palo Alto, Neal became friends with Ken Kesey, who had just had his book *One Flew Over the Cuckoo's Nest* published.

As Neal added LSD and other new drugs to his diet, I discouraged his visits home. I had no desire to meet his new friends nor have them influence our children. So far, I had seen no demonstration of a better way of life by the young rebels, and I was having enough trouble with ordinary adolescents and my own feelings of inadequacy in dealing with them. So I did not respond with enthusiasm when Neal offered to bring the great author Kesey to meet us. I asked him to come alone or not at all, and he did so until my fears subsided.

The group of friends that collected around Kesey called themselves 'The Merry Pranksters,' and occasionally one or another of them would come along with Neal when he was without a car. The one Neal seemed to consider the least threatening to me, and therefore the one we saw most often, was Ron Bivert, who owned a bookstore in Santa Cruz and had quiet good manners and clean clothes—even if his hair was cut in the style of the comic strip hero, Prince Valiant. All the Pranksters had nicknames, and Ron's was 'The Hassler.' Understandably, the children got a big kick from the names as well and from the escapades Neal recited; no wonder, I thought, since most of them sounded on a junior-high level.

One day Neal told us about the proposed trip they all wanted to take around the country in Kesey's wildly painted bus. It was not simply a prank, Neal hastened to explain, but a serious mission to enlighten the rest of the United States, and the whole thing would be filmed and made into a movie of great social significance.

The plan actually materialized, and we had some peace during their absence, but in far less time than I had expected, Neal was back. The Hassler came with him to tell us about the great success they had achieved. He had taken a shoebox full of photographs along the way, and we all poured over them. Not surprisingly, the Pranksters had encountered a good deal of rednecked stiffness, fear, suspicion and prejudice on the trip, and I found myself recognizing some of my own attitudes in the faces that lined the streets of the cities they had passed through.

Weeks extended into months; we heard reports that the movie was being edited professionally, but that various problems were holding it up. By now my defenses had lowered enough to allow Kesey to visit, and one time he came home with Neal and assured me seriously that it would be a great film and that Neal would make a lot of money. But in the end, fun and games triumphed; the editor was 'turned on' to LSD, and, with wanton destruction of film and equipment, the movie was abandoned. As far as I could see, they all believed the purpose of life was spontaneous 'experience,' so at least they'd had that.

The children reveled in Neal's visits. He'd tell us of the group's hilarious encounters with the police, like the time he'd sweetly conned an officer into pushing the bus out of the middle of a busy thoroughfare while Neal directed the traffic. Sometimes I had to laugh myself, but if Neal got carried away and began salting his tales with too much description of the group's drug or sex capers, I'd nudge him or kick him under the table. There would be cries 'Oh, *Mom,*' and the three pairs of shining, adoring eyes would temporarily dull. I began to see the writing on the wall.

My influence was weakening, and the school system was more an adversary than an ally. John was not performing well in his studies, in spite of his 'genius' I.Q., and so was branded a 'poor achiever'; the school's method of correction was 'punishment,' sentencing him to classes which offered even less intellectual stimulation rather than more. I tried every way I could to motivate John, without success. Eventually I tried to pass the buck to Neal, and sent a letter to Kesey's cabin in La Honda where he was living. All my insecurity and anger came to the fore:

... Now I believe a possible explanation for John's trouble has come to me ... Here's the picture as I see it: Could it be that John's father, whom

385

he loved more than anyone, has rejected all the values I try and inspire in him and has chosen a way of life in which none of these values are important or needed? John has been told repeatedly that his father, too, has a brilliant mind, and I can tell him you are the most miserable of men, but is he going to believe it? Why should he, when all he ever sees or hears is that you lead the most carefree hilariously delightful existence—no dull books, no rules, no responsibilities, no respect for law—free to do just as you please . . . You didn't even lose the love of your family and can see them whenever you've nothing better you want to do. When you're through telling them how great you are and how much fun your activities are, you can just eat, sleep or watch TV. Now, how can anything top that? . . . I tell you all this because, though I doubt it will help now, I want you to stop building the big glorious pictures of life that you have been . . . John *loved* the bus tour, naturally. No doubt he can't wait to join the happy band—and his books are less and less appealing. So, here we go again. If you can't contribute something of value, don't come at all.

I can't say what the effect on him would be if you vanish, should you choose to, but I do know what is resulting from the present visits, and that, at least, must stop . . .

There was no reply, but Neal stopped coming by so often, and even began the considerate habit of calling me in advance to see if a visit would be convenient.

This was all during the time that Neal was frequently in and out of jail, so there were longer periods without communication, let alone support, moral or otherwise. I had carefully explained to Neal that the $200-per-month child support which the divorce settlement had awarded was only a figure my lawyer had suggested in order to preclude any argument from the judge, and that he was not to feel bound by it. Nevertheless he harped on it continually, keeping track to the penny how much he owed me. All he actually *did* about it was bother other people and ask them for money for us.

On his earlier trip East, Neal had evidently expected Jack to give him a sizeable sum of money. What he had received was $10.00, Jack pointing to the size of his phone bill as an explanation. With Allen, Neal fared better as a rule. I cringed to see him go from con-man to beggar.

Neal covered a lot of ground in these last four years. He went East again in the summer of 1965; this time he did not write to me, and I supposed he'd run out of excuses. From a letter to Ken Kesey I learned that Neal was still guilt-ridden about us and even considered taking a job driving a truck for a few weeks in Chicago.

Anne was living with the Keseys at La Honda, and wrote to Neal to keep him posted about his friends and about her own lonely vigil:

. . . I didn't think you'd really gone, and now I'll just wait and see what happens. I'm glad you didn't take me with you, as I am having a great time here, trying to seduce, unsuccessfully, every male member of the gang. Everyone misses you especially me . . . And I never had such a gorgeous time as we spent together at the Lish's. There's lots of things I want to say like if you love me why did you leave, etc.

Faye [Kesey's wife] is trying to help me endure, and be clear, if you'd only believe how hard I'm trying, and I love you so very much. . . . I'm helping paint the bus, washing and cleaning for Faye. It's a beautiful morning; the Hermit gave me some white powder he thinks is ground up aspirin, but, in your spirit (and mine) I gobbled it up, and I must admit that I haven't got a headache . . . Oh, I missed you that night when you left . . . I kept thinking you were coming back. . . . Ken wrote a story about you before the bus trip, which I typed, and June helped, too. It's good. The part about you was very revealing and showed how others look at you, again, which is not at all the way I see you, for I see you as my love not as a character, running wild. I'll copy it out for you. He loves you, too:

Cassady and crew have arrived, banging on the gate, and he didn't go to sleep last night with his mind on freedom. 'Been up for days, Chief, since we were out here last. In fact in great shape, and look here, *three* to bring, now what do you think of that?' Anne and Sharon on each side, and to this usual twosome he indicates that he may have added the blonde Swede, trying burlesquely to put his arms around all three. 'Oh, no, no, no,' admonishing himself, breaking away, becoming confidential about a score, or two bucks for some minor repair on some ailing vehicle somewhere, making my refusal somehow inevitable by the tone of his asking, always skilled at wheedling a 'no' from me, as one of the orneriest old farts to ever draw breath, as well as being one of the most phenomenal testimonies of the hidden human potential, talking and moving while doom cracks under his feet, a ball of burning time.

. . . My, my, shame and a pox on your harem. I wish we were married; the ring is on my right hand now. This typewriter is labeled 'Neal's Printing Co.,' and they're playing 'I can't get no satisfaction.' That's true alright! They just hid the last of the IT290 and I tried to follow Babbs & the Hermit to see if I could get any, but was sidetracked by the foxy Mt. Girl . . . they just played 'I got you, Babe.' We should stop believing all the unhealthy things that seem to be. After all we're still alive . . . Please come back and tell me to come to you and how . . .

Sharon was a mousey girl in glasses and Buster Brown shoes; Neal often took up with such women hoping to help them. Few were saved, and this fact became another guilty burden on his suffering soul.

Neal wrote Kesey a twenty-two page description of his trip, and inserted an answer to Anne, commenting on every thought she'd expressed and saying that her love was the nourishment of his life:

'Thanks for the little quote from Ken. I don't think it'll ever be that way again (all those girls, I mean).'

Neal often spoke about getting away from Anne, as he did about all of us, yet in his expression of sentiments like these, he held out the lifeline of hope, and none of us could let go. The same names kept cropping up in his correspondence; others were added, but few subtracted. A girlfriend of long standing in Salt Lake City was still on the list. He visited her each time he traveled, once even taking Anne with him. Anne told me they had been to the races, and that while she had remained seated, Neal and the other girl had held up a betting window at gunpoint: I doubted the story, or at least Neal's involvement.

Fifty-nine

Perhaps Neal's spells in jail were a welcome escape from the devotees who yearned for him in so many near and far places. Could it be, I wondered, that he had at least overcome his fear of police and prison? Or was the fearlessness part of a total surrender of his will to live? I heard he was taking more chances in cars, driving carelessly and rolling them on purpose.

Anne was always waiting for Neal to get out, and often wrote me long letters filled with her hopeless love:

> ... but I love him & so we greet each other joyfully and part painfully ... Besides we both feel responsible for the low condition the other's sunk to, and we should forgive each other ... I know if he'd love you, I mean like a *man*, not a spiritual overseer, I'd forgive him not loving *me* ... He'll never love & respect me like he does you, but if only he'd not hate me ... I'd like to see you ... and you are my only friend, really, if I may so presume ... Last night I turned down my landlord, trying to become a lady—(like Neal tells me you are) waiting for him to return at midnight. He didn't, of course, and the rent's not paid ...

I'd reply with motherly advice and sympathy.

When Neal was in jail, Anne probably enjoyed the short time when she could be sure of where he was, and how well I remembered how his drug-free letters could be all that any girl could wish for. He wrote them to me, too, filled with the old brilliance, zeal, reassurance and vows; for pages and pages he wove the pattern of another dreamy future: '. . . knowing, as we do, when all is said, that what I truly want is only to succeed as husband and father . . .' or

I pray each nite that *we* might find our way clear to remarry & still live up to our missions—mutual and otherwise. I'm just about ready to go forth as a real man; not thinking of self first any more, or just meeting the need, but truly inspiring & helping as I know I can—& must! Have so much to tell you . . . P.S. Please, love, search your heart; is there still room for me? *Love*, Neal.

In the spring of 1966 Neal had written me a birthday letter that brought the words of his spiritual life-reading resounding in my ears; and I was to remember them often during the short time left to him. Dr. Gordon, Dr. Hunter's 'seventh-plane teacher,' had said:

. . . There is very little we can tell you that you do not know . . . you have brought back a strong memory and are reliving your past—groping for a higher path . . . you want your family to know that you think of them first—this is your pattern—and you have given them a light few parents could have shared with their children . . . How difficult freedom is to perform . . . Strange, you have always led, but you have always felt you followed—but they wrote about *you* . . . you are standing on a precipice—do not be frightened—You live in the NOW—and—tomorrow—may not—be—your—gift. . . . You will feel you can pull down the curtain—and you will move into a spiritual existence that will consume you—free you—not easy—your soul will shake with volcanic—when you see the greatness of the inner you—you will walk a different path . . .

Neal's positive and glowing words were as welcome to me as ever, but I knew what he hoped for was impossible. When he was off drugs I knew how sincerely he believed his words and how urgently he wished them to be true—as I did—but his jail-inspired desires were no match for his chemical needs.

The Pranksters were now busy running up and down the coast going to colleges or other gatherings and giving shows they called 'Acid Tests.' The customary ingredients were Kool-Aid spiked with LSD and anything else available, loud rock music, lots of Day-Glo paint and splashing colored lights. From what I could glean from Neal's efforts to make some sense of them, these events consisted largely of a lot of sensory self-indulgence and pointless nonsense, not to mention danger.

What a waste of time, energy and creativity, I thought. Why wasn't

Kesey writing books for the benefit of mankind? His first was beginning to carry weight toward a reform of the mental health facilities. *That* was the way to change objectionable factions in society, surely, rather than the kind of influence he was exerting over young minds now.

Then while Neal was in jail in San Mateo, Ken was arrested for marijuana possession; with a previous 'bust' still pending in Palo Alto, he staged a suicide and fled to Mexico. What next? I wondered. The careless performance was soon unmasked by the police; Ken had added an automatic felony to his blooming record. That summer the group, Neal included, went down to Mexico to find him. I received obscure postcard messages and strange wobbly notes on old scraps of paper, often with small amounts of money, U.S. or Mexican. In one of his more lucid letters, Neal informed me he was finally free of Anne and had sent her back to the States. I couldn't tell what magic formula had made this possible at last, and Anne's letter a few weeks later gave no clues. She was braving it alone in Venice, California, a seaside town I'd been told was rapidly degenerating into a hippie-haven:

Dear Carolyn,
I held off writing as long as possible, due to the fact that our friendship is a fluke, so it isn't easy to disregard the implications. But I do miss you, and I've been playing the races again (and losing) and going to sex orgies (imagine—30 people all copulating in plush Hollywood pads) and painting (one painting—all breasts, beads & eyelashes) and water skiing and swimming—and going out with handsome bachelors, movie actors, & a bank robber! in Cadillacs and Mercedes, and I can't complain except I'm trying to catch a man of my very own, and, to that end, it's not very wise to contact Neal, by proxy or otherwise. (I wonder if I deserve my very own man?) My horoscope today said to take any advice, but since I lost my last $ at the racetrack yesterday, and the rent isn't paid, nobody has offered any advice! . . . I'm afraid my luck may have changed, and if so, I have enough sleeping pills to leave this life. So I'm for accepting a 'no' or a beating & my heart is pure, and the next time you hear of me, let's hope it's my funeral or wedding and put an end to this disgrace. P.S. I'm invited to the bullfights in Mexico with a real, blue-eyed darling Mexican bullfighter!

I figured she's postpone her suicide until after the bullfight, but mad as she seemed, it was impossible for me to censure her. There was something very real and honest about her, and I loved her 'pure heart' for it.

Kesey wearied of exile, and the group sneaked him back into the

United States, 'to rub salt in the wounds of J. Edgar Hoover,' he said. Then occurred another of those extraordinary coincidences which were changing so profoundly my ideas about fate and destiny. Neal was traveling back from Mexico with Kesey in the fall of 1967. He had never before telephoned me when 'on the road,' but on this occasion he called from Texas; he had nothing in particular to say and there seemed to be no justification for such an expensive call. But then he mentioned in passing that he was going to San Antonio the next day. Unbeknown to Neal, our daughter Cathy had married a boy who'd been drafted and posted to San Antonio; what's more, again quite unknown to Neal, Cathy was about to give birth. So Neal's chance call to me resulted in his arriving at Cathy's bedside just after the delivery of his first grandson.

Neal came to see me on his return, and told me that Kesey was planning a big Halloween party, the last of the Acid Tests, and everyone was to be in costume so Ken could conduct it without detection. It was to be a 'graduation' from acid, and Kesey planned some charade to reassure the authorities: he would now inform the young folks that maybe it would be better if they did not indulge in LSD after all. Neal urged me to come. I would never have gone alone, but when I told Helen about it she was curious and said she'd accompany me; neither of us had seen any of the psychedelic world first hand, only descriptions in the media, and as mothers of teenagers we felt a certain obligation to check it out for ourselves.

On the big day, Helen and I went to Gavin's to await directions from Neal. I now had even less desire to see or hear Neal 'perform'; whenever I heard of him behaving thus, I squirmed in embarrassment for him and couldn't help thinking of the tragic professor in the film *The Blue Angel*, whose obsession resulted in his degradation into the role of a performing bear. Neal apparently exploited his brilliant mind by talking incessantly 'on three levels at once' (as Gavin pointed out), and it was too much for me. (When he and I were alone together and he'd start to talk like that, I'd attempt to stay with him and his lightning thoughts until my mind would spin with the effort and I'd have to beg him to be quiet, something which took an even greater effort on his part. What I did digest made perfect sense, but it took too much concentration to follow all the leads.)

Neal telephoned two or three times during the afternoon to keep us posted on the attempt to find a suitable location for the party. We had heard on the radio that Ken had already been apprehended, but Neal said everyone had pitched in and bailed him out for the evening, so the general excitement was at an even higher pitch.

Helen and I were far from bored while we awaited news. At Gavin's there was always a perpetual stream of visitors, usually the sort of individual seldom encountered elsewhere. On this occasion we were visited by 'the champion swimmer of China,' who jogged in wearing short-shorts, announced that he had just ridden his bike to Santa Cruz and back—150 miles—asked us to guess his age and jogged out. In the living room Gavin was entertaining a strange pear-shaped man, well dressed all in black with a bald head and a Fu Manchu mustache, soft features and protruding eyes. He was languidly waving a pudgy hand while talking, and on his index finger shone a gigantic topaz ring. After Gavin had walked him to the door, we pounced. 'Who was *that* queen, Gavin?' Helen asked, and Gavin reacted with spluttering apoplexy. 'Queen, queen? Why, he's one of the *most* virile men I know—has a lovely wife, children—why, how could you think—?'

'Gee, I thought so, too, Gavin. Why all the masquerade, then, and that obscene rock on his hand?' Gavin's response made continuing irresistible.

'Oh, my.' Gavin sighed and sank back in his chair. 'That was Anton LeVey, the leader of the Satanist Church. You remember, Carolyn, we stopped to see him on the way back from the Highland Games last summer? And he wasn't home, so I couldn't show you the occult furnishings and booby-traps in his house—nor his pet lion.'

'Oh, yes, I remember—'

'Lion?' Helen interrupted looking blank.

'Yes, he has a pet lion,' explained Gavin, 'but the neighbors are objecting to his roars, so he may have to put him in a zoo. I never heard him roar, but I do remember sitting next to him at the dinner table one night, and the thing began licking the side of my head. Well, you know their tongues are so *rough*—like metal files—I thought my ear would come right off. I remember asking Anton if he could stop him from doing that, and Anton said, "Oh, just hit him in the mouth, and he'll stop." I wasn't about to hit that great five-hundred-pound beast in the mouth!'

Neal called again and informed us that the party was to be held in a warehouse in the Mission District; he'd call again later and tell us how to find it. Suddenly it seemed odd that Neal hadn't come up to Gavin's to see us.

Gavin explained: 'He knows I'm angry with him, that's why. The last time he was here, he picked up the phone and began calling long distance. I told him he was welcome to use the phone any time he liked, but I'd appreciate it if he wouldn't make toll calls—you wouldn't *believe* my phone bill—it's astronomical! And, do you know, he got so mad, he *threw* the telephone at me? I never knew Neal to do a thing like that before.' Gavin was right. Neal's temper was getting shorter and shorter, and it frightened me to think what he might do next.

Gavin's houseboy Cappy came in and told us that a friend of his had been in 'Q' with Neal and could he bring him in to meet me. I agreed, of course, and Cappy ushered in a short, swarthy man. He had graying black hair which was brushed back from his forehead and hung to his shoulders in wisps. Around his brow was a thick band of braided leather. He had a short grisled beard and mustache and no top teeth. He was wearing boots and nondescript trousers, but his coat was a naval officer's summer khaki, too small and tightly buttoned.

I said, 'You knew Neal?'

He nodded. 'I've just recently been released. This last time I was in for eight years.'

'Oh?' I inquired sociably. 'What for?'

'Murder.' His tone was equally sociable.

It was getting late. Helen and I discussed whether or not we felt up to acid graduations in the Mission District followed by the long drive home after dark.

'Why don't you come with me, instead?' Gavin asked. 'Anton came over to invite me to a Black Mass he's conducting tonight—it's Halloween, you know, and the Mass is being held in the Wax Museum.'

'What's a Black Mass?' Helen and I chorused, but Gavin didn't hear us; he had gone over to his desk to find the invitation.

'Let's see—I don't know if I can bring guests . . .' and he studied the wildly decorated card. 'It doesn't say, but I'll call Anton.' When he'd hung up, he said, 'No, Anton says one of you would be all right, but guests must be restricted to pairs—absolutely!' So that settled that. (When home again, I looked up 'Black Mass' in my occult encyclopedia and called Helen. 'I found out why only couples are allowed at a Black Mass,' and I read her the lurid description. We broke up into laughter; what would have happened if two such dumb females had found themselves in the midst of such a ceremony?)

So, with guardian angels in attendance, we headed for home; but finding it still light, we agreed to stop off at the warehouse and decide then if we wished to stay. I wanted to see Neal, and I'd promised the kids a report on the party.

When we arrived, we recognized Mountain Girl sitting outside on a car fender, nursing her baby. We asked for Neal, and she said he had been there but had left. 'He'll be back sometime.'

Inside it was dark and gloomy. A few rows of old theater seats were arranged to our right, so we sat down to await developments. As I'd often noticed, Neal and his friends had nothing if not time. We waited and waited.

A few Pranksters ambled about, some setting up musical equipment, others lolling on mattresses. We saw Kesey's cousin, who, like the other members of the fold, wore white coveralls festooned with American flag patches, and were surprised at how many small children there were around. There were lots of teenagers, too, all in bizarre outfits, although we couldn't tell whether or not they were special costumes for Halloween. The sound system worked all right, and eventually the band came on but not Ken's friends, The Grateful Dead, as he had hoped, because they'd had a previous engagement.

When the 'spontaneous' replacement band wasn't playing and shouting over the p.a., someone did things of an electronic nature, and I wondered if the idea was to ascertain just how much human ears and nerves could tolerate. Further conversation was impossible; it was an effort just to think. Now the center of the hall was crowded with squirming, wildly leaping bodies, and a few wiggled in the wings near us, their faces devoid of expression, their eyes glazed or closed.

Kesey strolled about in front of us. He had changed into white tights, red boots, and a red and white satin cape, with a red, white and blue sash across his bare chest—his Superman outfit. He didn't see me, or at least he gave no sign of recognition, and he was evidently in no hurry to get on with the ceremony itself.

We had to move aside as the area was invaded by TV cameramen, who began to climb around and over us, and in their wake followed a half-dozen elegantly dressed men and women, craning their necks to view the scene. They were far more animated than anyone else in the room.

When I could stand the pain in my head no longer, I looked at Helen and she reached for her bag. Neal had not returned, and we were sure he wouldn't miss us. It took the whole ride home in the crisp night air to shrink my head to its normal dimensions and return my ears to ordinary sensitivity. Helen, too, was silent until we were nearly home. 'God,' she said, 'that's a far cry from our idea of fun at their age!'

At home we watched the late news, and needless to say what the cameramen had filmed had been edited in such a way as to give the impression of a wild and depraved Bacchanalian rite. It angered us considerably.

Sixty

———

Neal's entanglements with the law had become just plain sloppy. There were no longer any issues involved; he simply indulged himself at will, paid the penalty and continued his disregard for any restriction. Apparently early Sunday morning was considered to be the best time for the authorities to trap offenders, and now we were periodically roused by two clean-cut, overcoated gentlemen inquiring as to Neal's whereabouts, a routine which continued long after his death. I began to feel paranoid and to refuse Neal asylum at home except in extreme cases, although it made me sad to see more bridges burned. He seldom called any more just for news or a chat, and when he asked to see me I agreed only when we could meet at a friend's. Above all, I never again wanted to witness an arrest, or to subject our home to suspicion and surveillance.

One day in the spring of 1966, Neal called me at work and asked to see me. I told him I was planning to attend a lecture in San Jose given by Hugh Lynn Cayce, and wondered if he would like to meet me there and see Hugh Lynn as well. He was delighted: 'Great! I'll see you at 7:30 *sharp*.' John was away for the night, so I asked Jami, now aged 16, if she'd like to come along.

We arrived a little early, taking seats near the back of the hall so we could catch sight of Neal at either entrance. We sat through the lecture, but there was no sign of him. This didn't surprise us, but we were disappointed. On the way out, we waited to speak to Hugh

397

Lynn, and here came Neal, striding toward us. He was wearing tan jeans, a light blue velour shirt, and Kesey's red cowboy boots. It was fun to see him dressed in something other than old work clothes, and he was quite tanned—something he had always insisted was impossible for his sensitive skin. He looked better and younger than I'd seen him in years. Jami and I broke into welcoming smiles, and he hugged us both. Then I saw Ken and a few of his friends standing by.

I turned to Neal. 'There's Hugh Lynn, do go say hello. He's been asking for you, and it's been so many years . . .' Neal went to him, but to my sorrow and chagrin, he affected a phoney bravado that Hugh Lynn was unable to penetrate with his sincere inquiries. I knew it meant Neal felt guilty for having failed this man who'd tried so hard to help, but I said nothing, of course.

When Neal rejoined us, he asked if we'd go with him to a friend's house for a little while. Jami was eager to go, and I thought it a good idea for her to see some of this group while I was along to supervise.

We drove to the address Neal had given us. Whoever lived there wasn't home, and a young girl was babysitting. Jami and I sat down in the living room, Neal paced about or stood on the hearth shifting from one foot to the other, preoccupied with something. Some of his friends were in the kitchen, others came and went, and another busied himself flirting with the babysitter. All I could make of it was that someone was telephoning to find the host and probably whatever else they lacked. It was approaching midnight when Jami whispered to me, 'What's happening?'

'What always happens, Jami, as far I know. Nothing. Waiting, hunting for someone or something and more waiting. It seems to be what Neal and his friends do best. You had enough?'

'Yes, let's go home,' she said, sighing with disappointment.

The next day Neal called again around noon. He and Kesey were going to a concert by The Grateful Dead, in Palo Alto, and he wanted to take John along to meet them. It was the last thing I wanted, but I knew John would be furious if he learned I'd denied him such a thrill. Neal promised not to drive, not to smoke marijuana, etc., etc., and that they'd get him home in time for dinner. I had to trust him. They collected John from school, and I spent the afternoon positive-thinking.

About five-thirty Kesey called me at work, telling me they were home safe and sound, and if I approved, they'd like to stay for dinner. 'Sure, Ken. I'll stop at the store on my way home. What would you like?'

'Now, just never you mind. You forget all about it and come straight home. I'll take care of everything.'

When I arrived home, I was handed a beer and told to stay out of the kitchen. While Ken's masterpiece was cooking, I filmed John, Ken and Neal playing catch on the front lawn. John had had a memorable afternoon, and Neal had kept his promises — 'Zonkers' having done all the driving. What a blessed relief it was, not to have to scold. Topping it all was a dinner as delicious as any I've had.

The following week, Allen called from San Francisco and asked if he could come for the weekend. It was his birthday. 'Is there a chance Neal can be found and persuaded to join us?'

I urged Allen to come and promised to do my best to find Neal. The Pranksters were between pranks, recuperating from their second Mexican trip or searching for new fields to conquer. Having so many of them in the area made me nervous; I hoped Neal's efforts to include the children in their activities would not become a habit, although the children, of course, wished otherwise. Their friends at school had become increasingly aware of Neal's identity, and they were all so struck with hero-worship of the whole gang that I was receiving less and less support for my uncordial attitude. In spite of Neal's good performance on the day of the concert, I knew better than to count on it every time. However, I was also ashamed of my former hostility toward Ken, who now impressed me greatly with his warmth and kindness, and I wished to make it up to him. Allen's request gave me an idea.

It was frightening, but after much weighing of the pros and cons, I decided this was a unique opportunity to accomplish several goals at once. I would invite the lot, not only Neal, and perhaps if the children and their friends were in the midst of these people, *en masse* and at ease, they might see them in a more realistic perspective and even gain some insight—not too dramatic, I hoped—into the reasons for my restraint. I told John and Jami to invite anyone they wished, and asked some old friends of mine and Neal's who had not seen him for a long time and who would be interested in meeting Allen and Ken as well.

Saturday morning I ordered a cake with 'Happy Birthday, Allen' on it, stocked up on hamburger, hot dogs, beer and wine, and turned my eyes heavenward.

Early in the afternoon Ken was the first to arrive. He was accompanied by a dark-haired girl named Paula and an 8-year-old, long-haired boy named Jason. Misgivings set in immediately—I had not expected to have to cope with a wild child. Paula explained why they had brought him: that morning they had gone to The Grateful Dead's apartment and found Jason alone; the band was in New York for a recording session. I broke in with 'He was living there *alone?*' but made an effort not to show my unhip outlook. 'Don't you know who his parents are?'

'We know *who* they are but not *where* they are,' Paula assured me. 'So I thought he'd like to come along with us.' Jason meantime had taken a lightning tour of the house and grounds, and apparently it would do.

'Where's Neal?' Ken asked.

'Haven't a clue,' I answered. 'Don't you know?'

'No. Guess I'll go look for him. Mind if I take Jami and John with me?' Both were tired of waiting for something to happen and leaped at the suggestion.

In about another hour Ken, Paula, and Jason returned. Ken slumped into a chair. 'Well,' he said, 'I've not only not found Neal, I managed to lose John and Jami.' I had to smile, and I was glad I could.

In a few more minutes, George Walker drove up in his convertible, Jami and John triumphantly seated up on the back of the rear seat, colorful scarves flying from their heads. George was wearing an outfit I assumed he'd acquired in Mexico—pants of a bright pink woven material with a jagged pin-stripe of alternating purple and yellow, a bright green satin shirt, and a bright yellow scarf around his neck. His blond hair was kept from his eyes by a flowered day-glo orange and yellow scarf. He was attentive, quiet and sweet to the kids, and he gave Jami a carved wooden comb as a souvenir of Mexico. Not long after, Neal turned up with Allen, driving the Dead's van covered with stickers advertising the band. Some of John's friends began to straggle in, wide-eyed with awe, and Jami drove off to get her friend, Kym. Everyone was excited but restless, waiting for a 'happening.' Allen's and Ken's groups had as yet not been very close, and I half-expected a conflict of egos.

Neal was behaving nervously and erratically and was in a foul mood, probably because he was trying to adhere to my rule of no drugs on the premises. At one point I made some thoughtless wifely remark that was intended to be jocular, and Neal's temper exploded—just the reaction I had gone to such lengths to avoid in the past. Oh, no—we couldn't have it now—the whole day would be ruined. I feared his anger, but I braved going to him and hugged him, muttering shushing noises. I could feel the wrench it cost him to surrender, but in a minute his stiffness relaxed, his arms went around me, and he dropped his head on my shoulder. 'Thank God,' I breathed.

Ken, Neal and the high-school boys retired to John's room and gathered together whatever instruments were at hand: guitars, harmonicas, maracas and drumsticks were about all we had to offer, and somebody else produced a flute. I knew the supply would be more than adequate for plenty of sound, but John and his friends began to scurry around in search of amplifiers. In the living room, Allen graciously read Kym's poems, wrote comments and reading suggestions, and Kym was floating on air. Then Allen and I sat on the floor while he unpacked a case of relics he had brought back from India and Tibet. With his usual generosity, he asked me to pick out anything we'd like to have. For his namesake, John Allen, he relinquished one of his own sets of finger cymbals.

Cathy had already had enough and left to spend the night at a friend's house, and now my friends began to arrive, among them George and Berylann Nelson, who also brought her mother—'Grandma Go-Go'—and her brother and sister-in-law with their two baby girls. All three women were psychic, and soon Berylann had 'amortized' one of Allen's relics, and her mother, Gloria, had read Kym's palm, after which she asked to see Allen's. I tried to discourage this entertainment since these friends had come to see and talk with us and Allen, not to furnish a sideshow, but Allen didn't understand Gloria's 'reading' anyway.

Jason burst in and asked if he could go swimming so politely that all my fears subsided, and George offered to watch him in the pool. Paula meanwhile had been anxiously telephoning to Santa Cruz every few minutes, telling me she simply *had* to find Hassler—she was crazy about him. After an hour or so she was successful, but how to get to him? Neal was always the answer to a maiden's prayer when she needed a ride, and instantly he volunteered to drive Paula the twenty-five miles over the mountains, and off they sped in the van.

Al and Helen Hinkle came with their two teenagers, and I felt better having Helen there. The patio was filling up. I looked up once to see a tall, distinguished-looking gentleman with a goatee come through the front door, proceed to the patio and sit on the sidelines for about ten minutes, then as quietly walk back into the house and out

401

the front door. Who could that be? He didn't look like a cop. I learned later he was the professor father of one of the boys, and had come to check out the great Allen Ginsberg.

The musical din was pretty constant from the back room. Then Neal returned in a cloud of dust and the tempo rose sharply. I realized immediately that he had not wasted the opportunity to get thoroughly stoned. He had stood it as long as he could, and technically he hadn't broken my rule. But seeing his strung-out condition, I needed a moment to recharge my firm determination to remain 'lovingly indifferent' throughout this day.

Everyone welcomed Neal joyfully, as always, and he went into the kitchen, yelling back at them all the while, then reappeared with a half-gallon carton of ice cream and a large plastic mixing spoon. With no break in his monologue, he stood on the raised hearth, slopping ice cream into his mouth, dripping it down his front and waving the spoon about to emphasize his words, melting ice cream flying about in all directions. It was yet another funny act that people would long recall, but it sickened me to see him in that state.

Allen was called to the telephone. An old friend of his, Alan Ansen, had arrived in San Francisco especially to see him. Normally I would have expected Allen to return to the city, but instead he invited Ansen to come to Los Gatos. An hour later he arrived.

Ansen was in his 60s and obviously homosexual, as was the friend who accompanied him. Someone let them in and cleared a space on the couch for them to sit. When I entered the living room, I noticed that any gaps between the wall-to-wall bodies were now filled in with beer cans, wine bottles, glasses or ash trays, with the babies asleep in the middle of the floor. Then I saw on the couch the apparition of two elderly gentlemen straight out of Wodehouse, exquisitely attired with spats, gloves and walking sticks, and with an expression on their faces of disdainful hauteur. I scrambled to hail Allen, who came swiftly to the rescue and escorted the two out to the patio and more air. I got the distinct impression of skirts being pulled aside as they stepped gingerly over and around the pulsating bodies on the floor. Helen was watching too, and when our eyes met we exploded in our usual private laughter.

The crowd began to thin out as the dinner hour arrived. Paul Robertson, a lawyer friend of Kesey's, told me he had to take his wife and child home as he was scheduled to perform at a Palo Alto nightclub later that evening. Ken and his other friends were preparing to leave, too, and Ken urged me to come to the performance. I hesitated, thinking it might be fun, but I knew I'd be a wet blanket and would never be able to hide my feelings if I had to watch Neal perform.

Those of us remaining had a dinner buffet followed by Allen's cake, and afterward John and his friends wanted to go with Neal and Allen to the nightclub. Since most of the boys were planning to spend the night with us, they didn't have to get their parents' permission and ganged up to persuade me to let them all go. I didn't care for this multiple responsibility, and I told John I'd really rather he didn't; but I could give them no sensible-sounding reasons without exposing my fears and lack of faith in Neal. They finally wore me down when I remembered the reason I'd started all this and the fact that I'd proved nothing yet. May as well go for broke. Reluctantly I gave in.

Neal, in no condition to drive, promised not to and to be careful of the boys and the law. Then he, Allen, John and his friends ran out to the van and piled in, Neal immediately jumping into the driver's seat, with Allen in the back dispensing the marijuana.

There was no longer anyone around to witness my defeat or offer solace, but there were plenty of glasses and ash trays to keep me busy. I went to bed around midnight, knowing sleep was out of the question. I tried not to listen to every car that passed, and turned my thoughts to positive if somewhat rote-like prayer. It helped considerably, but of all the bad nights I had known, this one topped the list. As it wore on, my imagination revealed hitherto unsuspected powers of invention. Two o'clock came and went. They'd be home soon; clubs closed at two. Three o'clock. Had they gone on to San Francisco for more? For worse? Places like Little Harlem reared up in my mind. Were they all in jail? In the hospital? Four o'clock. How could I possibly have allowed this, risked this? What a fool I'd been. By 5:30, I was a shivering, wrung-out rag, but at last John was home and his friends, too. Whatever horrors they'd been exposed to I'd deal with another time; I pushed my anxieties away and slept.

Peace and order returned, but what had I gained? At dinner the following evening I asked John and Jami for their impressions. Both of them admitted to a certain amount of disillusionment, now that they had seen their idols as ordinary people. My sacrifice had not been in vain. We did not, however, discuss Neal. John and the other boys had told me they'd enjoyed the evening. The band in which Paul played was great, they said, and Paul could play two saxophones at once. During the break, the Pranksters had taken over the stand with their mind-blowing noise and nonsense, thrashing away on the instruments

403

none of them could play. Neal had taken the mike and darted among the tables talking on his three levels in a steady stream. I shuddered and asked no more.

Some weeks later, I felt strong enough to ask John what they had done from 2:00 to 5:30 in the morning. 'Oh, was it that late?' he asked. 'Well, we went to some house—I think it was in Palo Alto. Dad and Ken disappeared, though I do remember Dad and Allen sitting in the kitchen part of the time. Dave, Steve and I just sat and looked at magazines, we didn't dare say anything or ask questions. When Dad and Ken came back, we split and got in the van to come home. Allen insisted Steve drive home . . .'

'Really?' I was surprised but pleased.

'Yeah, he was terrified of Dad's driving,' John laughed. 'Poor Steve—just 16—brand new license. But the van was stuck in a ditch, see, and Steve kept stalling it and spinning the wheels and saying "I don't want to drive," so Dad took over "to get us out." ' John giggled again. 'I was sitting next to him in the front seat with Steve, and everyone else was in back. Dad would come to a red light and pretend he wasn't going to stop, then he'd wink and grin at us. Allen and the others would scream, *'Neal*—it's a *red light!'* Dad would roll back a little, but keep on sneaking out, just enjoying getting everyone frantic—nothing coming the other way, of course, and I knew he knew what he was doing—but—' he hesitated, casting a sheepish look at me '—I guess my laughing only encouraged him.'

'No doubt,' I agreed. 'But Steve said Neal never looked at the road, and kept turning round to talk to Allen with his hands off the wheel.'

'Yeah, oh, well, yeah, but he *always* does that—pounding on the wheel to the music—you know how he is.'

'Yes,' I sighed, 'I do.'

Recently, someone asked John to appraise his feelings for Neal. He said, 'Well, all I know is I'd rather have had him for a father than anyone else I've met.' By now, too, it was safe for John to tell me some of the times they'd shared together when he was a boy. On one occasion, Neal was home and had joined John and his neighborhood friends in their games. They had decided to borrow a friend's go-cart, though the friend wasn't home, and ride down the steep driveway of his house. Neal, arms and legs akimbo, was having his turn when the family returned. The boys still howl remembering Neal looking at the ground penitently as the mother soundly scolded his behavior. 'I can understand the boys,' she said, 'but a *grown man*, a *grown man!*'

Sixty-one

When Neal had returned from Mexico he had collected another girl. I didn't meet her, but I heard from Gavin that she had much in common with her predecessors: 'They have such *terrible* fights, I can't see how they *survive*.' This girl went by her initials, J.B., and was the daughter of a wealthy family in Erie, Pennsylvania. Like many of her peers, she did not see eye to eye with her family in matters of lifestyle, though their money was acceptable. She had left the Pranksters for a visit home at the time of our party, but she still telephoned me frequently to discuss Neal. She talked for as many hours as I could stand, telling me what Neal needed and how she was going to straighten him out. 'Good,' I responded, 'I certainly hope so. I'm all for it.' Like Diana, when she spoke of Neal it was with a tone of authority and ownership, and I realized she knew Neal even less than had Diana; but by now I'd learned not to argue. Like Anne, she talked a lot about astrology, but she had an additional talent: she heard voices.

The few times I saw Neal after the party made me wonder if she hadn't been giving him some kind of 'treatment' already. His mind had taken a definite turn for the worse. He would be perfectly lucid and logical one minute, then say in all seriousness, 'I've been getting acquainted with the Devil, you know. Oh, I realize you don't believe in him, but there really is one, and I talk to him frequently. He lives in the hills above Redwood City.'

Then there was the time I was driving him to the highway to hitch-hike, and as we turned onto the main road, he said, 'I can influence people with my mind now. Honest, I've really got it perfected. Watch, I'll show you. See that woman who just passed us? She's going to turn on her lights—*now*. See?' And he smiled in triumph. The woman was descending the hill in front of us and had hit her brakes so, sure enough, her tail lights went on. I sneaked a glance at Neal; he had to be putting me on—I hoped. But he was deadly serious, and I became even more wary.

I also discovered he was keeping a short hop ahead of the law again. I thought something was wrong when he began hitch-hiking so often; he had rarely needed to in the past because he could always find a car somehow. More often than ever we had visits on Sunday mornings from the two gentlemen in overcoats, and my fears for him increased. Surely, if they apprehended him now, he would be sent back to San Quentin. But I wasn't sure how it worked; I only knew Gavin had warned him repeatedly. After letting him come home for the party weekend, I now had to start insisting again that he meet me elsewhere.

One day Neal opened up to me and reviewed his lamentable condition. 'Then why do you hang around with those people?' I asked.

'That's just it. I can't help it anymore. I don't know where else to go. I'm a danger to everyone—to myself most of all. I keep swearing I'm going to stop making an ass of myself, but then I get in a group and everyone stares at me, waiting for me to perform—and my nerves are so shot, I get high—and there I go again. I don't know what else to do—it's horrible.' His voice broke, and with it my heart. I was as helpless as he. He had postponed his own 'about face' for so long, had gotten no closer to his source of strength, and now I felt sure it was too late. When he was gone, I had to try and keep him out of my mind. 'Let others do as they may, as for me . . .' was the way it had to be. The more he demonstrated the ravages of his life, the more determined I was to find a way. I needed no other inducement.

One Sunday morning some months later, he telephoned, his voice weak and trembling. 'Carolyn, I'm sick . . .'

'Do you want to come home?' What had happened?

'Could I, please?'

'Of course, Neal, if you're sick. Where are you?' He said he was at the home of a lawyer friend in Larkspur, a small town north of San

406

Francisco, and I said I'd call Al Hinkle and see if he'd drive me up.

'Yes, darling — hurry, please.'

Reliable Al came right over and picked me up. It was early afternoon when we found the house. The wife told us Neal was asleep upstairs; her husband had gone to wake him when they saw us arriving. I tried to find out from her what was wrong with Neal, but apparently he had concealed his problem, for she said only, 'Just tired, I guess. He's been asleep since he arrived last night.' After a long enough time to make me impatient, Neal appeared, a little drawn but otherwise looking normal. He was very nervous and anxious to get away.

When we got to the car, Neal climbed into the back and lay down, reaching forward for my hand. He closed his eyes and clenched his teeth, his forehead perspiring, and I could see he was controlling something with great difficulty. Al chatted genially as though everything were like old times, and I knew Neal appreciated his homey strength as much as I did. Occasionally Neal would try to answer or comment, but though he smiled, his teeth would chatter if he unclenched them, and he was shivering in spite of the heat.

When we reached home, Neal appeared to relax much more. He sank down on the couch and was able to talk, persuading Al to stay for a cup of coffee.

Neal said he'd been at Ken's farm in Oregon the night before, and the usual party was in progress. He had suddenly become unbearably overwhelmed by the whole scene and had run out of the house and straight to the highway to hitch-hike home, not stopping for his jacket, his cigarettes, anything. 'I simply couldn't stand it another second.' Timid flickers of hope stirred in me whenever there was a major upheaval such as this, for it seemed to me that a sudden and dramatic illumination was now Neal's only chance of rescue.

Al offered a practical suggestion. He told Neal that there had been personnel changes in the top echelons of the railroad, and perhaps now Neal could get his job back. They were desperate for trainmen, and one with as much experience as Neal would be really valuable.

Neal accepted the challenge with enthusiasm, but his voice was oddly flat. 'Yes. That's it. Go back to the world of peace and sanity and regular work. Ah, yes.'

Then and there Al telephoned a conductor friend who knew Neal and who worked an early morning commuter train from San Jose to San Francisco. The conductor agreed to come and pick up Neal the following morning, drive him to the depot and give him a ride on his train. In the city he would steer him to the proper authority. Perfect. Neal removed his shirt, shoes and socks, his high spirits returning. When Al left and Neal stood at the door rubbing his bare tummy and smiling goodbye, it was as though I'd been rocketed back fifteen years.

Neal took his clothes back to John's room where he would sleep, and I sat on the couch and gazed out at my hills. Could this really be? Was it possible it could all drop away? But my old dream didn't really stir: it had been buried too long.

Neal stood over me. 'Where's John? Where's John?' His voice was full of alarm, his eyes wide and black.

'Why, Neal, I told you, John's spending the night with Jim, and Jami's at Kym's.'

Neal clutched his temples, wheeled around and walked swiftly to the back of the house, moaning, 'Oh, my *God*, I've killed my son, I've killed my son!' A sob caught in his hoarse throat.

I followed him, my heart racing. In John's room he had thrown himself on his knees beside the bed, held his head in both hands and rocked back and forth, sobbing. I put my hand tentatively on his shoulder, but he recoiled slightly, saying gently in a normal voice, 'No, please, please—just leave me alone. I know, there's nothing you . . . I'm all right, really . . .'

I couldn't sit still anywhere, so I fidgeted around the house, praying silently and listening. Once again Neal strode down the hall to the living room, grabbed his head and then his crossed arms as he bent over, straightened, flung back his head and continued to repeat, 'I've killed my son! I've killed my son!' What could he mean? What was in his mind? I had a flashed vision of John being chopped to death by the blades on a chariot wheel. Could it be that life that Neal was remembering? I wished I could question him, but he went back to leaning on John's bed, rocking himself and muttering unintelligibly through his sobs. Why was there nothing I could *do*?

Then the front door opened and John and Jim ran in and made straight for John's room. I gasped and ran to intervene, but as I reached the hall, I saw Neal emerge from the room as the boys approached. He smiled, ambled out and greeted them warmly. Then he turned to me. 'Say, I'd better polish my black shoes for tomorrow. They're still here, right?'

'Yes, dear, but I'll polish them for you, as I always did.'

Neal stood leaning against the kitchen doorframe, as cool and charming as he once had been, while I placed newspaper on the stool and worked on his shoes. I experienced another of those strange time lapses or relapses. John paused to say goodbye before he left to spend the night at Jim's house.

'Goodbye, son,' Neal called after them. 'I'll see you tomorrow night after work.' I put the polish away and began to prepare dinner for the two of us. I thought it an odd coincidence that both Jami and John were going to be out for the night; they didn't stay overnight with friends very often and hardly ever at the same time.

Now Neal was staring out the front window, and I could sense his nervousness returning. At dinner he picked at his food, something I'd never seen him do before, and he didn't seem aware of my presence, deep as he was in his own thoughts. Then abruptly he stood up, pushing back his chair.

'I've got to wash my hair,' he said flatly, and bolted into the bathroom and turned the shower on hard.

My apprehension increased as I cleared the table and listened. Neal was in the shower, but he wasn't washing his hair. Instead, he was yelling and pounding on the walls, clearly audible over the rushing of the water. I was frightened. I went to the phone and dialed Silent Unity in Missouri, something I've never done before or since; I had to do *something*. A degree of calm returned when I heard the soothing voice say, 'We will pray, knowing that your husband is surrounded by the protection of God and enfolded in His love. His mind is healed.'

I sat at the table again, my eyes on the bathroom door, and repeated over and over the affirmation, blotting out all other thoughts and holding my fear at bay. In a minute, the shower stopped. Now I could hear Neal pacing back and forth in the bathroom, continuing his one-sided conversation with the Devil, but more quietly now.

In another few minutes, he came out, his face pale but composed. He sat down at the table beside me and reached for his shirt, for the tiny Bible he always carried in his pocket. He closed his eyes, opened the book at random and began to read: 'Be not thou envious against evil men, neither desire to be with them. For their hearts studieth destruction, and their lips talk of mischief.' He stopped, gazed at me open-mouthed, looked mournful and nodded. Then he continued: 'Whoso keepeth the law is a wise son; but he that is a companion of riotous men shameth his father. He that turneth away his ear from hearing the law, even his prayer shall be abomination . . .' Neal slowly closed the book and whispered, 'You see?' Then, 'I want to go to bed. Don't leave me.'

I turned down one of the beds in John's room while Neal took off his jeans; then he climbed in. 'Please stay with me, darling,' he said sadly, looking at me with woeful eyes. The twin beds were head-to-head in the corner, so I lay down on my stomach on the other, my arm outstretched to Neal. He grasped it with both hands, laid his cheek against it, and was instantly asleep. I stayed in that position until my arm was numb and I had to extricate it from his grip. Never had I seen him in such a deep sleep. There was no sign of breathing, unusual with his troublesome nose, and if I hadn't felt some warmth I'd have thought him dead.

Thus he remained all night, and at six o'clock the next morning I woke him as he had requested, even though I was doubtful he would go through with his work plan. But he jumped up, alert and agreeable. He dressed carefully, shaved, and fussed with his hair as of old, while I made a big breakfast. By all appearances, he was perfectly normal and ready for a day in the life of the average conductor. I didn't dare mention the night before. Slurping the last of his coffee, he saw his ride turning in the drive, kissed me wetly and ran out, yelling back, 'Remember, I'll be back tonight, darling, after I get hired.'

I closed the door and sat down to think. Did I want to start this all over again? Could he possibly get hired, and if he did, would his conversations with ghosts or whatever continue? I felt it unlikely that he could return to the railroad so simply, or that he would stay with it if he did, but sometimes I hated to be right.

Two weeks later John and Jami spent a day in San Francisco with some of their friends. They came home in the early evening and ran to me excitedly to tell me they had accidentally run into Neal. They'd been walking up a street near the Haight–Ashbury district when they'd seen Ken's bus park and the Pranksters get out. Neal was behind the wheel. Both John and Jami greeted him warmly, but he was casual and off-hand, showing no surprise to see them. They asked him where he'd been, why he hadn't returned home and whether he'd been hired by the railroad. Neal paused to think, then said, 'Oh, yeah, that. No, I didn't go. The cops arrested me—just got out.' He went on fiddling with something on the dashboard.

Ken called to them, 'Come on. You want to come with us?'

Jami said that as usual there had been a lot of marijuana around, but that whenever she and John had been with Neal and were offered some they always sensed he would prefer they didn't indulge, and so, wanting to please him, had refused. On this occasion Jami had tried a couple of whiffs of laughing gas, but hadn't liked it. This was welcome news to me. Then Jami, close to tears, said Neal hadn't recognized her. He kept talking affectionately to her friend Kym and calling her 'Jami.' It hurt her deeply, not so much for herself, but because she knew how Neal would feel if he ever realized what he'd done. I hoped he never would.

The next afternoon I was sitting in the living room reading, when I noticed that the same car had passed the house two or three times. Getting up to look more closely, I saw Neal was driving the car, with a girl sitting beside him. I walked out to the road. Neal backed the car at my approach but made no sign of parking. When I reached the car he leaned forward to see past the girl. His chest and feet were bare; he wore nothing but jeans.

'What are you doing, Neal? Why don't you come in?'

'Get in and we'll talk.' He looked so strange—grim, yet as though he had a secret to impart, and also angry. The girl, who looked about 18, stared at me accusingly.

I tried to be chummy and casual, but grave forebodings quickened my heartbeat. 'No thanks, I'll stay here. What's up?'

Neal's face grew rigid. He clenched his jaw and spat out, 'What about your *daughter*, eh. Taking *drugs*! Yeah—in the city yesterday.'

I frowned, blinked, shook my head. 'What? What do you mean?'

Neal churned the car back and forth, swaying me with it. 'Get in.'

'I don't want to get in. If you've something to tell me, park the car and get out. I don't understand.'

Now the girl chipped in. 'Jami, your daughter, was taking drugs. How come you let her? She really shouldn't, you know, she's too young for that.' She flipped her cigarette ash while I gaped at her. It was all crazy—and especially since I realized they were talking about Kym.

'Look, Neal, I know all about it,' I said, not too sure that I did. 'I wasn't there, but I understand *you* were—her father—why didn't you stop her?' I did my best to ignore the adolescent and her supercilious gaze.

Neal didn't answer. He looked angry still, but confused now, too. I was growing frightened; by the look of the two of them I could only guess that they must have dashed impulsively all the way from San Francisco to tell me this urgent news. What sort of torture was Neal going through?

'Is that all you've come for?' I tried to sound gentle, tried to reach him somehow. 'It's *all right*, Neal. Jami's all right. Thank you for telling me, but don't worry. I must go in now, goodbye.' I turned and

411

ran back to the house and, thank God, Neal gunned the car and sped away.

By 1967 we no longer received special messages or contributions from Neal on holidays or birthdays, but I knew, if he were able, he would be thinking of us, and we included him in our thoughts and prayers all the more. For several months I had been urging him to go to Mexico and be free of the danger of being hunted down. I guessed the net was closing in. J.B. had called to say she had rented a house in San Miguel de Allende; he was welcome to use it, and it had a typewriter and everything he'd need. She herself wouldn't be able to get there until after the Christmas holidays.

When we didn't hear from Neal at Christmas, I thought perhaps he'd gone, and felt relieved. I was wrong. He telephoned the last week in December and asked if I would see him on New Year's Eve. This wasn't one of our special dates anymore, and I wondered why he wouldn't be spending it with his friends or some girl. Could he be contemplating another new beginning? Whatever his purpose, I agreed to meet him at a friend's, not counting on his turning up.

As I prepared to leave for our meeting, I thought it curious that I still felt a rise in excitement at the thought of seeing Neal alone, even though I held out no real hopes. But since he had chosen the date, perhaps he would be romantically nostalgic. By the time I arrived, I had worked myself into a sentimental and expectant state. There was another couple already there, with whom our friend and his wife planned to celebrate, and I surmised by their appearance and dazed expressions as we were introduced that they had all jumped the gun somewhat.

Neal was there, too, seated in a chair on the other side of the room, and I went to sit on the couch opposite him, flashing my most appealing smile. He greeted me casually, and I peered at him, fearing he hadn't recognized me. He had, but he was certainly little moved. He was listening to the music, gazing into space, and now and then would make a remark that might have been aimed at anyone or no one. Then he started humming, his glance occasionally falling on me as though I were a passing pedestrian. I made a few efforts at establishing contact and failed. There was nothing to do but sit and wait, and since I wasn't in whatever world they were in, repartee was limited. My romantic expectations were turning into equally romantic feelings of rejection, even though I knew them to be unjustified. Throughout the agonizingly slow dinner, Neal waved his fork to the music, hummed between mouthfuls and continued to gaze over my

412

head. I tried to look at a magazine, but the lighting was too dim. At long last the dishes were collected and the company departed, finally leaving us alone as they'd promised.

I looked at Neal, seeking a reason for his urgent summons, but I was still not included in his field of vision. After a minute or so, I said, 'Well, if this is all you wanted to see me for, I have other things to do at home.' And I rose from the couch. Neal didn't speak, but got up and gently pulled me back down, then stretched out with his head on my lap. Closing his eyes, he clasped my hand to his chest and said, 'Please, please tell me about the children—about yourself—everything you've been doing.' His voice sounded weary.

I dredged up all the trivia that makes up the daily lives of a growing family. Although his eyes remained closed, he was more responsive now, and if I paused or sounded as though I couldn't possibly care, he'd prod me by repeating my last two words or asking a question. For a time, I felt compensated, but soon I became bored, and I didn't want to comment too deeply on the problems with the children, most of which were a result of my having to cope alone. I tried to shift the talk to him, but he was evasive or answered only in monosyllables.

'Neal, aren't you going to go to Mexico, after all? Really, you *must*.'

'Yeah, yeah,' he sighed. 'But I have to go to the city first and get money.' Another delay? Why was he dragging his feet?

'Oh, Neal,' I wailed, 'every day and every trip to the city increases your chances of arrest. Surely you know that?'

Instead of answering, he announced matter-of-factly, 'I have to take a bath.'

He got up and went into the bathroom. Not knowing quite what to make of this move, I followed. He said no more, started the water, undressed and climbed into the tub. I sat on the edge in case there was anything else on his mind. He leaned his head back against the wall, folded his hands across his chest, gazed into space for a minute, then closed his eyes and resumed humming.

I concluded that the audience was at an end. 'Well, Neal. I guess I'll be going.'

'Yes, ah—thank you, dear—' His eyes were still closed, but he patted my arm.

'Goodbye, Neal. Hap—Happy New Year.'

'Mmmmm.'

I drove home, thoroughly depleted and feeling as though I'd been pouring energy into a void and receiving nothing in return—an unusual feeling after seeing Neal; people were always commenting on how much of himself he gave to others. I wondered if now he had given all of himself away and only the broken shell was left.

Three weeks went by, and I heard no more. I hoped no news was good news. Then he telephoned. He was in Los Angeles at the home of a couple who, like countless others, had met and responded to his charm but little understood his true nature. (They published an underground pornographic paper and, in their ignorance of Neal's disgust for such things, had been puzzled when Neal hadn't leaped at their offer of a job.) I pleaded with him to stop tempting the law, to go to Mexico, stay at J.B.'s house, relax in the sun and get healthy. 'Then you'll be able to write again. You can do it, honey. Do it for us if not for yourself.'

Was he listening? There was a pause, then, 'I'm coming home.' His voice was—quiet, his tone conveyed finality. Oh, God, what now?

I swallowed the lump in my throat and tried to be casual. 'Now, Neal darling, you know all about that . . .'

'I'm coming *home*.' More determined, more final, only a hair's breadth away from a scream.

Don't say that, stop saying that . . . Why was he doing this, making me say no again? He'd witnessed before what it did to me. I remembered the time after the divorce, when he'd stopped at the door on his way out for the umpteenth time and said, 'Please, can't I come back?' With no warning I had collapsed onto the nearest chair and disintegrated into great wrenching sobs. I was caught completely off guard, and both of us were surprised, but I couldn't control myself. He had bounded over to kneel beside me and hold my heaving shoulders. When I forced out my voice, it was too loud. I knew the children could hear, and I couldn't help it. 'Great God, Neal, haven't you any idea what it means to me to send you away? Don't you know yet it's the *last* thing I want to do? Stop making me reject you over and over and over. Don't ask to stay—you know I have to send you away—Please—' Neal had kissed my wet face and hurried out of the house. It was the only time the children had heard me cry, and they never forgot it.

So now he was asking again, and in such despair. What could I say? There was no hope left in me for a life with him; but wasn't there anything I could do to soothe his torment? No, nothing.

'No, Neal, dearest. Please go to Mexico and get well. *Then* come home. You know we'll be waiting.'

'I've got to come home *now*.' I could hear the effort he was making to control himself, and my hands were shaking, too.

'Neal, please—' I wailed.

There was a long pause. 'Well . . . maybe . . . maybe by my birthday . . .' He mumbled the rest, but there was a trace of defiance in his tone.

'Yes, Neal. God be with you.' He hung up sharply.

Later I heard he had been refused entry at the border because of his appearance, but had managed to connect with a film crew who had taken him in with them.

He had delayed so long that, before he got to San Miguel, J.B. had already arrived, and she had called me to find out where he was. I had told her what little I knew, but I could not explain his reluctance to get there. 'It sounds like the perfect place for him.'

'Well, anyway,' she'd said cheerfully, 'my voices tell me he's going to be all right.'

'Oh? That's good news. The last times I've seen him, his mind has been pretty well muddled. I'm afraid the drugs have taken their toll.'

'Not at all. He's going to be completely cured. He'll write again and get steadily better. Within the next six months, they say.' She was confident.

'That's fine, J.B. Do keep those positive thoughts, and I'll try to support them.'

The next time J.B. called it was less than two weeks later. It was a Sunday morning, the 4th of February 1968. In a state of semi-shock, she told me Neal was dead.

'Thank God,' I breathed. 'Released at last.' Perhaps J.B.'s voices had spoken the truth after all.

Sixty-two

Jami, John and I were finishing breakfast when J.B.'s call came. After I had hung up I quietly told them what had happened, although they had guessed, and we sat in silence for a few moments, of one mind and one prayer. Of course, it didn't sink in all at once; it took months to hit home. Neal had been absent for so much of our life, there was no sudden change in our routines. Only as time passed did we miss him and remember how much he had been a part of us. Whenever I couldn't stem the weeping that came over me occasionally, I knew it wasn't for him, but for the golden light that had been his gift and for the dream I had never got to hold.

The same afternoon, J.B. called again, bless her. I had completely forgotton about the mechanics of death, and I knew nothing of them, not even in this country, let alone a foreign one.

'What shall I do?' She was asking *me*? But she sounded much more sensible and efficient now, and said she'd take care of the arrangements. 'Well, J.B., he has to be cremated. Can you arrange for that?'

'Cremated? Why cremated?'

'Never mind why, he made me promise. Just find out how to go about it, okay? And, my dear, I can't thank you enough. What would I have done without you?' She could speak Spanish and knew the town, so if she could function normally, I knew she'd be more useful than I. Ken's lawyer friend, Paul Robertson, graciously came up with the necessary financial help.

For my part, I had to think about who to inform. First, the Hinkles, who felt much as I did, and then Allen and Jack. The phone number that Allen had given us had been changed. His new one was unlisted, and I was at a loss as to how to reach him. The New York operators and their supervisors were admirably diligent in protecting his privacy. But I *had* to succeed, and in the end a Spanish-sounding operator agreed to call him, give him my message and ask him to call me back. Allen was subdued, fatalistic, sad. He'd known death before.

Next I called Jack. He wasn't home, but the operator left a message with Stella, his wife, asking him to call me. Monday rolled around and Jack had still not rung. Why not? I debated with myself and wondered all day, finally deciding to try again. I couldn't have him hearing about Neal's death some other way, like reading it in the paper. This time Jack answered the phone. I had only just blurted out the news when Stella began yelling behind him, 'Jacky, Jacky, stop it . . .

He shouted at her, 'Shut up. Neal is dead.'

There was a scuffle and she came on the phone, overwhelming me with apologies for not having given Jack my message. 'But, you see, if I don't do something, he'd spend all his money on telephone bills . . . I had no idea . . .' I sympathized with her and told her I was glad that Jack had someone protecting him from himself.

Jack came back on the phone, considerably sobered, and said all the beautiful things I wanted to hear about Neal—but he still wouldn't believe Neal was really gone. 'It's just a trick. He's hiding out someplace, like Tangier.' Each time I'd try and get him to see it was for the best, he'd cut me off and rhapsodize some more.

For days and weeks, J.B.'s calls and confusion mounted. She gave me three different versions of the cause of Neal's death and the circumstances preceding it, the only constant being that she and Neal had had a fight the evening before, soon after his arrival, and he had left the house in anger. 'You see,' she repeated often, 'whenever he got mad at me, he identified me with you.' I let it pass.

Her first version had been that Neal had been high on 'reds' at the time of their battle and had stormed out to go to a wedding where he had had a lot of alcohol. I knew Neal was familiar with the end result of that combination. Would he have done it on purpose? Was that what he'd meant by 'maybe by my birthday'? I doubted it, knowing how he felt about suicide, but he might have taken a risk, not caring, or perhaps he was so mentally out of it he didn't realize what he was doing. No laboratory analysis of his body was reported. Much later I learned that, because drugs had been involved, the authorities wanted no part in it. Perhaps it was just as well. I preferred to think the God within him had mercifully relieved Neal of a burden which was too great for him to carry or transcend. I had always dreaded the idea of Neal as an old man; it would have been grotesque—he personified youth to everyone who knew him.

(Fifteen years were to pass before I learned that Neal had gone from the wedding to retrieve the luggage he'd left at the Celaya train station upon his arrival a day or two before. He had walked only about a quarter of a mile before collapsing beside the railroad tracks.)

J.B. herself gave me cause for concern. She could often 'see' Neal and hear him. When she looked in a mirror, she saw his face instead of her own. My anxieties increased. Maybe I should go tend to it myself. But I couldn't leave work that long, and I had no money. I had to trust her.

J.B. called again a few days later. 'Are you sure I should have him cremated? He'll have to be shipped to Mexico City for that.'

I sympathized with her for the hassle it involved, but said, 'Yes, J.B., I'm sorry, it's a must. The theory is, you see—and Neal very much hoped it's true—that the fire purifies the body and makes a quicker and easier transition possible for the soul's release. Since we can't prove it one way or the other, I'll have to follow Neal's wishes, don't you agree?' She sighed but said she'd try.

Not being familiar with everything that J.B. was obliged to take care of in accordance with Mexican custom, yet being all too familiar with her mental quirks and her great attachment to Neal, I became convinced I'd never see the ashes.

After nearly four months had passed, J.B. telephoned from Los Angeles. She and the ashes were safely within the boundaries of the United States, and she said she'd fly to San Jose. I agreed to meet her at the airport. One more leg of the journey to go. Would she change her mind?

On the evening of J.B.'s arrival, my friend Florence who was living with me at the time came with me to pick her up. J.B. had said she'd be wearing jeans, but that was the only clue to identification she offered. It was dark, and as we turned into the terminal drive, I had to swerve to avoid a mound of rags and hair cacophonically blowing on a harmonica. 'Hunh, you don't often see hippies here,' Florence observed. I cruised slowly past all the exits from the lighted terminal, and we both scanned the few passengers for a girl in jeans. There was none in sight. At the same instant and with the same thought, Florence and I turned to look at each other, and I drove back to the entrance and pulled up beside the huddled figure sitting on the curb. It was J.B. She pocketed the harmonica in the folds of a large poncho and turned to pick up a woven satchel and a shoulder bag, all the while holding tight to a large wooden box cradled in one arm. She managed to climb into the car without dislodging it, and all the way home she hugged it to her. There was no doubt in my mind as to what that box contained.

We chatted amiably and more or less coherently on the drive home, with the emphasis on my thanks to her, which were indeed sincere — and, I did so hope, justified. At the house I ushered J.B. in, closed the door, and turned to her smiling.

'Here, I'll take your burden from you now. You've been simply wonderful. I still can't thank you enough.'

I held out my hands, but she hesitated, looking from Florence to me and back, weighing the situation. I thanked God there were two of us. With reluctance, J.B. slowly handed over the polished box. Not wishing to show her my suspicions, I put it down on a nearby table.

'Let's have a glass of wine, shall we? It'll give you a lift after your tiring trip.' I went to the kitchen, Florence settled herself and lit a cigarette, and J.B. sat cautiously on the edge of her chair.

Neal and I had come to believe firmly that there is no death except for the flesh, and that grief and mourning only slowed down the progress onward and strengthened whatever might bind the soul to earth. This feeling was a great comfort to me now. J.B., on the other hand, was inclined to the view that the box on the table contained the Neal she had known.

At the end of the evening, as the three of us were about to head for our respective beds, I picked up the wooden box, saying as off-handedly as possible, 'I think I'll put this away now. I don't think we want it in the middle of the living room, especially when the kids come home tomorrow—a bit morbid, don't you think?' And I smiled at J.B. as I started for the back of the house. She half rose from her chair, but sank back without answering. Was she going to fight me for it? Not yet. I put the box of ashes in a metal filing cabinet and locked it.

The next morning J.B. rose early, and strode briskly about the house while I cooked breakfast. She seemed cheerful and made an effort to be friendly. 'Say,' she accosted me in the kitchen, 'did you jump into my body last night?' I dropped a spoon. And that was only the beginning. By the time we'd finished eating, I was starting to twitch. She had sounded at least capable of sensible communication during most of our telephone calls, but now I was having difficulty connecting each of her sentences with the one before it, and she would suddenly burst into convulsions of laughter or song. I recognized a few references to astrology and various occult phenomena, but what was she *saying*? My head swam with the effort to respond.

She kept up this performance throughout the day, always skillfully sidestepping my attempts to 'help' her with her onward travel plans, while I worked on a large painting, the strain tying my stomach in knots. About once an hour, she'd discontinue her erratic conversation and say, 'Where are the ashes?' Each time I'd respond like a parrot: 'They're put away now, J.B. Let's forget about them and not be morbid.' She'd say, 'What will you do with them?' And I'd say, 'I don't know yet. I'll have to think about it and consult the kids. These ashes are not Neal, of course, but let's say symbolically he is home now as he asked to be—and loved.' Nausea threatened each time I had to repeat the scenario, but I held firm: 'They're put away and there they'll stay.' This was possibly the longest day I can ever remember.

Eventually, after preparing dinner and at my wits' end, providence intervened in the form of an old friend, Paul. He was a large, strong man, not at all aggressive, but J.B. needn't know that. (She would have recognized him as a Leo of the pussycat variety had she known him.) He stopped by to return a book he had borrowed, and I immediately pressed him into service. Three months earlier Gavin had offered to put J.B. up, and now Paul agreed to drive me and J.B. to San Francisco.

I put the dishes in the sink and said cheerfully, 'Come on, J.B., I know you're anxious to get moving. Gavin told me he hoped you'd visit him on your return, and Paul here has agreed to drive you there—save you the fare—isn't that great?' I was struggling into my coat by now, and Paul and I headed for the door, holding it open for her.

Slowly, she gathered her things together, her mind working furiously, I could tell. 'May I see the ashes one more time?'

'No, J.B., I'm sorry. I told you—do try and transfer your thoughts of Neal from the ashes to his living spirit. He'd prefer that, I'm sure, and you'd be much happier, too, right? Ready?' I went through the door and Paul waited for her to precede him.

On the way to the city, she entertained us with her harmonica, obviously having had lessons from the Pranksters.

At Gavin's, there was another brief setback. In front of J.B. and several guests, he said that he no longer had any room available. I was near panic. Would I have to take her back? Then a young man, whom I shall forever think of with undying gratitude, spoke up with extraordinary chivalry and offered his room to J.B. for the night. Pressing my advantage, I said that Paul and I must hurry home— 'Work day tomorrow, you know.' Gavin walked to the door with us, and I gave him a brief summary of the tribulations I'd experienced with the ashes. He understood immediately and forgave my rudeness in trying to dump J.B. on him without warning. He smiled wryly, recalling the battle which had taken place over D.H. Lawrence's ashes in New Mexico: 'Frieda mobilized a bunch of Navajos to see that Mabel's Pueblo Indians didn't waylay the ashes on their way from Taos to the Lawrence ranch near the Colorado border. I heard the story from both sides!'

The ride home was one long sigh of relief. It was over.

Two weeks later, the doorbell rang. I opened the door to find J.B. standing on the stoop. 'I want to say goodbye to Neal. I want to see the ashes once more. I'm going to tour the country tomorrow.' She had hitch-hiked all the way from San Francisco to see those ashes. See them—or collect them? In one sense, I felt she had some right, considering her part in the story, but I was still afraid of a battle over them, which I could not stomach. I stood in the doorway. She brushed past me into the hallway, but I stood there firmly, not closing the door.

'No, J.B., I'm very sorry, really, but I've told you again and again. You can treat death any way you wish, but since you knew Neal such a very short time, I feel I have a better idea of how he'd feel about this. Honor Neal some other way, if you like, but leave his ashes out of it.' I was quite frightened of her now. If she'd go this far, how much farther? I still believed she wanted to get those ashes for herself.

We stood eyeing each other. She leaned back against the door jamb. 'How well you must have known him. How fortunate all your years together. You know what a fine man he was and how he loved his children.'

'Yes, J.B., I do. And I think it would grieve him for us to fall out in any way—especially over this.'

She accepted her defeat and walked away down the drive and up the road to the highway.

Condolences arrived day by day, all emphasizing the tremendous effect Neal had had on people's lives. Some were from individuals I had never met, and I was doubly touched by these, because Neal had made so many friends in his later years who had been unaware of his family's existence. There were inspired poems from young people, and a moving letter from Gordon Lish as well as one from his former wife. The national press took little notice of Neal's passing:

SAN MIGUEL de ALLENDE, Mexico, February 4, 1968 (AP) Neal Cassady, 43, of San Francisco, a former railroad conductor and long associate of prominent members of the beatnik and hippie generations, has died here. Police reports said Cassady was found unconscious but still alive early in the morning along the railroad tracks. Cassady was a friend of novelist Jack Kerouac and the poet, Allen Ginsberg.

But the underground press and local papers were exceptionally fervent in their eulogies. Without judging Neal's personal merit, Ralph Gleason, in the *San Francisco Chronicle*, commented, '. . . Only the underground press mourned this remarkable man, who was intimately involved with two major novelists and a major poet.' And that was the least one could say.

From the time of Neal's death Jack telephoned more frequently, but he was rarely sober and it was always in the wee hours. Sometimes he'd say, 'Neal's not dead, you know—he *couldn't* be. Naw, he just wanted to get away,' then another time he said, 'Ah, Neal—I'll be joining him soon.'

'Jack—don't.'

'Yes, I will. It won't be long. I'm gonna join him.'

'Please, Jack. Don't talk like that. Why don't you come visit me?'

'Can't. Can't hardly get myself to the bathroom for a leak.'

'You seem to be able to make it to the refrigerator okay.'

'Yeaah,' he'd laugh. 'You know what I drink now? Boilermakers. The best whiskey an' the best beer for a chaser—I have my little glass here now, m'dear—yep, really grrreeaat . . . But, ah, yes—if I were with you now—ah, ha—we'd sit by the fire, you'n me, eh? an' we'd talk again like we usta . . .' He'd be silent until I'd think he'd fallen asleep.

'Well, Jack, in that case, you'll have to go back to wine—I don't like whiskey.'

'Mhmm, yeah, well—I ain't goin' nowhere—'cept with Neal.'

'Have you been writing?' Again I'd try to change the subject.

'Hmm, yeaah . . .' he'd brighten sometimes, '. . . just finished one.

It's about two little boys hitch-hiking through the South.'

'Really, Jack? Not autobiographical?'

'Nope. Jack—fict-shon.'

'Well, Jack, that's really fine!' How phoney could I be? 'Now, see? You've got all that self-analysis out of your system, and you can start a whole new career! I'm *so* glad. I've always thought you could write beautiful imaginative fiction—more like *Dr. Sax* . . .' In my heart I was saying, 'Can he really still do it?' It didn't seem possible in his condition. He seemed to be *trying* to destroy his life and talents. But I didn't want to be sad. I was sick and tired of lamenting. Damn it, I still wanted to live happily ever after!

The following Easter eve I was invited to a dinner party by some prominent local people who had varied interests and were acquainted with many creative artists. I had a thoroughly good time. I usually hate parties, especially when I know almost no one there, so for me it was a rare treat to meet a group of people all of whom were active, optimistic and uncritical—no chips on their shoulders, no axes to grind. Maybe, just maybe, a new life was going to open up for me!

The *joie de vivre* of that evening was an exhilarating tonic, but I rather overdid the wine, and when I ran into my house at two-thirty the next morning I was more than ready for bed. Gratefully I lowered my throbbing temples to the cool pillow. It took a few minutes for the whirling to stop and the giddy stimulation of the evening to subside but when it did, I was totally out.

I heard the ring of the telephone from a long way off—or had it rung only in my head? I dashed stumbling, toward the counter in the kitchen that held the phone. My head descended and sank on my elbow.

'H'lo,' I whispered.

'Go pour yourself a glass of wine and talk to me.' Jack's voice was mellow, slurred and cozy, ready for a nice long chat. Oh, where was his wife when I needed her?

'Oh, Jack, no—please, not tonight—I just can't tonight. I've just crawled into bed with a terrible headache. I've had way too much wine already—I simply *can't* . . .'

'Aw, come on—I wanna talk to you.'

'Please, Jack, I really can't, I mean it—have a heart!' My teeth were chattering and I shook with cold. 'Call me tomorrow, please—in the daytime. I'll be glad to . . .' I hung up and scurried back to my warm bed. The phone rang out again.

'Hey, you can talk to me—go get a drink.'

'Jack—no—please—tomorrow, okay? I'd love to talk to you, you know that, but this is the worst possible time—honest—think of *me* now, Jack, please? This once? Couldn't you do that for me?' I felt my righteous indignation rising, and I hung up. Good grief, it must be six or seven in the morning in Florida—had he been at it all night? Well, hell, *one* time he could consider me. Right though I believed I was in my head, I knew it wouldn't wash with my emotions, but I was too beat to fight back.

The telephone rang again, and I pulled the pillow over my ears and gritted my teeth. Oh, Jack, dear Jack, have mercy—*please* understand!

He never called again, and seven months later he did join Neal, just as he'd predicted:

ST. PETERSBURG, FLA., October 31, 1969 (UPI) Novelist Jack Kerouac, 47, father of the literary 'Beat Generation' in the 1950's and reluctant godfather of today's hippie movement, died today of a massive abdominal hemorrhage. Kerouac, of French-Canadian extraction, soared to fame after publication of his novel *On the Road* in 1957. He wrote 18 books which sold several million copies and were translated into 18 languages, Kerouac and poet Allen Ginsberg were the prophets of the beat movement which flowered in San Francisco & New York.

I felt strangely lonely and remote from his death at first, even resentful. Then I realized I'd not been near Neal or Jack when either of them died. Other women had tended to the business of their passing, yet in my life I'd been closer to those two than anyone I'd known. It was right. Alive I knew them, and alive they would always be to me. 'Let the dead bury the dead; our concern is with the living.'

But it pleased me when Allen wrote to me after attending Jack's funeral and I felt somebody recognized my part in his life:

. . . How are you and yr children tonight? Jack's funeral very solemn. I went with Peter & Gregory & John Holmes in Holmes's car, saw Jack in coffin in Archambault funeral home on Pawtucketville St. Lowell, some name and funerary home from Jack's own memory—& pall bore thru high mass at St. Jean Baptiste Cemetery—Jack in coffin looked large headed, grim-lipped, tiny bald spot top of skull to finger touch on his brow, fingers wrinkled, hairy hands protruding from sportsjacket holding rosary, flower masses around coffin, U-shaped wrinkled furrow familiar at his brow, eyes closed, mid-aged heavy, looked like his father had become from earlier dream decades—shock first seeing him there in theatric-lit coffin room as if a Buddha in Parinirvana pose, come here left his message of Illusion-wink & left body behind.

Sad I didn't call you before, but too much woe, life & business on my desk till this dusk. Take care of yourself . . .

424

Every word pained me with horror; his description more intimate than even I would have allowed myself to note if I'd been there. How thankful I was that I had not been present.

For Jack, of course, there was more public notice than for Neal, but not all of it was kind. The media praised Jack now for his work, but condemned his life, whereas Neal had produced no 'work' and had led a life opposed to every social decree. True, the underground press was kinder to Jack than the majors, and the *Village Voice* of New York carried a beautiful tribute, but they also published a ruthless and scathing denouncement of him. Why was there this need in people to tear down the heroes they themselves had created? Why did they feel they had the right to consider them their property, subject to their approval or contempt? A few years later this trend was given a hideous manifestation in the form of a caricature of Jack as he had supposedly looked near the end. I opened the *Esquire* magazine in which the painting was reproduced and burst into tears, not so much for Jack as for the poor soul who had gained either satisfaction or income from such a disgusting display of callousness.

Back in my own backyard, no sooner had I shuddered and dismissed J.B.'s morbidity than Diana's took over. She called and called from New York, at first telling me all the things I should do about the funeral for Neal, and then saying I should split the ashes with her.

My blood boiled even more than it usually did when I was forced to be in contact with this female, and I had no difficulty understanding *her* meaning. 'Damn it, Diana, won't you ever quit? Who do you think you are, anyway? You knew Neal for only one of his forty-three years. Your marriage was void, Neal never saw your son except just after he was born, and all of it happened *twenty years* ago. Where do you get off telling *me* anything? And wanting part of his ashes is sickeningly morbid. Good God, woman! I shouldn't have had him cremated, I should have chopped him up in little pieces and passed him around to all his women, like relics. Yuuck—it is *revolting!*' And I hung up.

I was ashamed of my outburst, it's true, and when she called right back, I said, 'Diana, listen. Once and for all, get this through your head: I don't want to discuss Neal's ashes—ever! Now, look, I don't want to yell at you, I don't want to be angry. Just be a good girl and *leave me alone.* I will not talk to you, and I'm going to hang up now.'

She wasn't listening; she just barrelled on.

'Diana—I'm going to hang up *now.*' And I did.

She called back. This time Florence answered, and she was too nice to hang up on anyone, so Diana ranted and raved for over an hour, giving out all sorts of fantasies, such as how Neal owed her $80,000 and my children weren't his (*'everybody* knew *that'*). Dear Lord, would she never get off my back?

How much I admired Anne Murphy during all this, her selfless and dignified adjustment to the death of the person who had been the very core of her being. She was still in bandages from an operation to increase her bust with silicone, a procedure she had subjected herself to in the hope that she could rekindle Neal's love for her. Her inital reaction had been brief: 'I almost killed myself,' she wrote, 'but, well, it's not right to do that. I'm going home for a visit, and I'll be at my mother's. If there's anything I can do, let me know. I'm so sorry. I hope you're OK. Thanks for the note . . .'

When she was settled at her mother's house, she wrote again:

I'm at my mother's now and wouldn't want to go to any funeral or wake. Still, if there's anything I can do for *you*, please let me know. He told me to try to be a perfect human being. That means paying bills, debts, and so I've got to earn some money. I still think he's alive sometimes. So grieving is destructive. And it's difficult to see people or places which confirm the negative. Then there's joy—thinking it's all a lie because he'll really be back, just teaching us or me a lesson. I can't go on any other way. I think you must be very sad and I wish there was something I could do. I'd do anything to have him alive again. Please try to find some happiness for yourself—you've lived for him so long, and you'll get and deserve such pleasure if you'd love someone else. I love you, Carolyn. And I wish you all the tolerance, patience and devotion you've shown, and love.

Anne

In another week Anne went back to Seattle and set out to carve a new life for herself. She never forgot Neal; he was still her inspiration, and when she felt insecure, she took trips to Mexico to find him. Needing him, she let herself believe he wasn't dead. Little by little she accepted the truth, drawing sustenence from what she'd known of him, and resolving to be worthy of the ideal he had sowed in her consciousness.

I spent another six months enduring Diana's persistent requests for the ashes, until I had to surrender or go mad. I agreed to give her some if she'd stop calling me. Yes, she said, of course, and I grasped at the bargain. Then she called to be sure I had her address, but it was only an excuse. Well, okay, I thought, if I let her talk and talk without resistance, maybe she'll get it all said.

But it was no use. She went on and on, repeating everything she'd told me a hundred times before. Finally I reached the point where I'd do anything to turn her off.

With the utmost revulsion, I opened the gray silken bag for the first and only time, and spooned a tablespoon or two of the contents into a little box, feeling as if I would faint any minute. 'There now,' I sighed, and I quickly wrapped and mailed the parcel to Diana.

It was an idle dream again. Every other day or so Diana called with a new idea of what she would do with the ashes when they arrived. First, they were to be placed in her family's plot in New Hampshire. 'Great,' I said. 'Do that. Goodbye.' But in another day or so—'Do you think maybe I should buy a tree in Washington Square and bury Neal under it?'

'Oh, good grief, Diana—you *know* how I feel. Do anything you want, but stop telling me about it. You're only getting a tiny spoonful.'

'Yes, I know. It's all I deserve.' Now that surprised me, coming from her. 'You know what I think I'll do?' Here we go again. 'I'm going to bury an old-fashioned quarter with him.'

'A what? Why?'

'You know—those old quarters that had an eagle on the back? Well, when you look at it one way it looks like an eagle, but going the other way it looks like a cowboy with a hard-on. Don't you think that is terribly appropriate for Neal? Really, Carolyn, isn't that a great idea?'

'Oh my God,' I groaned.

Soon after Jack's death, Diana called again. It was a particularly bad moment, and I let fly. Blast the woman!

'Will you shut up a minute? Don't you ever think of anything except what happened twenty years ago? *Twenty years*, Diana. My God, woman, what are you doing with your life?' And on and on, condemning her without pause.

And then a strange thing happened to me. Right in the middle of all this rage, it was as though I heard a click somewhere inside of me, and without any change in my angry tone, I went right on yelling, but now—I *loved* her! I began to feel warm, melting and joyous, and I listened to myself incredulously: 'Now, lookit, Diana—life is to *live*— you're a young woman still—yes, you are—God gave you *life*, not age, and you're attractive—you used to be a model, remember? Well, remember things like that—let the dead bury the dead—concern yourself with the living. Life is so great, Diana—come on, now, quit all your moaning and complaining and get out and use your good brain and good looks. And you've been blessed by knowing Neal! Use the gift he gave you—for good! For living!' Now I couldn't think of enough hopeful, positive things to say to her. She had mumbled a time or two, but mainly she'd been quiet as never before—she had always talked right through me. Could I possibly have reached her at last? 'Do it for Neal, Diana. It's what he'd have wanted you to do, don't you agree?'

'Yes—I think so. Would you send me something—some literature?' I could hardly believe my ears. She was excited too, just as I was, and it felt good. I hoped a seed had been planted, and I vaguely wondered if Neal had had anything to do with this.

We ended the conversation dripping with compliments, sweetness and light. And I was ecstatic. By golly—I bet I was free of her at last! How funny—here I was, forever preaching that you can only change your environment by changing your own mind and by non-resistance, yet I'd never even thought to apply it to Diana.

She soon gave me the chance to test my new attitude. In a few days she called again, this time to tell me she had received the ashes. 'Thank you very much,' she said warmly, sincerely. 'You know they arrived on my husband's birthday, and my daughter put them beside his plate with his other gifts!' she squealed with delight. I held my breath. 'But I rescued them just in time! And now, I've finally decided what to do with them. I want your approval.'

I sighed. Nothing had changed with her, after all. But I at least felt only bemusement now—not defiance or anger—and enormous relief.

'Okay, Diana, let's have it. What are you going to do?'

'Well, I have just telephoned Jack's wife in Florida. Of course, she doesn't know who I am, but I asked her if I could bury Neal's ashes in Jack's grave.'

I couldn't help an involuntary spasm. 'And what did Stella say?'

'Actually, she sounded pleased. She said she hadn't been able to afford a proper tombstone yet, but when she sells the house in Florida, she'll be coming back to Lowell, and she wants to do it then. She said I could meet her there. Isn't that wonderful?'

'Wonderful, honey.'

'We'll have a nice little ceremony, you know, something simple, and maybe I'll get a plaque—something about Neal being buried in Jack's heart. Don't you think that would be fitting?'

'Anything you say. Do it any way you like. You have my blessing.'

'Yes, I think it will be nice. Now—I'd like to do something for you.

I'll place a bet for you on the Derby. I've really gotten into it. Which horse do you want to win? Pick any one you like. Two dollars, okay?'

'Lovely. Put it on the third choice, Di, in memory of Neal.'

INDEX

Note: CC in the index stands for Carolyn Cassady; NC for Neal Cassady, AG for Allen Ginsberg, JK for Jack Kerouac.

431

433